The Nonprofit Handbook
Second Edition

Gary M. Grobman

White Hat Communications
Harrisburg, Pennsylvania

Published by White Hat Communications.

Copies may be ordered from:

White Hat Communications
PO Box 5390
Harrisburg, PA 17110-0390
(717) 238-3787
(717) 238-2090 (fax)
Web Site: http://www.socialworker.com/nonprofit/nphome.htm

This publication is intended to provide general information and should not be construed as legal advice or legal opinions concerning any specific facts or circum-stances. Consult an experienced attorney if advice is required concerning any specific situation or legal matter.

Contact the author in care of White Hat Communications, or by e-mail at: *gary.grobman@paonline.com*

Printed in the United States of America.

Editing: Linda Grobman

Library of Congress Number: 99-64921
ISBN: 0-9653653-2-8

Table of Contents

Foreword

Joe Geiger
Executive Director
PA Association of Nonprofit Organizations

Congratulations! You have decided to be a part of the fastest-growing segment of business development in the United States. You are considering joining, or have already joined, hundreds of thousands of other nonprofits in the United States. They come in all sizes, shapes, and colors. The nonprofit sector's heritage includes helping in an emergency, encouraging the human spirit, educating and shaping values and goals and being the first to offer a hand.

You have chosen to be a vital link in developing the fabric of the community. From the time our ancestors landed on Plymouth Rock (or staffed the Welcome Wagon that greeted those who did), people have worked together in formal organizations to better the human condition. The nonprofit sector has always been in the forefront of improving our society and the human condition.

Today, the nonprofit sector is in a very challenging period. Nonprofits are experiencing ever-growing scrutiny and demands for accountability. Service demand is increasing. There is more competition for charitable dollars. The public and government both are demanding that nonprofits improve their efficiency. This book will help you respond to these challenges.

As the chief executive officer of PANO, I am pleased to be a part of the second edition of *The Nonprofit Handbook*. Every week, callers to PANO ask questions: Should we start up? Should we merge? Should we go out of business? I am pleased to have a practical tool that can help answer these questions. This book will help you keep on track. It is also an extraordinary resource for those who already manage or serve on the boards of nonprofit organizations. With practical advice on fundraising, communications, lobbying, personnel management, grantsmanship, and scores of other issues, it is a must for every nonprofit executive to have.

This book is based on *The Pennsylvania Nonprofit Handbook*, which has been revised and expanded since the fifth edition was published in 1999. There are new chapters on mergers, change management, quality, and the Year 2000 problem. And, this edition also includes a chapter devoted to the significant developments affecting nonprofits that have occurred since the previous edition. Here, in one place, is a useful summary of the seismic events of the last year or so—from publication of the IRS intermediate sanctions regulations to enactment of the Volunteer Protection Act.

In summary, *The Nonprofit Handbook* is at the top of the list of essential tools to have on your bookshelf. In summary, this book is must reading. While it will have value as a reference tool to be consulted when needed, I highly recommend that you read the book cover-to-cover to familiarize yourself with the panoply of issues facing the modern nonprofit in every state of our United States.

J.M.G.
June 1999

Introduction

Americans of all ages, all stations in life, and all types of disposition are forever forming associations. There are not only commercial and industrial associations in which all take part, but others of a thousand different types—religious, moral, serious, futile, very general and very limited, immensely large and very minute. Americans combine to give fetes, found seminaries, build churches, distribute books, and send missionaries to the antipodes. Hospitals, prisons and schools take shape in that way. Finally, if they want to proclaim a truth or propagate some feeling by the encouragement of a great example, they form an association. In every case, at the head of any new undertaking, where in France you would find the government or in England some territorial magnate, in the United States you are sure to find an association.

—Alexis de Tocqueville
Democracy In America
1835

Little has changed about the American propensity to form benevolent associations in the 164 years since de Tocqueville wrote the above words. The modern charitable institution, however, may bear little resemblance to the typical charity of the 19th century. Burgeoning demands for services, increased government regulation, keen competition for funds, the advance of technology, demographic changes, and the public's changing perception of our institutions have all worked to increase the challenge to those in leadership positions with nonprofit organizations.

Virtually every single American is touched in some way by the services of this country's nonprofit organizations. Organizations such as churches and synagogues, civic groups, hospitals, day care centers, libraries, colleges, symphonies, art museums, the Red Cross, Salvation Army, and the American Cancer Society work in partnership with government and the public to improve our lives and those of our neighbors.

The nonprofit sector's participation in the American economy is impressive. According to Thomas McLaughlin, writing in his 1995 book *Streetsmart Financial Basics for Nonprofit Managers*, nonprofits account for at least 6% of GNP and employ 7% of the workforce. In January 1999, the Internal Revenue Service released a study indicating that after adjusting for the effects of inflation, assets and revenues of nonprofit tax-exempt organizations more than tripled, to $1.9 trillion and $.9 trillion respectively, between 1975 and 1995. In fiscal year 1997, there were 692,594 organizations in the United States with 501(c)(3) status, and 141,776 with 501(c)(4) status.

Most Americans recognize the value of nonprofit organizations in society. Of 120.4 million individual tax returns filed nationally in 1996 by individuals and couples, 31.6 million claimed a tax deduction for charitable giving, totaling more than $86 billion in deductions, according to the IRS. Many more billions of dollars were donated by persons who do not itemize, or who do not bother to declare the value of their charity on their tax returns. The business community also donates billions of dollars each year to charitable institutions.

According to the latest (June 1999) annual report of *Giving USA*, published by the American Association of Fund-Raising Counsel Trust for Philanthropy, total charitable giving by individuals, corporations, and foundations increased by 10.7% in 1998 over the previous year, to an estimated $174.5 billion. Additionally, billions of hours annually are volunteered to nonprofits. According to the latest (1995) statistics on volunteering compiled by Independent Sector, 93 million Americans, half of all adults, volunteer an average of 4.2 hours each week with nonprofits. This totals 15.7 billion hours in volunteer time. The dollar value of this amount is an estimated $201.5 billion, based on a 1995 estimate of $12.84/hour of value (which has been revised to $13.73/hour for 1997). As those who volunteer can attest, the value to society, such as the relief of human suffering, far exceeds the dollar value.

It is difficult to foresee and anticipate all of the barriers that stand in the way of a nonprofit organization's creation and survival. One thing is certain—there will be barriers. Forming and running a nonprofit corporation, or any corporation, is a major challenge. Yet it is proven that the accomplishments such organizations can achieve far exceed what any single person, operating without an organizational structure, can achieve alone.

Starting and running a nonprofit corporation in the 21st century requires political acumen, immense technical skill, vision, physical and mental stamina, and, perhaps most of all, luck and a sense of humor.

In the fall of 1984, the Internal Revenue Service, because of a computer glitch, lost $300 million in federal tax withholding payments of 10,000 companies. Even after the snafu was discovered, thousands of the companies received curt letters threatening that the government would seize their property and bank accounts if the tax payments were not made within 10 days. As a nonprofit executive who was on the receiving end of one of these letters, I can certify that "maintaining a sense of humor" was not easy at that time. Yet in the years since that IRS debacle, several more calamities beyond my control afflicted the nonprofit I ran.

There were times when running a nonprofit was no picnic. And then there were times when it was the most fun I ever had. I would like to think that if a publication such as *The Nonprofit Handbook* had been around when I first started, my job would have been easier.

Purpose of the Handbook

As one might expect, a plethora of laws, regulations, court decisions, and other government policies apply to nonprofit corporations.

The purpose of this handbook is to provide answers to questions such as:

1. What does one have to do to form a nonprofit corporation?
2. What are the advantages and disadvantages of incorporating?
3. How does a nonprofit organization qualify and apply for 501(c)(3) status?
4. What kind of paperwork is involved in typical nonprofit operations?
5. What should be in a nonprofit corporation's bylaws?
6. How does a nonprofit organization qualify for discount bulk mailing privileges?
7. How does a nonprofit organization qualify for a state sales tax exemption?
8. Can a nonprofit organization engage in unrelated activities that generate income?
9. Will the tax exemption of a nonprofit organization be at risk if it engages in lobbying?
10. What steps need to occur for merger with another nonprofit corporation?

This handbook cannot purport to answer every conceivable question, but it does attempt to provide sources for answers to many of the questions posed by nonprofit board members and staff. It also provides primary source material on important state and federal laws and regulations, sources for some of the most useful government forms, and sound advice about many nonprofit management issues.

For each state and the District of Columbia, this Handbook provides basic information about incorporation, lobbying registration and reporting, income and sales tax exemptions, and registration to conduct charitable solicitations. The names and addresses of the appropriate government contact offices are provided. This second edition also provides the addresses of useful Web sites where additional resources may be found.

Who Can Use This Book

This handbook will be a useful reference to—

a. Those who are considering forming a nonprofit corporation.

b. Those who need to keep up-to-date on laws, regulations, and court decisions that affect nonprofit organizations, including executive staff and board members of existing nonprofit organizations.

c. Those who will benefit by the advice included in this handbook on running a nonprofit organization, such as fundraisers, lobbyists, public affairs consultants, staff and leadership of funding organizations, and government officials, in addition to those who serve as the staff and board members of nonprofit organizations and their associations.

This is the second edition of this publication. Every effort has been made to make this *Handbook* as useful as possible, and free from errors. It is the intent of the author to seek corrections as well as suggestions for improving this publication, and to incorporate these contributions in future editions. A survey/order form has been included in the Appendix to provide feedback to the author and the publisher.

Acknowledgments

The author gratefully acknowledges the contributions of scores of individuals and organizations to this book. Among them are Kathleen Steigler and Linda Grobman, who edited the first edition of the *Pennsylvania Non-Profit Handbook*, on which this book is based; Michael Sand, who wrote the chapter on boards as well as the chapter on applying for grants; and Bob Mills, Esq., who completely rewrote and expanded the sections on volunteer and staff liability. Thanks are due also to those who reviewed and edited specific chapters of the previous edition, including Terry Roth, Esq.; W. Barney Carter; George Bell, Esq.; Bill Knoll, Classification Reform Instructor for the U.S. Postal Service; Otto Hofmann, Esq.; Phil McKain; Jim Fritz, Esq.; Bob Mills, Esq.; Frederick Richmond; the late Steve Zneimer; Jim Redmond; Elizabeth Hrenda-Roberts; Ron Lench; Christine Finnegan; Joan Benso; Dick Shelly; John Briscoe; and Ken Wickham. Independent Sector, and the Internal Revenue Service Public Affairs Office in Philadelphia also cooperated in the researching of this publication.

I am also appreciative of the contributions to this publication that were made by Gerald Kaufman, a nonprofit consultant from Philadelphia, whose essay on governance of nonprofit charities and chapter on nonprofit ethics deserve to be shared with every board member and staff person who is affiliated with a charity. Dr. Pam Leland of Seton Hall University for her thoughtful chapter on how to respond to property tax exemption challenges. Joel Cavadel, an attorney from York, PA, made many contributed to the section on mergers and consolidations, for which I am most grateful. Some of the material in the chapter on change management was adapted from material on outcome-based management jointly written by Frederick Richmond and me, and from material on large group intervention that Gerald Gorelick and I wrote together.

Barbara Trainin Blank did her usual thorough and professional job of editing and proofreading, and additional proofreading of this edition was provided by Linda Grobman.

Finally, a word of thanks to the Pennsylvania Association of Nonprofit Organizations, particularly to its executive director, Joe Geiger, for participating in this second edition. PANO is fast becoming the single address for Pennsylvania charities without their own statewide associations to turn to for information, products, services, and training.

G.M.G.
July 1999

Chapter 1
The Decision to Incorporate

> Synopsis: Among the advantages of incorporating an organization are limits on liability, lower taxes, and increased organizational credibility. Among the disadvantages are loss of centralized control, and increased paperwork, time and expense of running a corporation.

Introduction to Incorporation

A corporation is a legal entity formed for business activities. Under state and federal laws, corporations are treated as a separate "person" for purposes of making contracts, paying taxes, and being liable for the consequences of business activity. A nonprofit corporation, also called a "not-for-profit" corporation in some states, generally is not permitted to issue shares of stock, and does not provide shareholders with dividends from the profits that are received from operating the business. While nonprofit corporations can and do make profits, these profits may not inure to the benefit of the "owners" of the corporation— the board of directors or trustees. Rather, these profits must be used to operate and maintain the organization. Some states place limitations on the types of activities that are the primary purpose of the nonprofit corporation.

Generally, there are three classes of nonprofit corporations:

1. Funding agency (e.g. United Way, Jewish Federation, private foundations)

The primary purpose of these organizations is to allocate funds, either those solicited as private donations or those already accumulated in an endowment or private fortune, for other agencies that provide actual services. Many of these organizations restrict their grants of funds to groups that provide a narrow range of services of interest to the funding organization. A Jewish federation is likely to make contributions solely to Jewish-affiliated organizations or others that principally serve the Jewish community. The United Way generally provides funding to social service agencies. Some foundations restrict their contributions to organizations promoting services for women, health-care related studies, or arts and humanities agencies.

2. Membership organizations (e.g. Common Cause, the Sierra Club, League of Women Voters)

These organizations exist principally to provide services (such as advocacy, information sharing, and networking) for their members, usually with a specialty of expertise.

3. Service agencies (e.g. hospitals, schools, day-care centers, family services)

These organizations exist to provide specific services to the public. They often charge fees on a sliding scale for their services to fund the bulk of their budgets.

Each type of organization operates differently in many significant ways.

The decision to incorporate is a mere formality for most leaders who envision a large organization with employees, contracts, offices, property, and equipment. Corporate status in general, and nonprofit corporate status in particular, provides many advantages. Maintaining an unincorporated organization with annual revenue and expenditures comfortably in five figures is cumbersome at best, if not impossible. It is at the low end of the scale where the decision to incorporate is most important.

It would be ludicrous to consider incorporation for the Saturday morning running group get-together, which collects two dollars from each of its eight members to pay for the refreshments after the run. Yet, when the group expands to three hundred members, dues are collected to finance a race, the municipality demands that the club purchase insurance to indemnify against accidents, and the club wants a grant from an area foundation to purchase a bus to transport its members to area races, then incorporation is clearly the option of choice.

Advantages and Disadvantages of Incorporation

The **advantages** of incorporation are the following:

1. Limited Liability. Of all the reasons to seek corporate status, this is perhaps the most compelling. Under all state laws, the officers, directors, employees, and members of a corporation, except under very limited and unusual circumstances, are not personally liable for lawsuit judgments and debts relating to the organization. Thus, the personal assets of the organization's executive director or board members are not at risk in the event there is a successful suit against the corporation, or in the event the organization goes out of business while owing money to creditors. Assets of an organization may be minuscule, while the individuals running it may have substantial assets. Corporate status protects those personal assets. Many people won't even consider participating in the leadership of an organization unless their personal assets are shielded by incorporation.

Many state legislatures have enacted laws that are designed to expand the liability protection afforded to nonprofit boards of directors and volunteers.

2. Tax Advantages. In the absence of incorporation, income accruing to an individual running an organization is subject to federal, state, and local taxes at the individual rate, which is likely to be substantially more than the corporate rate. In the case of nonprofit incorporation, organizations can be exempt from many taxes, depending upon the type of organization. For organizations that are charitable, educational, religious, literary, or scientific, 501(c)(3) tax-exempt status is particularly attractive (see Chapter 8). Most state laws exempt corporations that have federal tax-exempt status from state corporate income tax. Certain types of charities may be exempt from state sales and use tax and local property taxes as well. Many types of charitable institutions, such as colleges and hospitals, which have substantial property holdings, would be taxed beyond their abilities to operate if they were denied tax exemptions. Many funding sources, such as government, foundations, and the public as well, will not make contributions to an organization that is not a 501(c)(3), since this status provides a tax-exemption to the contributor, and assures that there is at least some minimal level of accountability on the part of the organization.

3. Structure, Accountability, Perpetuity, and Legally Recognized Authority. When people and organizations interact with a bona fide corporation, they have confidence that there is some order and authority behind the decision-making of that entity. A reasonable expectation exists that the corporation will continue to honor agreements even if the principal actor for the organization dies, resigns, or otherwise disassociates himself or herself from the organization. They know that there is a legal document governing decision-making (as detailed in the bylaws), succession of officers, clear purposes (as detailed in the Articles of Incorporation), a system for paying bills, accounting for income and expenses, and a forum for the sharing of ideas on policy and direction from the corporation's board members. So long as the necessary papers are filed, the organization will continue in perpetuity regardless of changes in leadership. This gives such organizations an aura of immortality that is seen as an advantage in planning beyond the likely tenure of an individual board chairperson or executive director.

4. Ancillary Benefits. Nonprofit incorporation can provide cheaper postage rates (see chapter 22); access to media (through free public service announcements); volunteers, who would be more hesitant volunteering for a comparable for-profit entity; and the so-called "halo effect," in which the public is more willing to do business with a nonprofit because of a real or perceived view that such an organization is founded and operated in the public interest.

5. Strength of Collegial Decision-Making. Decision-making in an autocracy is clearly easier and more efficient than in an organization run as a democracy. Yet, there is a value in making decisions by building a consensus among a majority of members of a board. Members of a board often bring different experience and talents and provide information that would otherwise not be available in making decisions. Issues are often raised that, if otherwise overlooked, could possibly result in disastrous consequences for the organization.

The **disadvantages** of nonprofit incorporation are the following:

1. Loss of Centralized Control. Many organizations are formed and run by a charismatic leader with a vision of how to accomplish a particular task or mission. Decision-making is enhanced without the distractions of the scores of issues that relate not to the actual mission of the organization but to the organization itself. The very act of forming a nonprofit corporation can be draining—preparing and filing Articles of Incorporation, negotiating bylaws, finding quality colleagues to serve on a board of directors, hiring qualified staff if necessary, and dealing with the myriad of personnel issues that emanate from hiring staff, preparing budgets, raising money, and preparing minutes of board meetings. Even finding a convenient time and place where the board can meet to assure that a quorum can be present can pose a troublesome and potentially overwhelming problem at times.

Incorporation is a legal framework that trades off the advantages addressed earlier in this section with some serious disadvantages. Decisions can no longer be made in a vacuum by one person without oversight or accountability, but are legally under the purview of a board of directors. Decisions have to withstand scrutiny of *all* persons on the board, some of whom may be hostile or have personal axes to grind. By definition, boards of directors are committees, and committees often make decisions that are compromises in order to mollify members with divergent viewpoints and competing interests.

For those used to making quick decisions "on the fly" and who revel in not having their decisions subject to second-guessing, modification, or otherwise being meddled with, then incorporation can be personally a shackling experience and can dilute one's control over the organization.

2. Paperwork, Paperwork, Paperwork. Even in the smallest nonprofit corporation, the paperwork load related to corporate status can at times be overwhelming. There are deadlines for virtually every filing. Keeping ahead of the paperwork wave requires discipline, commitment, and a sense of humor. Forms get lost in the bureaucracy, misfiled, or lost in the mail.

Failure to handle this paperwork can result in criminal penalties, in some cases. There are penalties for missed filings (e.g., failure to file a timely 990 federal tax return results in a $20/day penalty, up to a maximum of $10,000, or 5% of the agency's gross revenues, whichever is smaller—and $100/day up to $50,000 for organizations with annual gross receipts exceeding $1 million). As soon as the first employee is hired, the paperwork wave accompanying that accomplishment almost requires the hiring of a second employee to file all the federal, state, and local government forms relating to employment.

In the first year, the filings can be intimidating, time-consuming, and frustrating. A new corporation must develop a bookkeeping system that is understandable by the accountant who will perform the audit and prepare the financial reports, pass resolutions, and file forms to open up corporate savings and checking accounts, order checks, file tax returns, and pay taxes. There are many federal, state, and local taxes that each require their own filing at different times of the year. A new corporation must also reconcile savings and checking accounts, prepare board meeting announcements and minutes, devise a system to pay bills, and establish a process for the reimbursement of expenses. Other tasks it must accomplish are to file forms to protect its corporate name, prepare an annual report, adopt a personnel policy, purchase office equipment, rent an office, prepare budgets, write fundraising letters, and find and retain board members.

The only consolation is that after a few years, one becomes familiar with the required filings. Then they become routine and just a minor nuisance.

Few of these tasks directly have an impact on the actual work of the agency, but typically they will consume more time during the initial year after incorporation than the actual mission of the organization.

3. Expenses in Money and Time. Significant resources are required to establish a corporation and run it efficiently. No law prohibits running a corporation from one's home with volunteer staff. Legally, the only monetary requirement for running a corporation is to pay a fee to file Articles of Incorporation. Yet, doing so often sets off a chain of events that dramatically increases the organization's complexity. Opening up corporate bank accounts, doing expense reports, filing taxes, and doing the paperwork described above are difficult to accomplish solely with volunteer labor. Raising the funds necessary to hire a person to do all of this work (in addition to coordinating the actual work involved in the purpose of the organization) adds to this burden, and requires even more filing and paperwork.

Many of these tasks would be required even in the absence of a decision to incorporate. But one can avoid much of the "wasted" time and energy by keeping "small." By keeping small, however, there is a substantial limit to what one can accomplish. Experiencing the disadvantages of incorporation is the cost one incurs in order to receive the substantial benefits.

Nonprofits and Private Benefit

Nonprofit corporation status provides many advantages over comparable for-profits. Yet this status is not conferred without a cost. Generally, nonprofits must operate differently and with different motivations than their for-profit counterparts. There is a general legal doctrine that prohibits nonprofits from acting in a manner that results in "private inurement" to individuals, i.e., the transfer of earnings or profits from the corporation to its "owners." The basic principle at work here is that a for-profit is intended to benefit its owners, whereas a nonprofit is intended to further a purpose.

There is nothing illegal or unethical about nonprofits selling goods and services and generating income. In the 1990s, nonprofits are becoming more sophisticated in finding new revenue sources to supplant the loss of government funds (see Chapter

2). Yet, nonprofits are distinguished from their for-profit counterparts by the destination of any profit.

Chapter 23 includes a list of many of the important differences between nonprofits and for-profits. In the 1989 text *Starting & Managing a Nonprofit Organization*, author-attorney Bruce R. Hopkins provides a useful chapter on the issue of private inurement in nonprofits.

Tips:

- Review your state's nonprofit laws and decide whether the organization is willing to be subjected to the limitations and accountability required by these laws.

- Avoid incorporating if it is essential to maintain complete control of the organization, and if it is possible to keep the scale of operations small.

- Contact someone who runs a nonprofit corporation of similar size and type envisioned for the organization. Ask questions about paperwork requirements, office equipment, rental space, and the benefits and pitfalls of running such a corporation.

- If leaning toward incorporation, identify potential incorporators/board members who are—

    a. Accessible, and not spread too thin among many other competing organizations
    b. Potential contributors to the organization
    c. Experienced fundraisers
    d. Knowledgeable about the issues of concern to the organization
    e. Respected and well-known in the community
    f. Experienced in legal, accounting, and nonprofit management issues.

Chapter 2
Steps to Incorporation

Synopsis: Organizational leadership must file the appropriate forms with the state in order to incorporate an organization. Among important decisions to be made are choosing the corporate name, choosing whether to have members, and choosing corporate purposes.

Introduction to Incorporation

While incorporation is a legal procedure, it does not require the services of a lawyer. However, lawyers with training and experience in state nonprofit law can be useful in reviewing, if not preparing, Articles of Incorporation and bylaws that are consistent both with statutory requirements and the purposes of the organization.

State libraries, law school libraries, and many public and private libraries have copies of state laws. Make sure in researching current law to refer to the most up-to-date supplement for use in the current year. This supplement will include all changes to laws made since the law books were first printed.

Choosing Incorporators

Incorporators are the persons legally responsible for forming the corporation. It is common for one person to serve in this capacity, although several persons may sign the Articles of Incorporation form as formal incorporators. Some states require more than one incorporator (see the state directory of this book).

Incorporators frequently play a more active role than solely being a name on the Articles of Incorporation filing. If they act to promote the interests of the new corporation (e.g. raise funds, recruit personnel, negotiate leases, or purchase property for the organization), their legal status is augmented by the responsibility of serving in a fiduciary capacity. This legal status confers on them the duty to take actions in the best interest of the corporation rather than in their own personal interest, and to disclose any conflicts of interest that may occur in their business dealings on behalf of the corporation.

By law, the incorporators make agreements on behalf of the corporation while it is in the process of legal formation. These agreements have no legal effect until they are approved by the corporation's board of directors once the corporation legally exists. As a result, incorporators who do make these agreements must make it clear to the other party that the agreement is not binding until the corporation exists as a legal entity and its board ratifies the agreement.

Once the Articles of Incorporation are filed and the state government agency with jurisdiction over incorporation (usually the Department of State) approves them, incorporators have no formal status, with one exception. They are invited to be present at the organizational meeting required by law, at which the board of directors is selected.

It is a common practice that the incorporators include members who will be serving on the first board of directors. Thus, care should be taken as to the qualifications of incorporators, as they may continue their association with the corporation as directors (see Chapter 4).

Choosing a Corporate Name

One of the most important and basic decisions in forming a corporation is choosing a corporate name. This name will be the organization's corporate identity, and the image created by it provides the first impression of those outside the corporation. "Short" and "descriptive" are two desirable characteristics in a corporate name. Many nonprofit organizations choose a name that gives the connotation of helping, or otherwise doing charitable activities in the public interest, rather than implying a for-profit motive. If the organization plans to apply for 501(c)(3) status, it should avoid names that would be suitable for organizations whose activities are clearly not eligible for this status. The organization may wish to consider suitable acronyms comprising the first letter of each word of its name, but cute or frivolous acronyms often give an unprofessional impression.

The process of having to change a corporate name after incorporating and operating as a nonprofit often results in time-consuming and costly activities, such as changing the logo (see Chapter 22); reprinting stationery, business cards, checks, and brochures; and changing all of the legal forms relating to Articles of Incorporation, bank accounts, and contracts.

For obvious legal reasons, the name must be unique, although it is usually legal to adopt a name similar to another existing corporation after receiving permission from that corporation and filing the necessary forms to do so. Typical state laws require that the name can be in any language, but require that it be expressed in English letters or characters. For more information about the limitations on corporate names, consult the state directory of this book.

Organizations may wish to perform a name search with the state agency of jurisdiction to ensure that no other corporation, active or inactive, is using an identical or similar name. Almost every state permits the name to be reserved for a modest fee prior to incorporation, typically for a 120-day period.

Many corporations also choose to do a national name search and take steps to register their names with the United States Patent and Trademark Office as trademarks. This can be done only for those organizations that will be marketing goods and services interstate. The fee is $245, which provides registration for ten years, assuming the owner certifies that the trademark has active status.

For more information or to obtain the correct forms, contact the Patent and Trademark Office:

Patent and Trademark Office
Trademark Assistance Center
U.S. Department of Commerce
Washington, D.C. 20231
(703) 308-9000
(703) 308-7016 (fax)

A pre-addressed postcard for obtaining this information is included in the back of this book.

Choosing Corporate Purposes

It is generally advisable to state broad corporate purposes in a manner that permits the corporation to grow and change direction without requiring its Articles of Incorporation to be amended. The purposes should be specific enough to permit the corporation to be eligible for 501(c)(3) status, if this is expected. Research similar organizations and review their Articles of Incorporation to obtain ideas on framing your own organization's Articles of Incorporation. Some states have limitations on how broad these purposes can be in the Articles (see state directory).

Choosing to Have Members or No Members

In general, it is desirable for most nonprofit corporations to have no members. This will assure that all power and authority will be maintained by the board of directors, and will prevent the difficult legal problems of expelling an individual member should that occasion arise. Outsiders, including those who would pay dues in exchange for participating in organizational programs and activities, can still participate in the activities of the nonprofit corporation without being legal members who are entitled to vote on the affairs of the corporation.

As with almost every issue, there are exceptions to this. Many organizations will find it desirable for each participant in the organization's programs and activities to have an equal voice in the internal governance of the organization.

Additional Provisions

Many corporations that wish to qualify for 501(c)(3) status add a provision that will facilitate tax-exemption approval. One such provision is a statement forbidding the corporation from engaging in partisan political activity on behalf of a candidate or substantially engaging in lobbying. The language for this provision can be adopted from 501(c)(3) itself:

> *"No substantial part of the Corporation's activities shall consist of carrying on propaganda, or otherwise attempting to influence legislation (except in accordance with Section 501(h) of the Internal Revenue Code). The Corporation shall not participate in any political campaign on behalf of or in opposition to any candidate for public office."*

Once the Articles of Incorporation are filed and approved, be sure that all actions taken on behalf of the Corporation will clearly indicate that they are actions for the corporation and not on behalf of individuals. Otherwise, such individuals may be personally liable for fulfilling the terms of contracts and other agreements, such as paying rent, staff salaries, telephone installation costs, and so on. One way to indicate that persons are acting on behalf of the corporation is to explicitly sign legal contracts and other documents as follows:

(corporate name)

By (individual's signature)

(individual's corporate title)

Corporate Mergers and Dissolution (See Chapter 26)

Each state has its own procedures codified in law for mergers and dissolution of nonprofit corporations. Both are substantially complicated. It is recommended that those considering either procedure consult an experienced attorney.

Tips:

- **Review the legal requirements of state laws for nonprofits to make sure the organization can and is willing to comply with them.**

- **Have a lawyer review, if not draft, the Articles of Incorporation.**

- **Include in the Articles of Incorporation additional provisions to enhance the prospects for achieving the appropriate federal tax status (e.g. 501(c)(3)) if such status is desirable (see Chapter 8).**

- **Choose a short and descriptive corporate name.**

Chapter 3
Bylaws

> Synopsis: Bylaws provide general policy guidelines for nonprofit corporations. There are statutory provisions that go into effect automatically in the absence of comparable bylaw provisions.

Introduction to Preparing Bylaws

Every corporation must have a set of bylaws that provides for its internal management and regulation.

The term "bylaws" may be defined as "the code or codes of rules adopted for the regulation or management of the business and affairs of the corporation irrespective of the name or names by which such rules are designated."

Perhaps the best advice on formulating organizational bylaws can be found in the publication *Robert's Rules of Order Newly Revised*, published in 1991 by Scott, Foresman, and Co. The 700 pages in the book contain an invaluable wealth of knowledge not only on parliamentary procedure but on organizational leadership. This book provides guidance on drafting certain bylaw provisions, and includes a sample set of bylaws. A more recent, 160-page edition of the book was published in 1993 ($8.95, Berkley Publications, ISBN No. 0-425-13928-X).

Certain provisions must by law be included in each state for nonprofit corporations. Beyond legal requirements, corporate bylaws are a necessary and important document, and great thought and care should be exercised as to what will be included in them.

Typical bylaws include provisions governing the following internal procedures and policies of the nonprofit corporation:

1. The purposes of the corporation, consistent with any federal tax law limitation or state laws governing lobbying or other activity
2. Limitations of liability of directors, consistent with state law
3. Types of officers
4. Terms, powers, and succession of officers
5. Location of principal office
6. Whether the corporation will have members, or whether all powers will be vested in a board of directors
7. How directors will be selected, and how vacancies will be filled
8. How many directors there will be
9. Length of, staggering of terms of, and limits on consecutive terms of the board of directors

10. Terms under which a member of the board of directors can be disqualified
11. Conditions under which the annual meeting and other regularly scheduled board meetings are held
12. How unscheduled meetings of the board can be called
13. Terms under which notice of board meetings must occur
14. What constitutes a quorum for the transaction of business
15. How many directors are required to approve an action
16. Whether actions of the board can be ratified through the mail or by conference call, or require directors to be present at a meeting
17. Power of the chairperson (or president) to appoint committees, and to provide for rules, powers, and procedures of such committees
18. Whether alternates can be empowered to represent directors, and who selects them
19. Who is responsible for preparing board meeting minutes and for storing and using the corporate seal on official documents
20. Who is responsible for keeping and reviewing the corporate books, and dispersing corporate funds
21. How amendments can be made to the bylaws
22. Terms and conditions regarding compensation, if any, paid to directors
23. What committees are authorized, and what powers and duties they have
24. The terms under which the corporation will be dissolved.

Legal Requirements of Bylaws

Each state law provides for some minimum standards with respect to bylaws of nonprofit corporations.

Most of these laws provide rules on many of the above bylaw options in the absence of explicit directions in the nonprofit corporation's bylaws. Thus, it is important to place provisions in the bylaws that will be intended to supersede these statutory legal guidelines, if the directors feel that the guidance provided in law is not acceptable to the corporation.

Among the provisions of bylaws that deserve the highest consideration and thought are the following, along with some comments about the issues they raise:

Quorum Requirements

A quorum is the minimum number of members or directors required to be present in order for a meeting to be held for the legal transaction of business. The purpose of a quorum requirement is to assure that actions are taken by a representative number of duly authorized participants rather than by an elite few. Standard advice, in the absence of relying on any statutory requirement, is to set the quorum at the minimum number of people who will be expected to attend a meeting, taking into account emergencies, adverse weather conditions, or conflicts with competing meetings. If the bylaws permit it, board members may participate in meetings and be counted as part of a quorum if they are in communication by speaker phone or by conference call.

Since actions cannot be taken legally at board meetings without a quorum present, it is best to begin with a conservatively low quorum requirement. Then change the bylaws to increase that number as appropriate. Otherwise, it is possible that the corporation will never have a quorum for its meetings, even if the sole purpose of the meeting is to change the bylaws to decrease the number of directors constituting a quorum.

Voting Rights

Boards need to vote in order to formally demonstrate that they have taken actions. Many organizations can be effectively run by consensus rather than formal voting, but even the most congenial and tolerant boards will eventually face issues that will divide them. In the absence of a provision in the bylaws, action may be taken at a board meeting with the approval of a majority of directors who are present at the meeting. There is nothing to prohibit a two-thirds vote being required to assure that actions are closer to representing a consensus. A two-thirds vote may be suggested for changing bylaws, or for changing membership dues requirements. Generally, a majority vote is sufficient for most routine board decisions, and avoids the inability to take positions and action that can occur as a result of a two-thirds voting requirement.

Selection of Officers

Many organizations are attracted to the democratic notion of offices being opened to all. With such a policy, any director can run for an office, ballots are prepared, and the winner is selected by the majority (or plurality) of voters from the board of directors or the membership at large. Other organizations feel that democracy puts at risk an orderly succession and threatens the existing power structure. Orderly succession can be accomplished by providing for a nominating committee, appointed by the chairperson, which selects a slate of officers. This slate is then perfunctorily approved by the full board. Both systems have their advantages and disadvantages.

Some organizations utilize a third alternative that combines the two. The nominations committee recommends a slate of candidates, but the procedures permit other candidates to run as well.

Executive Committees

Board meetings may occur at regular intervals, but issues arise in the interim that demand immediate attention. In such cases, it is valuable to have a mandated procedure for taking legally legitimate actions in the absence of board meetings. The mechanism to accomplish this is the executive committee, provided for in the corporate bylaws. While the executive committee typically is comprised of the corporation's officers, many state laws authorize executive committees comprised of one or more directors appointed by the board. Typically by law, the executive committee has all of the power and authority of the full board with the following exceptions:

- The executive committee cannot fill vacancies on the board.
- The executive committee cannot adopt, amend, or repeal bylaws.
- The executive committee cannot have powers inconsistent with the resolution passed by the board establishing it.

A sample set of bylaws that could be sufficient for many newly formed, small nonprofit corporations is included as Appendix A.

Tips:

- **Review state law with respect to corporate bylaws. Identify which provisions are required, which provisions apply only in the absence of a different provision in the bylaws, and which act to pre-empt the statutory guideline.**

- **Give careful consideration to the more important bylaw provisions, such as—**

    - **Quorum requirements**
    - **Succession of officers**
    - **Powers of the executive committee**
    - **Voting by the board of directors**

- **Have an attorney review the bylaws to assure that they are in compliance with state law, and ensure that the organization's desires with respect to internal decision-making will be consistent with efficient operating procedures.**

- **Schedule an organizational meeting to approve the bylaws, and distribute a draft of proposed bylaws before this meeting.**

- **After a final version of the bylaws is approved, provide a final copy of the bylaws to all members of the board of directors.**

Chapter 4
Nonprofit Boards of Directors

Synopsis: It is a critically important function for nonprofit organizations to find and retain qualified, experienced board members and officers. Board meetings generally have a routine order of business and provide the forum for making organizational policy.

One important requirement of a nonprofit organization is the formation of a board of directors. The board has the responsibility to set policy for the organization in accordance with the applicable laws and to see to it that the policies are implemented.

Board Formation

The size of the board should depend on the needs of the organization. If the board's role is strictly policy-making and the policies are implemented by a qualified staff, a small board might be more appropriate. However, if extensive board time is required for fundraising or implementing programs, then a much larger board would be in order.

The number of board members is set in the bylaws. One effective technique is to set a minimum and maximum number of board members and to allow the board to determine its size within these parameters. Then the board can start small and add members as the need arises.

The term of board members must be included in the bylaws. Board members should have fixed terms of office. One common practice is for all board members to have three-year terms, with one-third of the members being elected each year. In this way, board continuity is assured. Some boards allow their members to serve unlimited terms; other boards wish to limit the number of terms to assure new members with fresh ideas.

The election process should also be spelled out in the bylaws.

Most organizations have a nominating committee that is responsible for recommending new board members to the full board. Additional candidates for board membership can be nominated either in advance or from the floor at the election.

The titles, duties, length of term, and process for the election of officers should be spelled out in the bylaws.

Organizational Officers

The elected officers of most organizations are similar:

Chairperson, Chair, or President

Leads the meetings of the organization. Appoints committee chairs. Either signs checks or delegates this duty to another individual.

Vice-Chair

Assumes the duties of the president or chair in his or her absence, or upon his or her death or resignation. In many organizations, is given specific responsibilities either in the bylaws or by vote. In some organizations, automatically becomes the next president.

Secretary

Either takes minutes at the board meeting or approves the minutes if taken by another individual. Responsible for all official correspondence.

Treasurer

Responsible for finances of the organization. Usually makes financial reports to the board and signs checks.

In some organizations, the officers are elected by the full membership. In others, the board of directors elects its own officers. Many organizations elect their officers to two-year terms, although one-year terms are quite common. Some limit the number of terms of officers.

Getting Good Board Members

Many organizations are finding it more difficult than ever to get excellent board members. This is due to factors such as the large increase in the number of nonprofit boards, the increasing number of women in the work force, and the fact that upwardly mobile professionals often relocate.

In order to assure excellence, many nominating committees are meeting several times during the year to search for potential board members rather than just once. One effective technique is to strive for a diverse board, and to list the types of characteristics desired. Some might be:

> *Expertise*: Some board members should have personnel management, fiscal, or legal expertise.

> *Ages*: It is helpful to have older Americans represented, as well as youth and individuals in between.

> *Races and Religions:* All major races and religions in the community should be represented on a diverse board.

Backgrounds: It would be helpful if some board members had corporate backgrounds, some were government leaders, and others served on the boards of other nonprofit groups.

Users of the service: Many boards include representatives of the client population being served.

The nominating committee or board development committee would search throughout the year for individuals with these characteristics who would then be asked if they wanted to be considered for board membership.

Each board should have a list of board member responsibilities. These might include attending board meetings on a regular basis, serving on at least one standing committee, and participating in fundraising. This list of duties should be provided to each prospective board member, and no board member should be elected who will not agree to meet these responsibilities.

Keeping Good Board Members

One technique for keeping good board members is to require all new board members to participate in an orientation program before they attend their first board meeting.

The first step in the process is to receive and review materials that all board members should have received previously. These include the following:

- Articles of Incorporation
- Bylaws
- Funding applications
- Personnel, fiscal, and other board policies
- Annual reports
- Names, addresses, phone numbers, and biographical sketches of other board members and key staff members
- List of committees and committee duties
- Minutes of the last several board meetings
- Audits, budgets, and recent financial statements.

The second step is to hold a meeting with the board chair and the executive director. This provides an opportunity to ask questions about the materials received, visit the staff offices and programs, get an update of current issues, and review board member responsibilities.

Other steps to encourage productivity of board members include the following:

- Give board members specific projects. A board member who serves as chair of a committee or who has specific fundraising responsibilities is more likely to stay active.

- Keep board meetings interesting.
- Thank board members for their work.
- Have social events periodically, in addition to formal board meetings.

One other technique is to remove unproductive board members quickly and then replace them with new and productive ones.

Other ways to increase board productivity include the following:

- Having a policy in the bylaws that missing a specified number of board meetings without a reason will result in automatic dismissal.
- Re-electing only board members who have been meeting their responsibilities.
- Calling board members who have not been active to ask them if there are any problems. In some cases, the chairperson should ask for their resignation if they do not agree to meet board responsibilities.

Board Responsibilities

Members of boards of directors have the following duties:

Personnel

The board hires the executive director. This is the board's most important responsibility. It then makes assignments to the executive director and monitors the Executive Director's performance. It is appropriate for the board or its Personnel Committee to do a formal performance appraisal of the executive director at least annually. The board approves salary scales and job descriptions for the other staff members who are hired by the executive director. The board approves the personnel policies for the organization.

Finance

The board approves budgets for the organization. No funds are expended unless the funds are included in a budget approved by the board. The board approves spending reports that are submitted to them on a regular basis.

Fundraising

All applications for funds are submitted to the board before being submitted to funding sources. The board also approves plans for special events fundraising, and board members are expected to participate in fundraising events.

Planning

Board members approve short- and long-range plans for the organization. They then monitor the effectiveness of the agency's programs to see if they have met the goals outlined in the plans.

Board Development

The board selects new board members and adopts procedures to see that excellent board members are selected and continue to serve.

Public Relations

Board members are aware of all of the organization's activities and encourage participation in appropriate activities by the community.

Advising

Board members advise the executive director on policy implementation as requested.

How Boards Function Effectively

Boards set policies only through a majority vote of their members at board meetings, unless the bylaws provide otherwise. For boards with staffs, one effective method of policy-making is to ask the staff to draft proposed policies. These policies are then sent to a board committee for review.

The chair of each committee should be a board member appointed by the board president. Members of committees are usually selected by the committee chair and may include non-board members.

All committees are advisory (except that the bylaws may permit the executive committee to act on behalf of the board between board meetings). Once a committee has approved a proposed policy, it is submitted to the board for approval.

Board members who wish a policy to be adopted begin the discussion by making a motion that a policy be approved. If another board member seconds the motion, discussion can begin; if not, the motion fails.

Once a motion is seconded, the chairperson opens the floor for discussion. Members are recognized by the chairperson before they may speak, and they can discuss only the motion on the floor. When the discussion has ended, the chairperson announces that a vote will be taken.

The easiest way to vote is by a show of hands. The secretary can then record the vote. If more than a majority approves a policy, it becomes the board's policy (unless the bylaws provide otherwise). It is the responsibility of the executive director to implement that policy.

The executive director receives instructions from the board at a board meeting. It is improper for individual board members to give assignments to any staff member without prior board authorization.

Holding High-Quality Board Meetings

One key factor in getting and keeping excellent board members is the quality of the board meetings. If board meetings are unproductive, board members tend to be unproductive.

An important technique for improving board meetings is to do as much planning *before the board meeting* as possible.

This might include:

- Sending a notice of the date, time, and location of the meeting to the members several weeks before the meeting. Even if the board meets the same day of each month at the same place and time, a reminder notice is important.

- Giving the board members the telephone number of the individual (usually the chairperson) to call if they cannot attend the meeting. In this way, the chairperson can get input on important items from individuals who cannot attend the meeting. Also, if a quorum will not be present, the meeting can be canceled in advance.

- Notifying members of important items to be discussed at the meeting. For major items, information or issue papers might be included in the meeting notice packet.

- Including as many written items as possible with the meeting notice rather than distributing them at the meeting. This includes the minutes of the previous meeting and the treasurer's report, for example. Members then have an opportunity to read items before the meeting, and members who do not attend the meeting are kept up-to-date more effectively.

- Developing a preliminary agenda before the meeting. Committee chairs who will be asked to report at the meeting should be notified. Background reports should be developed for important issues.

The board meeting should start on time. Once the members know that every board meeting starts on time, it is much more likely that they will be prompt. Each board meeting should start with the distribution of a written agenda. The agenda should be as detailed as possible, listing each separate item to be voted on.

Once the secretary announces that a quorum is present, the chairperson asks all those present if there are any additional items for the agenda. Thus, there will be no surprises and the chairperson can run the meeting more effectively. The chairperson has the option of referring new items to committees or postponing items until future meetings.

The order of business at most meetings is as follows:

- *Approval of the minutes of the previous meeting.* A formal vote is needed to approve the minutes. Minutes should be distributed to all members and should not be read aloud at the meeting.

- *Chairperson's Report.* The chairperson should state before each item which items are informational and which require board action. The chairperson should remind the members that only policy-making recommendations require board action.

- *Executive Director's Report.* This report should be in writing. If it is lengthy, it should be distributed before the meeting. The executive director should then highlight important aspects of the written report and take questions.

- *Committee Reports.* Committee reports should be in writing unless they are very brief. After giving the report, the committee chair should make specific motions when board action is required. Only policy items require board action; no board action is required when the committee chair is simply providing information.

- *Unfinished Business.* The only items belonging in this section are ones raised at previous board meetings. The chairperson should remind the members when the item was raised originally and why it was postponed.

- *New Business.* Major items of business are discussed as part of the chairperson's report, executive director's Report, or committee reports. At the beginning of the meeting, members are asked if they have additional agenda items, and the chairperson has the option of placing some of these items under New Business.

- *Good and Welfare.* Many organizations provide an opportunity for members and guests to make short announcements, raise issues to be discussed at future meetings, or to comment on items of interest.

- *Adjournment.* No formal action is needed. The chairperson announces the date, time, and place of the next meeting, reminds the members of steps to be taken before the meeting, such as committee meetings, and adjourns the board meeting.

After the board meeting, the minutes are sent to board members for their review. The minutes must include a list of attendees and the motions made and votes taken. Additional information may be included at the pleasure of the board. Many organizations include only the minimum required, and the minutes do not include individual comments made at the meeting. While the minutes need not be taken by the board secretary, they should be distributed under the signature of the board secretary.

Relationship Between Board and Staff Members

The board of directors sets policy for the organization. Several examples of the types of policies set by the board are provided above. The only way policy can be set is by a majority vote of the board at a board meeting (unless the bylaws provide otherwise).

The executive director (or the chief executive officer of the organization) attends all board meetings, and is responsible for implementing the policies set by the board. The executive director hires other staff members (whose salary levels and job descriptions have been approved by the board) to assist in implementing these policies.

When an item arises at a board meeting, the chairperson rules whether the item is a policy matter. If so, a vote of the board is required in order for action to be taken. If the item is not a policy matter, no board vote is taken. The purpose of the discussion is to provide guidance to the executive director on non-policy matters.

The executive director researches sources of funds and writes grant applications. Before a grant application can be submitted to a funding source, it should be approved by the board.

Certain types of communications between board members and staff members are not appropriate. For example, individual board members may not give assignments to staff members. Assignments are given to the executive director by vote of the board at a board meeting. The executive director is responsible for assigning tasks to other staff members.

Staff members should not complain to individual board members about programs, assignments, or policies. Complaints should be made according to specific procedures established by the board.

When a board member volunteers to help out in the office, that person must be treated as a staff person and no longer wears the "board hat." The executive director remains the person to make assignments to that person.

Tips:

- Develop a list of typical decision areas that are likely to arise in the course of routine corporate operations and reach a board consensus on whether the decisions should be made by—

  a. The executive director alone.
  b. The executive director, in consultation with the board.
  c. The executive director, in consultation with the board chairperson.
  d. The board alone.
  e. The chairperson alone.
  f. A committee of the board.

  Review, revise, and update this list annually.

- Consider adopting a policy on the responsibilities and privileges of board members, and include a conflict-of-interest policy.

Chapter 5
Strategic Planning

> Synopsis: Formal strategic planning is not for every organization. All stakeholders must be committed to successfully develop and implement a strategic plan. Although such plans require a major investment in money and time and have other institutional costs and risks, the benefits include enhancing the agency's ability to respond to internal and external threats.

Introduction

Strategic planning is a formalized process by which an organization makes a study of its vision for the future, typically for three years or more from the present. A strategic plan is an important management tool for agency leaders to consider the effects of advances in technology, changing markets for its services, the effects of government funding cutbacks, or the emergence of other organizations (both for-profits and nonprofits) that provide similar, competing services.

Agency CEOs often are so involved with putting out fires and responding to the exigencies of day-to-day operations that it is a luxury to set aside time to think about the position of the organization even a year into the future. An agency's board is often ill-equipped to consider changes in agency structure and operations in the context of a regular board meeting.

Purpose of Strategic Planning

In his 1994 book *The Rise and Fall of Strategic Planning,* Henry Mintzberg lists four reasons organizations do strategic planning: to coordinate their activities, to ensure that the future is taken into account, to be rational, and to control. Strategic planning is designed to suggest remedies for agency problems before they blow up. Deep cuts in government grants, changes in markets, advances in technology, competition from for-profit businesses, and changes in demographics in an agency's service area all crystallize the need to change the basic way an agency does business.

Virtually all successful large for-profit businesses engage in a formal strategic planning process. The conventional wisdom is that businesses that do so, regardless of whether they are for-profit or nonprofit, are more successful over time than those that do not. However, Mintzberg cites scores of academic studies that show mixed results as to the benefits of strategic planning in business and industry, and concludes that the value of strategic planning is nebulous at best.

Putting that aside, a periodic strategic planning process provides the framework for a long-term assessment of emerging threats, and the opportunity to develop creative strategies to respond to them. The intent here is not to encourage or discourage nonprofits to engage in a formal strategic planning process; rather, it is to raise issues to consider in the event that this endeavor, for whatever reason, is under consideration.

Strategic planning requires the investment of both money and time. For most nonprofits, both are scarce. Thus, it is important that agency leaders systematically evaluate whether the benefits of preparing, updating, and implementing a periodic strategic plan outweigh the costs. Strategic plan preparation often involves the hiring of an outside consultant, plenty of meetings, and the involvement of board members, agency staff, and other agency stakeholders for an extended period of time.

The strategic planning process is fraught with danger. The contents of a final strategic plan often are totally at odds with the vision of the agency leader who first suggested preparing one. The planning committee dynamics are often uncontrollable by the people who provide the agency with leadership. Agency leaders may be uncomfortable sharing the agency's dreams and aspirations, its "dirty little secrets," and proprietary financial projections with a professional outside consultant, and may be even more reticent with community members of the planning committee. Yet, many agencies that successfully complete a strategic planning process improve their performance. Participating board members feel a renewed connection and bond to both the agency and their colleagues. Agencies that don't plan for the future, whether in a formalized process or informal board retreats, often suffer the consequences.

Strategic planning in the for-profit sector has been popular for several decades. In the for-profit world, strategic planning has the advantage of having each member of the committee, virtually by definition, already in agreement on the basic mission of the organization; that is, in short, to make as much profit as possible. There will be differences, of course, as to the methods used to accomplish this. In a nonprofit, there is not always agreement on the mission from the outset. In a hospital situation, for example, some planning committee members may view the mission as providing quality health care to the community. Some may feel it is to teach medical students, advance life-saving technology, increase "market share" by gobbling up other health care institutions, or serve populations not served by other institutions.

In a for-profit setting, the outcomes are easily measurable—net profit and market share are statistics easily compiled. In the nonprofit sector, consumer satisfaction, community benefit, and image in the community often are considered more important than bottom-line net revenue, and are difficult to measure satisfactorily. In the nonprofit sector, board members may actually be concerned if the institution is making too much net revenue and not providing services to sectors of the market that would clearly result in revenue shortfalls. It is the nature of nonprofits that the institution is not motivated by private profit motive and, in theory, this can create conflicts. As one commentator wryly suggested in response to President Bush's *Thousand Points of Light* program, it's all right to be one of the "thousand points of light" and do good deeds, but someone still has to pay the light bill. As a result of government cutbacks, tensions are mounting within nonprofit boards as they wrestle with difficult decisions concerning how to ease the financial crunch while maintaining traditional markets.

Making the Decision to Develop a Strategic Plan

The motivation for initiating a strategic plan comes from many sources:

Board Members. Board members who have participated in successful strategic planning as a result of their service on other nonprofit boards are often the source for initiating a strategic plan. Board members who run their own businesses or work for for-profit companies that routinely develop strategic plans also may raise this issue. Many who serve on nonprofit boards see strategic planning as a management and governance tool equal in importance to budgeting, and cannot imagine an organization that doesn't initiate a formal process to look inward at least once every half-decade.

Funders. Some funders require the development of a strategic plan before they make grants to nonprofit charities. These funders want evidence that their contributions will be used prudently and cost-effectively, and will influence the direction of the organization. A strategic plan developed as a result of such a requirement by a funder would obviously highlight changes in the organization's programs that are the direct result of the contribution.

Retirement of a Long-Term CEO. Many nonprofits were started by visionary leaders who ran the organizations from the seat of their pants. This "old school" of doing business may no longer be valid. New agency leaders, many with MBAs, believe that nonprofit organizations are businesses, and the same management techniques they learned in business school are applicable to the philanthropic sector. The new school recognizes that the bottom line remains the principal concern of the agency, whether or not the bottom line is interpreted as the net revenue at the end of the year or the number of satisfied clients served. The old school agency executive is often skeptical, if not fearful, of strategic planning. Perhaps his or her vision of the agency has never been challenged, and a formal process to evaluate the agency from top to bottom, from the mission statement on down, is a threat to executive autonomy. In some cases, that skepticism is justified.

Once a new generation assumes the mantle of leadership, there is motivation to rebuild the agency from the ground up, starting with the mission statement and proceeding, in some extreme cases, to changing the model of the copying machine. A strategic plan is often the vehicle for the new leadership to assert its authority and provide a mechanism for a higher level of executive accountability.

Agency Trauma. More often than not, it is an organizational crisis that triggers the decision for a strategic plan when an agency has no regular process to prepare one. The resignation or firing of a CEO is a traumatic event for any nonprofit. Sometimes, this event has occurred because of underlying unresolved issues and problems that may have developed and been inadequately addressed over many years. In the case of the involuntary separation, the organization's leadership has the opportunity to reshape the organization before a new executive takes over and molds the direction of the agency. Other traumatic events that may trigger the initiation of a strategic plan are the loss of a major funder, the establishment of competition from another nonprofit or for-profit, major damage to, or aging of, the agency's physical plant, liability suits, or quantum advances in technology that call into question the future demand for services by the agency.

Benefits of Strategic Planning

1. It permits discussion of issues in a proactive rather than reactive mode. Usually developed in an atmosphere that encourages creativity and brainstorming, the strategic plan may not only include concrete directions, but also provide an institutional set of core values. In a typical board meeting, there is simply no time to engage in a meaningful discussion about the long-term future of an agency, unless the board governance model recommended by Gerry Kaufman in Chapter 6 is followed. Many nonprofits are operating on the edge of financial chaos, often one failed grant application away from having to lay off staff or fold entirely.

2. It requires an action plan to solve real problems faced by an agency. The action plan is a template that the staff can use to implement the policies and desires of the board. Many CEOs complain that the board helps with solving problems, but fails to provide direction on the core values of the agency. A strategic plan explicitly includes those core values, and assists the CEO in creative strategies for solving current problems and anticipating future ones.

3. It provides a formal mandate for the reallocation of resources to respond to changing conditions, and the means to obtain additional resources if required. A successful strategic planning process that develops an aggressive plan to attack problems often energizes a moribund board.

4. It builds inter-board relationships that might not otherwise exist, and creates a partnership among the board chairperson, board members, staff, funders, and other stakeholders. Each has a role that is defined in the plan and, if bought into, the added responsibilities increase the available resources of the agency. The social contact that occurs at many board retreats, particularly those designed in bucolic settings away from the hustle and bustle of the agency, cement personal relationships among participants. This improves the bond between the agency and its leadership.

5. It provides a mechanism for the board, staff, and agency stakeholders to become more informed about the activities and problems faced by the agency. It promotes, in many cases, a frank discussion by the agency executive of problems that might not be shared in a conventional board meeting context. Many CEOs welcome the process in that it takes a burden off their shoulders and shares it with the agency's "owners" and constituents.

6. It provides an opportunity to focus on the forest rather than the trees. It is easy for a CEO to become lost in the mundane issues of personnel, budgeting, office management, board relations, and public relations, and virtually ignore issues relating to the actual purpose and mission of the nonprofit.

Costs of Strategic Planning

1. **Money.** Serious strategic planning costs money, a scarce resource for most nonprofits. Many nonprofits recognize that it is useful to have a trained, dispassionate consultant to assist in the planning process. There are costs to schedule planning meetings and travel to those meetings. Many organizations recognize the value of eliminating outside distractions to aid brainstorming, and thus schedule planning meetings at staff retreats held at attractive, isolated campgrounds, conference centers, business resorts, or hotels. There are costs of photocopying and printing all of the planning documents. There are opportunity costs, as well, because staff and board resources are diverted from other duties.

2. **Time.** Any realistic strategic planning process requires the allocation of precious staff and board resources. Meeting preparation, meeting attendance, minutes, preparation of draft and final strategic plans, and hiring a consultant all take time. It is not uncommon for a strategic planning process to take more than a year.

3. **Potential bad will.** As with any process, things can go wrong. Bad group dynamics can result in painful meetings and destructive outcomes. It is not unusual for a group to spend an entire four-hour meeting arguing over trivial words in a mission statement. This can be painfully frustrating for committee members more interested in developing an action plan to solve agency problems. Strategic planning may bring board factions into collision, and meetings can degenerate into a test of wills. This may be healthy in the context of a committee rather than having a drag-out fight at a board meeting, but it means that to have a constructive planning process, personal baggage must be dealt with first. If the final strategic plan is not implemented, board members who participated may feel that the agency wasted their time, and may not be as likely to participate in future efforts, or even may resign from the board. Current staff members may feel threatened that their jobs are at risk, and may look for other employment.

4. **Loss of Agency Initiative.** A formal strategic plan may diminish an executive's initiative and quick response to changing conditions, because the preferred course of action is not in the strategic plan. The strategic plan may become outdated quickly and stifle a more-appropriate response to changing conditions that were not anticipated in the plan. In addition, strategic planning often involves the board not just in setting objectives and outcomes, but also in determining the methods that should be used to achieve those objectives and outcomes. Many feel that this is the role of staff, not the board, and making it the role of the board takes away the flexibility necessary for executive staff to function effectively.

A Sample Strategic Planning Model

The intent of this chapter is to give a cursory review of what a strategic plan is, its costs and benefits, some advantages and disadvantages, and some issues that often arise when nonprofits consider initiating a strategic plan. It is recommended that other specific resources be consulted when exploring the need for a strategic planning process, and several excellent sources are included in the bibliography. The following is one model for developing a strategic plan, and is a hybrid put together from several theoretical models.

Step 1. Decide whether to develop a strategic plan.

Consider the costs and benefits mentioned earlier in this chapter, and also the following questions:

- Is there enough time and money to allocate for this planning process now?

- Is the agency prepared to implement whatever plan eventually is approved, or will it sit on the shelf?

- Do we have a commitment from the agency's executive director, board chairperson, board members, and other stakeholders to develop a plan, or will we just be going through the motions?

- Are the agency's short-term problems so overwhelming that the agency is wasting time planning for the future when its continued existence is seriously threatened by current problems?

Step 2. Build the infrastructure necessary to develop a plan.

a. Appoint a planning committee of the board. Include creative board members, funders, the CEO, chief financial officer, clients, and opinion makers from the community. Consider that any committee of more than 10 becomes unmanageable. Some strategic planners recommend that the entire board serve on the committee.

b. Compile and distribute articles and related material on strategic planning to the entire board. (For information on reprints or rights to photocopy this chapter or other copyrighted materials, contact the publisher of the material.)

c. Decide on whether the facilitator/consultant will be a board member or a private paid or volunteer consultant. A board member already knows a lot about the organization, its strengths and weaknesses, its personnel, and all other members of the committee. On the other hand, that board member brings with him or her prejudices about colleagues and staff, and often has a point of view or hidden agenda that is not held at arm's length. A private strategic planning consultant has the experience to keep the discussion focused and follow the agenda. There are many consultants who have experience working with nonprofit agencies in designing the planning process itself, participating in orientation sessions for the planning committee, serving as a referee for dispute resolution, helping the committee reach consensus when that is desired, neutralizing oppositional or disruptive participants, and providing technical assistance.

A good consultant can organize the process and provide logistical support so that the agency board and staff will not be absorbed by the planning process mechanics. On the other hand, a bad consultant may influence the process beyond what is desirable, and constrain the participation of committee members. One must be careful to assure that the plan, if written by a consultant, is not a tepid re-write of the plan the consultant developed for a previous client, which may have only minimal relevance to the current client.

It is good advice to informally survey comparable organizations to check out potential strategic planning consultants. Statewide associations may also be helpful in identifying consultants. Of course, it is vital that any contract between the organization and the consultant spell out exactly what services are required, the timetable, and the level of participation required by the consultant.

Step 3. Decide how many years the strategic plan will cover.

In general, small nonprofits choose a shorter time frame than larger nonprofits, perhaps two-four years for smaller agencies, compared to larger institutions, which prepare five-year plans.

Step 4. Put in writing the timetable and the process.

This includes the steps that are required and who is responsible for accomplishing each task. Among the tasks are:

- appointing the committee
- hiring a consultant or facilitator
- leading the orientation of the planning committee
- picking the meeting site
- scheduling the meetings
- writing the first draft of the plan
- providing the procedures to review and revise the draft
- writing the final plan
- developing the process for the planning committee to approve the final plan
- formulating the review and the process for the full board's approval of the final plan.

Step 5. Prepare a memo on what is expected of the strategic planning process.

This memo to the planning committee should highlight the major problems that are to be resolved by the strategic plan, such as how to review and update the mission statement, how to respond to potential cuts in government funding, how to respond to the new location of a for-profit competitor, how to deal with a change in the demographics of the people in the area served by the agency, and so on. The memo should note whether the planning report should be a consensus document (that does not meet unanimity) or rather majority rules after all points of view are heard.

Step 6. Have the agency board endorse the planning process, and allocate funds necessary for it to proceed.

Step 7. Appoint the committee, appoint or hire the facilitator/consultant, send out orientation materials, and schedule the first meeting.

The first meeting

The first meeting is usually an orientation session, which includes some of the following components:

1. A review of the purpose of the committee, the timetable, future meeting schedule, meeting the facilitator.

2. A review of the agency's current mission, history, short-term problems, long-term threats, staff resources, programs, activities, strengths and weaknesses, major successes and failures, core values of the organization, financial status, future commitments. The agency's CEO and CFO should be present to answer questions from the planning committee, and ask questions of the facilitator to establish ground rules for the planning process.

3. An analysis of the needs of the stakeholders, including those currently receiving service, and scenarios about how those needs may change. For example, is the population served by the agency changing demographically? Is government funding likely to drop? Is the community becoming poorer, limiting future fee-for-service revenue and requiring more non-fee revenue?

4. An analysis of institutional limits: population served by geography, age group, income level.

5. An identification of what in the above can be changed by the organization as a result of strategic planning and what is the result of forces beyond the control of the agency.

The second meeting

The second meeting begins the brainstorming of the committee. This meeting examines the mission statement, and reviews potential changes to that statement that, in some cases, might have been unrevised for decades. The facilitator may list various problems on the horizon of the agency, with the planning committee serving as a focus group—such as funding problems, changes in markets, competitors, outside threats from changing social, economic, political, or technological conditions, or demand for services. The planning committee is given a homework assignment to come to the third meeting with suggestions for solving these problems.

The third meeting

The third meeting consists of brainstorming on action strategies that will solve the problems identified at the first and second meetings. The facilitator lists each strategy, and includes a table with the costs and benefits of each, the probability of success, and the pros and cons. Each strategy for each problem may be ranked based on the committee's assessment as to the value of the strategy.

The fourth meeting

The committee develops an action plan, with a timetable for implementation that includes coming up with the resources necessary to implement the action plan. The plan also includes a procedure to review the progress made in implementing the plan.

In the above model, a draft strategic plan can be accomplished with four three-hour meetings.

In *Managing a Nonprofit Organization*, Thomas Wolff outlines six levels in the linear model of strategic planning. In the linear model, the planning committee considers one level before proceeding to the next. This contrasts with the integrated planning model, which provides for many of these levels to be considered simultaneously, recognizing that the end result is interdependent upon each of the earlier levels.

Level 1. The planners consider the mission statement, which describes the purpose the organization is trying to achieve.

Level 2. Agency goals are developed, providing the general direction in which the organization intends to go.

Level 3. Objectives and targets are set, indicating the outcomes the organization hopes to achieve.

Level 4. Strategies are formulated to meet the objectives and targets. These are the methods and ways the organization plans to achieve those outcomes.

Level 5. An action plan is developed to implement the strategies.

Level 6. An evaluation is performed after implementation, to review whether the outcomes were achieved and whether the strategies were successful.

For example, a hypothetical nursing home might have a planning document that, in an abridged form, is as follows:

Level 1. To provide quality long-term care services to the aging population of Anytown, for the purpose of improving the quality of life for those who need institutional care.

Level 2. To reduce the operating deficit and become the long-term care institution of choice in the community by improving quality of care.

Level 3. Increase non-fee revenue by 50%, and improve the cash-flow situation by taking advantage of accounting productivity. Improve government reimbursement by 25% within three years.

Increase private pay residents from 30% to 50% within the next five years.

Level 4. Issue charitable gift annuities and hire a development staff member.

Hire a lobbyist to assist the statewide association to advocate for continuing the Medicaid intergovernmental transfer program.

Hire a marketing associate to place advertisements in publications read by active, upscale, middle-aged persons whose parents may be in need of long-term care services.

Level 5. Investigate the feasibility of marketing charitable gift annuities, and hire a consultant by July 15 to develop a program for residents and their families.

Aggressively go after accounts receivable, delay accounts payable for an additional 30 days, eliminate programs that are not profitable, increase fee-for service; increase fundraising; become entrepreneurial by selling subscriptions to a newsletter.

Place an advertisement in the state chapter of the Society of Association Executives newsletter to hire a registered lobbyist.

Hire a marketing associate by June 15, and use endowment funds for seed money, and assume the new staff member will generate at least enough income to finance his or her salary.

Level 6. One year after final approval of this report, require the executive director to prepare a progress report on whether the goals outlined in level 2 are being achieved, and what mid-course corrections to Level 5 are required in order to meet the targets of Level 3.

The process of planning each level can be discussed and refined for two hours or nine months. The parameters differ, obviously, for a hospital with a half-billion dollars in gross revenue, compared to a charity with $50,000 in gross receipts.

The actual plan may be written by the facilitator, the chairperson of the planning committee, or staff in consultation with the board and facilitator. In every case, the planning committee should review a draft of the plan before submitting its final version to the board. The board reserves the power to approve, disapprove, approve with changes, or send the plan back for revision.

Some of the changes that may be recommended by a nonprofit agency strategic plan are:

1. a mission change
2. a change in the character of services provided
3. a plan to expand or downsize staff
4. a plan to expand or sell capital equipment and/or physical plant
5. a plan to expand fundraising
6. a plan to retrain staff
7. a plan to move the agency's location
8. a plan to seek a merger with similar organizations
9. a communications plan to improve or renovate the agency's public image
10. a plan to hire a lobbyist, or form a statewide association representing agencies with similar problems or uncertainties
11. a plan to establish a for-profit subsidiary
12. a plan to seek, or refuse, government grants
13. a plan to liquidate the agency
14. a plan to professionalize the agency, or deprofessionalize it—e.g., a decision by a hospital to substitute nurse aides where registered nurses were used formerly
15. a plan to change the governance of the organization—increase or decrease board membership, change quorum requirements, change voting requirements, change committee structure, change the powers of officers
16. a plan to change the compensation structure to reward and improve productivity
17. a plan to change the agency's market niche
18. a plan to change into a for-profit
19. a plan to modernize the name of the agency.

Some components of a strategic plan may be:

1. a five-year projection of staffing patterns
2. a five-year projected budget
3. sources of revenue to implement changes called for by the plan
4. a marketing strategy
5. a schedule for periodically updating the strategic plan
6. a schedule for evaluating whether the plan is being implemented effectively and whether the strategies provided in the plan are successful
7. a physical plant/equipment plan
8. yearly updates to the plan.

Chapter 6
A Transforming Model for
Nonprofit Board Leadership
By Gerald Kaufman

Overview

The nonprofit sector in the United States has undergone substantial changes over the past 20 years. There are many factors that are responsible for this change. The nonprofit sector itself has grown enormously over the past decade, fueled by the tremendous increase in fees and government funding. The nonprofit sector's funds are no longer predominantly from charity; only 18% of the revenue of the sector, excluding religion, came from philanthropy in 1990. The remainder came from fees (51%) and government (31%).

Society now relies on the nonprofit sector to deliver health and social services, participate in economic development, build housing, feed the hungry, educate and protect children, provide art and cultural experiences, and convey many other services. The sector no longer primarily dispenses charity, but rather provides essential services to all people, regardless of their income level.

Increased government funding has brought with it all of the trappings of bureaucracy: rules and regulations regarding internal management and financial accounting; program operation manuals governing all aspects of client treatment; and a strong emphasis on reimbursement for a detailed defined set of services, often overshadowing the organization's original mission, and narrowing the vision.

Providing services to individuals, although essential, does not translate into building strong, safe communities. The rise in numbers and importance of community development corporations and the resurgence of the settlement house movement may be vehicles for some community building.

Boundaries between the nonprofit sector and government and the for-profit sectors are eroding. Many parts of the nonprofit sector are becoming quasi-government. Large corporations and nonprofits are forming partnerships to solve community problems or to enhance the corporate image. This trend challenges the responsibilities, independence, and traditional values of the nonprofit sector.

Individual nonprofit organizations have become larger and more complex, often requiring sophisticated, professional management. An increasing number of them are using the most modern technology and marketing tools to raise money, attract clients, and influence public policy. In this climate, small community-based organizations have difficulty competing.

One result of the growth in size, complexity, and importance of the nonprofit sector is increasing scrutiny by the press, the public, and governments at all levels. Public officials are raising questions about whether nonprofits are being operated in the public interest or for private gain. Challenges to tax exemptions, particularly in Pennsylvania, are occurring in many jurisdictions. The IRS is increasing its auditing and oversight of nonprofit, tax-exempt organizations.

Disclosures of one well-known major charity's excessively high salary and perks for its executive director and similar scandals have led to the lessening of public confidence in the nonprofit sector, according to a recent Gallup poll.

Current Board Functioning

In many instances, boards of directors continue to operate as if change of this magnitude had not occurred. Too often, as one author put it, boards "... fall into trivia, short term myopia, meddling in staff work, and other failings. They do so even when composed of intelligent, experienced, caring members."

Professionally staffed, large, complex organizations tend to pursue funding without too much regard to mission. In these situations, boards often evaluate executive directors on the basis of the fund balance at the end of the year, rather than the accomplishment of the mission.

Ideally, the essential role of boards of directors is assuring that nonprofit organizations are mission-driven, governed by a board of citizens responsive to the community that they serve, based on the values of altruism, community and diversity, operated in an ethical and prudent manner, and providing citizens an opportunity to participate in the civic life of the community.

When one observes boards and board committees or reads minutes of meetings, one sees that much time is spent listening to reports. Committees meet to listen to appropriate staff members report on the subject matter under the committees' jurisdiction.

These meetings typically involve several telephone calls between the staff and the committee chairpersons, resulting in preparation of a report and an agenda by the staff. The meeting might take several hours of discussion and, as a result, some minor changes might be made to the report. The same process is repeated at board meetings, with many or all of the committees reporting. In addition to committees, the executive director and treasurer also make reports.

The line between board and staff roles and decisions is blurred. Too often, when the board is asked to take some action, it is of a trivial nature that should have been made by the executive director, such as: what kind of computer to buy, what insurance agent to use, what color the invitations should be for the fundraising dinner, what the sign-in and -out requirements should be for employees, and on and on. Some boards get involved in more weighty administrative decisions such as hiring staff, signing all checks, and approving grant proposals. In these instances, although much time is involved, seldom are the recommendations of the executive director not followed.

All of this activity gives many board members a sense that they are doing important work. But much of it is rubber stamping at best, or destructive interference in responsibilities of staff at worst. Others, however, frequently complain about the mind-numbing details that occupy board meeting time. As a result, board attendance is frequently low and quorums hard to assemble. What these activities largely amount to is reviewing what has already occurred, and they have little relevance to what are uniquely the board's responsibilities.

A major complaint of many executive directors is the enormous amount of staff support that these board activities require, and a feeling that much of it is meaningless. Another point of conflict often is around fundraising, with the executive director's expectations of the board seldom being fulfilled.

Boards also do some important work, such as composing the mission statement or engaging in strategic planning. Here, too, boards often defer to executive directors and give pro-forma approval to executive directors' efforts. However, some boards engage in strategic planning over extended periods of time, even as long as a year, involving themselves in the minute details of program operation.

Most board members receive little or no training as to their role or what is expected of them, other than being told that they "make policy," approve budgets, and have a fiduciary obligation for the fiscal integrity of the organization and for fundraising. This often translates into: routine approval of the annual plan and detailed financial reports prepared by the staff, receiving and reviewing the annual audit, and selling a few tickets to the annual fundraising event or helping to arrange a silent auction.

Another function performed by many board members is to act as volunteers in some aspect of the organization's programs. Although this is a worthwhile activity, it has nothing to do with board members as governors of the agency.

There is often tension between boards and executive directors concerning access to information. Boards spend so much time on trivia because they have not articulated what is important to them. They may look at anything and everything because they are not sure what they are looking for. Boards complain that they don't get enough information, or they get too much and don't know what to do with it. Executive directors complain that boards demand information and then they don't read it. If the nonprofit sector is to be the strong value- and mission-driven sector that the public expects and its history and role in society demand, strengthening and emphasizing the centrality of boards of directors is essential.

A New System of Board Governance

If we are to transform nonprofits into much more effective and accountable organizations, we must redefine the role of board governance. In this new world, we need a model of board governance that will assure that nonprofit organizations will be operated with vision on behalf of the community they serve, in an ethical and prudent manner, producing results that justify the costs.

John Carver, the father of this model of board governance, in his book, *Boards That Make A Difference*, defines board governance as follows:

> *Board leadership requires, above all, that the board provide vision. To do so, the board must first have an adequate vision of its own job. That role is best conceived neither as volunteer-helper nor as watchdog but as trustee-owner. Policy Governance is an approach to the job of governing that emphasizes values, vision, empowerment of both board and staff, and the strategic ability to lead leaders.*

The concept of trustee-owner is central to this new system of board governance. Every nonprofit exists for the benefit of the "moral" owners and the board functions as trustees on their behalf. The board's job is to define who those moral owners are. In the case of a legal services agency, the owners might be all low-income people living in the community that the organization serves. For a low-income housing development group, the owners might be, at one level, all of those needing decent low-income housing; but, at another level, the owners are all residents of the city, because a healthy society is one in which everyone is housed decently.

Every nonprofit exists for those who would benefit from the realization of its mission in its broadest sense. Boards of trustees operate nonprofit organizations in trust for these moral owners. The *primary* responsibility of boards then is not to support the staff, but rather to assure that the organization fulfills its fiduciary obligation to the owners.

Board members may also act as volunteer-helpers but they do that as any non-board member would, not as trustee-owners. The board has certain, defined watchdog functions, but that should not take up the majority of its time as it does now in so many organizations.

While everyone in an organization makes policy at some level, the question is what policies are the board's? Policy is defined as, "The values or perspectives that underlie actions." The following is a short summary of the four areas that define the board's job and for which written policies are required:

1. Ends or Outcomes. The board must determine how the world will be different as a result of the activities of the organization. To do that, the board must decide what human needs will be met, for whom, and at what cost. The board should formulate these ends policies starting at the broadest level—the mission statement—and continue from the next broadest formulation to a point where they are willing to stop and delegate the balance to the executive director.

The mission statement is a statement about outcomes. Outcomes are not activities; they are the results expected from the activities of the organization. Under this model, boards are concerned with results or ends, and their obligation as owners of the organization is to assure the production of worthwhile ends.

Practices, methods, activities are means, not ends. Boards should stay out of staff means, except to say what means are not acceptable, which will be discussed below.

A typical nonprofit mission statement might be that it provides "high-quality services to the mentally retarded" or "shelter and supportive services for the victims of domestic violence." These are statements about activities, not about outcomes. Boards must decide what they expect the agency to accomplish, and what results are expected from these high-quality services.

An example of a results-based mission statement might be to prepare the mentally retarded for "independent living in the community." In that instance, the board might further specify that independent living includes job readiness, household mainte-nance, knowledge of community resources, and other skill areas that the board believed were necessary to enable the clients to live independently in the community. What means the staff put in place to achieve the ends should not be a matter of board concern.

Private and government funders often dictate staff means by requiring very specific programs, activities, and methods. Under these circumstances, if boards are clear about ends, then staff can negotiate with funders about means. If staff believes that programs prescribed by funders will not achieve the results or ends determined by the board, then the organization should refuse the grant or contract or the board should revise the ends policies.

Such an approach will counteract the seduction for nonprofit agencies to pursue whatever funding is available, whether or not the funding will accomplish the reason for the organization's existence.

In the area of domestic violence, for example, there are studies that show that if police are trained to intervene strongly with an abuser, the repetition of domestic violence can be substantially reduced. However, most domestic violence agencies are paid to provide only shelter and treatment for the abused partner.

Under this model, boards would grapple with the question of what outcomes the organization is expected to achieve and would regularly monitor the agency on that basis. Outcomes might include reduction of abuse, independent lives away from their abusers, temporary respite, or preservation of families.

The formulation and reformulation of ends policies will occupy much of the board's time and, to perform that role, much of a board's attention will be focused outside the organization. The board will need to inform itself of community needs and how those needs are changing, whether there are other organizations it should be collaborating with, how changes in public policy are likely to affect the mission, and whether the organization should merge with other groups to better accomplish the mission.

2. Executive Limitations. These policies articulate the board's values regarding how the executive director manages the organization. Executive limitations policies are proscriptive; that is, they are expressed in negative terms, and state what the board will not permit in the following areas: treatment of staff and volunteers, financial planning (budgeting), financial condition, asset protection, board awareness, and information. These are the usual areas of board concern with the means the executive director uses to manage the organization.

Under this model of board governance, boards do not get involved in the program activities as governors of the organization, other than to assure themselves that the activities are achieving the desired ends. (Board members may get involved in the activities as volunteers working under the supervision of the appropriate staff person, and in those instances they are not acting in their board member/governor capacity.)

If boards determine the ends to be attained and then ordain the means of attaining them, it is not reasonable to hold the executive director accountable for the outcomes. Executive limitations narrow and define the board's involvement in staff means.

Under traditional board operations, boards prescribe from time to time how the executive director is to operate the organization. A typical example is the formal adoption of a set of personnel policies. At other times, board members suggest what kind of telephone system to install, how often the newsletter should go out, fundraising ideas, marketing strategies, or even how to run a staff meeting.

Board actions or suggestions are scattered through the minutes over the months and years, often forgotten. The executive director may not be sure whether the board is directing the executive director to take some action, or merely offering suggestions, and many of these ideas and suggestions just float out in limbo. On the other hand, some board members may interpret a suggestion as a board directive and later criticize the executive for not complying.

Executive limitations place the responsibility for operational details where it belongs, on the executive director, other than the values of prudence and ethics that the board has identified as important limitations on the executive's authority. These policies regarding executive limitations normally can be written in five or six pages and provide the basis for clearly defined and targeted monitoring of executive director actions.

Boards, under this approach, free themselves from the operational minutiae and the impossible and endless task of monitoring all details of programs and management. With executive limitations in place, the board will have identified what is really important to it and confine its monitoring accordingly.

Thus, instead of boards drafting or even approving personnel policies, executive limitations would state what it would not allow in the treatment of personnel. For instance, board-drafted personnel policies normally include a detailed grievance procedure for employees. Executive limitations would simply state that the executive director shall not fail to have a policy permitting employees to submit a grievance to the board.

Other examples of value-laden executive limitations are prohibiting discrimination regarding hiring or promotions, sexual harassment, and making purchases over a certain amount without competitive bids. Boards should not concern themselves with matters that do not involve their values, such as what holidays the staff has off, whether the organization has flex time, or other details of staff operation properly in the province of management.

Executive limitations policies free the board for the much more important and exciting work of defining the organizational ends, of envisioning the future. The staff, in turn, has much more time to do the work necessary to reach the vision.

3. Executive Director-Board Relationship. This set of policies describes what is expected of the executive director (achievement of ends policies and non-violation of executive limitations), and how and when the policies of the board will be monitored. The executive director is evaluated on the performance of the agency, not on individual performance.

A fundamental principle is that a board monitors only against criteria previously set. The board monitors against these pre-set criteria in one of three ways, depending on which criterion is being monitored: executive director's report regarding ends and executive limitations; external report, such as an audit; and direct inspections of documents or locations. A monitoring schedule, with times and manner of monitoring, is included in this set of policies.

4. Board Process. These policies describe how the board is going to govern itself. They include the role of the president, committees, board job description and board internal dynamics. The board job products are linkage with the ownership, written governing policies, and assurance of executive performance. Optional products include fundraising and government relations or advocacy.

An important principle is that the board speaks with one voice and relates to one employee, the executive director. Board holism is fragmented by the use of traditional board committees, which normally concern themselves with some aspect of staff operations and, therefore, accomplish little other than rubber stamping staff recommendations or interfering with staff work. Under this model of governance, board committees are used to help the board do its job, not the staff's job.

If the board is to speak with one voice, it is not acceptable for individual board members to direct employees or the executive director to take action or produce reports, unless the whole board has spoken on the subject. This principle alone could save many organizations countless hours and substantial staff stress.

Conclusion

This approach to board governance defines the jobs of the board and executive director; gives boards leadership responsibilities to determine the mission and vision of the agency; keeps boards out of operations by focusing them on ends, not means, other than to assure themselves that the means used are prudent and ethical. The executive director is an active participant in the discussions leading to the adoption of all of the policies.

The move to this model of board leadership takes time, and it takes letting go of old habits and processes. Boards will need outside assistance in making the transition. Board meetings will be different, and those board members who like dealing with administrative and program details might be somewhat uncomfortable. The major emphasis for selecting board members will be on people with vision who are connected to the broader ownership.

By implementing this model of board governance, the board and staff of nonprofit organizations will be united in a common vision and mission, will have delineated clear boundaries between the board and staff concerning staff methods and activities, will be in closer touch with their "community" and other parts of the external world, and, above all, will be producing worthwhile outcomes rather than inputs.

An important consequence of this model is that many organizations will need to be much more collaborative with others in order to fulfill their missions and attain their ends. A "drug-free community," or similar world-changing mission, is not possible without the involvement of many other groups and organizations.

Governance is not about managing an organization, but about creating a world. Governance is about dreaming.

Gerald Kaufman, the author of this essay, is a nonprofit organizational development consultant based in Philadelphia. He is headquartered at 126 W. Mt. Airy Avenue, Philadelphia, PA 19119 and can be telephoned at (215) 247-5070.

Chapter 7
Nonprofit Organization Ethics

> Synopsis: Nonprofit charities have a special obligation, both legal and moral, to uphold the highest standards of ethical practice, to be accountable to their boards and the public, to avoid conflicts of interest, and to treat their employees with dignity.

Introduction

Nonprofit organizations, especially those qualified under section 501(c)(3) of the Internal Revenue Code, occupy a special and unique place in American society. Their uniqueness has many attributes.

All such organizations are supported by the nation's taxpayers: they are exempt from federal and state income taxes; contributors, for the most part, can deduct their contributions from their federal income tax (and from their state income taxes in most states; they are eligible to have their postage subsidized by the federal government; and many are exempt from state and local sales and property taxes.

In our highly competitive, individualistic society, the nonprofit sector provides a way to express our humanitarian values, to preserve our cultural heritage, to promote various causes, to educate, and to enlighten. It is often through coming together in nonprofit organizations that our citizens exercise their constitutional rights to petition their government, free speech, assembly, and freedom of religion. Nonprofits play a unique role as the intermediary between the citizens and their government.

Maybe most important of all, nonprofits formulate much of the moral agenda for society. One only has to think of the environmental movement, rape crisis and domestic violence centers, public subsidies of arts and humanities, public awareness of AIDS and support of AIDS programs, and countless other issues that people coming together in voluntary organizations were able to put on the nation's agenda.

Historically, the primary distinguishing characteristic of the nonprofit sector is that it is mission- and value-driven. Nonprofit organizations exist to accomplish some social good, however that may be defined. A set of values and assumptions underlies this view of the voluntary sector including altruism, cooperation, community, and diversity. The privileges granted to the sector and public expectations are grounded in this belief.

However, there is a trend away from this traditional source of values towards a for-profit value system that emphasizes competition, survival, market share, growth for growth's sake, and, above all, emphasis on the bottom line. This shift is fueled in part by increasing government contracting as nonprofits face more responsibilities, scarce resources, the influence of board members from the corporate community, the demands of funders, and the increasing number of trained "managers" who come into the nonprofit sector without being imbued with its traditions and values.

Some economists view the nonprofit sector as a form of business that is the result of the failure of the market in the private and public sectors. These economists overlook the place of the independent sector in the civic life of our society.

The following are some issues relating to ethics that are appropriate for nonprofit boards and staff to consider:

1. Accountability

Accountability often is overlooked in discussions about ethics. Because of the unique status of 501(c)(3) organizations, they have a special obligation to the public to be accountable for the results of their activities that justify their tax exemptions and other privileges. Organizations should continually challenge themselves by asking if the outcomes produced are worth the public investment.

Nonprofit boards of directors have a special obligation to govern with integrity. Governing with integrity means that the organization recognizes that it is accountable to the public, to the people it serves, and to its funders. Accountability includes the concept that nonprofit organizations exist only to produce worthwhile results in furtherance of their mission.

In addition, accountability encompasses a core system of values and beliefs regarding the treatment of staff, clients, colleagues, and community. Yet, organizational survival needs too often undercut core values. Although everyone in the organization is responsible, it is the board's ultimate responsibility to assure that its values are not compromised, and that the activities are conducted within acceptable limits.

A more subtle issue of accountability is seldom discussed. Staff will sometimes pursue grants and contracts, or engage in direct solicitation campaigns, for the primary purpose of growing. Boards sometimes ask whether the executive director "grew the organization" as the primary criterion for measuring success. Boards have an obligation to ensure that all activities support the organization's mission.

2. Conflict of Interest

A potential conflict of interest occurs any time organizational resources are directed to the private interests of a person or persons who have an influence over the decision. Examples might include the leasing of property owned by a relative of the executive director or a board member, the board awarding itself a salary, the organization hiring a board member to provide legal representation, or the executive director hiring a relative or a board member's relative.

A conflict also can occur when the person or persons making a decision expects something in exchange from the person in whose favor the decision is made. One example of this is the case in which an executive director retains a direct mail firm, and the executive director's spouse is hired by that direct mail firm shortly thereafter.

With regard to board members, the cleanest approach is to adopt a policy that does not allow any board member to profit from the organization. It is the duty of every board member to exercise independent judgment solely on behalf of the organization. For example, suppose a board member who owns a public relations business successfully argues that the nonprofit needs a public relations campaign and then is hired for the campaign. The board member's self-interest in arguing for the campaign will always be subject to question.

Suppose in the above example the board member offers to do the campaign at cost, and that is the lowest bid. It may be that even at cost, the board member's firm benefits because the campaign will pay part of the salary of some staff members or cover other overhead. It may be perfectly appropriate to accept the board member's offer, even though it is a conflict of interest. However, it is absolutely essential that the board have a procedure in place to deal with these types of issues.

Some organizations permit financial arrangements with board members, provided that the member did not vote on that decision. Given the good fellowship and personal relationships that often exist within nonprofit boards, such a rule can be more for show and without substance.

A similar problem can cause a conflict in the awarding of contracts to non-insiders. There may be personal reasons for one or more members of the board or the executive director to award contracts to particular persons, such as enhancing their personal or professional relationship with that person.

There are instances when it is appropriate to have a contract with an insider, such as when a board member offers to sell equipment to the organization at cost, or agrees to sell other goods or services well below market value. Here, too, the organization should assure itself that these same goods or services are not available as donations.

It is essential for the board to confront and grapple with these issues and adopt a written policy to govern conflict of interest in order to avoid the trap of self-dealing, or its appearances.

3. Disclosures

There are many ethical issues and much disagreement within the nonprofit sector regarding how much disclosure is required to those who donate to charitable nonprofits. The first obligation of every organization is to obey the laws and regulations governing disclosure. Nonprofits have a legal and ethical obligation to report fundraising costs accurately on their IRS Form 990, to obey the requirement regarding what portion of the cost of attending a fundraising event is deductible, and to comply with state charitable registration laws and regulations.

Nonprofits face a more difficult ethical issue when deciding how much disclosure that is not required by law to make, particularly if the organization believes that some people may not contribute if those disclosures are made.

In the for-profit corporate world, the Securities and Exchange Commission demands full, written disclosure of pertinent information, no matter how negative, when companies are offering stock to the public. There is no comparable agency that regulates charitable solicitations by nonprofits. Nonprofits must be very careful to disclose voluntarily all relevant information and to avoid the kind of hyperbole that misrepresents the agency.

Another difficult issue is whether fundraising costs should be disclosed at the point of solicitation. The costs of telemarketing campaigns or of maintaining development offices are sometimes 80%, or even higher, of every dollar collected. Some argue that people wouldn't give if these costs were disclosed. Others argue that if the soliciting organization cannot justify these costs to the public, and in many cases they are not justifiable, then the organization is not deserving of support.

There are recognized ethical standards regarding public charitable solicitations promulgated by the following:

National Charities Information Bureau
19 Union Square West
New York, NY 10003-3395
(212) 929-6300
http://www.give.org/index.cfm

Council of Better Business Bureaus
4200 Wilson Blvd.
Suite 800
Arlington, VA 22203
(703) 276-0100
http://www.bbb.org

A different set of ethical issues exists around disclosures to foundation and corporate funders. For instance, what is the obligation of disclosing changed circumstances after the proposal is submitted and before it is acted upon, such as when key staff have announced plans to leave? If the organization knows that the changed circumstance might affect the decision, is it unethical not to disclose it?

4. Other Issues

Accumulation of Surplus

If funds of a charitable nonprofit are to be used for charitable purposes, what is a reasonable amount of surplus to accumulate? The National Charities Information Bureau suggests a ceiling of twice the current year's expenses or the next year's budget, whichever is greater.

Organizations should consider the circumstances under which it is appropriate to disclose to prospective donors the amount expected to be used to accumulate a surplus. Clearly, if a major purpose of the solicitation is to build a surplus, that should be disclosed.

Outside Remuneration

Executive directors and other staff often are offered honoraria or consulting fees for speeches, teaching, providing technical assistance, or other work. The ethical issue is whether the staff person should turn the fees over to the nonprofit employer or be able to retain them. Potential conflicts can be avoided if the policy is based on the principle that all reasonably related outside income belongs to the organization. Thus, an executive director's honorarium for speaking to a national conference would revert to the employer, but his fee for playing in a rock band on weekends would be his or hers to keep.

An argument against this principle is that the employees' usage of their spare time should be of no concern to the employer. The argument on the other side is that the line between employer's and personal time is not so easy to draw. Is it ethical for an employee to exploit the knowledge and experience gained on the job for personal gain? Are we buying only time from our employees, or do we expect that we are getting the undivided professional attention from that person?

If the board or executive director is silent on this issue, the assumption is that earning outside income is a private matter. It makes sense to have a clear policy on outside income before an employee is hired.

Salaries, Benefits and Perquisites

Determining an appropriate salary structure is perhaps the most difficult ethical issue in the nonprofit sector. Ethical considerations arise at both the high and low ends of the salary spectrum.

If an organization is funded by grants from foundations and corporations or by government contracts, the funders can and do provide some restraint on excessive salaries. However, if the nonprofit is funded primarily by individual donations or fees for service, such constraints (other than, perhaps, those relating to the intermediate sanctions regulations of the Internal Revenue Service—see Chapter 30) are absent.

Boards fall into an ethical trap if they reward executive directors based on the amount of income received, rather than on how well the mission is accomplished. A board can consider many criteria when setting the salary of the executive director. These include the size and complexity of the organization, what others in similar agencies are earning, and whether the salary is defensible to the public. Some nonprofits include proportionality in their salary structure by limiting the highest paid to a factor of the lowest paid (e.g. the highest can be no more than three times the lowest).

As a result of enactment of the *Taxpayers Bill of Rights 2*, there are now *legal* as well as ethical restrictions about paying excessive compensation (see Chapter 30). Ethical management of employees requires that each person be treated with dignity and respect, provided a salary that can provide a decent standard of living, and a basic level of benefits, including health coverage. A potential, critical conflict arises when a charitable organization working to spread its social values treats its staff in a way that conflicts with its organizational values.

Conclusion

There are many other ethical issues that nonprofit organizations will confront on a regular basis, such as: personal use of office supplies and equipment; personal use of frequent flier mileage; the extent of staff and board diversity; and the use of private discriminatory clubs for fundraisers, board meetings, or other events. The list is endless.

There are many excellent publications on the subject of ethics. A few of them are:

1. A series of articles by David E. Mason in *Nonprofit World*, published by the Society for Nonprofit Organizations.

The Society For Nonprofit Organizations
6314 Odana Road; STE 1
Madison, WI 53719-1141
(608) 274-9777

2. *Making Ethical Decisions (34 pages, $6.95 plus $3.25 shipping and handling).*

Josephson Institute of Ethics
4640 Admiralty Way
Suite 1001
Marina del Rey, CA 90292
(310) 306-1868

3. Ethics and the Nation's Voluntary and Philanthropic Community.

Independent Sector
1828 L Street NW
Washington, DC 20036
(202) 223-8100

What is important is that nonprofit organizations consciously engage in discussions about ethics and values on a regular basis, recognizing that the charitable nonprofit sector has a special obligation to uphold the very highest standards. Boards of directors of charitable nonprofits have an important role in this regard. Boards cannot play a more important role than assuring that nonprofits are accountable, and that they operate as mission- and value-driven organizations.

Many who choose to work in the nonprofit sector do so because the stated values of the sector and their personal values are in harmony. It is critical that such people be vigilant against the erosion of those very principles that attracted them to the work.

Only in this way can the public be assured that the charitable nonprofit sector remains worthy of its privileges and that the sector continues to occupy its special and unique place in our society.

Tips:

- **Challenge yourself and your organization to hold yourself up to the highest ethical standards, avoiding even gray areas of conflicts of interest and appearances of conflicts of interest.**

- **When in doubt, ask yourself, "How would I feel if my family and friends read about this on the front page of the daily newspaper?"**

- **Obtain salary surveys published by your state chapter of the American Society of Association Executives (ASAE) and determine whether anyone in the organization has an unreasonable salary.**

- **Demand that all business relationships with the organization be at "arm's-length," and obtain at least three bids on any work that costs at least $1,000, even if a board member claims that he/she will provide the product/service at cost.**

Chapter 8
Section 501(c)(3) Tax-Exempt Status

Synopsis: Federal 501(c)(3) tax-exempt status is valuable not only because of the tax advantages to the nonprofit corporation, but to the organization's contributors. Corporations with this status may not substantially engage in lobbying or engage in partisan political activities.

Achieving 501(c)(3) status should be the principal objective after filing the Articles of Incorporation for virtually all nonprofits organized and operated for religious, charitable, scientific, literary, or educational purposes, testing for public safety, fostering national or international amateur sports competitions, and the prevention of cruelty to children or animals.

The federal regulation implementing Section 501(c)(3) tax-exempt status states (Reg. §1.501(c)(3)-1(d)):

> *"(d) Exempt purposes. (1) In general.*
> *"(i) An organization may be exempt as an organization described in section 501(c)(3) if it is organized and operated exclusively for one or more of the following purposes:*
> > *(a) Religious,*
> > *(b) Charitable,*
> > *(c) Scientific,*
> > *(d) Testing for Public Safety,*
> > *(e) Literary,*
> > *(f) Educational, or*
> > *(g) Prevention of cruelty to children or animals.*
> *"(ii) An organization is not organized or operated exclusively for one or more of the purposes specified in subdivision (i) of this subparagraph unless it serves a public rather than a private interest. Thus, to meet the requirement of this subdivision, it is necessary for an organization to establish that it is not organized or operated for the benefit of private interests such as designated individuals, the creator or his family, shareholders of the organization, or persons controlled, directly or indirectly, by such private interests..."*

For nonprofits whose activities are eligible, designation by the Internal Revenue Service for 501(c)(3) tax-exempt status is a major objective to be achieved as quickly as possible. This status confers several substantial benefits to the organization:

1. The nonprofit will be exempt from federal income taxes other than unrelated business income taxes (UBIT). The current rate of federal corporate income tax is 15% on the first $50,000 in taxable income, 25% on the next $25,000, 34% on the next $25,000, 39% on the next $235,000, and 34% on the rest up to $10 million. While many nonprofits will not

generate large amounts of net revenue, particularly in their early years, it is a major advantage to have the option to capture this net revenue for future expansion, venture capital, and covering future operating deficits.

2. Persons contributing to the nonprofit can take a deduction on their own income taxes for their contributions. Since the incremental tax rate for middle- and upper-income persons on adjusted gross income for the tax year 1998 is 28% (on income of $25,350-$61,400 for singles, $42,350-$102,300 for married filing jointly), 31% ($61,400-$128,100 for singles, $102,300-$155,950 for married filing jointly), 36% ($128,100-$278,450 for singles, $155,950-$278,450 for married filing jointly), and 39.6% (higher than $155,950 for singles and $278,450 for married filing jointly), this represents an attractive incentive for persons to leverage their own contributions with the "tax expenditure" contributed by government.

3. Many major donors (such as United Ways and certain foundations) will not make contributions to organizations that do not have 501(c)(3) status.

4. The designation of 501(c)(3) status indicates a minimal level of accountability, policed by the Internal Revenue Service, which is a useful governmental stamp of approval of the charitable activities of the organization.

5. In some states, qualifying 501(c)(3) organizations may elect to self-insure for purposes of complying with unemployment compensation laws (see Chapter 11).

There are several disadvantages:

1. A 501(c)(3) may not engage in partisan political activity on behalf of political candidates.

2. Such organizations may not substantially engage in lobbying or propaganda.

3. Such organizations have a higher level of accountability, and must, as all 501(c) exempt organizations, make copies of their 990 tax returns available in their offices upon request (see Chapter 30).

4. There is a substantial application fee ($500 in most cases), and this fee is not refunded if tax-exempt status is denied.

Although not always the case, most incorporators of nonprofits have some altruistic motive for incorporating. The motives of the incorporators cannot be for personal gain. As one might expect, the motives are usually of an "eleemosynary" nature, i.e., for the betterment of society.

Many nonprofit corporations are formed because a person or group of persons is frustrated with the lack of government action to solve a problem that, in that person's view, should be solved by government. Congress historically has recognized that government cannot do everything for everybody even when the cause is just. Instead, Congress provides an opportunity for citizens to form organizations to do the activities themselves. They are rewarded by having certain privileges, such as the tax-exemption, provided that the activity falls within a statutorily enumerated list of activities.

Section 501(c) of the Internal Revenue Code lists more than 20 classes of activities that can qualify a nonprofit corporation for tax-exempt status. A list of these classes is provided in this chapter. Only one of these classes, 501(c)(3), permits a tax deduction for contributions made to organizations in that class, and requires that such organizations not engage in substantial lobbying or propaganda activities, or in political activities that advance the cause of candidates.

501(c)(3) status is not granted pro forma. There are stringent requirements for approval. Because of this, 501(c)(3) status is prized, and is viewed by many in the public as a stamp of approval by the federal government. The fact is that 501(c)(3) status does not necessarily imply government's endorsement of the organization's activities. In 1997, the federal government granted 47,015 501(c)(3) applications, denied 226, and took "other" action on 17,761, many of which were eventually approved after additional information was provided.

How To Apply for 501(c)(3) Status

To make application, an organization needs the following forms and booklets from the Internal Revenue Service:

- Form 8718—*User Fee for Exempt Organization Determination Letter Request*

- Form SS-4—*Application for Employer Identification Number*

- Form 5768—*Election by an Eligible Organization to Make Expenditures to Influence Legislation*

- Package 1023—*Forms and instruction booklets for applying for 501(c)(3) tax-exempt status*

- Publication 557—*Tax-Exempt Status for Your Organization*

The above forms and booklets can be obtained at any local IRS office (see Appendix C for addresses). They can also be ordered by calling a toll-free number (1-800-829-3676).

According to the IRS, it takes about eight-and-a-half hours to complete the basic form and several more hours to complete supplemental schedules. It also takes several hours to learn how to complete the forms. It is advisable to be as careful as possible in completing the forms, since the wrong phrase can result in denial. Legal advice in applying for tax-exempt status is recommended, particularly from those with experience in what the IRS reviewers will be considering.

Some organizations are exempt from having to file the 1023. Among them are:

1. Those that will have gross receipts of less than $5,000 annually.

2. Bona fide religious institutions.

3. Certain groups affiliated with a parent organization that already has tax-exempt status, and that will send a letter extending its exemption to them.

Federal law expects that an application for 501(c)(3) status will be filed within 15 months after the end of the month in which the Articles of Incorporation are filed. If the organization files on time and the application is approved, 501(c)(3) status will be retroactive to the date of the Articles of Incorporation. There is a form to file if the 15-month deadline is not met. For more information about this option, see IRS Publication 557.

Fees

There is a $500 application fee to file the form 8718, *User Fee for Exempt Organization Request,* which must be submitted with the 1023. New organizations expecting gross receipts of not more than $10,000 for each of the first four years, or existing organizations that have not had gross receipts of that amount in each of the last four years, can qualify for a reduced fee of $150. The fee must be paid by check, but a corporate check is not required.

Several commercial publications offer step-by-step advice on filling out applications for 501(c)(3) tax-exempt status. Among the best is *How to Form your Own Non-Profit Corporation* by Anthony Mancusco (Nolo Press, 950 Parker Street, Berkeley, CA 94710).

A Short History of Tax-Exempt Status

In ancient times, government, whether secular or non-secular, recognized that certain activities assisted the role of government and were deserving of tax exemptions. Several thousand years ago, some of the best land in the Nile Valley was set aside tax-free by the Egyptian pharaoh for the priests of Osiris.

Modern tax-exemption law has its roots in England, with the passage of the Statute of Charitable Uses in 1601. According to *Unfair Competition? The Challenge to Charitable Tax Exemption,* by Harrison Wellford and Janne Gallagher, current U.S. tax-exemption law draws its roots from an 1891 court case in Britain *(Commissioners of Income Tax v. Pemsel)* that provided a judicial definition of charity strikingly similar to the American legal standard.

The modern federal tax-exemption can be traced to 1863, when the income of charities was exempted from a corporate tax enacted to finance the Civil War. The 1894 Income Tax Act was eventually declared unconstitutional. Yet it served as the precedent for exempting organizations that were for "charitable, religious, or educational purposes." Such exempt organizations were recognized only if they relieved poverty and were not permitted to generate outside income.

A 1924 Supreme Court case, *Trinidad v. Sagrada,* decided that for purposes of tax-exempt status, the destination of the funds, rather than the source, was the key determinant. This case involved a religious order that sold food, wine, and other goods to support its school, mission, church, and other operations. Thus, tax-exempt organizations were permitted to run profit-making enterprises provided that the net profits were funneled to tax-exempt purposes. This policy was revised by Congressional enactment of an "unrelated business income tax" (UBIT). From 1909 to the present, many other categories of tax-exempt status were added by federal statute (see below).

Tax-Exempt Status Other than 501(c)(3)

The Internal Revenue Code provides more than 20 other categories of tax-exempt status besides 501(c)(3). Those who wish to file for tax-exempt status under section 501(c) for other than 501(c)(3) need to request Package 1024 from the IRS.

Among the other categories are:

501(c)(4)—civic leagues, social welfare organizations
501(c)(5)—labor, agricultural, or horticultural organizations
501(c)(6)—business leagues, chambers of commerce, trade associations
501(c)(7)—social clubs
501(c)(8)—fraternal beneficiary societies
501(c)(9)—voluntary employee beneficiary associations
501(c)(10)—domestic fraternal societies and orders that do not provide life, sick, or health benefits
501(c)(11)—teacher retirement fund associations
501(c)(12)—benevolent life insurance associations and other mutual businesses
501(c)(13)—cemeteries and crematoria
501(c)(14)—credit unions

501(c)(15)—mutual insurance companies
501(c)(16)—farmers' co-ops
501(c)(17)—unemployment compensation benefit trusts
501(c)(20)—prepaid group legal services organizations
501(c)(25)—title holding corporations or trusts.

With limited exceptions, these organizations have the same federal tax benefits as a 501(c)(3). One major difference is that with few exceptions, contributors cannot deduct the amount of their contribution from their personal income tax payments. For many of these organizations, there is no limitation against lobbying activities, and most are permitted to engage in partisan political activity (although there may be a substantial federal excise tax associated with political expenditures).

Chapter 9
Insurance and Liability

> Synopsis: All nonprofit corporations must have workers' compensation insurance and participate in the unemployment compensation program. It is advisable for nonprofit corporations to purchase general business insurance. Many state laws have lowered the liability threshold for directors and volunteers of certain nonprofit corporations.

General Liability Concerns of Nonprofit Corporations

Murphy's Law has many variations and corollaries. In its simplest form, it states that "if something can go wrong, it will." No one can foresee catastrophic events, and even if one could, it is virtually impossible to protect a corporation against all possible eventualities.

A nonprofit corporation, like a business corporation, should do everything in its power to mitigate the effect of claims against the corporation. The corporation, like any other business, could suffer personal injury or property damage claims caused by floods, fire, theft, earthquake, wind damage, building collapse, and slips and falls, just to name a few. Legal claims against corporations tend to be of the low-incidence, high-risk variety. These claims do not happen very often, but when they do, the results can be disastrous.

Nonprofits are exposed to legal risks in many other areas. They engage in typical business transactions on a routine basis. They arrange for conventions, seminars, and other meetings. They publish newsletters. They are also employers with the attendant risk that hiring, advancement, or firing decisions may be challenged based on contract rights, discrimination, or fraud. A nonprofit corporation could be exposed to the antitrust laws if its membership has a competitive advantage. Such nonprofit corporations could conduct various kinds of programs that permit their members to self-regulate, such as by business or professional codes, product standards and certification, or professional or academic credentialing, to use but a few examples.

As this chapter will indicate, nonprofit corporations should consider basic general liability insurance to cover personal injury and property damage claims. Consideration also should be given to purchasing directors and officers (D&O) insurance to protect their volunteer leadership from personal legal claims. Finally, a similar but broader type of insurance policy dealing with general professional liability protects not only officers and directors, but all association volunteers and staff as well.

General Business Insurance

Employee lawsuits, floods, fire, theft, earthquake, wind damage, building collapse, loss of business income, pollution, riot, lightening, war, landslides, nuclear contamination, power failures, falls, electrocution...the possibilities are endless for natural disasters, accidents, and crime. Fortunately, generic business insurance policies will protect a corporation from all of these plus scores of other potential but unlikely occurrences. If the organization is willing to accept a reasonable deductible (an amount of damages the corporation pays before benefits are provided on the remaining amount of damages), a policy may cost as little as a few hundred dollars. It is a worthy investment to make, if only for peace of mind. Most policies include defending corporate leaders in the event they are sued for whatever reason relating to business activity. Prices for basic insurance are competitive. Be sure the corporation has liability and medical expenses coverage of at least $500,000, and that the policy will cover the legal costs of defending and settling suits against the corporation and its staff.

Workers' Compensation Insurance

Every state has a workers' compensation law. The purpose of worker's compensation is to provide income to workers injured on the job and to pay their medical bills. In exchange, the employee gives up the right to sue the employer. Contact your state's Department of Labor or equivalent to learn about the requirements for purchasing this insurance.

Unemployment Compensation Insurance

The state unemployment compensation program is a job insurance program. Its purpose is to provide some limited protection against loss of income for workers who lose their jobs through no fault of their own. Contact your state Department of Labor or equivalent to learn about the requirements for participating in this program.

Federal Unemployment Taxes

Nonprofit corporations other than those with 501(c)(3) status are also subject to Federal unemployment taxes (FUTA). Businesses receive a credit on the amount of unemployment taxes paid to the state. The FUTA tax is paid by filing a 940 FUTA tax return. Quarterly deposits may be necessary, depending on the amount owed. These deposits are made in the same manner as federal quarterly withholding deposits.

Liability of Officers, Directors, and Other Volunteers

Nonprofit corporation volunteers may suffer from the same potential liability for actions in performance of their duties as individuals involved with business corporations. Furthermore, as managerial people, volunteer officers and directors of nonprofit corporations are bound by the same basic principles governing their conduct as directors and officers of profit-making business corporations. They owe a fiduciary duty of reasonable care and the duty to act in the corporation's and its members' best interest. This involves a duty of loyalty or good faith in managing the affairs of the corporation.

Generally, this duty requires individuals to use due care in the performance of their duties for the corporation to act in good faith in the best interest of the corporation as a whole and not for the interests of some but not all of the members, and a duty to avoid activity or transactions in which the individual has a personal interest. In short, in this litigious society, courts are tending more and more to impose responsibility on officers, directors, and volunteers of nonprofit corporations— including hospitals, charities, and educational institutions— for anti-trust problems, tort liability, and similar areas of liability exposure.

Volunteer Protection Act

Although few successful lawsuits have been brought against nonprofit corporation volunteers, the possibility that lawsuits can occur presents a "perception problem." At the federal level, the Volunteer Protection Act (VPA) was signed into law by President Clinton in July of 1997, with an effective date of September 16, 1997. The intent of the law is to provide limited legal immunity for the volunteers of charities who are involved in accidents that occur in connection with their charitable service. It would extend this immunity unless the person intentionally caused harm to others or showed flagrant indifference to the safety of those who were injured. The immunity does not extend to activities not authorized by the charity, nor to hate crimes or sexual offenses. It encourages states to grant liability immunity to nonprofit organization volunteers who are acting in good faith and within the scope of their official duties.

Personal or Professional Individual Insurance Coverage

Many nonprofit corporations purchase either Directors and Officers (D&O) insurance to cover directors and officers, or a broader type of policy sometimes referred to as professional liability insurance, to protect not only officers and directors but all association volunteers and staff. Although premiums for this type of insurance continue to be high, it is expected that the decrease in exposure afforded by the recent statutes will result in lower claims, and, eventually, lower premiums.

Tip:
- **Seek legal counsel before making any corporate decisions with respect to liability suits and claims.**

Chapter 10
Fiscal Issues

Synopsis: All nonprofit corporations must keep certain financial records and provide a financial summary. There are three levels of financial verification—audit, review, and compilation. *Line-item* and *program* budgets are the two major forms of budgeting utilized by nonprofit corporations.

Bookkeeping

Both state and federal law require corporations to record all expenses and income in an organized format. This can be done using one of many popular computer programs or manually. Several basic decisions need to be made. First, the corporation must decide on the period for its fiscal year. Because federal law requires the 990 nonprofit tax return to be filed within four-and-a-half months after the end of the fiscal year (technically, by the 15th day after the fifth month after the end of the fiscal year), that alone can determine when to begin the fiscal year. Other factors to consider are the fiscal years or the announcement date of grants of major funding sources, using a calendar year for simplicity, or beginning the fiscal year as soon as the first corporate income is received.

A second issue is deciding whether the bookkeeping system will be on a "cash" basis or "accrual" basis. Cash basis financial reporting is based upon when income was received and deposited and when expenditures were made. The "accrual" method factors in "accounts payable" and "accounts receivable" (i.e., when there is a legal obligation to pay someone in the future). Most novices find the cash basis easier and simpler. The accrual method, on the other hand, gives a more realistic picture of the actual financial situation of the organization, and thus complies with generally accepted accounting principles. This decision should be discussed with the organization's accountant, or whoever is likely to prepare the tax returns and annual financial report. This is the time when the foresight of placing a certified public accountant or two on the board of directors can pay dividends.

Some funding agencies may have other accounting and bookkeeping requirements that must be considered.

Audits/Fiscal Accountability

There are three levels of financial verification. In descending levels of scope, they are audits, reviews, and compilations. The level of financial verification required is often determined by the nature and source of funding for the organization. Many government grants explicitly require a minimum level of financial verification in their contracts. Such a contract may be a "pass-through" of funds from another source, and the original source may need to be tracked down to determine whether it has its own requirement. It is good advice to request this information, in writing, from any contracting agency that provides the organization with grant funds.

Each of the three financial verification levels requires that all organizational funds be kept segregated and all transactions be accounted for. Thus it is never good organization policy to sign over an incoming check payment to a third party. Instead, deposit the check into the organization's account and then write a new check to the third party. While ignoring this advice may save the time of making a deposit and writing a check, it will result in a loss of "paper trail" necessary to determine who paid what to whom, when, and for what.

In the absence of an overriding requirement in a contract, federal, state, and local governments require an audit report when the funds in the contract are $100,000 or more in any single year. State and local governments generally require a review if funding is between $25,000 and $100,000 annually. If funding is less than $25,000, a compilation report is usually acceptable.

Audit Report

The highest level, an audit, is a complete arm's-length verification of the accuracy and reliability of account statements and financial reports. Records are systematically examined and checked to determine how they adhere to generally accepted accounting principles, management policies, and other stated policies. The purpose of independent audits is to eliminate bias, self-interest, fraud, and unintentional errors. While an auditor can never obtain *absolute* proof of the representations made in a financial statement, the standard used is that of a "reasonable man" (or woman) who has "adequate technical training and proficiency as an auditor," according to the American Institute of Certified Public Accountants. Auditors have a professional code of ethics to ensure their independence from the management of the corporation. Although they are paid a fee by the corporation, they are considered to be responsible to the public rather than to their corporate clients.

The American Institute of Certified Public Accountants has prepared a comprehensive publication entitled *Audit Guide* specifically to assist nonprofit corporations in preparing for their annual audits. This Guide can be purchased for $40.50 ($32.50 for members), plus $6 for postage and handling from:

American Institute of Certified Public Accountants
Harborside Financial Center
201 Plaza Three
Jersey City, NJ 07311-3881
1-800-862-4272 (for orders)
(201) 938-3000 (for general information)
http://www.aicpa.org

Many government agencies have audit requirements for recipients of their grants. So do many foundations and other umbrella fundraising organizations.

Audits are often required by major umbrella fundraising organizations, with exceptions when the revenues are relatively small.

The Financial Accounting Standards Board (FASB) has issued rules that affect the content of financial statements. These new rules took effect for most small nonprofits in 1996. Financial statements must include a statement of financial position (balance sheet); a statement of activities (revenue and expenses) that includes changes in net assets and any change in restricted and unrestricted net assets; and a statement of cash flow showing how money was obtained, spent, borrowed, repaid, and so on. Although these new rules do not have the force of law, they must be followed in order to have your financial statement certified as "prepared in accordance with generally accepted accounting principles." The board also issued rules changing the way multi-year contributions are recorded and requires certain volunteer services to be recorded as revenue, particularly if those volunteer services would otherwise have had to be purchased.

Review

A second standard of financial verification, called a "review," is the application of analytical procedures by the accountant to the financial data supplied by the corporation. It is substantially narrower in scope than an audit. Much of the information supplied by the corporation is accepted at face value, although there may be a spot check to see if there are any glaring errors or any inconsistencies between expenses recorded and the checks that are written. The examination of internal control and the proper allocation of income and expenses is similar to that of an audit report. Unlike an audit, the review will not include a formal auditor's "opinion" as to the compliance with generally accepted accounting principles.

Compilation

The third level of financial reporting/verification, a "compilation," calls only for the proper classification of assets, liabilities, fund balances, income and expenses, from information supplied by management. Third-party verification of assets and liabilities is not required, although internal supporting documents may be used in their place. "Spot checks" are employed only when the accountant is aware of inconsistencies in other areas of the examination. As in a review, the accountant will not render an "opinion" on the accuracy of the report.

In the absence of legal requirements, it is good policy for nonprofits that expend more than a few thousand dollars to have at least a review. Many nonprofits have certified public accountants on their boards who may be willing to arrange for a review of the corporation on a *pro bono* basis.

Budgeting

Some nonprofits can exist for years using volunteer labor, donations of stamps, in-kind printing and other services. and have no need to raise money or make any expenditures. Others are more likely to have some staff and pay office rent or, if not, still have expenditures for workshops, postage, printing, telephone, and other typical corporate expenditures. The annual budget document is the blueprint for both spending and income. A poorly conceived budget can lead to the corporation's demise. On the other hand, a well-conceived, realistic budget, can be the catalyst for program planning that will provide a corporate life for many fruitful, productive years.

There are two major types of budgeting used by nonprofit corporations. Both have their advantages and disadvantages.

Line-Item Budget

The line-item budget is as it says—a list of various categories and the amount the corporation expects to spend for each category. Corporations, from the largest to the smallest, have some of the same categories in a line-item budget. Among the most common are:

1. salaries
2. consulting services
3. professional services
4. taxes
5. benefits
6. telephone
7. postage
8. printing and photocopying
9. travel and entertainment
10. workshops and conferences
11. bank fees
12. dues
13. subscriptions and publications
14. data processing
15. equipment
16. equipment maintenance and repair
17. legal services
18. insurance
19. rent
20. miscellaneous
21. office supplies
22. maintenance and repairs

23. security services
24. utilities
25. bookkeeping and payroll services

As an expense is incurred, the amount of the check is entered in a journal prepared for this purpose, coded by the expense category. At the end of each month, the amounts of each category are aggregated on a ledger sheet called a "monthly summary." The monthly totals should be compared to the budget in each category to determine whether spending patterns are consistent with the budget.

Program Budget

The second type of budgeting is called a program budget. The program budget also contains various line-items, but the difference is that *each* major program of the corporation is provided with a line-item budget. For example, if your corporation is having a conference, then the conference itself has a budget. Printing, postage, and telephone costs are attributed to the conference. Printing and postage costs may be associated with another program as well, such as a newsletter. Each program of a nonprofit, such as conferences, newsletter, membership, or publications, has its own budget. The advantage of the program budget is that one can determine quickly the incremental savings that will accrue if a particular program is eliminated. The disadvantage is it is not easy to allocate overhead costs (such as salaries and rent) to various programs.

It is not unusual for nonprofits to combine the two types of budgeting—to have a general line-item budget, but to allocate some spending in all categories to certain programs. For small nonprofits, line-item budgets are the easiest to prepare and follow, and program budgets provide better information.

Expense Reimbursement

Organizations incur expenses. Many of these can be conveniently paid by corporate check. Many others, should the organization desire, can be paid by corporate credit card, which is particularly useful for travel expenses. It is not atypical for newly formed organizations to require two signatures on checks. This is not unreasonable for recurring expenses that can be processed well in advance, such as paychecks, federal withholding, rent, major equipment purchases, and taxes. It does present problems when making small, but reasonable, purchases on-the-spot. An expense reimbursement system should be designed to provide protection against one person making unilateral decisions on spending, but needs to be flexible enough to keep the organization from being hamstrung when trying to pay a $25 telephone bill.

One suggestion is to set up an "imprest account" to pay routine office expenses, requiring only one signature. The authorized person (such as the executive director) has a reasonable sum to disburse from this checking account, which is entirely separate from the "master" checking account. The imprest account is replenished from the master checking account using a check that requires the usual two signatures, only upon a review by the chairperson or treasurer (or both) of what was expended, including supporting documentation such as receipts. The account should provide an amount needed not only to pay reasonable expenses for the month, but enough to cover expenses for part of the following month, since several days or weeks may elapse during the processing of the expense report.

The organization leadership should provide general guidelines as to what types of expenses are acceptable for reimbursement, and what expenses should be absorbed by the staff. For example, hotel accommodations in any city can range from $30-$300. A dinner can be purchased for three dollars or $75. Many organizations refuse to make decisions concerning what is appropriate, and instead provide a per diem allowance. The staff member then must absorb costs that go beyond this amount.

Many other expense issues arise that require board policies. How much should be reimbursed for mileage? What if a spouse attends a conference with a staff member and shares a room, resulting in an incremental cost increase? How will expenses be reimbursed that cannot be directly documented with a receipt? All of these issues can be resolved on an ad hoc basis, but it is useful to think about the nature of expense reimbursement before it creates problems. Many organizations have failed because their budgets were depleted by discretionary spending in the absence of an expense policy.

Chapter 11
Personnel

> Synopsis: Nonprofit corporations with staff should have a written personnel policy. There are a number of state and federal laws that apply to nonprofit operations and many standard forms that must be filed in order to comply with these laws.

Whether a nonprofit corporation has one salaried employee or hundreds, a written personnel policy can avoid disputes that, in some cases, can destroy an organization even before it gets off the ground. Obviously, a personnel policy for a small organization will be less complex than for a large one. It is advisable to review personnel policies of several organizations of similar scope and choose among the provisions that are sensitive to organizational needs. It is not necessary to reinvent the wheel, but *having* a wheel is important.

Qualified and trained personnel are an organization's most prized assets. Staff members need to feel that the organization is flexible enough to respond to their individual needs. Conversely, the organization must have the ability to operate efficiently, effectively, and economically, and to treat all employees fairly and equally. A balance must be attained, and each organization can best determine for itself where the balance lies.

Before hiring the first employee, among the issues to consider and to develop policies for are:

- Should staff be paid employees of the corporation, or should the corporation hire a consultant? (Note: federal and state law permit persons to be hired as "independent contractors" rather than employees only if two conditions are met: the individual must be free from organizational control or direction over the performance of the services provided and must be customarily engaged in an independently established trade or business.)
- What should the job descriptions of staff be?
- How much should each staff member be compensated? Should a staff person be paid on a salaried basis or by the hour?
- If an office is established, what should the office hours be, and where should the office be located?

It may be advisable for the organization to have a personnel committee. The role of this committee is to study the issues raised in this section, develop a personnel policy for ratification by the board, if appropriate, and to serve as the adjudicating body to resolve grievances by employees.

After a decision is made to hire employees, some of the issues to consider for inclusion in a personnel policy are the following:

1. **Hiring policies (see Chapter 12)**—How should job vacancies be advertised? Will there be affirmative action to recruit minorities? Should the search be national, statewide, regional, or local? Should current employees be given preference in hiring for vacant positions?

2. **Firing policies (see Chapter 12)**—What are the conditions that permit dismissal without appeal, such as "for cause"? Will there be severance pay? Will placement services be provided? Will notice be given of unsatisfactory job performance before dismissal?

3. **Probationary periods of employment**—Should there be a period of probation during which an employee can be terminated without access to any grievance procedure or will not be entitled to receive benefits, including leave?

4. **Sick leave, vacation, personal days**—How many days will be accumulated and how? Will a doctor's note verifying the sickness be required?

5. **Holidays**—Which holidays are paid holidays and which are optional? What is the policy with respect to the observance of religious holidays?

6. **Personal days**—How many personal days will be permitted, and how will they be accumulated? If not taken, will they be "cashed in" upon retirement?

7. **Overtime policies**—Which classes of employees are eligible for overtime pay? Is overtime mandatory if requested by the corporation? Will overtime be compensated in salary or compensatory time?

8. **Compensatory ("Comp") time**—Should comp time be granted in lieu of overtime pay? Should it be required for routine doctor/dentist appointments?

9. **Full-time vs. part-time status**—How many hours per week qualify the employee for benefits?

10. **Health insurance**—Is there a group plan? Will gross salary be increased if an employee is covered by the health insurance policy of a spouse and desires not to be covered by the organization?

11. **Pension**—How long does it take for an employee to be vested? What is the employer and employee contribution required?

12. **Life insurance, and other benefits**—Is there a menu to choose from?

13. **Employee evaluation**—Who performs the evaluation? Under what conditions may employees exercise their legal rights under state law to examine their employee files? Who has access to personnel files?

14. **Merit salary increases; COLA increases**—What are the criteria used for salary increases, and how often and by whom are salaries reviewed?

15. **Continuing education benefits**—Who has authority to approve requests? What are the time and cost limitations? When do employees become eligible?

16. **Staff training/orientation**—Is a pre- or post-employment physical or other examination required? Is there a formal review for new employees concerning staff personnel policies?

17. **Maternity leave**—What documentation is required? What is the maximum leave the employee may take without losing the job?

18. **Bereavement leave**—How long will such leave be, and what relatives will be included in the policy?

19. **Family and medical leave**—For what purposes will this leave be granted, what documentation is required to accompany a leave request, will the leave be paid or unpaid, and what will the effect be on unused sick leave and vacation (see #17)?

20. **Pay for jury duty, military leave**—What is the organization's policy?

21. **Sabbatical leaves**—After how many years will employees qualify, for how long, and will this be paid or unpaid leave?

22. **Expense reimbursement documentation**—How shall expenses be filed and what expenses are eligible? Is there a flat per diem for out-of-town travel or reimbursement? What amount will be reimbursed for mileage?

23. **Notice required for resignation**—What is the minimum notice required and what are the sanctions for not complying?

24. **System for resolution of employee grievances**—May employees appeal to the board of directors? Is there a committee for this purpose?

25. **Disciplinary sanctions for rule-breaking**—Is there provision for suspension with or without pay?

26. **Prohibition against secondary employment**—What types of outside earned income are prohibited or permitted?

27. **Telephone policy**—What is company policy with respect to personal calls at work, including long-distance reimbursement?

28. **Payroll**—Will salary be provided weekly, every other week, or monthly?

While the issues may seem overwhelming, a small organization may only have need for basic policies such as hours of operation, vacation and sick leave policy, benefits provided, and holidays. The rest can be determined on an ad hoc basis by the executive director, in consultation with the board's chairperson and/or the personnel committee, if there is one.

Major Federal Laws Affecting Employers

Taxpayer Bill of Rights 2 (P. L. 104-168)

This law was enacted on July 30, 1996, but its provisions relating to excessive income are retroactive to September 1995. It includes "intermediate sanctions" provisions that authorize the Internal Revenue Service to levy excise taxes on excessive compensation paid out by 501(c)(3) and (c)(4) organizations, and to also penalize nonprofit managers who authorize such excessive compensation. The new law also provides for increased public disclosure of financial documents (see Chapter 30).

Fair Labor Standards Act of 1938 (52 Stat. 1060, 29 §201 et seq.)
Enacted in 1938, the law provides for a minimum wage, controls child labor, and requires premium pay for overtime.

Equal Pay Act of 1963 (P.L. 88-38, 29 § 206)
Requires that men and women performing equal work be paid equally.

Civil Rights Act of 1964 (P.L. 88-352, 28 §1447, 42 §1971, 1975a-1975-d, 2000 et seq.)
Prohibits discrimination, including employment discrimination, on the basis of race, color, religion, sex or national origin. Includes prohibition of certain questions being asked by prospective employers at job interviews.

Equal Employment Opportunity Act of 1972 (P.L. 92-2615 §5108, 5314-5316, 42 §2000e)
Amends the Civil Rights Act by expanding anti-discrimination protection.

Age Discrimination in Employment Act of 1967 (P.L. 90-202, 29 §621 et seq.)

Prohibits discrimination against persons age 40-70, as revised by the 1978 amendments.

Immigration Reform and Control Act of 1986 (P.L. 99-603, 7 §2025 and other references)

Requires employers to certify that their workers are not illegal aliens, and prevents discrimination on the basis of national origin.

Employee Retirement Income Security Act of 1974 (ERISA) (P.L. 93-406, 26 § 37 et seq., 29 §1001 et seq., and other references)

Requires accountability and reporting related to employer pension plans.

National Labor Relations Act of 1935 (49 Stat 449, 29 §151 et seq.)

Authorizes workers to form unions and other collective bargaining units.

Pregnancy Discrimination Act of 1978 (P.L. 95-555, 42 §2000e(k))

Amends the Civil Rights Act (that prohibits discrimination on the basis of sex) to change the definition of "sex" to include "because of or on the basis of pregnancy, childbirth, or related medical conditions."

Drug-Free Workplace Act of 1988 (P.L. 100-690, 41 §701 et seq.)

Requires organizations receiving federal contracts valued at $25,000 or more to certify that they will provide a drug-free workplace, notify their employees of actions taken against those who violate drug laws, and establish a drug-free awareness program.

Americans With Disabilities Act of 1990 (P.L. 101-336, 29 §706, 42 §12101 et seq., 47 §152, 221, 225, 611)

Prohibits employers with 15 or more workers from discriminating on the basis of disability.

Family and Medical Leave Act (P.L. 103-3, 29§2601 et seq.)

Requires businesses with 50 or more employees to provide certain workers with up to 12 weeks annually of family or medical leave to care for a sick spouse, child, or parent, or to care for a new child.

Sample State Laws Affecting Nonprofit Employers (examples from Pennsylvania)

Solicitation of Funds for Charitable Purposes Act (10 §161.1 et seq.)

Provides for regulation and disclosure of organizations that raise funds from the public for charitable purposes.

Child Labor Law (43 §41 et seq.)
Prohibits the employment of persons under 16 with limited exceptions, and provides labor standards for the employment of persons 16-18.

Corporation Not-for-Profit Code (Nonprofit Corporation Law of 1972 and Nonprofit Corporation Law of 1988—15 Pa. C.S.A. §7101 et seq.; §7301 et seq.; and 15 Pa. C.S.A. §5101 et seq.)
Contains codified statutes that apply to all nonprofit corporations in Pennsylvania.

Directors' Liability Act (42 §8361 et seq.)
Reduces the liability for directors of nonprofit corporations.

Equal Pay Law (43 §336.1 et seq.)
Requires employers to provide fair wages for women and persons 16-21, and to keep records of hours worked and wages paid to their employees.

Pennsylvania Labor Relations Act (43 §211.1 et seq.)
Protects the right of employees to organize and bargain collectively.

Human Relations Act (43 §951 et seq.)
Prohibits discrimination because of race, color, religious creed, ancestry, age or national origin.

Employee Records Inspection Law (43 §1321)
Requires employers to make employee records with respect to qualifications for employment, promotion, additional compensation, termination, or disciplinary action available for inspection by the employee or his/her agent during business hours, and permits the employer to require that the inspection take place during the employee's or agent's free time.

Lobbying Registration and Regulation Act (Act 93 of 1998)
Requires persons receiving compensation to advocate the passage or defeat of legislation to register with the State Ethics Commission, and to disclose certain expenditures and contacts.

Minimum Wage Act (43 §333.101 et seq.)
Sets the Pennsylvania minimum wage.

Pennsylvania Workmen's Compensation Act (77 §1 et seq.)
Provides for a worker's compensation program (see Chapter 9).

Unemployment Compensation Law (43 §751 et seq.)
Provides for unemployment compensation to workers who lose their jobs through no fault of their own (see Chapter 9).

Standard Paperwork for Corporations with Employees

Federal Forms

1. Form SS-4, Application for Employer Identification Number—This is the first form to be filed when hiring an employee. Once this form is filed, the Internal Revenue Service will establish an account for the organization and assign a federal tax number (EIN). This number will be the organization's account for paying taxes and is requested by other government authorities for tax purposes. It is requested by most foundations and grant makers as well. This form should be filed at least a month before the number is needed. To obtain this form, call the IRS toll-free at 1-800-829-3676.

2. Form W-4—Employee's Withholding Allowance Certificate—Each employee must file with the employer a copy of form W-4, which documents the number of exemptions and additional federal withholding. The information in the W-4 enables the employer to calculate how much should be withheld from gross salary (not including state and local withholding).

3. Circular E—Employer's Tax Guide—Employers need to obtain a copy of this publication (order by calling toll-free 1-800-829-3676), in order to calculate the amount of federal income tax withholding, Social Security withholding (for calendar year 1999 set at 6.2% of gross wages up to $72,600), and Medicare withholding (for calendar year 1999 set at 1.45% of gross wages, without any ceiling). The amount of wages needed to earn a Social Security credit is $740 in 1999. Workers thus will need to earn $2,960 in 1999 to earn the maximum four credits for the year. Most workers need 40 credits to be eligible for retirement benefits.

4. Form 8109 Federal Tax Deposit Coupon Book—These are coupons the corporation sends with payment for the federal withholding described above and the required federal payroll taxes. The employer is required to match the employee's contribution to Social Security and Medicare. Thus, the check should be made out for the total of federal income tax withholding plus 15.3% of gross wages and salaries of all employees, consistent with the ceilings noted above on Social Security and Medicare. Form 8109 is also used for the payment of other taxes, including Unrelated Business Income Tax (UBIT), and Federal Unemployment Tax (FUTA). These tax payments are due by the end of the month following the month in which the payments are withheld. Most corporations file their tax deposits with a local bank, making the check payable to the bank. A bank that accepts federal tax deposits can provide information on the procedures for filing correctly.

5. Form 941—Employer's Quarterly Federal Tax Return—Each quarter, the IRS will send a form for reconciling federal tax payments that were deposited for the previous quarter. The final line will indicate if the corporation owes any payments to the IRS.

6. Form 940—Employer's Annual Federal Unemployment (FUTA) Tax Return—This form must be filed if more than $1,500 was paid in wages during any calendar quarter or if the organization had one or more employees at any time in each of 20 calendar weeks.

7. Form W-2—Wage and Tax Statement—This statement is given to all employees on or before January 31 and details their gross salary and amounts withheld in federal, state, and local taxes during the previous year.

8. Form W-3—Transmittal of Income and Tax Statement—This return looks like a Master W-2, and aggregates information for all employees. It is filed with the Social Security Administration accompanied by one copy of each employee's W-2.

9. Form 990—This is the tax-exempt nonprofit corporation's tax return.

10. Form 990-T—This is a supplement to the tax-exempt nonprofit corporation's 990 tax return that reports gross income of $1,000 or more from unrelated business income during the fiscal year.

11. Form I-9—This form is kept by the employer for each worker to certify that the workers are citizens, nationals, or aliens legally authorized to work in the United States. If you need more than 100 copies, you can purchase them from the Superintendent of Documents, PO Box 371954, Pittsburgh, PA 15250-7904 or call (202) 783-3238. Smaller quantities can be obtained from any local Immigration and Naturalization Service office, or by calling 1-800-870-3676. A pre-addressed postcard for obtaining this form from the regional office serving the Washington, D.C. area is included in the back of this book. A *Handbook for Employers* (M274) explaining the responsibilities of employers with respect to the I-9 form is available free from any local INS office or U.S. Border Patrol Office, or may be purchased for $1 from the Superintendent of Documents.

12. Form 1099 MISC—This form must be filed if the organization pays more than $600 in the calendar year to those who are not direct employees. One copy is given to the individual on or before January 31. The other is sent with similar forms to the IRS on or before February 28, using **Form 1096** as a transmittal form.

Chapter 12
Hiring and Firing

> Synopsis: Nonprofits have options for staffing their agencies. A planning process is necessary when hiring and firing employees, and there are legal requirements for doing so. There is a continuum for disciplining employees short of termination.

Few can argue with the view that a nonprofit's human capital is its most important resource. The executive director influences the direction, morale, image, and financial stability of an organization. Yet, even the least senior employee can have a significant impact, negative or positive, on the organization. Employees can be creative, nurturing, versatile, ingenious, inspiring, and team building. And they can be disruptive, destructive, infecting morale, and creating scandal that can ruin the reputation of a charity that took decades to foster.

The recent episode involving a national United Way executive is just one example of how a single individual can stain an entire sector. The shock waves from the New Era Philanthropy scandal are continuing to be felt. As our society becomes more litigious, poor performance by an employee can have disastrous consequences. Many human services nonprofits who work closely with the aged, children, and the disabled have experience with defending the actions of their employees in court, and are at risk for damage suits in the millions of dollars. In some cases, this may be a matter of life and death for at-risk clients. The responsibility for choosing staff in a nonprofit should not be taken lightly.

Each hired employee is an investment by a nonprofit not only in the salary paid to him or her. The chemistry of an organization is changed by a new hire, and bad hiring decisions can haunt a nonprofit for many years or destroy it completely.

In recent years, nonprofits have lost the stereotype of having certain characteristics compared to their for-profit counterparts. That stereotype often viewed nonprofits as—

- less hierarchically structured
- less willing or able to fire non-productive employees
- more informally managed
- paying less and providing fewer benefits for longer hours
- more altruistically managed, with less emphasis on the bottom line
- more interested in their employees' personal satisfaction

There is plenty of evidence that this stereotype is no longer valid, or is at least becoming frayed at the edges. Nonprofits today face the same competitive and financial pressures to succeed as their for-profit counterparts. Nonprofits are becoming more comfortable hiring MBAs and those with for-profit business experience to manage their enterprises, where once social work degrees were the educational pedigree of choice.

Many of the jobs available in the nonprofit sector are equally available in the for-profit sector. For example, both often require a CEO, accountants, legal staff, supervisors, receptionists, government relations personnel, public relations officers, and administrative assistants and secretaries. For many of these jobs, the actual tasks performed by nonprofit employees are indistinguishable from those performed by for-profit employees.

Regardless, it is important to recognize that those who apply for jobs offered by nonprofits may retain the stereotypical image. It is useful to consider whether a prospective employee may have an unreasonable expectation of working for a nonprofit. This can be assessed during the job interview.

Hiring requires a positive attitude, which is often missing on the part of the hirer. First, if the hiring is being done to replace a fired employee, or resigned employee, the hirer often is distracted by the disruption caused by the separation. The hirer often is in a position of having to perform a task that is not pleasant—putting aside current responsibilities to perform the job search and interview. Few, if any, managers enjoy this process.

Before embarking on hiring a new employee, it is useful to do some planning that considers:

1. What are the tasks and duties the new employee will perform?
2. Are these tasks absolutely necessary?
3. Could someone already in the organization perform these tasks? Do these tasks require special education, professional credentials, and/or experience that are currently lacking?
4. Can we obtain these services through means other than hiring an employee? (see below)
5. How long will it take to hire a new employee, and will these duties still be required at that time?
6. How will these tasks change over time?
7. What can we expect in productivity of this new hire?
8. What support services will this person require? For example, will we also have to hire a secretary or administrative assistant?

Options—Advantages, Disadvantages, Legal Considerations

Hired Staff—The Sunday paper classifieds are usually filled with hundreds of job openings from nonprofit organizations who have decided to hire full-time staff.

> **advantages**: Employees have the most stake in the organization; they tend to be loyal, may work additional hours, and be flexible in doing tasks not in the job description when necessary.

disadvantages: Employees must be paid even when work is not required, require payroll taxes and expensive benefits, are paid for vacations and when sick, possibly disrupting work flow.

Paid Contractor—private for-profit companies and individuals market their services to nonprofits to perform tasks that are intended to obviate the need for hiring full-time workers.

> **advantages:** The nonprofit does not have to withhold income, Social Security, Medicare, state and local taxes, or pay unemployment and Social Security taxes. Contractors can be hired for short-term or long-term projects and can be terminated easily, do not require year-round benefits (although the equivalent is often built into the contract price), and do not obligate payment by the nonprofit unless the job is completed successfully. The contractor may have skills and resources that the nonprofit would not otherwise be able to afford except on a temporary basis.

> **disadvantages:** It may be legal only under certain limited circumstances. The Internal Revenue Service publication 15-A *(Employer's Supplemental Tax Guide)* provides details on the 20 factors that indicate whether an individual is considered an employee or an independent contractor. Independent contractors sometimes charge steeply in that they must cover overhead and marketing, and make a profit.

Volunteers—unsalaried workers, some who may be there not solely because they are altruistic and want to help, but because they may be fulfilling educational requirements, or disciplinary requirements ordered by a court (see chapter 13).

> **advantages:** They do not require a salary, and they are there not for a paycheck but, with rare exceptions, because they want to be.

> **disadvantages:** They do not have the paycheck as motivation, generally work fewer hours than employees, and may leave the organization on short notice.

Temporary Hires— hiring people for short-term employment without a promise that the employment will continue beyond a certain date.

> **advantages:** They permit the organization to respond to seasonal fluctuations in workload.

> **disadvantages:** The recruitment and administrative burden of temp workers can be substantial.

Outsourcing to another organization—either contracting with an employment service for temporary workers, or contracting with an outside organization to perform the functions, for example, a payroll and accounting service, which could otherwise be performed by an employee bookkeeper.

advantages—The organization can avoid the expense and administrative hassles of hiring employees.

disadvantages—Outsourcing is often more expensive on an hourly basis than would be the case if a person is hired temporarily.

Process in Hiring

Search Process. Many nonprofits, through their personnel committees, develop a procedure to hire new employees. Search committees are often authorized by the board to develop job descriptions, prepare job notices, cull through résumés to identify several candidates to interview, and recommend a candidate to the board. Others entirely delegate the process to the executive director (unless, of course, it is a search for an executive director). In either case, the basic steps remain the same:

1. **Prepare a job description.** The job description is a useful planning document for the organization. It also allows prospective employees to decide if they are interested in, and capable of, performing the duties expected of them.

2. **Prepare a job notice.** The job notice provides standard information such as job title, description of the job, education and/or work experience required, salary range, deadline for application, and the person to contact. Decide whether the notice will request applicants to send résumés, or file applications provided by the organization.

3. **Advertise the job.** Jobs may be advertised in daily newspapers, trade journals and publications, the newsletter of your state association, through the State Job Service, with educational institutions, online through the Internet, and, most importantly, internally.

4. **Review the applications.** Develop a process for reviewing and ranking for the purpose of deciding who gets invited for interviews. Remember to send a letter to those not interviewed, informing them that they were not successful.

5. **Interview candidates.** The interview should be a dialogue, not a monologue by the interviewer. Let the candidate talk, so that the interviewer can make judgments about how articulate the candidate is. It is useful to be friendly, ask a few softball questions first, and perhaps make a comment about something interesting on the résumé, such as a hobby, professional association membership, or award. Ask about any years that appear to be missing on the résumé.

There are questions that should be asked by the interviewers, and questions that by law cannot be asked. Among the questions that may be asked are:

- What background and experience make you feel you would be suitable for this particular position?

- What is your educational background, and how has that prepared you for this position?

- What has attracted you to apply for a position with this organization?

- What experience, education, or background prepares you for this position that would separate you from other applicants?

- What former employers or teachers may be consulted concerning your abilities?

- What are your long-term professional goals?

- What are the two or three things that are most important to you in a new professional setting?

- What motivates you to perform? How do you motivate those who work with you or for you?

- What are some of your most important accomplishments in your previous position, and what did you do that was special to achieve them?

- Describe a situation in which you had a conflict with another individual, and what you did to resolve it.

- Are you more comfortable working with a team on a group assignment, or by yourself?

- What are your significant strengths and weaknesses?

- Why are you shifting direction in employment?

- Where do you see yourself professionally in five years?

- How do you feel about your current/previous employer(s)?

Among questions that you may not ask are:

- questions relating to an applicant's race, sex, sexual orientation, national origin, religion, or age

- questions relating to physical and mental condition that are unrelated to performing the job

- questions that provide an indication of the above, such as the number of children, the applicant's maiden name, child care arrangements, height/ weight, whether the applicant is pregnant or planning to have children, the date the applicant graduated from high school, and whether the applicant is a Sabbath observer

- whether the applicant has ever been arrested or convicted of a crime, without proof of business necessity for asking.

6. **Select the best-qualified candidate.** This is different than selecting the best candidate. The best candidate within the pool of applicants may be identified easily, but if that person is not quite up to the task, it is a mistake to hire him or her. It is better to begin the search again, or try to find another way to have those duties performed without taking a chance that a bad hiring decision will harm the organization, perhaps irreparably.

7. **Verify information from the résumé and interviews; investigate references.** Under laws in some states, you cannot refuse to hire an employee based on a prior criminal conviction, unless that conviction specifically relates to the prospective employee's suitability for employment. Even in that case, the applicant must be informed in writing of a decision based on that, in whole or in part. For some nonprofit jobs, particularly those involving children, state law requires a State Police background check. It is not unusual for job candidates desperate to make their résumés stand out to embellish their educational or professional qualifications. A few telephone calls can ferret out many of these. This is a wise investment; someone who is dishonest enough to fudge qualifications on a résumé is likely to be just as dishonest when it comes to other professional issues. Investigating references can often turn up reasons for not hiring someone. It is good practice to request permission from the applicant to check references, and to contact previous employers. While a candidate may refuse for personal reasons to permit contact with a previous employer, it is sometimes, but not always, an indication of a flawed relationship.

Among the questions that are appropriate for prior employers are:

- How long did the applicant work for you?

- What was the quality of work of this applicant?

- What level of responsibility was the applicant given?

- How did the applicant get along with coworkers?

- Did the applicant show initiative and creativity? In what ways?

- Was the applicant a self-starter, or did he/she require constant supervision and direction?

- Was the applicant punctual?

- Is there anything you can tell me that would be relevant to my decision to hire or not hire the applicant?

8. **Make an offer to the candidate and negotiate salary, benefits, and other terms of the offer.**

9. **Put the offer in writing once the offer is successful.** Use a contract, if necessary or desirable. Once the contract is signed or the offer is otherwise accepted, notify other candidates that they were not successful, and arrange to orient the successful candidate.

Firing

The loss of one's job is often the most stressful and traumatic event in a worker's life, with the exceptions of the death of a close family member or divorce. For most managers, having to fire someone is unpleasant at best, and often traumatic. In many cases, it represents a failure not just by the affected worker but by the organization.

Managers must be careful how the firing is done; employee lawsuits over firings are becoming more common. When a nonprofit is unionized, even firings for the most egregious offenses may be challenged. It is also important to make sure that there is authority to fire. For example, the board chairperson may not fire the executive director without authority from the board, unless the bylaws provide for that. The executive director may not fire the communications director, for example, unless the organization bylaws and/or job description of the executive director makes it clear that he/she has this authority.

Planning Issues

Before firing an employee, it is important to do some advance planning. Among the issues to consider are how to deal with the workload performed by the fired employee, the effective date of the termination, what to tell coworkers about the action, how to ensure that the employee will not take away sensitive files and other materials, what to tell the employee about health and life insurance continuity and pension benefits, how to deal with separating personal property and organization property, how and when to terminate e-mail addresses and passwords, how much severance pay and other benefits to offer, and whether any letter of recommendation will be provided.

When to Fire

It is usually appropriate to summarily (without warning) fire an employee for gross misconduct that threatens the organization. Examples of this are drinking on the job, the conviction of a serious criminal offense, the willful destruction of agency property, stealing from the agency, or causing harm to others (such as clients or other employees). Most unacceptable behaviors that eventually result in dismissal are not as abrupt, and it is only after the manager has attempted a series of mitigation efforts that have failed that the employee is told to leave. Among these behaviors are unexplained absences, chronic tardiness, insubordination, laziness, and general poor job performance. Many nonprofit managers are close to their employees and shy away from taking appropriate discipline. They need to realize that the health of the organization requires discipline, and that they are getting paid to assure that the organization functions. Problem employees inhibit otherwise productive coworkers.

Discipline Short of Firing

Poor performance on the job may be the result of many factors. These might include personal problems of the employee, miscommunication by the manager, or skills required to perform the task that, for whatever reason, the employee does not have. Each of these has a remedy and, if the manager is flexible, dismissal can be avoided. For example, the birth of a child or serious illness of a spouse or other close family member can leave a valued employee unable to function. Some time off, flextime, counseling, or temporarily decreasing duties can all help. Continuing education can improve job skills. Improving communication from the manager, either "coaching" on how to do the job better, or at least providing some feedback on what is going wrong, can avoid nasty firing episodes. Most employees want to do well, and many believe they are doing well but are never told that their professional work is actually considered poor by those who evaluate and manage them. For some employees, however, discipline is required.

Discipline Continuum

1. **Verbal communication.** Short of the gross misconduct referred to in the beginning of this section, this should always take the form of informal communication by the manager. It should be verbal, and one-on-one—definitely not in front of coworkers. The manager should explain the problem and seek an explanation from the employee of what the manager can do to help improve the worker's ability to perform. In many cases, this will be enough. Make a notation in your records when this communication was provided and what was said, and whether the employee acknowledged the problem and agreed to improve his or her performance.

2. **Written warning.** If there is no appropriate response to the verbal communication (e.g., the employee continues to show up to work late or misses reasonable deadlines), a written memo outlining the problem should be shared with the employee. It should not be accusatory, but should state that the employee is engaging in behavior that is unacceptable, needs to be changed, and that this memo follows up on a verbal communication.

3. **Written formal warning.** This involves a formal memo to the employee from his or her immediate supervisor, similar to the written warning, but notes that this new memo will become a part of the employee's permanent personnel file. The memo should make it clear that the person's job may be in jeopardy unless there is

significant progress measured by a certain date, and that this progress will be evaluated on or shortly after that date.

4. **Suspension without pay.** Some employees just won't comprehend the seriousness of being late or being disruptive unless there is a real financial penalty attached. A one-day suspension, without pay, makes it clear that the manager has authority to take action, and that permanent suspension (i.e., firing) is possible.

5. **Firing.** This is the last resort. In the larger nonprofit, this may actually have a beneficial effect on other employees if they feel that this troublemaker is hurting the organization. In the smaller organization, firing is rarely beneficial in the short term; a poor employee is often much more productive than no employee at all. In the nonprofit organization, firing should always be for cause. It is not appropriate to fire your administrative assistant who has been faithful, loyal, and productive for 10 years just because the daughter of your college professor moved to town and needs a job, even if the administrative assistant has a contract that provides for employment "at will." Even if there is no avenue for the fired employee to appeal, a nonprofit manager should be convinced that the firing is called for, and could be defended in a court of law if necessary. Some may have to defend the firing in court, or before a grievance panel of some kind, such as a human relations commission. In recent years, courts have considered "wrongful discharge" suits and have awarded damages to fired employees who were dismissed unfairly. If in doubt that the firing is both legal and appropriate, consult an attorney.

How to Fire

1. It is common courtesy to make sure that the fired employee is the first to know, other than those up the chain of command who must know or be consulted first to obtain dismissal authority.

2. Fire the person in private, in a one-on-one situation.

3. Explain to the person why he or she is being fired, and point out the previous attempts to reach accommodation. But don't turn the meeting into a debate or let the person plead for his or her job. That time is too late. Explain that the purpose of the meeting, in addition to letting the person know about the firing, is to share productive information about procedures and benefits.

4. Explain applicable company procedures and benefits, such as severance pay, outplacement services, the effective date of the firing, when to turn over keys and files, and COBRA benefits. COBRA (the Consolidated Omnibus Budget Reconciliation Act of 1985) permits employees who retire, are laid off, who quit, or who are fired for reasons other than gross misconduct to continue to qualify for group health coverage for up to 18 months after termination, provided they pay the premiums. The manager may make suggestions about other jobs.

5. If appropriate, arrange for an exit interview, permitting the employee the opportunity to share information about the organization, job description, coworkers, job function, and so on. While this exit interview may not always be pleasant, the information provided may be invaluable.

Chapter 13
Volunteers

Synopsis: Volunteers are a crucial strength for nonprofits. They can be highly motivated, and can save organizational resources. There are significant disadvantages as well. Effective strategies for volunteer recruitment, training, and retention are presented.

Introduction

Nonprofit organizations rely on volunteer assistance to perform organizational functions from receptionist to board chairperson. Indeed, the term "voluntary sector" is a working synonym for "nonprofit charities."

Nonprofit organization budgets rarely permit salaries for all needed employees. During times of economic uncertainty, nonprofit organizations are particularly vulnerable to budget cutbacks, ironically at the very same time that the demand for their services increases. Using volunteers is an effective way to stretch limited organizational resources, build community support, improve communications, and tap hard-to-get skills.

The changing demographics of the '90s—more single-parent households, more two-parent working families, more women in the workforce, an increasing incentive to continue working to maintain income rather than retiring—demand that volunteer recruitment, training, support, and recognition change to meet new realities.

National statistics provided by Independent Sector validate the view that citizens are volunteering more and more. According to statistics compiled by that organization, 48.8% of adults in this country provided volunteer service in 1995. This compares to 45.3% in 1987. The monetary value of this service was $201.5 billion in 1995, based on 20.3 billion hours of volunteer work. The average volunteer donates 4.2 hours/week. A 1995 survey commissioned by Independent Sector indicates that the plurality of volunteer work assignments are with churches, synagogues, and other religious organizations (17.2%). The second leading category of beneficiary agencies is "informal" (13.5%), followed by education (11.6%), youth (10.2%), health (8.8%), human services (8.4%), work-related (5.2%), recreation (4.9%), environmental (4.7%), public/societal benefit (4.5%), arts (4.1%), and political (2.5%). All other categories comprise 3.4%.

Volunteerism is alive and well in the United States. New public-private sector initiatives are strengthening the institutions that promote volunteerism. Partnerships are developing in schools, colleges, religious institutions, and the private sector. Successful volunteer programs tap "non-traditional" sources of volunteer strength. More and more, these partnerships are being directly encouraged by government.

Federal legislation signed on September 21, 1993, the *National and Community Service Trust Act* (P.L.103-82), provides additional incentives to promote volunteerism among the young and not-so-young, and pay them living and educational stipends as well. The federal budget for this program was $472 million for FY 1999. On February 1, 1999, President Clinton proposed increasing this amount to $585 million for the fiscal year beginning October 1, 1999. This amount would fund 69,000 AmeriCorps slots, with the expectation that the number would increase to 100,000 by 2002. In the past four years, more than 100,000 citizens have served in these positions. The total proposed budget for the Corporation for National Service for FY 1999-2000 is $848 million. This funds three programs—AmeriCorps, Learn and Serve America, and the National Senior Service Corps. Interested organizations should monitor local newspapers and the *Federal Register* for RFP announcements, regulations, and briefings.

Benefits and Considerations of Volunteers

Among the benefits of using volunteers are:

1. They do not require salaries or fringe benefits. While this is the most obvious advantage, there may be other financial savings as well.

2. They are often highly motivated. Volunteers are there because they want to be, not because it is their livelihood. If it was "just a job," volunteers might be somewhere else.

3. They can speak their minds without fear of loss of a livelihood. Volunteers can often be a useful sounding board. They are often less shy about speaking out than a paid employee might be.

4. They may bring skills to the organization that it may not otherwise be able to find or afford.

5. They may have a network of community contacts who may be a source of contributions, expertise, prospective staff, or additional volunteers.

Other considerations are:

1. Just because volunteers are not on the payroll does not mean that the organization incurs no costs. Volunteers need telephones, work space, equipment, supplies, desks, and virtually everything else besides a paycheck. Training and orientation costs are just as high as for salaried workers.

2. Volunteer retention is often a problem. Paid employment elsewhere may replace volunteering. Family commitments or other duties may intervene. A volunteer can be easily captured by competing interests.

3. Volunteers, just like paid staff, dislike dull, repetitive, uninteresting work, and are more likely to do something about it quickly.

4. Volunteers are generally available for fewer hours per day and have a higher turnover than salaried employees. Many, such as students, volunteer for specific time periods and for short terms. They often require more hours of training and supervision per hour of productive work than employees.

Nonprofit Organization Volunteer Policy

To maximize the effectiveness of volunteer help, a carefully planned strategy is recommended.

Volunteer Job Description

Individuals are more likely to volunteer to assist an organization if they have specific information about the tasks they are being asked to perform. Before requesting volunteer assistance, develop a detailed job description that includes at least the following information:

1. Examples of duties to be performed
2. Specific skills or training needed
3. The location where the duties will be performed
4. The hours per week required
5. The time period (e.g. weeks, months) the duties will be performed
6. The supervision or assistance that will be provided
7. The training that will be provided.

Volunteer Recruitment

Active recruiting is required to maintain a dedicated volunteer pool. The following are some ideas for generating volunteers:

1. Pass around a sign-up sheet at community speaking engagements where potential volunteers can indicate their interest. Be sure to provide space for addresses and telephone numbers, as well as space to indicate specific skills or interests.

2. Include information about volunteer opportunities in any public relations brochures, media stories, newsletters, and public service announcements. Many local newspapers have a regular column devoted to nonprofit organization volunteer opportunities.

3. Ask users of the organization's services if they would like to volunteer, if this is appropriate.

4. Target solicitation of potential volunteers to groups in the community that are likely to have time to share. The retired, schoolchildren, and church groups are excellent sources for volunteers.

5. Post volunteer opportunities on your Web site and on general sites that permit the posting of volunteer opportunities, such as IdeaList (see pages 161-162).

Interview potential volunteers as you would potential employees. Be sure their interests are compatible with the organization's. Find out what their motivation is for volunteering. Is it to perform a service or advance a cause? Is it to develop marketable job skills and make contacts? Is it to have a place to "hang out" and have access to a telephone? A volunteer can have the same organizational impact, negative or positive, as a paid staff member. The fact that a person is willing to work for free does not automatically make him or her the best candidate for the "job." The organization should not lower its standards in any way. Make sure that expectations are clear and performance is reviewed.

Tell potential volunteers about the organization and obtain basic information about them, such as their skills, training, and interests. Ask about their time availability. Once satisfied that the right volunteer is matched with the right job, review the volunteer job descriptions with them and ask them if they are ready to volunteer for specific assignments.

Orientation

Make certain every volunteer receives a complete orientation before starting to work. In some instances, a group of volunteers may participate in a formal volunteer orientation program. In other situations, a one-on-one orientation at the work site is appropriate. Make sure to include the following:

1. Overview of the organization's mission.
2. Description of the specific task to be performed.
3. Confirmation of the hours required.
4. Statement of whom to contact if help is needed.
5. Individual to contact if an assignment will not be completed as scheduled.

Rewards

While volunteers don't receive a paycheck for their services, they should receive other types of payment. Remember to thank them for the work they perform. Both informal thanks and periodic formal award ceremonies to thank volunteers are appropriate. Encourage volunteers to attend training programs to update their skills. Include them in agency social events. Remember that extra "payments" to volunteers will pay off in effective service to the organization.

Virtual Volunteering

A growing number of organizations are harnessing a new source of volunteers—those unable or unwilling to work on site, but who are eager to participate in volunteering for their favorite cause by working from their home or work computer. Virtual volunteering has obvious advantages for those who are elderly, disabled, caretakers, or who otherwise are restricted in their mobility or willingness to travel to a volunteer site. And for many others who are too busy or otherwise unable to commit to a specific time and place for their volunteering, this non-traditional method opens up opportunities.

Virtual volunteers are being used to design and update Web sites, prepare newsletters, respond to requests for information, research reports, and prepare advocacy materials. Virtual volunteering has appeal to those who are too busy to make a commitment, but have the ability to fit in volunteer work from home on an ad hoc basis—provided they have a computer and a modem. While there are some limitations involved in virtual volunteering (such as no hands-on supervision or the lack of face-to-face interaction), advances in technology are providing opportunities for people who otherwise would not make a volunteer commitment to volunteer. An eye-opening feature on virtual volunteering appeared in the April 17, 1997, issue of *The Chronicle of Philanthropy,* and I expect that it won't be too long until this nontraditional strategy becomes traditional.

Impact Online, an organization founded in 1994, administers a Virtual Volunteering Project. You can find information about how to begin, and even locate volunteers at this site, which can be found at: *http://www.impactonline.org/*

World Wide Web Resources (see additional resources in Chapter 20)

IdeaList
http://www.idealist.org/

This site, sponsored by the New York-based Action Without Borders, is an excellent online resource for nonprofits, and boasts the participation of 16,000 organizations in 130 countries. Nonprofit organizations can join for free, although a donation is requested. Member organizations may post information about their address, mission, contact person, telephone number, Web site URL and e-mail address. The organizations arc categorized by 40 types to facilitate searches by the public. Organizations post information about volunteer opportunities available, a job description, what skills are requested, and the dates that the volunteer is needed. Organizations may also post information about events and materials, such as newsletters, annual reports, and other publications. Although not required, there is an application form for posting organizations used to verify the information.

Support Center for Volunteer Management
http://www.genie.org

Click on "answers" and search for "volunteer management" from the pull-down menu and then click "open sesame" for the current FAQs relating to volunteer management. This site is an excellent resource.

Energize, Inc.
http://www.energizeinc.com/supervising.html

This is a "virtual appendix" to Energize's book *What We Learned (the Hard Way)—About Supervising Volunteers* by Jarene Frances Lee ($21.95). At the time of this review, six volunteer supervisors in a variety of settings posted practical advice. The page includes information on how to post your advice as well. There are other useful documents viewable at the site (see *Planning for a Volunteer Center* at *http://www.energizeinc.com/art/avolc.html*)

TIPS:

- **Interview all prospective volunteers.**

- **Make sure their duties are clearly defined, expectations are clear, and their performance is reviewed.**

- **Have a policy for volunteer termination or reassignment just as for paid employees.**

- **Consider having a formal awards ceremony for volunteers.**

- **Perform an "exit interview" with volunteers who leave or are terminated.**

Chapter 14
Charitable Solicitation Registration

> Synopsis: Most states require charities to file registration forms before engaging in fundraising solicitations. A Unified Registration Statement is available to streamline submissions, which is accepted by 32 states and the District of Columbia. Organizations must still submit individual financial reports to these states.

Introduction

All but 10 states in the United States regulate charitable fundraising. State laws requiring charities to register and to provide information about fundraising activities to the government is not a recent development—for example, the Pennsylvania General Assembly enacted a law to regulate fundraising back in 1919. Many states during the 1980s and 1990s enacted tough laws regulating charitable solicitation. This trend was motivated by abuses in virtually every state in which unscrupulous organizations posed as charities. Engaging in deceptive practices, these organizations generated contributions from the public that were intended for charitable purposes. Some of these organizations took names similar to reputable charities, and diverted most, if not all, of the proceeds of their solicitation to line their pockets. Other abuses involved professional fundraising organizations that would solicit business from bona fide charities, offering to raise funds in exchange for a percentage of the contributions received. Even if the charity received a minuscule percentage of what was raised and the charity benefited—it was at the expense of an unwary public.

Abuses such as these continue to this day. But state laws have made it tougher for deceptive practices to occur, and have given law enforcement officials new authority to take action to enjoin illegal or deceptive fundraising activities. Perhaps as important, these laws have provided the public (and the media) with easy access, often a toll-free telephone call or mouse click on a Web site away, to information about charities, their leadership, and how much of the money they contribute is actually being funneled to the charity and used for charitable purposes.

The State Directory of this book summarizes the charitable solicitation statutes in each of the 50 states and the District of Columbia. All but a handful of states require charities to register and provide reports that are made public.

From the perspective of most bona fide charities, these laws are a positive development—despite the prospect of costly and burdensome reporting requirements. The public, generous with charitable giving, was becoming more cynical with each fundraising scandal. As one mainstream charitable association (United Way of Pennsylvania) explained in its newsletter on why it testified in support of the 1990 Pennsylvania charitable solicitation law:

"United Ways and hundreds of other legitimate charities, which are 'squeaky clean,' are adversely affected and risk loss of public credibility and confidence as a result of a small but growing number of 'charitable' fundraising efforts which raise money solely or primarily for personal gain under the guise of charity."

While most of these laws are weak in prescribing a minimum threshold on what percentage of donations are required to be actually put to use for charitable purposes (rather than paying the expenses of professional fundraisers), the public policy philosophy is more along the lines of "a little sunlight is the best antiseptic."

While one can find patterns of similarity, each state that regulates charitable solicitation has its own law, regulations, and forms for registration, registration renewal, and expense/fundraising reporting. Many states also require registration and reporting for professional solicitors and fundraising counsels, and require those who make their living in this manner to post a bond with the state.

For charities that raise funds in more than one state (and as a result of the increasing prevalence of charities using the Internet to raise funds), complying with the requirements of each state can be problematic, expensive, and time-consuming. While the information provided in the State Directory is helpful, the requirements change without warning in some states. For several years, national and regional charities have legitimately complained about the impracticality of keeping up with the legal requirements for solicitation law compliance. An innovative project has addressed this concern.

The Unified Registration Statement

The National Association of Attorneys General and the National Association of State Charities Officials have developing the Unified Registration Statement (UCS). This document can be downloaded from the Internet *(http://www.nonprofits.org/library/gov/urs/c_urs210.htm)* in PDF file format. This format requires the use of an Acrobat Reader, which can be downloaded free at thousands of Internet sites, including this site. Although each state regulating charitable solicitation maintains the practice of providing its own individual registration form, 32 states and the District of Columbia will accept the UCS for registration purposes—all but six (Alaska, Arizona, Florida, North Carolina, Utah, and West Virginia) of the states that require registration. Six of the 33 jurisdictions that accept the URS (Arkansas, Georgia, Maine, Mississippi, North Dakota, and Tennessee) require a supplement filing to the UCS. These supplemental forms are not extensive, and are available on the Internet as an appendix to the UCS forms.

Charities may print out the PDF file directly from the Internet (or save it to disk for printing out later), fill in the information, and file it with each participating state. Instructions are provided at this Web site for printing or saving the file. A version of the form in HTML can be found on the Web site to review, but this version is not acceptable for printing out and submitting to state regulatory offices.

The URS is continually being updated and improved in response to comments provided by the charities and state regulators that participate. As of press time, the latest version of the form was 2.10, which was made public on April 30, 1999. You should verify that the most current form is being used by checking with the Web site:

http://www.nonprofits.org/library/gov/urs/

As of June 1999, the District of Columbia and following states accept the URS for registration:

Alabama			
Arkansas	Maine	New Hampshire	Pennsylvania
California	Maryland	New Jersey	Rhode Island
Connecticut	Massachusetts	New Mexico	South Carolina
Georgia	Michigan	New York	Tennessee
Illinois	Minnesota	North Dakota	Virginia
Kansas	Mississippi	Ohio	Washington
Kentucky	Missouri	Oklahoma	Wisconsin
Louisiana	Nebraska	Oregon	

Each state has individual exemptions and exclusions from registration requirements (based on, for example, the type of organization or the amount of fundraising conducted annually). Also, each state requires different supporting documents to accompany the URS, and charges an individual registration fee. Charities may still submit the state's individual registration form, but most charities soliciting in several states that accept the URS find it much more convenient to submit the standardized form.

The general Unified Registration Statement, version 2.10, consists of 22 questions on three pages. It requests:

- general information about the charity
- whether there was a previous legal name used
- information about misconduct by the organization's officers, directors, employees, or fundraisers
- a list of states where the charity is registered and the dates and type of solicitation conducted
- information about the organization's federal tax status
- methods of solicitation
- information about the purposes and programs of the organization for which funds are being solicited
- the names, titles, addresses, and telephone numbers of officers, directors, trustees, and principal salaried executives
- information that describes relationships (such as financial interest or relationship by blood, marriage, or adoption) between organizational leaders and professional fundraising organizations, suppliers, or vendors
- information about felony or misdemeanors committed by the organization's leaders
- the names of those who are responsible for custody and/or distribution of funds, fundraising, financial records, and those authorized to sign checks

- banks where funds are deposited, along with the account number and bank telephone number;
- the name and address of the accountant/auditor
- the name and address of the person authorized to receive service of process
- whether the organization receives financial support from other nonprofit organizations, shares revenue with other nonprofits, whether anyone owns an interest of 10% of greater in the organization, or whether the organization owns a 10% or greater interest in any other organization (and explanations for all of these)
- whether the organization uses volunteers or professionals to solicit directly to the public
- a list of professional fundraisers, solicitors, fundraising counsel, or commercial co-venturers accompanied by information about their services, compensation arrangement, contract dates, dates of the campaign, and whether that person/organization has custody or control of donations
- the amount paid to these persons during the previous year.

Financial information about the charity, including:

- contributions in the previous year, fundraising costs in the previous year, management and general costs
- fundraising costs as a percentage of funds raised
- fundraising costs plus management and general costs as a percentage of funds raised.

Note that the URS can be used only for registration and registration renewal, not for the annual financial reporting required by almost all states that regulate charitable solicitation. A separate project is in the process of developing a standardized reporting form for annual financial reporting.

The use of the Internet for fundraising has raised legal questions that previously were not relevant. For example, is a charity in Pennsylvania that is not registered in Utah violating the Utah solicitation if it puts a general solicitation on its Web site, and receives contributions from someone in Utah? This area of law is not clear, and it will likely take several years, if not decades, for a body of case law and statutory law to provide guidance to charities wrestling with these questions.

Chapter 15
Fundraising

Synopsis: The basic rule of fundraising is to ask—ask the right people at the right time in the right way. There are many conventional and creative ways to raise funds for a nonprofit organization.

ASK.

The rest of what is needed to know about fundraising—the amount to ask, who to ask, when to ask—are technical details that will be expanded upon in this chapter. However, the simple asking of funds for an organization is the major point of this chapter, since it is rare, but not unheard of, that funds are sent to an organization unsolicited.

Most states require organizations to register *before* they raise funds for charitable purposes. Before launching a formal fundraising campaign, refer to Chapter 14 and the State Directory at the back of this book to assure compliance with current state law.

How Much to Ask For

There are enormous differences in fundraising techniques if one is trying to raise $10 million for a new hospital wing or $633 to finance the costs of filing Articles of Incorporation, 501(c)(3) application, and a roll of stamps. There also are many similarities.

First, the organization must start with a reasonable budget plan. How much is needed to finance the organization's first-year activities? Will it have paid staff? Staff salaries, benefits, and payroll taxes generally are the largest line-items in any budget. The next decision that determines the order of magnitude in an organization's budget is having a separate office, which requires rent, telephone, furniture, equipment, and office supplies.

A good practice is to prepare three budgets:

1. A "low-end" budget, which assumes a minimum level to get the organization off the ground. The organization would cease to function if revenue did not cover expenses in this budget.

2. A "middle-end" budget, which is as realistic as possible, and considers the likely availability of funds for the year, and

3. A "high-end" budget, which assumes there is a millionaire "angel" who loves the organization so much that he/she is willing to keep writing checks to keep it comfortable.

In asking for money, one should tailor the "pitch" to the demographics of the contributors. It helps to understand the motivation of the contributors as well. People give money for a reason. It may be because they share the organization's motivation for starting up. It may be they feel guilty because otherwise they would not be doing anything to address a problem. It may be they desire power in the organization that they can get only by being a contributor. They also may be looking for ways to get a tax deduction, align themselves with a popular cause, or to become immortal (such as by contributing an endowed chair or building wing that would have their name on it). They may be contributing to an organization because they want a particular organizational leader to be their friend or to contribute to their own favorite cause.

The most successful fundraising is done by requesting contributions from people who have money to give away, who both know and respect the organization (or someone on its board or staff), and who are given reasons for contributing that are sensitive to their private motivations.

It is a good idea to select some board or advisory committee members based on their ability to tap funds from their friends and associates. Many of their well-heeled friends will write a check to virtually any cause solely because that influential board member picked up the telephone and asked them.

It is important to ask all board members to make a contribution to the organization. Many will be delighted to do so, recognizing that the organization, to be successful, does need some start-up funding, and it would make them look foolish if the organization is stillborn as a result of lack of seed money. It is not unusual for external funding sources to consider the extent to which board members participate in making contributions. Therefore, a participation percentage of board member contributions may be as important, or more so, than the dollar amount raised from board members.

Always suggest an amount when asking for a donation. Of course, the solicitor should consider the ability of the person to give that amount. The solicitor also should give examples of how that specific amount will be used to benefit the organization (e.g., "your $2,000 donation will purchase the computer system the office needs...").

IRS Substantiation Rules

The federal *Omnibus Budget Reconciliation Act* (OBRA), enacted in 1993, imposed new requirements on charities and donors with respect to substantiation of donations for contributions made beginning with the 1994 tax year. The law requires charities to provide a contemporaneous written acknowledgment of contributions of $250 or more when requested by a donor; the donor may not take a charitable tax deduction without having such a written acknowledgment. The practical effect is that charities are sending these statements routinely to their donors as a part of a "thank you" letter. The written acknowledgment must include the amount of cash paid or a description of property transferred by the donor, a statement of whether the donor received goods or services in exchange for the donation, and a good-faith estimate of the value of such goods and services, if any.

The law requires charities that provide goods or services in exchange for the donation, if the donation is in excess of $75, to provide in writing a statement to the donor that the deductibility of the donation is limited to the excess of the amount donated over and above the value of the goods and services provided, and an estimate of the value of those goods and services that were provided by the charity. For example, if your 501(c)(3) organization holds a fundraising dinner and you estimate that your costs of catering and entertainment is $45 and you charge $100 per ticket, you must disclose to ticket holders that they can deduct the contribution of $55 per ticket purchased. IRS Revenue Ruling 67-246, 1967-2 C.B. 104 provides examples of fact situations that require this disclosure.

December 1996 final draft regulations issued by the IRS provide some guidance to charities on several issues. First, charities may ignore benefits provided to members that can be used "frequently," such as gift shop discounts, free or discounted parking, or free or discounted admission to the organization's facilities or events. Second, free admission to members-only events can also be ignored if the cost per person does not exceed $6.90. For those who pay more than $75 for a membership package that offers more benefits than a membership at $75 or less, then only the benefits offered to those with membership costs of $75 or less can be ignored when taking the charitable deduction. If an organization offers free admission to a fixed number of events in exchange for membership, then the IRS's interpretation is that the fair market value of the admissions must be deducted from the value of the contribution.

Charities must provide written substantiation of a donation to volunteers who wish to claim as a deduction the cost of unreimbursed expenses of $250 or more. The regulations also require that institutions such as colleges that raise money by offering their alumni the right to purchase hard-to-get athletic tickets must consider 20% of the payment for the tickets as the fair market value for the right to purchase the tickets. This amount may not be deducted.

There are many gray areas with respect to substantiation issues, and the IRS has not been totally clear in providing guidance to charities. It makes sense to consult an attorney familiar with this issue if there is any question about whether your organization is in compliance with IRS requirements.

Sources of Funding

Among other sources for funding are:

1. **Umbrella Fundraising Groups** (e.g. United Ways, Jewish Federations, Catholic Charities, Junior Leagues, and similar service organizations)

In addition to providing an important source of funding, membership in a federated fundraising organization provides added visibility and community endorsement. This is especially important for those agencies that lack name recognition. While membership in a federated fundraising organization carries no iron-clad guarantee that funding levels will be sustained or increased (especially in a recessionary and highly competitive fundraising environment), member organizations fulfilling priority needs can count on relatively stable funding.

Although members sometimes chafe at accountability, program, and fundraising requirements imposed by umbrella organizations, few would trade their federated funding for total independence. While it sometimes appears that existing member agencies have a total lock on funding, the trend in recent years has been toward funding "cutting-edge" programs that are highly responsive to critical community needs.

2. Foundations

Major foundations usually require written proposals, many of which can be time-consuming to prepare, and there is a time lag between application (and a response to questions from the foundation on issues that were not adequately covered by the application) and when the check is in the mail. Other foundations are run by benefactors who establish the foundations for tax purposes. The benefactor may write a check as soon as the request for funds is received. Most foundation proposals can be prepared by someone without special training or education. The trick is to research the kinds of organizations and activities of interest to the foundation and tailor the grant application to that information. It is also vitally important to tailor the submission to the application guidelines of the foundation, since many proposals are rejected on technical grounds even before they are judged on their substance. Many local libraries have sections devoted to foundation fundraising, including research materials with the names, addresses, and the types of funding provided by each foundation.

According to *The Art of Fund Raising* by Irving R. Warner, foundations are responsible for just five percent of philanthropy. However, the individual gift may be quite substantial, and the awarding of a major gift by a name foundation can have benefits beyond the financial reward. It can serve as a catalyst for other grants and give the beneficiary organization increased credibility.

3. Direct Mail

The key to direct mail fundraising is a mailing list of people who are likely to consider making a contribution. Professional services sell mailing lists categorized by various interests and demographics. Organizations may wish to send a few newsletters to such a list, and then follow up with a direct mail appeal. If an organization is a membership organization, its members are among the first who should receive an appeal for voluntary contributions. After all, they have already indicated their interest in the organization's activities and are most likely to know what the organization is doing and how its funds are being spent.

Others to include on solicitation lists are the following:

a. Persons who benefit from the service provided by the organization and families of such persons, provided this is appropriate
b. Individuals who are in attendance at speaking engagements
c. Persons who make contributions to similar organizations.

A fundraising letter should appeal to some basic instinct that will make the reader have an irresistible urge to run to his or her checkbook and write a check to the organization. Appeals that honestly portray the needs of the organization and the importance of the services it provides are a basic component of direct-mail letters. Among the most popular appeals are those that generate:

a. **Guilt**. Make people feel guilty that they are not participating in solving some urgent problem.

b. **Affiliation**. Appeal to the need to belong to an organization that is doing something worthwhile.

c. **Self-interest.** Find some way to show that by helping the organization, donors' own lives will be improved in some way.

d. **Ego**. Make prospective donors feel they are wonderful people only if they make a contribution.

e. **Idealism**. Appeal to the idea that the world or community will be a better place for everyone and only a chosen few selfless people will help this cause.

f. **Religious need to give to charity.** Religious organizations have relied on this for years, but many secular organizations find this line of appeal equally effective for certain target audiences.

4. Businesses

Many organizations receive operating funds and in-kind contributions of services, equipment, and supplies from businesses in their communities. Among these businesses may be:

a. Employers of board members

b. Suppliers of goods and services to the organization

c. Businesses that make contributions to other organizations in the community

d. Businesses that sell goods and services to board members, members, or clients

e. Major employers in the community.

Rather than visiting a business "cold," it is effective to involve representatives of businesses in the organization's program before asking them for funds. Among ways to do this are:

a. Have business representation on the board

b. Establish a "business advisory committee" consisting of local businesspeople

c. Invite business representatives to an "open house" to see the organization in action

d. Place business representatives on the organization's mailing list. Send them the newsletter and newspaper clippings about the organization's accomplishments

e. Invite business representatives to speak to the organization's board or membership about their products and services.

Many business corporations have established foundations that are staffed to consider funding applications from charities.

5. Telephone Solicitation

Similar to direct mail, telephone solicitation is effective if done with the right list of names and correct telephone numbers. A college making calls to its alumni using student volunteers will certainly have a much better response than making calls at random. Similarly, an organization is well served if it can tailor calls to those with a likely interest in the purpose of the organization.

6. Government Grants

During the 1980s, federal government grants to nonprofits, particularly for social services, plummeted. Yet there are millions of dollars in federal and state grants to nonprofits that still go begging for takers. The trick is to identify the source of funds and determine eligibility. The *Catalog of Federal Domestic Assistance* is available in many libraries. It can also be found on the Internet, in searchable format, at *http:// www.gsa.gov/fdac/*.This document provides a summary of available federal grants and the qualifications and conditions for applying.

Government grants usually are accompanied by lots of paperwork and operational requirements, some of which may be inconsistent with the manner in which an organization intends to operate. Some analysts view a 1991 U.S. Supreme Court decision (*Rust v. Sullivan*) as clearing the way for the federal government to impose even greater restrictions on how government funds may be spent. If applying for government grants, learn about any additional requirements in order to be in compliance with law.

7.   Revenue-Generation Other Than Voluntary Contributions

The following are strategies used by nonprofits to increase income:

- Newsletter subscriptions
- Newsletter advertising
- Annual fundraising dinner
- Reception for a famous person or someone well known in the field of expertise of the organization/testimonial dinner
- Sale of publications
- Sale of services
- Sale or rental of mailing lists (make sure the buyer will use the list in a manner consistent with the organization's goals and will not resell the list to others)
- Small games of chance (provided they comply with state regulatory laws)
- Wills and bequests
- Social events (e.g., bus trips to sports events)
- Newspaper advertising to request contributions
- In-kind donations
- Card calling (using board and organizational members to do peer one-on-one solicitation)
- Fees from workshops and conferences
- Sale of exhibit space at workshops and conferences
- Special fundraising events such as bake sales, flea markets, and running races.

Hiring a Consultant

There are hundreds of honest, hard-working, professional fundraising counsels who will, for a fee, provide an organization with fundraising advice or even handle all fundraising. There also are hundreds who are not reputable. Most states regulate this industry, and there are opportunities to obtain information about counsels before making a hiring commitment.

Tips:

- Review other organizations' solicitation materials and use effective presentations as a model for solicitation.

- Keep a file of newspaper clippings about benefactors in the community and others who would have a potential interest in the work of the organization. A few well-placed and well-timed telephone calls can be effective in reaching these influential people.

- When applying for grants, ask the funding source for grant application forms and instructions.

- Involve everyone in the organization in the fundraising effort—it is not prudent to isolate fundraising from the programs the organization funds.

- Always thank each donor, regardless of the amount received. A $2 check from an individual may have required as much personal sacrifice as a $1,000 check from a wealthier contributor.

Chapter 16
Writing Effective Grant Proposals

Synopsis: Grant applicants should research the grantor before applying. They should not deviate from the format of the grant application except with express permission. There is a formula to follow for effective grant applications that, among other components, emphasizes the needs of the community rather than the needs of the applicant.

Introduction

Competition for government, corporate, and foundation grants is increasing. At the same time that funding from government sources for human services is shrinking, the demand for human services is skyrocketing. Charities are becoming more sophisticated in how they seek alternative sources of funding. Many are hiring development staff with specialized training and experience in obtaining grants. Others without the resources to make such a major investment are forced to do what they can. The purpose of this chapter is to provide a framework for the preparation of proposals for those without substantial grantsmanship experience.

It is often useful for grant seekers to develop the attitude that the relationship between themselves and the grantors is collaborative. True, all of the wonderful plans you have in mind will never come to fruition without the funds. However, the grantor needs the creativity, dedication, staff resources, and vision provided by the grant recipient. A grant proposal that is seen as simple begging is not as likely to be as successful as one that encourages the grantor to become a partner in an effort that will have substantial benefits to the community and to society.

Before embarking on a costly and time-consuming search for grants, verify that the purpose of the grant is consistent with the mission of the agency. Some organizations apply for grants simply because the money is available and obtainable, and they have a scheme to win it. However, the successful grant application may result in the organization losing its focus if the grant is inconsistent with the direction of the organization. Even if the grant's purpose is consistent with the mission, consider whether the project is viewed as constructive by agency stakeholders, such as members of the board, clients, and staff. It may be useful to convene a focus group to gauge whether the grant would truly be beneficial to the agency and its clients.

In addition, organizations should consider cash-flow issues, grant eligibility, the politics of the grant, and the source of the grant. The check from the funder may arrive months after the agency has committed itself to hiring staff and paying other project costs. Is a source of funds available until the grant funds are received? Are there laws or other grant requirements that must be adhered to that, for any reason, you are unable or unwilling to honor? Have the grants being applied for been promised informally in advance to other organizations? Does the grantor have a reputation for making unreasonable demands on organizations it funds?

Researching the Grantor

Once you believe a funding source may have funds available, do not begin to write the grant application until you have tried to find out the answer to several questions from the funding source. Try to obtain an interview with a representative of the funder before beginning to write the funding application. You should have the following information before beginning the proposal-writing stage:

1. The application format

Why write a 30-page application when a three-page application would have been funded? Why write a three-page application and not get funded when a 10-page proposal would have been accepted? Many government agencies will send you a *Request for Proposal* (RFP) that will outline exactly what should be included in the application. Many larger foundations will provide specific instructions. If you are given written instructions by a funding source, do not deviate from these instructions without permission. One major reason grants do not get funded is that the writer does not follow the instructions to the letter. Even minor deviations can make the proposal ineligible. If you believe a particular instruction does not apply to your situation, request written permission from the funder to make changes.

2. Motivation of the funding source

Many funding sources specialize in awarding grants for specific purposes. You will not receive a grant from such a funder unless the proposal clearly is responsive to the vision and mission of the funding agency. When applying for a government grant, for example, obtain and study the legislative history that led to a funding appropriation. When applying for foundation funds, be sure to obtain the donor's funding instructions. Many corporate and family foundations have a priority listing of the types of programs they fund and will be glad to share this information with you.

3. The amount of funds awarded by the grantor per award, and the amount of total funds awarded

This will be extremely helpful information if you can obtain it. In many instances, a government agency has a specific allocation of funds for a particular program. Large foundations set specific priority areas and make general allocations in the priority area. Foundation directories that provide this information are available in most public libraries. It just makes no sense to develop a grant application if the funds awarded by the source are too small.

4. Successful applications that were funded in previous funding cycles

Perhaps the best indicator of the types of funding applications that will be successful is a review of actual applications that have been funded. A strong argument can be made that government agencies have an obligation to provide you (as a taxpayer) with copies of funded applications. While you may have to review the applications at the agency's headquarters or pay for duplication, you should be able to review past grants.

Many foundations will provide a list of the previous year's grants and the total of each. You can contact the individual agency and ask for a copy of its funded application. While lists of past grants are often difficult to obtain from businesses, many annual reports and business newsletters include a list of grants that have been awarded and their sources.

5. The names of individuals making the funding decisions and their backgrounds

When writing a grant application, it is important to know who will be reviewing it. If the reviewers have extensive expertise in your field, you will not have to define every term. In many instances, however, a foundation trustee or a business official on the allocations committee will not have any knowledge of your particular field. You will then have to carefully explain your services in layman's terms, spell out every abbreviation, and define each technical term you use.

6. The criteria used in making the grant selection

Knowing the selection criteria can be crucial in determining how to write a grant. Many grantor agencies have limited amounts of funds and will give preference to smaller grants. Others will make the selection based on non-cost factors and then negotiate the cost of the proposal. Knowing whether it will be helpful or harmful to have political officials contact the grantor agency is important information.

Sections of a Grant Application

1. Cover Letter

Many grant applications specifically request a cover letter and define what information should be included. If this is not specifically prohibited by the grant application format, write a short cover letter on agency stationery that:

- Is addressed to the individual at the grantor agency whose name, title, agency name, and address are absolutely correct

- Contains a one-sentence description of the proposal

- Provides the number of participants, jobs obtained, or other units to be funded by the grant

- Lists the total amount of funds requested

- Provides the name, address, and telephone number of the individual at the agency to contact to request additional information.

2. Executive Summary

Include in this section a succinct summary of the entire proposal.

3. Introduction

Provide important information that may not otherwise appear anywhere else in the grant application. Items you might include are the following:

- Your agency's mission
- How long you have been providing the type of service included in this program
- Brief history of your agency
- Major indicators that you are capable of operating programs efficiently and effectively
- If there are eligibility requirements in the proposal, state that you are eligible to receive the funds
- Statement of your I.R.S. Section 501 tax-exempt status
- Outline of letters of support from past clients, representatives of cooperating agencies, and legislative officials (The letters themselves should be included as appendices to the application.)
- Statement of how you will obtain funding for the program at the end of the grant period.

4. Need

For a grant to be funded, the agency must demonstrate the need of the individuals in the community for the service to be provided. What is the extent of the need and how is the need documented? The need described should be the need of the individuals in the community for the services, not the need of the agency. Rather than stating "We need a counselor because our agency doesn't have one" or "The funds for the one we had were cut back by the government," estimate the number of individuals who need counseling services. The need should be the need in your coverage area. While national or statewide figures might be given, if you serve a particular county, the estimate of need for that county should be provided. The need should be the need for the particular service you are providing. If you provide services for victims of domestic violence, for example, the estimated number of victims of domestic violence should be provided rather than unemployment figures or other available statistics. The need should be quantified. How many individuals do you believe are eligible for the particular service you provide in your coverage area?

Common sources of data are the following:

1. Census Data—Make certain you are using data from the 1990 and later censuses. In most cases, 1980 data is outdated.

2. County Planning Commissions—Call the office of your county commissioners to find the number for your county's planning commission.

3. State Agencies—The Departments of Education, Health, Labor, and Human Services, or their equivalents, are all excellent sources of data.

4. Local Governments—Local police departments are excellent sources of crime data, and local school districts can provide educational information.

5. Self-generated data—In many cases, you can provide the data from sources within your agency. Sources might be:

- Waiting lists
- Letters from potential clients requesting a service
- Letters complaining that a particular service is not in existence
- Testimony at public hearings
- Information obtained from questionnaires administered to present clients asking them to list other services they might like
- Community surveys.

5. Objectives

Objectives are the proposed results of the project. Objectives should have the following characteristics:

- They are measurable. How many individuals do you estimate will participate in your program?

- They are time-based. How many individuals do you estimate will participate in your program in the next three months? In the next year?

- They are realistic.

The information to measure objectives can be obtained as part of your program. Do not list objectives in your proposal if the information to measure them would be impossible to obtain if the proposal is funded.

6. Project Description

Here is where you will outline your program. An easy way to remember what to include is the 6 W's of program writing:

1. Who? Who are the clients? How are they selected? What are the restrictions (e.g., age, income, geographic)? Who are the staff members?

If you are asking the funding source to pay for new staff members, include a job description and a qualifications statement that lists the educational, experience, and other job requirements. If you are applying for funds to continue existing staff, include a résumé and a biographical statement for each staff member.

2. What? What services will be provided? For educational programs, include a course outline. You may include relevant sections of an operations manual. For other programs, a narrative outlining the services would be appropriate. Still others might provide a "day in the life of a client." What outreach efforts will be made?

3. Where? Where will the services be provided? Give addresses of all main and field offices. If you will be obtaining new space with the program funds, what type of space are you seeking?

4. When? What are the hours that services will be provided? On which days during the year will services be provided? It is also useful to provide a timetable for project implementation.

5. With whom? What other agencies are participating with you in the provision of services? For example, include agencies referring clients to you for service. Outline the agencies to which you refer clients. It is important to obtain letters from the other agencies confirming any relationships you are describing.

6. Why? Why are you providing these services rather than alternatives? Are you providing any unique approaches to the provision of services?

7. Budget

If it is not clear from the grant application forms, ask the funding source how much financial detail is required. Many businesses, for example, may only require the total amount you are going to spend. On the other hand, most government agencies require a line-item budget that includes a detailed estimate of all funds to be spent. Such a budget might be set up to include the following:

1. Personnel costs (salaries, fringe benefits, consultant and contract services)

2. Non-personnel costs (travel, space, equipment, consumable supplies, and other costs such as telephone, postage, and indirect costs)

Some grantor agencies may require your agency to contribute a matching share. If you are permitted to include in-kind or non-cash expenditures, use the same budget categories as above. In the personnel category, for example, you would list the worth of the time volunteers are contributing to your program. In the non-personnel category, you would include the market value of the equipment donated to your program.

8. Evaluation

Inform the funding source that you will be conducting an evaluation of the services you are providing.

1. Detail who will participate in the evaluation process. Outline the participation of board members, staff members, clients, experts in the substantive field, and representatives of the community in the evaluation process. Some grantors require an independent evaluator.

2. Explain what will be evaluated. List some of the issues the evaluation team will consider. For example, the evaluators will review whether the need was reduced as a result of providing the services. Were the objectives met? Were the services provided as outlined in the Project Description section? Will the budget be audited by an outside firm and, if not, who will review the receipts and expenditures?

3. Specify what type of evaluation will be provided. Provide in as much detail as you can how the program will be evaluated. If formal classes are provided, include the pre- and post-test you will use to evaluate the classes. If a client questionnaire will be used, attach a copy to the application. Describe how the program data will be reviewed in the evaluation process. Include a description of the audit or the process you will use to review the budget items.

9. Conclusion

In no more than two or three paragraphs, summarize the proposal's main points and the reasons the community will be improved as a result of successful completion of the project.

When you have finished writing your grant application, ask yourself the following questions before you send it to the funding source (in plenty of time to meet the application deadline):

- Is it free of the jargon of your field?
- Are all abbreviations spelled out the first time you use them?
- Have you followed all of the instructions in the Request for Proposal (RFP)?
- Are all words spelled correctly? Remember that your computer's spell-checker only tells you that the words you use are English, not that they are the correct words.
- Is your application interesting to read?
- If you were the grantor agency, would you fund it?

Finally, get the application in the hands of the grantor before the deadline. The fundraising field is replete with horror stories about multi-million dollar proposals that were not even considered because someone put the application in the mail and it didn't arrive until well after the deadline. Make sure there is enough postage if the application is mailed. It is highly recommended that applications be either hand-delivered or sent by overnight courier, such as Federal Express or Airborne Express. Make several office copies before submitting the original, and be sure that you provide the number of copies requested by the grantor.

Chapter 17
Lobbying

Synopsis: Lobbying by nonprofit corporations is not only legal, but should be encouraged. There are effective strategies to communicate with legislators in person, by letter, or by telephone. All states require lobbyists to be registered and report expenditures.

Lobbying is the time-honored tradition of communicating with elected or appointed officials for the purpose of influencing legislation and other public policy. The word itself derives from the outer room of the legislative chambers where paid professionals congregated, seeking to button-hole legislators before they cast their votes. In recent years, the term has developed a pejorative character as the public, justified or not, perceives special interest lobbyists as using their influence to work against the public interest.

Whether referred to as "advocacy," "government relations," or "lobbying," it is a right afforded by the First Amendment to the U.S. Constitution relating to freedom of speech, as well as the right to petition to redress grievances. Many of the public policy decisions made in Washington, state capitals, and cities and towns have a direct effect on nonprofit organizations and the interests and clients they serve.

Many nonprofits are expressly created to advance one cause or another considered by a government body.

Organized lobbying is an effective way to communicate an organization's views on a pending issue, to promote a favorable climate for those served, and to directly influence the outcome of decision-making. Lobbyists are employed by organizations who view themselves as working in the public interest—speaking for the poor and disenfranchised, improving the environment, establishing programs to serve the disabled, or expanding government support for vital human service and community needs.

Legal Requirements for Lobbying

Federal Requirements

The *Lobbying Disclosure Act*, PL 104-65, was enacted on December 19, 1995 and provides major changes in registration and reporting requirements for lobbying the Congress and the Executive Branch. The bill also includes a provision (Section 18) that places restrictions on the lobbying by nonprofit civic leagues and social welfare organizations, among others, which receive federal funds. The effective date of the act was January 1, 1996.

The act defines "lobbying contact" as—

> "*any oral or written communication (including an electronic communication) to a covered executive branch official or a covered legislative branch official that is made on behalf of a client with regard to—*
>
> *(i) the formulation, modification, or adoption of Federal legislation (including legislative proposals);*
> *(ii) the formulation, modification, or adoption of a Federal rule, regulation, Executive order, or any other program, policy, or position of the United States Government;*
> *(iii) the administration or execution of a Federal program or policy (including the negotiation, award, or administration of a Federal contract, grant, loan, permit, or license); or*
> *(iv) the nomination or confirmation of a person for a position subject to confirmation by the Senate.*

The act defines "lobbyist" as—

> "*any individual who is employed or retained by a client for financial or other compensation for services that include more than one lobbying contact, other than an individual whose lobbying activities constitute less than 20 percent of the time engaged in the services provided by such individual to that client over a six month period.*"

A packet of materials, including a copy of the *Lobbying Disclosure Act*, registration and expense reporting forms, instruction booklets for filling out the forms, and answers to frequently asked questions, are provided by contacting the following:

Secretary of the Senate
Office of Public Records
232 Hart Senate Office Building
Washington, D.C. 20510
(202) 224-0758

Unless they are self-employed, individual lobbyists do not register with the House and Senate. The new law requires registration by lobbying firms, defined as entities with one or more employees who act as lobbyists for outside clients. A separate registration is required for each client. A typical nonprofit that has one or more employees who engage in lobbying activities is required to register, provided that its expenses attributable to lobbying exceed $20,000 in a semi-annual period (either January 1-June 30 or July 1-December 31).Registration is required no later than 45 days after a lobbyist first makes a lobbying contact or is employed to do so, whichever is earlier. To register, the organization files a Form LD-1 in duplicate with the Secretary of the Senate and the Clerk of the House:

Secretary of the Senate
Office of Public Records
232 Hart Senate Office Building
Washington, D.C. 20510
(202) 224-0758

Clerk of the House
Legislative Resource Center
1036 Longworth House Office Building
Washington, D.C. 20515
(202) 225-1300

Registration discloses general information, a description of the registrant's business or activities (e.g., social welfare organization), a list of employees who act or are expected to act as lobbyists (an employee is not considered a lobbyist if he/she spends less than 20% of his/her time lobbying), an indication of the issues to be lobbied (selected from a list of 74 general categories, such as "welfare"), and the specific issues to be addressed, including specific bill numbers or executive branch activities.

Expense Reporting Requirements

Registered organizations are required to file two semi-annual reports. The first report, due August 14, covers the period January 1-June 30. The second report, due February 14, covers the period July 1-December 31. One copy must be filed with each of the two offices. Organizations employing lobbyists must report whether their lobbying expenses were less than $10,000 or more. If lobbying expenses were more than $10,000, the organization must make a good-faith estimate, rounded to the nearest $20,000 of their lobbying expenses during the reporting period. Organizations must also file a separate sheet on each general lobbying issue that was engaged, specific information about each bill or executive branch action, the Houses of Congress and federal agencies contacted, and the name and title of each employee who acted as a lobbyist.

State Requirements

Every state has individual registration and reporting requirements for lobbyists. Consult the state directory in the back of this book for the requirements in your state. Don't rely on this book for the legal requirements, as they may have changed since this book went to press. Always contact the office that administers this state law for reliable information.

Effective Strategies for Lobbying and Advocacy

- Know Your Legislators—Give them the information they need to help the nonprofit organization meet its objectives.

- Identify Key Contacts—Survey the organization's network to discover who has a personal or professional relationship with key public policy decision-makers, and who contributes to political campaigns.

- Target Decision-Makers—Pay special attention to legislative leadership, the majority and minority chairpersons of relevant committees, and their staffs.

- Use Local Resources—Identify constituents connected to the organization, and match them up with their legislators for advocacy contacts.

- Schedule Lobby Days—Many nonprofit organizations and other groups schedule a Capitol Lobby Day. Such events typically include a briefing on an important pending issue by an organization's executive director, a rally and/or press conference in the Capitol, scheduled office visits to local legislators and legislative leadership, and a closing session to exchange information gleaned from those visited.

- Schedule Press Conferences—Non-governmental organizations can hold press conferences in the Capitol or on the steps of the Capitol.

- Circulate Petitions—While viewed as one of the least effective forms of lobbying, the presentation to a legislator or government official of a petition signed by thousands of persons is a worthy "photo opportunity" and may get some coverage.

- Present Awards—Many nonprofit organizations present a "Legislator of the Year" or similar award to recognize key legislators for their interest in the issues of concern to that nonprofit. These awards further cement a positive relationship and ensure continued access to that legislator.

- Arrange Speaking Engagements—Most legislators are delighted to receive invitations to address groups of their constituents. Such gatherings provide opportunities to educate the legislator on issues of interest to the organization.

- Provide Contributions—Money is still considered to be the mother's milk of politics. While corporations, by law, cannot make contributions themselves, individuals and corporation-affiliated Political Action Committees (PACs) may and do. Those that make contributions find their access to public policy makers is vastly improved. As a general rule, the more an organization's activities are perceived to be in the public interest, the less need there is to rely on making political contributions to develop access and to deliver the organization's message.

- Request Public Hearings—Public hearings held by a legislative committee provide an opportunity for media coverage, a forum for an organization's point of view, and a way to galvanize support for an issue. Having an organization's clients fill a hearing room sends a clear message to the committee members and staff.

While it is true that the suggestion by a committee chairperson to hold hearings on an issue may be a strategy to delay or kill a bill, public hearings can nevertheless be utilized by the organization to focus attention on an issue. A hearing can generate public and media support. It can provide a forum for improving the proposal, thereby minimizing opposition to the legislation.

501(h) Election

The U.S. Congress in 1976 enacted a law that expanded the rights of nonprofits to lobby. However, it was not until August 30, 1990, that the IRS and Treasury Department promulgated final regulations to implement this law. In the preceding 14 years, there had been a pitched battle between nonprofits and the Congress. Nonprofits fought diligently to preserve their rights to lobby under the Constitution and the 1976 law. Some in the executive branch also sought to deny those rights. The principal issue is the definition of the term "substantial," since the law prohibits 501(c)(3) nonprofits from carrying on "substantial" lobbying activities.

The regulations permit electing organizations to spend on lobbying, on a sliding scale, up to 20% of their first $500,000 in expenditures, and up to 5% of expenditures over $1.5 million, with a $1 million ceiling in each year. Organizations can spend no more than a quarter of their lobbying expenses on grassroots lobbying (communications to the general public that attempt to influence legislation through changing public opinion).

These regulations exclude certain expenditures from lobbying, including—

1. Communications to members of an organization that brief them on provisions of legislation, but do not urge that they take action to change those provisions.

2. Communications to legislators on issues that directly affect the organization's own existence, such as changes to tax-exempt status law, or lobbying law.

Of major importance to nonprofits, the organization would no longer be subject to the "death penalty" (i.e., the total revoking of their tax-exempt status) for violations. There is a system of sanctions replacing that.

All 501(c)(3)s must report the amount they spend on lobbying on their 990 tax returns.

IRS Regulations on Lobbying

The August 1990 regulations of the Treasury Department with respect to lobbying are quite complicated. An excellent 57-page publication, *Being a Player: A Guide to the IRS Lobbying Regulations for Advocacy Charities,* is available from The Alliance for Justice, 2000 P Street, Washington, D.C. 20036.The guide explains in clear and precise terms what is permitted under these regulations, and includes many sample forms and worksheets. The cost is $15. Obviously, the booklet will need to be updated to reflect the new requirements of the *Lobbying Disclosure Act*.

Contacts With Legislators

1. Visiting a Legislator

- Make an appointment, if at all possible

- Arrive promptly, be warm and courteous, smile, speak for five minutes or less on a single issue

- Don't threaten or exaggerate your political influence (if one is really influential, the legislator will already know)

- Listen carefully to the legislator's response and take notes; be polite, but keep the legislator on the subject

- Leave the legislator with something in writing on the issue, if possible

- Request that the legislator do something to respond to the organization's position—vote in a specific way, take action on a problem, or send a letter to legislative leadership requesting action

- Follow up the meeting with a thank-you note, taking advantage of this second opportunity to reinforce the organization's views and remind the legislator of the action requested

- Do not feel slighted if referred to a staff member—legislators often have last-minute important meetings or unscheduled votes. Staff members are valued advisors who, in some cases, have as much influence (or more) than the legislator in the process and may have more time to help.

2. Writing to a Legislator

- Restrict letters to one issue; be brief and concise

- Clearly indicate the issue of concern, the organization's position on it, and the bill number, if known

- Write the letter in a manner that will require a written response and include a return address

- Use facts to support positions, and explain how the issue affects the organization, its members, and the community

- Use professional letterhead, if appropriate; type the letter, if possible, or write neatly and legibly

- Try not to indicate that the letter may be a form letter sent to scores of other legislators

- Make the letter positive—don't threaten the loss of votes or campaign contributions

- Follow up after the vote on the issue to indicate to the legislator that the organization is following his or her actions with interest and that it appreciated or was disappointed by that vote.

3. Telephoning a Legislator

- Speak clearly and slowly

- Make sure that callers identify themselves in a way that will permit the legislator to reach them or the organization by letter or telephone

- Follow the guidelines listed above for writing and visiting, which are equally appropriate for telephoning.

Tips:

- **Those who expect to spend a substantial amount of time in legislators' offices should register as lobbyists, even if they feel the law may not require them to do so. The judge of whether the person doing the advocacy is in compliance with lobbying laws will not be that advocate.**

- **Comply with all state and federal reporting requirements.**

- **If the nonprofit corporation is a human service provider, invite local legislators to tour the facility and observe the services being provided.**

- **If the corporation is a membership organization, invite local legislators to speak to the membership.**

- **Encourage members to make individual contributions. It is good advice not to get involved in partisan politics, particularly if the corporation has 501(c)(3) status. Those who do choose to participate in partisan politics should be scrupulous about separating personal political activities from the corporation and not using corporate resources for partisan political activities.**

- **Download and review the comprehensive, 158-page second edition of *The Nonprofit Lobbying Guide* that Independent Sector has posted for free access on its Web site at:** *http://www.indepsec.org/clpi*

Chapter 18
Political Activity by Nonprofits

Synopsis: Charities are proscribed by law from engaging in electioneering. However, many political activities, such as candidate forums, questionnaires, awards, and compiling voting records, are not only permissible but are important activities for charities and other nonprofit organizations.

Introduction

Volunteer leaders and executives of nonprofit organizations are, generally, key opinion makers and play an important role, both in their organizations and in their personal lives, in shaping public policy. Many elected officials got their first taste of community service by serving as nonprofit board volunteers. Many elected officials continue to serve on nonprofit boards, and their expertise and political influence are often of great value.

Yet, there has been an historic concern that nonprofits, particularly nonprofit charities, may be using taxpayer-financed subsidies to unduly influence the outcome of elections. This concern has been codified in federal and state law that, in general, prohibits 501(c)(3) organizations from engaging in political activity, and places severe restrictions on other tax-exempt organizations. Some state laws mimic federal law, prohibiting corporations and unincorporated associations, other than Political Action Committees (PACs) and other organizations formed solely for political activity, from making contributions or expenditures in connection with the election of a candidate.

A 501(c)(3) organization by federal law explicitly may "not participate in, or intervene in (including the publishing or distributing of statements), any political campaign on behalf of, or in opposition to, any candidate for public office." No corporation, nonprofit or for-profit, may make campaign contributions. Moreover, any expenditures by a charity, for or against a candidate, can result in the loss of the organization's tax-exempt status, the assessment of a large excise tax, and potential fines against the charity's executives and volunteers. Charities may not endorse candidates or oppose candidates for public office. Generally, a person is considered to be a candidate for public office when he or she makes a public announcement to that effect, or files a statement with the elections commission of an intention to run. Expenditures made prior to that time or after the election are not considered to be political activities.

Department of Treasury regulation §1.501(c)(4)-I(a)(2)(ii), as amended in 1990, expressly forbids 501(c)(4) organizations from engaging in direct or indirect participation in political campaigns on "behalf of, or in opposition to, any candidate for public office" as part of its definition of "social welfare." However, a subsequent IRS Ruling (Rev. Rul. 81-95, 1981-1 C. B. 332) has interpreted that this regulation does not impose a total ban on political activity by 501(c)(4)s. The level of political activity that is permitted by 501(c)(4)s without jeopardizing their tax exemptions is still unclear. What is clear is that the political activity by the organization must not be a substantial part of its activities, and the activity must be consistent with the organization's social welfare mission, according to the May 1992 *Harvard Law Review* (p. 1675), which provides substantial guidance and applicable case law on this complicated legal issue.

Among the types of expenditures that may be considered political activity are candidate travel expenses, fundraising expenses, polls, surveys, candidate position papers, advertising and publicity, and money paid to the candidate for speeches or other services. Expenses relating to non-partisan voter registration drives are not considered political expenses.

Individual Political Activities

Volunteers and agency staff of charities have the same First Amendment rights as anyone else. There is no prohibition against such persons making political contributions, volunteering to work on a campaign, signing letters of support (provided any reference to their charitable organization affiliation clearly indicates that the reference is for identification purposes only), and issuing statements on a candidate's behalf. Moreover, the resources of the charity cannot be used for electioneering. Charitable organization leadership and staff should not write letters on a charity's stationery in support of a candidate. They should not turn the offices into a *de facto* campaign office for the candidate, using the telephone, copy machine, computer, and other resources, even during non-business hours.

Penalties

Beyond the sanctions of loss of tax exemption authorized by the 1954 Revenue Act, the Revenue Act of 1987 increased the sanctions available to the IRS in enforcing the prohibition against political activities. It also provided the IRS with the authority to seek an injunction to bring about an immediate cessation of violations that are deemed to be "flagrant." Most political campaign expenditures by 501(c)(3)s and 501(c)(4)s are now subject to a 10% excise tax applied to the organizations and a 2.5% excise tax (up to $5,000) applied to each of the managers of the organization who knew that a political expenditure was being made. This tax only applies if the expenditures were willful, flagrant, and not due to reasonable cause. If the illegal expenditure is not corrected, an additional 100% tax is imposed on the organization and 50% (up to an additional $10,000) on each manager who knew of the violation. Correcting the violation means that the managers tried to recover the contribution and took steps necessary to stop future violations.

While this area of law has a substantial gray area, there are several important general rules to be aware of in guiding an agency's quasi-political activity. Each case decided by the IRS is fact-specific, and their rulings provide only general guidelines.

The best advice for charitable organization leadership and staff is to provide a wide margin for error when contemplating engaging in political activities and not to engage in any activity that would even raise the specter of being improper, even if such an activity falls within the legal framework provided by current case-law.

Quasi-Political Activities

Among the most common issues raised by charities are the following examples of border-line, quasi-political activities:

1. Voting Records. There is nothing illegal about a charity annually publishing a compilation of voting records of the Congress or the General Assembly. Some guidelines to follow are that the compilation should not be released only before an election and should list the voting records of all of the public officials or those in a relevant region (rather than selecting out only those who are up for re-election, or who are targeted by the organization because they consistently vote for or against the organization's public-policy positions). It should also involve a wide range of subjects, not imply approval or disapproval of the public officials, and should not be disseminated beyond the membership or mailing list of the organization, i.e., the general public.

2. Questionnaires. It is not only permissible but advisable for charities to communicate with candidates, informing them of the organization's positions on issues and requesting their views. When candidates run for office, it is a vulnerable time for the shaping of their public-policy positions. Many regret the positions they have taken during the election in response to a seemingly innocuous questionnaire. However, the use of these responses by an organization can be troublesome.

The IRS has ruled (Rev. Ruling 78-248) that it is permissible for charities to send a questionnaire to candidates and publish the answers in a voter's guide. However, the charities should make an effort not to demonstrate obvious bias in the questions, or to favor one candidate over another by making editorial comment. Organizations with a narrow range of interest, such as a pro-life or pro-choice group, are more in jeopardy by publishing the results of a questionnaire than groups with a broader range of interests, such as the League of Women Voters. If viewed by the IRS as a back-door method to influence how your constituency votes, then questionnaires could place an organization's exemption in jeopardy.

3. Public Forums. Many 501(c)(3) organizations have a Candidates' Night to permit their volunteers and staffs to meet the candidates and question them about issues. This is not illegal, and is expressly permitted by the IRS, provided it ensures "fair and impartial" treatment of the candidates (Rev. Rul. 86-95). However, such programs should be conducted with common sense. The moderator should be someone who can be even-handed. All *bona fide* candidates should be invited, although it is not a prerequisite that they all accept the invitation for the event to be scheduled. Organizational leaders should refrain from making editorial comments about the positions of the candidates. Any account of the event in the organization's newsletter or other publication should be even-handed and should refrain from making editorial comment in favor of, or in opposition to, a candidate's views.

4. Mailing lists. The mailing list of a charity may be a valuable asset in the hands of a candidate. Many organizations get substantial revenue from selling, or renting, their mailing lists. There is no prohibition against selling a mailing list to a candidate for public office. However, giving a mailing list to a candidate is tantamount to making a political contribution. Also, all candidates must be given the same opportunity to purchase or rent the mailing list; no favoritism is permitted. As noted elsewhere in this publication, the sale or rental income from organizational mailing lists is potentially subject to federal unrelated business income tax, despite recent court rulings that decided they are not.

5. Awards. Many charities give "Legislator of the Year" or "Public Citizen of the Year" awards or similar citations to elected officials. However, making such an award just prior to an election in which the awardee is a candidate may be considered improper electioneering. From a practical viewpoint, even if this is done without any intention to help that candidate, a charitable organization's volunteers or contributors who may not like that particular candidate could view it as a disguised attempt at electioneering. It is a good policy to avoid providing awards to candidates during election periods.

Note: The above analysis is not intended to serve as legal advice about any particular set of facts, but only as a review of currently available reference materials on this issue. Consult a lawyer for a definitive answer to any particular legal problem.

Tips:

- If you as a nonprofit executive are a "political animal" who *must* get involved in partisan political activity, find another entity, such as a PAC or a political party committee, to channel those energies. Never use your organization's stationery for political purposes.

- Seek experienced and competent legal counsel before engaging in any political activity that falls into a gray area.

- Use permissible political activities to the advantage of the organization, such as candidate forums, candidate questionnaires, and awards to public officials.

Chapter 19
Communications

Synopsis: Organizations need to effectively communicate their objectives, activities, and accomplishments to attract funding, participation, and public support. Publications, media contacts, and workshops are among the methods used to communicate organizational interests.

Introduction

A well-planned public relations/communications strategy is important for two reasons. First, the organizational leadership has made a major investment in forming a nonprofit corporation, and a solid public relations effort will promote the organization's purposes. Second, few newly-formed nonprofits begin with a silver spoon in their mouths. The first few years often are a fight for survival financially.

There is a "Catch-22" at work here in many cases. New organizations must accomplish something useful quickly to obtain the credibility necessary to attract financial assistance. Yet the organizations often need this financial assistance to accomplish their missions.

Public relations thus serves an important internal function. It promotes the organization in a positive light and generates the essential public support needed to perpetuate the organization. An organization may be quietly successful in changing public opinion, advancing a legislative agenda, or providing vital services to worthy clients and its members. But if the right people—the board, funders, and potential funders and leadership—are unaware of the organization's successes, then its continued existence may be at risk.

Menu of Standard Nonprofit Communications Tools

An organization may be shy about tooting its own horn. But if it declines to do so—carly and often—then its horn may be taken away. There are thousands of creative ways to get the name of an organization in front of the public in a positive context. Among the conventional techniques nonprofits use are the following:

1. Organizational Brochure

Each nonprofit organization, from the largest to the smallest, should have an organizational brochure. The brochure should clearly include the name, address, and telephone number of the organization, e-mail address, Web site address, its mission, its purposes and principal interests, its affiliations (if any), its federal tax-exempt status and ways to make contributions, the names of its board members, advisory committee, and key staff people, and its major accomplishments. The organization's logo should appear on the brochure (see Chapter 22). If the organization is a membership organization, the brochure should provide information on dues and how to join.

The brochure should be distributed with all major fundraising solicitations. It should be a standard component of press packets, and be distributed at speaking engagements made on behalf of the organization. All board members should have a supply of brochures to distribute to their friends and colleagues who may be interested in joining, contributing, volunteering, or assisting in other ways.

2. Organizational Newsletter

The organization should, no less than on a quarterly basis, publish a newsletter for distribution free-of-charge to all board members, all dues-paying members, significant opinion leaders on the issue(s) of interest to the organization, political leadership (such as members of the General Assembly, local members of Congress, and local elected officials), the media, current and potential funders, and colleagues in the field.

Among the items the newsletter may contain are—

- Recent board decisions.
- Legislative action in Washington, the state capital, and municipal government of interest to the membership and clients.
- Schedules of upcoming meetings, workshops, conferences, and training sessions.
- Messages from the executive director and/or board president.
- Articles contributed by experts on the board or from the membership about issues of interest to the readership.
- Articles about organizational accomplishments such as grants received, advocacy accomplished, coalitions joined, and letters of commendation received.
- Profiles of people involved in the organization.
- General information about the status of issues of interest to the organization.

The newsletter need not be fancy, but should be as current as possible. It is advisable to select a creative and descriptive name for the publication and establish a master layout, so that subsequent issues will have the continuity of similar design.

The newsletter is often the only contact hundreds of influential people will have with an organization. As such, it is vitally important to present a professional, accurate, and aesthetically pleasing format. The newsletter should be carefully proof-read and *all* typographical and grammatical errors eliminated. Make sure articles on one page continue correctly on subsequent pages.

Headlines should help busy readers find their way through the newsletter. Tricky headlines can be annoying. Double-check all headlines for appropriateness. Double check all names, telephone numbers, and addresses included in the newsletter.

3. News Releases

The media annually provide millions of dollars in free publicity to nonprofit organizations. The typical mode of communicating with the media is through the mailing (or faxing) of a standard news release. The news release is a pre-written "news" article that includes the name, organization, and work telephone number of the key organizational contact person at the top. If the release is *really* important, include the home telephone number as well. The release should be dated, along with "For Immediate Release" or "Embargoed Until (insert date/time)" as appropriate.

Examples of topics for news releases can be the following:

a. An organization's official comment on a new law or legislative proposal, new regulation, or court decision affecting the organization's clients or members.

b. An accomplishment achieved by an organization.

c. The release of a study or survey commissioned by an organization.

d. The hiring or promotion of a staff member, or change of leadership within an organization.

e. Awards given by or to an organization.

News releases are distributed to those who are most likely to print or broadcast them. A news release to a TV or radio station should be no more than six or seven sentences, nor more than two double-spaced pages for the print media. Most news releases will be edited before final publication or broadcast, although many neighborhood newspapers will print news releases word-for-word.

The basic style of the body of a press release is the following:

a. Precede the text with a catchy, descriptive headline.

b. Put the most important sentence first.

c. Place subsequent facts in descending order of importance.

d. Include suitable quotes of organizational leadership when appropriate. The quotes should express a view/opinion, rather than providing a fact that could appear in the release narrative.

e. Make sure the text answers the basic questions of "who," "what," "where," "why," "when," and "how."

4. Press Conferences

Organizations with a story of major interest to the public may want to consider holding a press conference. To do so, a media advisory is distributed in the same manner as a news release, telling the press where and when the press conference will be held, the subject, and speakers. It may be helpful to make follow-up calls to the news desk of the local newspapers and broadcast stations. At the press conference, written materials (a press packet consisting of a copy of a written statement, the organization's brochure, and materials relating to the topic of the press conference) should be distributed.

Another good idea is to arrange for a black-and-white photo of the organizational representative speaking at the press conference. The photograph may be accompanied by a picture caption and sent to media outlets not covering the press conference. Don't forget to include a press packet, as well.

A banner with the organization's logo, draped in front of the podium, creates a photograph that is useful for future annual reports, newsletters, and related publicity. Take into account that 1-hour commercial photo developers may require several days to develop black-and-white film.

5. Public Service Announcements

Many TV and radio broadcasters regularly broadcast public service announcements (PSAs) for nonprofit organizations free-of-charge. PSAs are an excellent and cost-effective way to get an organization's message, and its name, to thousands of viewers and listeners. The last line of such an announcement can be: "This message is brought to you by (the name of your organization) and this station as a public service." The rest of the announcement can be a 30-second sound bite of information of interest to people—how to obtain a free service, how to avoid health and safety risks, or even how to join or volunteer for your organization while accomplishing some vital objective in the public interest. Before preparing a PSA, check with a potential broadcaster for the technical specifications relating to the form and format of the announcement. Some stations may be willing to *produce* your announcement without charge, as well as broadcast it.

6. Conferences and Workshops

Well-planned conferences and workshops can serve a useful public relations function. A one-day conference can bring together interested lay leadership and professionals in a shared field of interest, introduce them to the organization, increase networking among the participants, and advance the organization's interests. The charge for the workshop can be set to cover all anticipated costs, or even to generate net revenue—provided it is planned well in advance and the plan is executed properly.

There are scores of major decisions to make in running a conference, such as choosing speakers who will generate attendance and excitement, preparing and distributing the conference brochure, selecting the site for the conference and arranging for exhibit space and advertising. There are hundreds of more minor decisions that need to be made as well, such as choosing the type of name tag to use, deciding who staffs the registration table, and choosing the luncheon menu. There are many sources of advice on how to run a successful conference, and many of these can be borrowed from the local library.

7. Intra-Organizational Communication

Board and key contacts need to know what is happening beyond what they read in the organization's newsletter. Periodically, it is useful to send out "Action Alerts" or "Background Briefings" that describe the status of a problem and what they can do to participate in its resolution. Some organizations have a specially printed piece of stationery for these messages. A sample letter may be included if the organization is encouraging its constituency to write letters. However, the organization should urge writers to use their own words rather than copy the sample exactly. The address or telephone number of the person they should contact should always be included.

8. Annual Report

Among the typical publications produced by nonprofit organizations is the annual report. Many nonprofits use this opportunity to supplement and embellish the financial information (provided they wish to make this public) with a report on the operations of the nonprofit during the fiscal year. The annual report can be professionally designed with fancy layout, fonts, charts, graphics, and color pictures, which imply progress and success in meeting organizational goals and objectives. It can also be a word-processed report photocopied on plain paper. In either case, it is an opportunity to communicate what the organization has been doing on behalf of its Board and membership, clients, funders, and the public, as well as its goals and plans.

9. Other Publications

Many nonprofits publish small booklets about various issues of concern, which are disseminated to their constituents and other interested parties. It is one more way to get the name of the organization in front of more people, and it is another effective way to communicate the organization's views to those whose opinions count. Subjects of such publications could be—

- The latest developments on issues of interest
- How to contact government offices

- How to lobby on behalf of the organization's issues
- The state legislature, and who serves on committees of interest to the organization.

These publications can also be considered the written equivalent of the public service announcement. Many institutions, such as hospitals, community centers, nursing homes, day-care providers, and libraries, will distribute these public relations booklets free of charge to the organization's target audience.

10. Membership/Board Surveys

Membership and board surveys can be, but may not always be, a useful tool to obtain information and feedback. The target of the survey may feel a sense of connection to the organization, and the survey will provide useful input from the membership. Member surveys can be tailored to suit the needs of the organization. For example, many advocacy nonprofits periodically survey their boards and/or membership to determine who among the board and membership has influence or personal relationships with key public policy decision-makers. Surveys can be used to gauge the effectiveness of organizational programs and activities.

Christine Finnegan, a managing editor at Morehouse Communications, adds this advice:

> "Be sure your survey goes to the right people, asks the right questions, and is easy to complete and return. If you don't plan to believe, abide by, or use the results of the survey, don't waste your time."

11. Speakers' Bureaus

Many groups, such as men's and women's clubs, fraternal organizations, educational organizations, membership organizations, and churches and synagogues, have speakers at their regular meetings. Organizational leaders may wish to proactively seek invitations to discuss the activities of their organizations with these groups. They may be the source of volunteers, donations, ideas, or simply good will and public support. Local newspapers (don't forget the "Shopper" newspapers) list many of these club meetings and their presidents. Addresses can be found in the telephone book, if they are not listed in the announcement. Members of the board can be deputized to speak on behalf of the organization. Many of them have associations with other organizations and clubs that would be delighted to host a speaker.

12. Newspaper Op-Ed Articles

Virtually all newspapers will print feature-length opinion articles on their Opinion/Editorial (Op-Ed) pages. Many will include a picture and a line of biographical material about the author. The Op-Ed page is usually the page most read by a newspaper's readership, along with the Letters-to-the-Editor page. It is an excellent forum to share an organization's ideas on an issue and bring attention to the organization. There are many cases in which a thoughtful Op-Ed article has resulted in legislation being enacted by Congress or the state legislature to address the subject of the article.

13. Letters to the Editor

Letters to the Editor are an effective way to "talk back" to a newspaper when the organization believes an article or editorial unfairly and erroneously shapes an issue. They can also be an effective medium to reinforce a position and permit the writer to expand on that position from the perspective of the organization. The general guidelines for writing letters to the editor vary from paper to paper, but usually provide for writing on a single issue, being concise (no more than three paragraphs), using non-threatening language, and providing information that might not be available to the readers from any other source.

14. Developing a World Wide Web Home Page

Thousands of nonprofit organizations are establishing home pages on the World Wide Web (see Chapter 20). These pages communicate information about donations; volunteer opportunities; products, services, and publications; and general facts about the agency. These pages can be prepared and maintained for very little cost and permit the general public to access information by computer modem from the privacy of their own homes and offices.

15. Forming a Coalition

There is strength in numbers. Two heads are better than one. Whatever the cliché, many organizations find a benefit in pooling their resources to accomplish an objective. One strategy is to form a coalition of other organizations to address an issue of critical importance. There are many advantages to doing this. A fuller discussion of coalition-building is provided in Chapter 21.

Chapter 20
The Internet for Nonprofits

> Synopsis: Nonprofits have an exciting, new resource in the Internet. Once connected, organizations can share information cheaply and quickly, and they can use search techniques to find information. Nonprofits can set up their own pages on the World Wide Web.

The recent explosion of useful resources for nonprofits on the Internet is perhaps the most exciting positive development for this sector in years. Thousands of nonprofit institutions whose leadership had barely heard of the Internet a few years ago are not only connected, but have their own World Wide Web (WWW) sites.

Nonprofit executives have taken advantage of this revolution in communications by using the Internet to troll for donors, lobby their members of Congress, advertise job openings, purchase office equipment and supplies, hold on-ine meetings and information sessions, market their services, check references of prospective consultants, distribute board documents, reserve library books, generate grass-roots advocacy letters to government officials, research new laws and regulations, and download the latest Supreme Court decisions, all without leaving their offices. Need a 990 tax return form? Download it from the IRS web site *(http://www.irs.ustreas.gov)*. Need driving directions to your board meeting for your board members? Have a computer generate not only the directions but even a map, and e-mail them *(http://www.mapblast.com)*. Have a general question about how to deal with a sensitive organizational issue? Ask for advice on the soc.nonprofit.org mailing list (view the frequently asked questions file for this mailing list, including subscription information, at *http://www.nonprofits.org)*.

In previous years, if you wanted to distribute a document to a board, you had to photocopy the document, collate it, stuff it in envelopes, put correct postage and mailing labels on the envelopes, and mail it. The recipient would receive it two-five days later. Time could be saved by faxing the document, or broadcast faxing it, to the list of recipients, but the cost of long-distance charges could be substantial. Via the Internet, the same operation results in almost immediate delivery of the documents to every person on the list, for the price of a local telephone call. The Internet is revolutionizing the way all businesses operate, and the nonprofit sector is finding that the benefits to the for-profit world are just as applicable to the nonprofit sector.

Having Internet access is like having your own private library, entertainment center, news and clipping service, private club, and nightly gala soirée, with several important differences—the library is the largest ever created in the world by a factor of perhaps 10,000, and you have a private genie to conjure up at will who can virtually instantaneously find and bring you almost any piece of information you want.

Saving money, while of prime concern to nonprofits, is only one advantage of utilizing the Internet. Perhaps the most exciting aspect is that nonprofit executives can communicate cheaply and efficiently with like-minded counterparts who may be in an office next door or on another continent. The culture of the Internet has developed so that it is easy for people who have something in common and information to share to find each other and begin a one-on-one or one-on-ten-thousand dialogue without having to laboriously screen out the other 80-100 million people who also are participating.

Many nonprofit executives report that attending a national conference results in serendipitous contacts with previously unknown colleagues, who generate new ideas, new strategies for solving problems, interchanges that promote innovation, collaboration opportunities among people otherwise separated by geography and useful social contacts. The Internet has become all this and more. The velocity of communication interaction among people has made a quantum leap as a result of the Internet. Nonprofits that don't take advantage of the new opportunities afforded by this emerging technology to save money, expand markets, and promote themselves may be left in the dust by competitors that do.

What is the Internet?

The Internet is a term that describes the connection among millions of computers all over the world. This connection supports communication between them as a result of a standardized connection protocol called TCP/IP (Transmission Control Protocol/ Internet Protocol). For the typical Internet user, all of the technical details are totally transparent; communicating from an Atari computer or a mainframe on the Internet makes no difference, provided each computer is running the same protocol.

The Internet was developed in the early 1970s by the Department of Defense for the purpose of providing communication that was disaster-proof. Initially, it was used by technical folks and academicians. It was clunky at best, used an obscure communications language, and the information shared was, at best, esoteric. Only in the last seven years or so has the Internet become a part of the popular culture and available to the masses. New communications software, commercial providers that market to the general public, the emergence of the World Wide Web, advances in technology such as high-speed modems, and competition in the industry have made Internet access popular. Millions without their own personal computers have access to the Internet through libraries, educational institutions, and the workplace.

Each resource on the Internet has an address to enable a user to find and connect to it. That address is called a URL (uniform resource locator). The URL has a standardized format that is useful in identifying its source.

Equipment Needed to Connect to the Internet

To make a connection to the Internet, five components are required:

1. A computer and monitor. The computer stores the communications software, provides the mechanism to download and store data from the Internet, provides a convenient way to dial into the Internet, and takes advantage of many new technological wonders, such as using the Internet to have real-time audio conversations. Although a printer is optional, you will find it useful to print out much of what you find on the Internet.

2. A telephone line. The Internet communicates by sending packets of data over the telephone line. A nonprofit may purchase a dedicated telephone line, which will be used only for computer communication. More typically, a nonprofit will either purchase a supplemental telephone line or, if online time is minimal, use an existing line. Many nonprofits go online using a separate line previously dedicated solely to the fax machine. Obviously, when online communication is occurring on the dedicated fax line, no faxes may be received or sent by the organization.

3. A modem. Most personal computers sold today have a built-in modem, typically 56k baud. The higher the baud rate, the more data can be transferred over the telephone line within a given time frame. A 2,400 baud modem is sufficient for the transfer of text, although large documents take proportionately longer. With the advent of the World Wide Web, which takes advantage of graphics, sounds, animations, videos, and other byte-intensive files, the modem speed becomes critical. The World Wide Web is almost unusable with a 2,400 baud modem. Many nonprofits find that even a 56k baud modem is not sufficiently fast, and there are technological breakthroughs that use special digital cable modems to provide data transfers several times faster than the conventional analog modems of most personal computers.

4. Communications software. A computer without communications software is like a car without an engine. It may look nice, but you aren't going to go far. Like cars, communications software can be a Volkswagen Beetle or a Mercedes. Fortunately, at least basic communications software is included in virtually every PC computer sold, in the form of the communications programs included in the Accessories folder of Microsoft Windows. There is an equivalent for MAC-based systems as well. Many PCs also include demonstration or full versions of communications software designed to connect to the Internet, provide e-mail management, a Web browser, FTP software, and a newsgroup reader. Among the most popular are: Internet Office!, The Instant Internet Kit, Internet Valet, Quarterdeck InternetSuite, and Internet In a Box. Many of the programs included in these packages may be obtained in some version for free from various sources; these packages will not connect you to the Internet without a monthly fee to a service provider.

5. Service provider. While it is possible to set up as one's own service provider and make a direct connection to the Internet, doing so is expensive, time-consuming, and technically difficult. The choice for almost all nonprofits has become to purchase an account with a commercial or nonprofit Internet service provider. Among the national service providers are CompuServe (1-800-848-8199), America Online (1-800-827-6364), Prodigy (1-800-776-3449), and The Microsoft Network (1-800-386-5550). Hundreds of local Internet service providers have sprung up to compete, and many charge less than the national companies, but for the most part provide fewer services. Typical costs for a service are $10-20/month. For that, you get access to the Internet and other content offered by the provider for a limited number of hours each month, and an additional charge for each hour online above that threshold. Almost all providers also offer the option of unlimited access to the Internet for a set monthly fee.

Practical Applications of the Internet

Among the most popular services and applications of the Internet are e-mail, the World Wide Web, FTP, Telnet, chat, newsgroups, and mailing lists.

E-mail: Most of the data transmitted over the Internet is in the form of electronic mail. These are text communications that are sent from one person to another. E-mail is a "store and forward" system that permits someone to send a message to someone else for later retrieval. Each Internet user is given an Internet address that is used to send and receive e-mail. E-mail messages also can have computer files attached to them. Experienced users refer to messages sent via the U.S. Postal Service as "snail mail." Letters are to e-mail what smoke signals are to long-distance telephoning. E-mail avoids playing "telephone tag" and for a fraction of the cost of faxing.

Mailing Lists: Mailing lists are a form of e-mail. Users who subscribe to a particular list may send a message on a topic of interest to that list. The message is automatically distributed as e-mail to every subscriber on the list. Thus, if you subscribe to the nonprofit mailing list *soc.nonprofit.org*, you can send a message to the list that gives details about your upcoming national conference on drug and alcohol abuse, and every subscriber will see that message as e-mail. Some mailing lists generate hundreds of messages a day and others perhaps one each day. If you are paying a server for each message, or have limited storage space for e-mail messages, it may be important to you to limit the number of lists to which you subscribe.

To subscribe to a mailing list, the subscriber generally sends an e-mail message to an administrative address in a standard format that automatically processes the request. The administrative address is different from the address to which messages are sent that are intended for the entire distribution list.

Some popular nonprofit mailing lists are:

CFRNET (communication among foundations, institutions, and business)
command: SUBSCRIBE CFRNET
address to subscribe: listproc@ripken.oit.unc.edu

FUNDLIST (fundraising)
command: SUB FUNDLIST
address to subscribe: listproc@hcf.jhu.edu

FUNDSVCS (fundraising)

command: SUBSCRIBE FUNDSVCS
address to subscribe: majordomo@acpub.duke.edu

ONLINE FUNDRAISING (fundraising)
command: SUB FUNDRAISING
address to subscribe: autoshare@gilbert.org

USNONPROFIT-1 (general nonprofit issues)
command: SUBSCRIBE NONPROFIT
address to subscribe: nonprofit request@rain.org

GRANTS (grants and foundations)
command: SUBSCRIBE GRANTS
address to subscribe: listserv@philanthropy-review.com

The command to subscribe is usually: "subscribe name of list firstname lastname" where firstname and lastname are your own names. The command is e-mailed, without any other message, to the administrative address.

Newsgroups: A newsgroup is another form of Internet communication that provides for group discussion of a narrow topic. It is like a bulletin board in the supermarket, where you have to take action to see it and read messages posted there, with an opportunity to post a reply for others to see. Sending a message to a newsgroup results in each subscriber of the newsgroup having the capability of seeing the message without receiving it as e-mail. Typically, someone makes a comment on a newsgroup, another person responds to the comment, and so on until there is a string of related messages on a topic. Simultaneously, others online will start another string of messages. All the messages are stored, often chronologically, and given a title, and viewers can pick and choose using a newsgroup reader (specialized software to facilitate reviewing newsgroups) to decide which messages to look at. One of the most popular newsgroups of interest to nonprofit organizations is: *soc.org.nonprofit.*

FTP: FTP, or file transfer protocol, is the tool used to connect to a computer and transfer files from one to the other. Using FTP, you can "upload" the file of your nonprofit's newsletter to the Foundation Center. Or you can "download" a list of the top 40 charities. For example, the Nonprofit Center may have a document called "Ethics of Fundraising." FTP connects your computer with the computer that has the file, so you can transfer it to your own hard drive or floppy disk and then print it out. As technology improves, more information providers are providing more user-friendly ways to upload and download files from their Web sites, and it won't be long before knowledge about FTP will no longer be necessary to successfully transfer files on the Internet.

Telnet: Telnet is the protocol to connect with a computer in a remote location and interact with it in real time, as if you were directly operating that computer on site. Using Telnet, one can use software that is locally unavailable, play games or engage in simulations with others who also are logged in. Like FTP, Telnet is also becoming an anachronism with the advance of more user-friendly information transfer technologies.

Chat: Chat is the Internet equivalent of ham radio. Using chat software, one can have a "conversation" with someone by using the computer keyboard, all in real time. What you type and the response of the other participant(s) appears on your screen simultaneously. It is possible to have a nonprofit board meeting entirely by chat. Most commercial providers provide for privacy among those who participate. More popular, however, are informal chats among those who just happen to frequent a chat room. More and more, these chat rooms are becoming specialized, so participants have something in common. Many Web sites, including those of nonprofit groups, use software, often provided free by commercial providers, that permits visitors to participate in chat. In return for the use of free chat rooms, the visitors often see advertising messages controlled by the software provider, not under the control of the organization that is sponsoring the individual chat room.

The World Wide Web

The World Wide Web (WWW) permits Internet users to link to resources on other computers, even if those computers are on the other side of the world. World Wide Web resources are reportedly expanding at the rate of 20% each month. The Web supports not only text, but graphics, photographs, full-motion videos, and sounds. Web pages are often formatted to give the appearance of an on-screen magazine, but there is one major difference. World Wide Web pages are formatted using computerized codes, called HTML (hypertext markup language), which permit the user to use a mouse or other pointer device to click on one part of the screen and be connected to a totally different World Wide Web page. These may be generated from a server on the other side of the world. For example, a World Wide Web page relating to libraries can be coded with links to libraries in hundreds of places. By clicking on one of these links, the computer's browser transports the user to the World Wide Web page of that library. To see World Wide Web pages and navigate through these links, "browser" software is required.

The Web contains information made available by people and organizations. No one is in charge of maintaining or organizing the Web, so what you see is only what someone else saw fit to make available. Using the Web is free and, so far, most of the content on the Web is free, as well. But an increasing number of sites are charging for access, and it is not unusual for organizations to provide limited access to a site free to the public, and restrict access to certain pages to their members or those who pay a fee.

World Wide Web History

"The World Wide Web" is probably the term most commonly thrown around in discussions of the Internet. You might see it abbreviated "WWW" or "W3." The Web was "invented" by physicists at the European Laboratory for Particle Physics (CERN). Their basic problem was that they wanted to find an easy way to cross-reference a document with its end notes and bibliography, which at that time, often required leaving the first document and searching for the second. The objective was to code the link to the second document at the same time one was viewing the first document. The Web you see now—with graphics that can be clicked on, flashy colors, and eye-catching animations and backgrounds—turned the WWW from what was a sterile, 1850s newspaper style to what looks more like a television or movie screen with an attitude.

The World Wide Web is exactly what its name suggests: a Web of interconnecting sites that span the world. Each "Web site" or "home page" belongs to, and is operated by (or abandoned by), some organization or person. Sometimes the terms "Web site" and "home page" are treated as synonymous, but there is a subtle difference. Web site refers to a collection of pages of a person or organization, while the home page is the main "gateway," "index," or table of contents to the rest of the Web site.

All Web pages contain only that information that the person or organization wants to make available to the larger Internet public. For individuals, it might be a self-description or a list of interests and links to their favorite Web sites. For an organization, it might be a description or advertisement of its services, or it could be information relating to its mission.

So imagine now, a global newsstand or television network in which each and every person has the ability to create his or her own "home page show." Some people use this ability to entertain, sell goods and services, or share news, ideas, or stories. Some home page shows are good, and some are pretty awful. Some are self-serving only and some altruistically offer the world some useful information and communication contacts.

Anyone with a Web browser can view these home page shows. Just as any brand of television shows the same program on the same channels, browsers show the same Web pages, even if the tint, contrast, and general layout may vary from browser to browser.

A key feature of the Web, with its millions of home pages, is the ability for each page to lead you to other pages. On almost any home page, you will see some text (or pictures) underlined (or outlined) and/or in colorful boldface. These are the "hypertext links" that, when clicked on with the mouse, trigger your browser to move along to another Web page. Note that sometimes one of the links will lead not to another Web site when clicked, but instead to an individual's e-mail address. A message form will appear, allowing you to write a message to the designated person. These are called "mailto" links.

The ability to create links is the magic of which the World Wide Web is formed, and is one way the Internet is different from television shows or newspapers. TV show producers generally want you to keep viewing their shows and not move elsewhere, and written publications are intended to be read in sequential order. The Internet is often referred to as "thinking in parallel," since it allows and encourages you to explore more in depth whatever diversionary routes you wish to take.

Deciphering a Web Address

A URL ("uniform resource locator") is the address for Web sites. Each Web page has a unique address. Typically, Webmasters organize the URLs of their pages in a manner similar to how directories and subdirectories are organized on a computer, by using forward slashes (rather than back slashes) to organize these pages. For example, a home page might have the URL:

http://www.organization.org/webpage.html

The home page might have a link to "press releases" with the URL:

http://www.organization.org/webpage/pressrel.html

The September 18, 1999, press release on the organization's Legislator of the Year award might have the URL:

http://www.organization.org/webpage/pressrel/091899.html

This is an important point to understand. Perhaps you are given the URL for a document and your browser gives you a "404" message (indicating that there is nothing available at that URL). Instead of giving up, you can try finding the page you are looking for by using the URL one directory higher, or two or three directories higher, as may be necessary. There are many times when you can find the information you are looking for even when you are given an incorrect URL.

Let's quickly deconstruct a Web address. The Web site address for White Hat Communications' The Online Nonprofit Information Center is:

http://www.socialworker.com/nonprofit/nphome.htm

The first thing you might notice is that there are no spaces. This is not a coincidence. No spaces are allowed in a URL, and this is why words are often separated by dots ("."), dashes ("-"), tildes ("~"), slashes ("/"), and underlines ("_").

Starting from the end, in the above address, the suffix, ".htm," indicates that the document is a Web page using HTML (hypertext markup language) codes. This is the code used to create Web pages, and these files usually end in "html" or "htm."

Next, each single slash mark ("/") lets you know that you are descending into further file directories in the person's server, just as you do in your own computer to find particular files or documents. This is useful to know, because there are times when you might know an address for a site that is likely to be in the ascending files. For example, suppose you wanted to find the main page for White Hat Communications. You could guess that the home page would be at *http://www.socialworker.com.* Entering this will, in fact, get you to the main page for White Hat Communications.

To "surf," "browse," or "navigate" the Web (these are all equivalent terms), you simply open your browser and type in the URL of a page, and from there explore various links. You can fully access the Internet's resources even if you hardly ever enter a URL by hand. Your browser will start you off at a default home page (usually the browser company's Web site), but you can set it to start at any site you wish—your own, a favorite organization's, or a favorite navigation launching point, such as the Yahoo! directory (*http://www.yahoo.com*). One browser feature you will come to rely on is the "back" button. Suppose you start to jump from page to page during your navigation, and realize that you have gone well off-track. The back button will retrace your steps as far back as you wish before going forward in a new direction. For a quick return to the beginning, you can always click the "home" button and begin anew.

Most browsers have a "bookmark" function that automatically records a favorite link for future use. Thus, in order to return to that page at a future time, you need only to click on the stored reference in the bookmark list, rather than having to type in the entire address.

Frames

A popular Web page development is the use of frames, a device that allows more than one HTML document to be displayed on your monitor at the same time. Usually, one frame will contain a "Table of Contents" consisting of links. When you click on one of the links, the referenced document appears in another frame, while the first frame remains on the screen. In essence, you are then viewing two Web pages in one. The page that is displayed in the second frame may be another page in the same Web site as the first, or it may be a page from another site.

A significant disadvantage of using frames is that many older Web browsers are not compatible with them. If you are using a browser that is not, and you try to access a page with frames, you will typically get an error message such as, "Your browser does not support frames. You cannot access this site." Some of these messages may have a link to a site that permits you to download, at no charge, a browser that supports frames. Your only recourse at this point is to download (or buy) a browser that supports frames. Some sites have a frames and a non-frames version, and we recommend that you provide both if you plan to build a site using frames, so you will not alienate (or lose as visitors) those who do not have a frames-compatible browser.

How to Find Resources on the World Wide Web

One of the complaints about the Internet in its early years was that you could find a plethora of fascinating data bases, files, and information, but it was almost impossible to find something you were actually seeking in advance. Commercial companies offered services to assist researchers in finding Internet resources, and often charged handsomely. Recently, that has changed dramatically with the development of powerful search tools, all of which can be accessed free of charge. Among the more popular search engines are Yahoo! *(http://www.yahoo.com)*, Lycos *(http://www.lycos.com)*, Excite *(http://www.excite.com)*, and Alta Vista *(http://*

www.altavista.com). Users access the search engine by connecting to its address, and then fill out an online form with the term or terms to search. For example, typing the term "nonprofit" in the Yahoo search engine generates within a second or two more than 500 responses in the form of links. Clicking on any one of these links transports you to the referenced page.

The search engine administrators usually provide a procedure for registering a new World Wide Web page with them so that it will appear in searches. Nonprofits that develop their own World Wide Web pages should register their pages with as many search engines as they identify.

Directories

A directory is analogous to a library card catalog. It organizes information on the Internet by preselected categories. You may find directories useful when looking for a specific Internet site if you know the site exists. For example, if you are looking for the site of Penn State University, using a search engine will likely provide a response of thousands of related possibilities, few of which will take you to the home page of that institution. However, using the Yahoo! Directory *(http://www.yahoo.com),* you can find the main category *Education* and work your way down through categories to find exactly the page you want (i.e., by clicking serially on the following: *Universities, United States, Public by State,* and *Pennsylvania* until you reach *Penn State University@).*

Web Rings

Web rings are linked groups of independent Web sites on a related topic. When you go to a site that is associated with a Web ring, you will find an area, usually at the bottom of the site's page, where you can click to go to the next site in the ring, the previous site, a random site in the ring, or a list of all sites on the ring. If you are hoping to find a number of related sites on a particular topic, you might check to see if there is a Web ring. You can search for Web rings by keyword at: *http://www.webring.org.* Other sites helpful for finding Web rings are Looplink *(http://www.looplink.com)* and The Rail *(http://www.therail.com).* Some find that it is easier to locate information about a particular topic through a Web ring search than through a conventional search engine. As of February 1999, there were more than 60,000 Web rings with more than 1 million sites. Among the Web rings you can find of interest to nonprofit organizations are those on domestic violence, AIDS, homelessness, disabilities, cancer, and premature babies.

Obtaining a Domain Name

A domain name is the part of the Internet address after the "@" sign. For example, my personal e-mail address is: gary.grobman@paonline.com. Paonline is my Internet Service Provider (ISP), and "com" indicates that it is a commercial provider. However, I could, for a fee, have this changed to: gary.grobman@whitehat.org without changing my ISP.

The uniform resource locator (URL) provided by an ISP is often quite long, and is not as elegant as an individualized URL that contains the organization's name. Most ISPs will, for a fee, provide an organization with its own domain name, or you can do it yourself by registering with the Internet Network Information Center (InterNIC). In either case, there is an initial $70 fee for the first two years, and an annual fee of $35 after that. This is in addition to any fees charged by your provider.

Applications must be submitted electronically, by filling out a template on the World Wide Web site of Network Solutions (*http://www.networksolutions.com*). You will need your name and address, the domain name you want to use (e.g., yourname.org) and the primary and secondary server Internet protocol number, which you can obtain from your ISP. Names are assigned on a first-come, first-served basis and are checked for prior use and for whether they are in some way objectionable.

Developing Your Own World Wide Web Page

There are thousands of commercial services all offering to design and administer World Wide Web pages for a fee. With a minimum of technical background, you can do it yourself. Software is available for free that works with popular word processing programs to convert documents into HTML language. The latest versions of most popular word-processing programs can save documents as HTML files suitable for posting on your Web site.

Once one knows the HTML codes to insert, one can even prepare a World Wide Web page entirely in Windows Notepad or other programs that create ASCII files, the simple files that consist entirely of text characters. Among the types of information that can be found on typical World Wide Web pages of nonprofits are:

> newsletter, annual report, press releases, brochure, how to contribute or volunteer, financial data, action alerts, job openings, information about board and staff members, publications, upcoming conferences and seminars, product catalogs and order forms, a way to e-mail the organization, and links to other organizations and government-based home pages related to the mission and purpose of the organization.

Internet Etiquette (a.k.a., Netiquette)

The culture of the Internet has developed over a short period of time and has changed as millions of new users have joined. Most servers have written rules about proper use of their service. There are general written and unwritten rules regarding the Internet. Among some of the more useful are:

- Don't type entirely in capital letters. This is considered the computer keyboard equivalent of "shouting," and can result in being flamed (being sent a threatening or denigrating unsolicited message).

- Don't put a message on a newsgroup, mailing list, or even personal e-mail that you would be embarrassed to have circulated to thousands of people. It just might happen.

- Don't send copyrighted material to a newsgroup or mailing list without permission from the copyright holder.

- Spend time "lurking" (the equivalent of listening quietly) on a newsgroup or mailing list before diving in by posting messages. Many groups and lists have a file associated with them called an FAQ (Frequently Asked Questions). Read it before posting your first message.

- Don't post clearly commercial messages on a newsgroup or mailing list. Announcements about new products are fine; sales pitches are strictly verboten and usually result in flame messages.

Problems With the Internet

The Internet is not without its problems. Consumer fraud exists, just as it does in the non-virtual world. Although newly developed software has improved the security of communications (particularly important, since financial information, including credit card numbers, is routinely sent through e-mail), it is not fool-proof. In general, all data are transferred through the Internet using ASCII files, which are virus-proof. However, viruses can be transmitted through attached files that are converted by coding software to binary files.

Copyright issues relating to electronic communication still are unresolved. Finally, the Internet has opened up an entire new world for exploration, and studies indicate that for some people, it may be psychologically addictive.

Numerous books, magazines, and media articles have been written exploring the costs and benefits of the cyberspace revolution.

Useful Internet Resources for Nonprofits

Thousands of charities and other nonprofits have their own World Wide Web sites. There are scores of interesting and handy gateways to them and other sites that have substantial resources of interest to nonprofit organizations. Perhaps the best thing about accessing these Web sites is they are free-of-charge to visit (other than the fee to your service provider for Internet access). Among them are:

1. The Internet Nonprofit Center
http://www.nonprofits.org

This site, first put online in 1994, is now under new sponsorship, the Evergreen State Society of Seattle, Wa. The site features a nonprofit locator, permitting users to search by name, key word, or ZIP code for all 501(c)(3) and (c)(4)s in the United States. The site's library includes publications and data about nonprofits and the nonprofit sector compiled by third parties, and also includes files of ethical standards published by the National Charities Information Bureau and the New York Philanthropic Advisory Services organization. The site includes files of current and back issues of *Nonprofit Online News*, and plenty of links to other sites of interest.

2. The Foundation Center
http://fdncenter.org/

The Foundation Center is an independent nonprofit information clearinghouse established in 1956. The Center operates five libraries, and provides materials to hundreds of public libraries (see Appendix E). The mission of the organization is to foster public understanding of the foundation field by collecting, organizing, analyzing, and disseminating information on foundations, corporate giving, and related subjects. Included at the Center's Web site is a weekly electronic newsletter called *Philanthropy News Digest,* published every Wednesday online, but which can be subscribed to by e-mail to arrive on Tuesday evenings. The site has a searchable archives, an excellent reference on how to prepare grant applications *(A Proposal Writing Short Course)* and standardized grant application forms. There is access to an online librarian who will answer your questions about where to find resources and basic information of interest to nonprofits. Just fill out the online form with your question.

3. GuideStar
http://www.guidestar.org

GuideStar, administered by the Williamsburg, Va.-based Philanthropic Research, Inc., publishes comprehensive reports about individual American charities. Its purpose is "to bring the actors in the philanthropic and nonprofit communities closer together through the use of information and communication technologies. GuideStar collects and analyzes operating and financial data from the IRS Form 990 and from voluntary submissions from the charities themselves." The database consists of more than 650,000 reports on individual charities, and the site is colorful, accessible, and well-designed. The database can be searched, at no charge, by any number of parameters, such as name, location, or type of charity. This is simply the best site on the 'Net for finding financial information about charities. Charities can provide their reports and update them online at no charge. The site also includes links of interest to charities and essays about philanthropy via the "GuideStar Forum" button. There is a page for nonprofits to post information, classified ads, online newsletters, and press releases. The News Spotlight has information about the voluntary sector, conferences, and links. The Resource Exchange matches donors, volunteers, and nonprofits who need them, and the Learning Center has files on how to be an informed donor, become a more effective nonprofit staff person, and more.

4. Nonprofit Managers' Library
http://www.mapnp.org/library/index.html

While much of this site is targeted to the needs of Minnesota nonprofits (such as local grant information), it is an excellent resource for all. There is a Nonprofit Job Board and a Nonprofit's Yellow Pages. The site boasts updated files on ethics, fundraising, communications skills, marketing, organizational change, risk management, strategic planning, and much more. There are numerous and useful links to outside organizations that make this site an excellent resource for those interested in grants, foundations, government information, and general information useful to nonprofits.

5. Philanthropy Journal Online

http://www.pj.org

This is the online version of a newspaper, based in North Carolina, that posts breaking news stories of interest to the nonprofit community. You can subscribe to the e-mail version for free.

6. The Nonprofit GENIE

http://www.genie.org

This site is a project of the Southern California Center for Nonprofit Management. Here you can find book reviews of nonprofit management books, plus 110 entries in a comprehensive Frequently Asked Questions (FAQ) for nonprofit managers, organized in nine general categories, such as insurance and strategic planning. There are plenty of interesting links to nonprofit resources as well.

7. The Chronicle of Philanthropy

http://www.philanthropy.com

The site provides highlights from this publication, which is the trade journal for America's charitable community. The tabloid-format biweekly is the number one source for charity leaders, fundraisers, and grant makers, and the Web site provides more than just a taste of what its subscribers receive in snail mail every two weeks. The site is updated every other week at 9 a.m. on the Monday before the issue date, and job announcements are updated on the Monday following that. The principal categories of this site are gifts and grants, fundraising, managing nonprofit groups, and technology. Each of these headings is further divided by a news summary, workshops and seminars, and deadlines. Also on the site are front-page news stories, a news summary, conferences, Internet resources, products and services, and jobs. Most of the articles consist of one-sentence summaries but are still useful, particularly if you don't have the $69 in your budget to subscribe to the publication for a year. The "Jobs" button transports you to a searchable database of hundreds of positions available. In some respects, this searchability makes the Internet version of the *Chronicle* more useful than the conventional version. There is also a handy directory of "Products and Services."

8. The Nonprofit Times

http://www.nptimes.com

This is the online version of the monthly tabloid newspaper, and has full-text articles from the latest issue, as well as classified advertisements.

9. Independent Sector
http://www.indepsec.org

This site is the first place to go for definitive statistics of interest about the nonprofit sector (click on *Facts and Figures*). It also has files on the Y2K problem, ethics, accountability and leadership issues (*Accountability and Effectiveness*), and even advice on how your organization can use the new philanthropy stamp in promotion campaigns. There is current information about new laws and regulations affecting charities, and public policy advocacy updates.

10. HandsNet
http://www.handsnet.org

Founded in 1987, HandsNet links more than 5,000 public interest and human services organizations using the Internet to promote collaboration, advocacy, and information-sharing by the sector. The public pages are updated daily, and the members-only pages are considered to be the most valuable around for nonprofits that engage in advocacy. The site's Action Alerts provide lots of government links, state-of-the-art information on current issues (most of which is provided by member organizations whose niche includes that particular public policy issue), capsule summaries, sources to find more information about the issue, sample advocacy letters, and information about new legislation. The Weekly Digest includes samples from hundreds of policy, program, and resource articles posted by members.

11. Nonprofit Gateway
http://www.nonprofit.gov

This site's strength lies in its convenient and user-friendly links to federal departments and agencies—executive, legislative, and judicial—and an easy-to-use guide to access publications of importance to nonprofits, such as the Federal Register, the Catalog of Federal Domestic Assistance, and access to the General Services Administration. It appears not to have been updated for at least two years. It has a grid of federal agencies that permits easy access to each agency's home page, page on grants, and its search page—a convenient feature.

12. The Contact Center's IdeaList
http://www.idealist.org/tools/tools.htm

This site is a great resource. It contains a searchable database of 10,000 nonprofit organizations (you can click on a form to add your organization to the database), a page on "Computing and the Internet," with links to free and low-cost servers, publications on Web site development, HTML tutorials, and a list of organizations that offer free products and services to charities. The "Tools for Nonprofits" button transports you to the Computing and Internet page, Employment and Internship Opportunities, and Fundraising. The fundraising page includes application forms for several grants and a "Proposal Writing Short Course." There are plenty of links to other organizations, although they are not attractively organized. The directory is organized geographically and by the organizations' areas of focus. Nonprofits that ask to be included in the directory are requested to make a $25 voluntary contribution, but otherwise the site is free.

13. Impact Online
http://www.impactonline.org

This site provides a posting area for nonprofits to advertise volunteer opportunities that can be performed online, and has excellent resources relating to "virtual volunteering." From the home page, click on "Virtual Volunteering" for cutting-edge information about harnessing the power of those who are homebound, those who are unable to commit to a specific time and place to volunteer, or those who are simply too busy— but who have valuable skills they are willing to share. The "Volunteer Match" may help you find suitable volunteers for your organization who can transcend the limitations of geographical inaccessibility, as well as general volunteering resources.

14. Philanthropysearch.com
http://www.philanthropysearch.com

This search engine tailored to the nonprofit community was launched on April 27, 1999. It is set up to allow nonprofit organizations to quickly find resources about charitable giving, volunteering, technology, and management resources. Nonprofits can register their site instantly with this search engine.

Chapter 21
Forming and Running A Coalition

> Synopsis: Many nonprofit organizations form and participate in coalitions to accomplish objectives that would be difficult to achieve by themselves. There are significant advantages and considerations to forming a coalition, and the fact that they flourish is indicative of their value. This chapter discusses the pros and cons of creating and/or participating in coalitions.

Introduction

The tapestry of advocacy efforts at the international, national, state, and local levels is replete with collaborative initiatives that bring together diverse interests to accomplish a common goal. As a nonprofit organization seeks to accomplish its mission, its leadership often finds the value of creating formal and informal partnerships among like-minded organizations. As in any endeavor, there are traps and pitfalls in creating and running a coalition.

While it is often said that "two heads are better than one," it is equally rejoined that "too many cooks spoil the broth." Both of these clichés often are equally valid when applied to a coalition, and it is important for an organizational leader to be able to assess which one applies predominantly before embarking on coalition-forming.

The Coalition

A coalition is a group of diverse organizations that join together to accomplish a specific objective that is likely to be achieved faster or better than if the organizations acted independently. There are many types of coalitions, and the structure is often dictated by political as well as financial considerations. The prototypical coalition involving state government issues consists of a convener coalition partner who has identified an issue, usually of direct importance to the convener's organizational membership.

The convener then "rounds up the usual suspects" by soliciting membership in the coalition from constituencies that will participate in the coalition. He or she schedules periodic meetings of the coalition at which members share information about the issue and develop a strategy to accomplish a specific goal of the coalition that, as is often the case, is the passage of legislation to solve the problem. It is not unusual for the coalition to continue even after the legislation it focused upon is enacted into law.

Structures of Coalitions

• *formal organization.* Some coalitions structure formally, creating a distinct nonprofit corporate structure, such as a 501(c)(3), which will permit the coalition to hire staff, seek tax-deductible contributions from the public, rent office space, and have a system of governance that parallels, in many respects, the constituent organizations that comprise the coalition. Obviously, one would not seek to create such a complex legal entity if the objective of the coalition was to be achieved in the short term. It is not atypical for a new 501(c)(3) coalition staff to spend much of its efforts raising funds to keep it in business rather than focusing on the actual mission of the coalition. Even if funding is stable, many formal coalitions spend an inordinate amount of time on intra-organizational issues, compared to achieving their stated purposes.

• *semi-formal coalition.* These coalitions consist of organizations that have some financial resources themselves, and are able to fund the activities of the coalition. While not incorporated as separate legal entities, these coalitions nevertheless may have office space and staff. The office space may be provided as an in-kind contribution from one of the coalition members, and the staff may or may not be an employee of one of the member organizations.

• *informal coalition.* Most coalitions are informal, consisting of a convener organizational leader, but with no dedicated organizational staff or budget, or separate bank account. The convener organization convenes the coalition, sends out meeting notices, holds the meeting in the convener's office, and staffs the coalition as a part of its routine organizational duties. Costs can be shared among coalition members, and the convener duty can be rotated among members. In general, member organizations are not bound by the positions taken by the coalition.

• *group networks.* A group network is a type of informal coalition that has been formed to serve an information-sharing function with less emphasis on coordinated action. These networks have no staff, no budget, take no positions, and are useful in raising the consciousness of participants about a particular issue or set of issues. These networks also are valuable in bringing people together to "network," and to build trust among organizational leadership. While efforts to coordinate action on an issue are often the result of a network-based coalition, the network itself often does not take a formal role in the coordination; rather, the discussions among the participants in and after the meeting result in the synergistic effects of the network.

Advantages of Forming a Coalition

• Coalitions focus attention among the media, opinion leaders, and those with advocacy resources on a specific issue. Any organization, no matter how large and powerful, has a limited ability to get its message across to the public, government officials, and the media. Building a coalition is an effective strategy to call attention to an issue, since messages not perceived to be important when heard from one organization may be considered important from another.

• Coalitions bring together experts on a particular issue. A convener of a coalition often has a burning desire to solve a particular public-policy problem and has well-developed organizational skills, but may lack the technical expertise to develop the solution. Creating a coalition is a strategy to bring together experts in the field who collegially can participate in developing a solution.

- Coalitions provide a forum to resolve turf issues and to limit destructive competition. Very few important public-policy issues are so narrow that a single organization is the only one with a direct interest in their resolution. Virtually any public-policy issue, particularly those that influence human services, affects a broad range of advocacy organizations, whether it impinges on children, schools, the environment, business, the disabled, or the aged. Trying to solve a problem without the "buying in" of key decision-makers is a recipe for disaster. Coalitions provide the framework for obtaining the cooperation of opinion makers who otherwise would be threatened by any effort to change public policy that violates their political turf.

- Coalitions provide credibility to an issue and the convener organization. One obvious application of this principle is the effort, often unsuccessful, of various extremist organizations not accepted in society, such as the KKK, to try to form or participate in coalitions that have a goal consistent with a community consensus. Another principle is that organizational messages viewed as self-interest are viewed negatively. When coalitions include organizations that are viewed to be acting in the public interest (such as those affiliated with the religious community or the League of Women Voters), an organization is better off having the message delivered by a coalition.

- Coalitions permit resources to be shared. Coalitions benefit by the resources of their membership, be it money, volunteers, staff, office equipment, or meeting space. It is more cost effective for an organization to form a coalition to permit resources to be shared, rather than having to pay the entire bill oneself.

- Coalitions provide a path to inform new constituencies about an emerging issue. For example, the religious-based advocacy community's constituency may not have access to detailed information about a specific state budget problem, other than seeing an occasional newspaper article. It is one thing for welfare recipients to write to their legislators requesting a grant increase, and another for middle-class taxpayers to write advocating for an increase based on economic justice, not self-interest. Coalitions provide a framework for expanding constituencies beyond those of the convener.

- Coalitions result in positive public relations for a convener coalition-builder. New organizations build respect by forming and running a successful coalition. While the "credit" for a success achieved single-handedly can be savored, achieving that success is often much more difficult than with help from a coalition. By bringing other organizations together and working for a common goal, those organizations learn to work with the convener, to build trust, to get visibility for the new organization, and to make it more likely that the convening organization will be invited to participate in other coalitions.

Disadvantages of Coalitions

- It is often difficult for members of a coalition to focus on an issue that is usually not the priority issue for any member of the coalition other than the convener.

- Coalition members who are not the convener often have an agenda different from that of the convener, and may seek to exploit the coalition for their own goals in a manner that may be inconsistent with the purpose for which the coalition was formed.

- Coalitions usually reach agreement on issues by consensus, which is sometimes difficult to achieve. When it is achieved, the result is often the lowest common denominator and dilutes the aggressiveness that might have been necessary to solve a problem.

- Coalitions require considerably more time to make decisions than would be required by the convener acting alone. Many coalition members require major decisions to be discussed by their own boards. There is a lag time between when a decision is requested and when a decision can be made by a coalition compared with an individual organization. Even scheduling a coalition meeting to discuss when a coalition consensus can be developed can be extremely difficult at times.

- Many important coalition partners have organizational difficulties that make them used to working independently rather than in coalition.

- Coalitions require organizational work (such as preparing agendas, mailing materials, and coordinating meeting times) that can be substantial.

To Form a Coalition or Not

There are many questions that should be answered, and an honest assessment made, in determining whether forming a coalition to solve a problem is constructive. Among them are:

1. What is the outcome I wish to achieve with this coalition? Is it realistic to achieve it by myself? Are the chances for success improved with a coalition?

2. Whose turf am I treading on by trying to solve this issue alone? Is there a more appropriate organization to form this coalition?

3. Are there constituencies in my own organization that will react negatively if I form this coalition?

4. How much will a coalition cost me in terms of money, time, focus?

5. Who should be invited to participate; who should not be invited?

6. Who are the experts out there I do not have access to unless I form a coalition?

7. Will my prospective coalition participants get along?

8. How will the coalition dissolve after my goals are achieved?

9. What kind of commitment do I need from participants, and is it realistic to expect to receive these commitments?

How to Form a Coalition

- Make sure that there are no irreconcilable major differences between coalition participants, either as a result of ideology or personal enmities.

- Identify all organizations that have a direct or indirect interest in the issue.

- Invite, if appropriate, organizations that would increase the credibility of the coalition.

- Make sure that the effort is not perceived to be partisan.

- Invite outside experts to either serve on the coalition or speak to it.

- Consider business, labor, education, religious advocacy, good government citizen groups, health, local government, state government, federal government, beneficiaries of success of the coalition's objective, provider associations, lobbyists, experts on the issue, community leaders, foundation and other grant-maker representatives, charities, and religious leaders as coalition members.

Tips:

- **Remember that if the objective of the coalition were the most central focus of all members of the coalition, they would have formed it first.**

- Respect the fact that your coalition is perhaps one of many, and keep meetings short with the agenda focused. Encourage all in attendance to participate, but don't dominate the discussion yourself or let any other participant dominate. Reach consensus as quickly as possible, and then move on.

- Delegate the work of the coalition to participants (such as by forming committees when necessary to develop a consensus).

- Make the meeting pleasant by being hospitable (such as providing soft drinks or lunch).

Chapter 22
Miscellaneous Administrative Issues

Synopsis: The offices of nonprofit corporations require computers, filing systems, and office equipment that are sensitive to organizational needs. The Postal Service offers discount postage rates to organizations that prepare bulk mailings in a manner consistent with its format and regulations.

Office Equipment

Many small nonprofit corporations are headquartered in the residences of their incorporators. There are obvious limitations to that, particularly if the corporation needs to expand its "shoebox" existence. For those who rent or own office space, some basic equipment items to consider (and budget for), are:

1. File cabinets (legal or letter size).
2. Postage meter, postage scales.
3. Typewriter, word processor.
4. Copy machine.
5. Fax machine.
6. Telephone system.
7. Telephone answering machine.
8. Computer, including CPU and keyboard, printer, monitor, and peripherals, such as modem, scanner, mouse, and Zip™ drive.
9. Electronic printing calculators.
10. Office furniture (including desks, bookcases, supply shelves, cabinets, chairs, lamps, end tables, coat racks, umbrella stand).

Staffing Patterns

Thousands of registered nonprofits operate effectively with no paid staff, while others, such as colleges and hospitals, have staff in the thousands. Salaries are by far the largest budget expenditure for organizations with paid staff. A typical "one man band" staff configuration has an executive director or director who performs all of the operations of the corporation. There may be the need for some part-time assistance to do bookkeeping or help with a special project on occasion, but it is not impossible for one versatile person to run a highly successful corporation. More typical is a two-person office—an executive/administrator and a secretary/clerk who performs the routine office management functions.

Nonprofits that can afford additional staff may have an assistant director, who may be responsible for publications, membership, or development (a euphemism for fundraising). Other typical generic staff positions of nonprofits are government relations representative, program director, publications specialist/newsletter editor, administrative assistant, public relations/community relations specialist, librarian, office manager, Webmaster, and data processor. Many nonprofits provide specific services. Hospitals will hire doctors, nurses, social workers, and lab technicians. Colleges will hire professors, deans, admissions officers, and custodians. The organization's mission may determine the types of specialists hired (see Chapter 11).

Many nonprofits choose to start small—hiring one staff member—and then expand with experience and fundraising, so there is a reasonable expectation that the budget can be supported in the long run. If a nonprofit is too ambitious at first, the staff may end up spending most of its time raising funds to support salaries rather than accomplishing the mission of the agency.

Stationery/Logo

Every nonprofit corporation needs to have stationery in order to provide a professional first impression. This stationery need not be fancy or expensive, although it is generally a good practice to print stationery on bond paper with some cotton content, which is heavier than the 20-lb. stock used in the copy machine. Most corporate stationery has a graphic (also known as a "logo") that is descriptive of the corporation. This graphic can also be used on the masthead of a corporate newsletter, on the Web site, on mailing labels, brochures, press packets, and other promotional literature. Paying an artist to draw a distinctive and creative logo is usually a good investment, although it is often possible to make one by using some of the popular "clip art" or graphics software programs. If you don't have a scanner, a computer store may be willing to scan logo art work, so it can be printed out in various sizes or "imported" into computer-generated publications as needed.

Filing Systems

The filing systems of nonprofit corporations usually evolve over several years, and are as individual as each corporation. Several factors should be considered in setting up a filing system.

Keep files of the corporation's internal operations separate from other files. For example, keep the files relating to tax-exempt status, corporation budget, office leases, insurance, taxes, Articles of Incorporation, membership, mailing lists, lobbying and charitable registration in a different place from files about general political and public-policy issues. A corporation should have correspondence files— one for "outgoing" and another for "incoming." One nonprofit always makes three copies of all outgoing correspondence—one for the "outgoing" file, one for the "incoming file" stapled to the incoming letter that generated the outgoing letter, and one for the subject file that relates to the issue of the letter. "External" files can be subject matter relating to the mission of the corporation. However, "internal" files will be similar from nonprofit to nonprofit. Among typical internal files are:

allocations, annual report, Articles of Incorporation, bank statements, board meeting agendas, board minutes, board meeting packets, bookkeeping, brochure, budget, bylaws, computer, dues structure, expenses, financial reports, grass-roots alerts, insurance, mailing lists, newsletters, office equipment, office leases, payroll, personnel, photographs, planning, postal service, press mailing list, press clippings, press releases, printing, grants, publications, speeches and testimony, special projects, tax-exempt status, taxes, and Web site. Some of these files will have sub-categories (e.g. newsletter—previous, newsletter—current), and others will be categorized by year.

Computer

Perhaps there remain a handful of nonprofit executives who are quite satisfied replying to correspondence the old-fashioned way—either writing replies using pen and paper, or banging out an answer on the same trusty Remington typewriter they used when they were in college. Many of them are satisfied with what they have—and don't begin to question this primordial existence until they are faced with having to bang out 3,000 "personal" letters asking for funds to save their jobs or tire of personally addressing 6,000 newsletters each month. The computer is, with good reason, a fixture in the modern nonprofit office.

The good news is that in the hands of a knowledgeable operator, a computer can do a variety of tasks and save thousands of expensive staff hours. The bad news is that they can be expensive and complicated to learn, may be vulnerable to the Year 2000 bug (see Chapter 27) and can "crash" at the most inopportune times.

Hardware/Software

This handbook provides only the most cursory review of basic decisions. It is geared to the small nonprofit interested in the advantages and disadvantages of purchasing a personal computer and the basic options.

Among many issues to consider when purchasing a computer system are:

1. Who will be using the system, and will they be sufficiently trained?

2. Is software available that is compatible with your hardware, and will this software be capable of providing the output you need?

3. Are you paying for features or capacity you are unlikely to ever need?

4. Is there sufficient follow-up support to answer questions, troubleshoot problems, and provide maintenance?

5. Is the system Y2K-compliant?

Basic Hardware Decision: Apple or IBM-Compatible

In the old days, these two types of computers were as incompatible as Beta format and VHS for VCRs. What once were uncrossable boundaries between these two hardware systems are now being crossed and integrated. Basically, the Apple-based MacIntosh ("Mac") computers are considered to be more "user-friendly," and employ a pointing device ("mouse") to choose among various options on a monitor. The operating system is usually a "graphical user interface" (GUI) that doesn't require the user to memorize all sorts of esoteric commands. On the other hand, IBM and IBM "clones" are generally less expensive and have more programs that are compatible, but require more knowledge on the part of the user. IBM and its imitators have developed software that imitates the user-friendliness of the Mac. Increasingly, the Mac-based hardware is permitting the use of files created using IBM-compatible software. Each system has those who swear by it and swear at it. The state-of-the-art is advancing so swiftly that this decision may become moot in the near future.

Microsoft Windows v. DOS (Disk Operating System)

Most IBM-compatible personal computers use one of two operating systems, which control how software and files are managed. Windows uses a "graphical user interface" system that utilizes a mouse to choose among various options— a "point and click" system. Windows supports "multi-tasking," allowing several programs to run at the same time, thereby increasing productivity. The latest version is Windows 98 and most general business software is Windows-compatible.

DOS uses keyboard commands for most operations, and is quickly becoming obsolete.

Typical Software for Nonprofit Personal Computers

There are thousands of programs available that are being used by various nonprofits. In general, there are several families of programs that are useful in a typical computer-based nonprofit office. Among them are:

1. Word Processing—WordPerfect, Lotus Word Pro, and Microsoft Word are among the most popular word processing packages. An advantage of word processing programs is that an entire document does not have to be retyped in order to make corrections or multiple copies. This is a major productivity enhancement if an organization desires to send a "personal" letter to 50,000 potential contributors. With a word processing program, an entire letter need not be retyped because of one error.

2. Spreadsheet—Lotus 1-2-3 and Microsoft Excel are among the most popular spreadsheet programs. In simple terms, the objective of a spreadsheet is to perform operations and calculations on numbers and automatically adjust a total when one number in a sum is changed.

Spreadsheets are indispensable for bookkeeping, budgeting, and similar documents. Many spreadsheets contain graphics capability that permits numerical data to be displayed in pleasing and informative formats.

3. Database—Dbase, Paradox, and Access are among the most popular database programs. The objective of a database is to sort data into various fields, which can then be used to generate mailing lists, store information that can be sorted, and perform other similar tasks.

4. Desktop Publishing (DTP)—Adobe PageMaker, Microsoft Publisher, and Quark Xpress are among the most popular DTP or page layout programs. These programs "import" graphics and output from word processing programs and can manipulate the result on screen in an eye-catching format. Text can be printed out in a variety of type faces and sizes, giving documents the appearance of having been professionally designed and typeset.

There are several software "suite" packages that provide the above types of programs all in one and are designed to work with each other. Before purchasing any software (which can be obtained for free from computer bulletin boards or cost thousands of dollars), it is best to seek advice from those who are knowledgeable about the advantages and disadvantages of each program.

Nonprofits affiliated with a state or national association should check with the staff of that organization to ascertain what software packages are used. Often, these organizations share data among their affiliates in only one format. While software is available to make conversions between formats and hardware configurations, substantial time, energy, and money can be saved by having compatible computer systems.

Computer Communications/Internet (see Chapter 20)

Computers with modems provide a gateway to communications with millions of other computers and their databases and bulletin boards, and permit you to send letters, computer files, and simple messages (i.e. e-mail) through the telephone wires. Commercial online services such as Microsoft Network, CompuServe, and America OnLine, provide news, weather, and other information valuable to nonprofits, bulletin boards that permit the sharing of experiences and problem-solving by those with similar interests and access to the Internet. The Internet is a network of computer networks. As many as 80 million people and organizations, including most governments, libraries, and institutions of higher learning, have connections to the Internet, affording virtually instantaneous communications among those connected. Using a commercial service permits communications between your personal computer and a computer on the other side of the world for the cost of a local telephone call. "Conversations" and "meetings" can be held in "real time" with each participant typing questions and responses into the keyboard.

Computer-assisted communication will revolutionize how business is conducted by nonprofits, and staff should be prepared to harness advances in technology to their advantage.

Credit Card Sales

Nonprofit organizations are businesses and have many aspects in common with for-profit businesses. They sell products and services, such as memberships, publications, counseling, and tickets to events. They also solicit donations from the public, and it is not unusual for many to be comfortable making these donations by credit card, either through secure forms on the Internet or, more conventionally, through the mail. Inexorably, we are becoming a cashless society, and the public increasingly relies on credit cards for financial transactions. Nonprofit organizations should consider whether having "merchant status" is advantageous.

Qualifying for merchant status for popular credit cards such as Visa, MasterCard, American Express, and Discover is routine for some nonprofit organizations. Organizations typically approach their bank to set up an account. You can find hundreds, if not thousands, of financial institutions willing to establish merchant accounts on the World Wide Web. One way to find them is to search under the term "credit cards" or "merchant account."

Startup fees, account maintenance fees, per-transaction fees, and the bank's percentage of sales commission for processing each transaction varies by financial institution, and may be negotiable. You will also need a system for transmitting the information about the transaction to the financial institution for processing, typically a terminal sold or leased by the financial institution, or computer software. The financial institution, within a few business days, credits your account for the amount of the sale after deducting transaction charges. You have to enter the card information and sales information into the terminal or software, and verify that the card is bona fide and the purchaser has not exceeded his or her credit limit. As you might expect, there is some paperwork involved, and inconvenience when a purchaser challenges a sale. On the other hand, entrepreneurial nonprofit organizations may lose out on revenue opportunities unless they satisfy the expectations of their customers.

Postal Service Issues

Nonprofit corporations typically generate a large volume of mail in the course of sending out annual reports, newsletters, program brochures, fundraising solicitations, surveys, grass-roots action alerts, and meeting notices. Mass mailings, as a result of U.S. Postal Service advances in technology, have become more complicated. Because of recent reforms that substantially change the way both organizations who qualify for nonprofit mailing status and others must prepare bulk mail, the USPS. has expanded its outreach by providing educational programs.

The Postal Service offers free training on how to process bulk mailings. Call the U.S. Postal Service's regional bulk mail center to get information on the next scheduled workshop.

General Postage Rates

The U.S. Postal Service publishes the *Postal Bulletin,* which details the latest rates, fees, and changes in regulations. Subscriptions to this bi-weekly are available for $108/year, and single copies are $7. A more comprehensive publication, *Domestic Mail Manual,* is published twice annually, and is available for $30. Copies of the latest edition are available from main post offices.

Postage Meters

Postage meters permit organizations to affix exact postage to letters and packages without the inconvenience of purchasing stamps of varying denominations. The postage is printed by the meter, and the organization pays in advance for the postage used. Most new postage meter systems permit postage accounts in the machine to be replenished by telephone/modem, although for older systems, this is done typically at the local post office. Postage machines are not sold but, in accordance with federal law, are rented by commercial companies. A license is required from the Postal Service, but the paperwork is handled by the vendor. Pitney-Bowes is the firm that developed the system and is the leader in the field. Competing companies can be found in the Yellow Pages under "Mailing Machines and Equipment." The cost of renting a machine is $24.75 per month and up, including a postage scale, depending on the system's sophistication.

Bulk Mail Permit Procedures

Organizations that desire to participate in the bulk-mailing program must first obtain an imprint authorization from the Postal Service. The one-time-only imprint fee of $100 is good for both first and standard class (formerly known as "third class") mailing. Mailing permits must be renewed annually, and there is a $100 fee for first class and $100 for standard class. The form to file is different for organizations seeking nonprofit mailing status. These organizations file a form 3601 with the Postal Service, while other organizations file Form 3624. The Postal Service automatically forwards the correct form when it is time to renew the permits.

A pre-addressed postcard for ordering these forms is included in the back of this book.

Having such an imprint entitles the organization to pay the postage in advance without having to affix postage to each individual piece of mail. The permit also provides a discount, provided there are a minimum of 200 pieces or 50 pounds in the bulk mailing and the mailing is sorted and processed in accordance with post office regulations. Each piece must be correctly ZIP-coded or it will not be accepted.

Once in receipt of the imprint permit, the organization can affix the imprint to mail pieces using a rubber stamp, or they can print it directly on the piece.

The bulk-mail discount can be large. The rate for a first-class letter rose to 33 cents per ounce and 22 cents for each additional ounce effective January 10, 1999. A comparable piece of mail sent standard-class bulk rate can be sent for a little more than half of that amount, depending on how it was prepared. There are substantial discounts to encourage bar-coding of bulk mailings.

501(c)(3)s (or organizations that have the characteristics of such organizations) may qualify for the U.S. Postal Service's Special Bulk Rate. The basic rate for letters under 3.2 ounces is 16.9 cents. However, this rate can be reduced further, depending on the nature of the presort and the destination.

Automation

Bulk-mail postage rates are substantially lower for mail that can be handled by automated equipment. For example, the rate per piece for a 5-digit bar-coded first class letter, up to 1 ounce, is 24.3 cents, compared with 30.5 cents for non-automated pre-sorted. Computer software is available at reasonable cost that will automatically place a U.S. Postal Service-compatible bar code on each label generated by your computer. Even if you do not have bar-coding capability, providing enough space for the Postal Service's equipment to optically read the address on each label and place its own bar code, while not reducing your postage rate, will qualify you for time-saving reductions in bulk-mail preparation. Consult the U.S.P.S. for more information about this "upgradable mail."

The entire system for presorting to comply with Postal Service regulations is too complicated to be described briefly. A thumbnail sketch of this system is provided below.

Size of Standard-Class Letter Mail

The dimensions of letter-size bulk mail are limited to the following:

length: 5 inches - 11 1/2 inches
width: 3.5 inches - 6 1/8 inches
thickness: .007 inches - .25 inches (enough to send a 20-page newsletter of 20-lb. paper, folded once)

Bundling

Bundles of sorted letters must be secured with at least one rubber band across the width of the bundle (the shortest distance), and at least two rubber bands (one along the width and one along the length) if between 1-4 inches in thickness.

Each bundle should be prepared by following steps 1-5 (Note that labels, rubber bands, and trays are provided free by the USPS. bulk mail center):

Step 1: Make bundles of letters with the same five-digit ZIP code, if at least 10 share the same ZIP code. Place a red "D" label in the bottom left corner of the first letter of each bundle.

Step 2: Make bundles of remaining letters with the same *first three* numbers in their ZIP codes, if at least 10 share the same first three numbers. These bundles need not be sorted by ZIP code within each bundle. Place a green "3" label in the bottom left corner of the first letter of each bundle.

Step 3: Make a bundle of remaining letters going to the same Area Distribution Center (ADC) if at least 10 share the same ADC. Place a pink "A" in the lower left hand corner of the first letter of each bundle. Note: The Postal Service in 1996 eliminated sorting by state and has substituted ADC sorting to make the mail move more efficiently. Contact the U.S. Postal Service for information about ADC groupings.

Step 4. Make a bundle of the remaining letters from the various ADCs, and place a tan "MS" label in the lower left corner of the first letter.

Tray Requirements

1. If there are 150 pieces or more with the same five-digit ZIP code, they are placed in their own tray. The USPS wants you to provide them with full trays. "Full" is defined as two-thirds full, so choose either a one-foot tray or two-foot tray in order to comply with this requirement. If you cannot provide a "full" tray at this step, combine the 5-digit tray with the 3-digit tray.

2. After completing step 1, if there are 150 pieces or more that have the first three digits in common, they are placed in their own tray. Do not combine the 3-digit pieces with the ADC pieces to create a full tray unless you are willing to pay a higher postage rate on the 3-digit pieces.

3. If, after completing steps 1 and 2, there are 150 pieces or more that go to the same ADC, they are placed in their own tray.

4. The remaining letters must be placed in a tray or left on top of the other trays.

5. Each bulk-mail processing unit has a list of local ZIP codes for which you can qualify for an even lower postage rate (12.1 cents per piece for 3-digits if at least 10 and 14.8 cents if less than 10 pieces to the same Zip). To qualify for this rate, these pieces must be separated out and placed in their own tray. Check with your local post office to obtain the ZIP codes that qualify for this rate.

6. Trays must be enclosed by a tray sleeve and bound with polyethylene strapping. Strapping material can be purchased from a commercial office supply house.

The trays must be labeled appropriately to reach the correct destination. The Postal Service can provide correct tray labeling information.

The applicable postage must be deposited in the organization's postage account balance is not enough to cover the postage for the mailing. A mailing statement provided by the Postal Service that identifies the organization, its bulk-mail account, and the number of pieces being mailed for each standard-class category, must accompany each mailing.

The bulk-mail operation is performed successfully by hundreds of for-profits and nonprofits alike every day. It can save thousands of dollars in postage compared with mailing every piece first class. It also saves the bother of affixing individual postage stamps. While it may appear intimidating at first, it becomes routine with practice.

In general, the Postal Service attempts to deliver standard class mail within ten days of receipt. Often, this mail is delivered just as expeditiously as first-class mail, although a four to five day time period for processing is not unusual. As a general rule, nonprofits should think twice before mailing anything standard class that absolutely *must* be received within 12 days after the organization delivers the mailing to the bulk mail center.

Only certain post office branches are equipped to process bulk mail. There are commercial services that specialize in processing bulk mailings. There are volunteer organizations that will offer to help nonprofit organizations do bulk mail, as well. The U.S. Postal Service has prepared a comprehensive publication titled *Preparing Standard Mail A,* updated January 1999. To order this publication (Publication 49), write to the U.S. Postal Service or contact your local post office.

Another USPS Publication, *Quick Service Guide* (Publication 95), provides specifications for bar-coding and OCR-related mail preparation. The Postal Service will most likely require all bulk business mail to be bar-coded within a few years. It is recommended that nonprofit organizations review this publication before building a database for a mailing list.

A pre-addressed postcard for ordering most of the forms and booklets described in this section is included in the back of this book.

Tips:

- When creating a mailing list, it is useful to have the list in Zip-code order or to be capable of sorting it in Zip-code order. Otherwise, letters must be sorted by hand to take advantage of the bulk-mail discounts.

- Most of the popular word processing programs will perform a Zip-code sort operation and create mailing labels, and virtually all of the database programs do. Many are capable of automatically inserting a bar code, which further reduces postage rates if printed in accordance with postal service regulations.

- Contact the U.S. Postal Service for help with bulk-mail preparation or rates. A useful telephone number is:

    1-800-238-3150—National Customer Support Center
    USPS Web site: http://www.usps.gov

Chapter 23
Nonprofits and Small Business Competition

Synopsis: Some small business advocates have charged that nonprofits have unfair advantages when they compete in the sale of goods and services. Legislation and regulations to remove these advantages are a clear threat to the ability of the nonprofit sector to function effectively.

An issue has emerged on the agenda of small business advocates that could jeopardize the ability of many nonprofits to perform their vital missions. Tracing its beginning to the early 1980s, the issue of alleged unfair competition between nonprofits and small business earned its first stamp of legitimacy when the U.S. Small Business Administration issued a report in late 1983 entitled *Unfair Competition by Nonprofit Organizations with Small Business: An Issue for the 1980's.*

Small businesses had, until then, complained with muted voices that nonprofit corporations possessed advantages in the marketplace that hindered the ability of small businesses to compete. Among these advantages were said to be:

1. Tax exemptions—the most tangible benefit of nonprofits;
2. Reduced postage rates;
3. Tax deductions for those who contribute goods and services to nonprofit organizations;
4. Use of venture capital—the ability to use contributions and non-taxable surpluses for expansion, state-of-the-art equipment, and seed money for new activities that may compete with private enterprise;
5. "Captured referrals"— "sweetheart deal" arrangements between affiliated nonprofits that eliminate competition from non-affiliated businesses;
6. Use of plant, staff, supplies, and equipment donated or funded by grants to spur unrelated business enterprises that may compete with small business; and
7. "Halo effect"—referring to the willingness of the public to do business with a nonprofit because of the perception that the organization is serving the public good rather than being operated for a private profit motive.

During the 1970s, nonprofit corporations were becoming increasingly sophisticated in their efforts to generate revenue. These efforts accelerated during the 1980s when many social service nonprofits were hit by the loss of government funding during the retrenchment of domestic spending under the Reagan Administration. Nonprofit hospitals were a particular target of small business owners, who resented the establishment of laundry and pharmaceutical services that competed with them. Small business advocates continue to complain that state government has no effective mechanism to track funds that may be channeled between a nonprofit agency and its for-profit affiliates.

Also targeted nationally were YMCAs and their Jewish counterpart JCCs. Some of the YMCAs and JCCs began marketing their lucrative health club services to an "upscale" market segment to generate revenues to cross-subsidize services provided to their more needier clients. Such facilities were caught in a "Catch 22." If they charged less than the market rates, they were accused of undercutting small business by taking advantage of their tax exemptions and other advantages. If they charged the same or more than the private health clubs, they were accused of operating just as any other business and thus not deserving of any tax exemption. Private health clubs across the nation, through the guidance of their associations, participated in legal actions against several YMCAs and instigated reviews by local taxing authorities designed to challenge the historical tax-exempt status of these facilities. An effort by nine private health clubs in the Pittsburgh area to challenge the tax exemption of the Golden Triangle YMCA in Pittsburgh was partially successful.

Colleges and universities garnered the wrath of small business owners who objected to college bookstores selling television sets and refrigerators, surplus computer time, engaging in testing service businesses, establishing travel agencies, or otherwise entering markets in direct competition with small business.

These small business owners found a voice in the Small Business Administration. On July 27, 1983, the Small Business Administration's Office of Advocacy held a one-day symposium on this issue, and followed up the conference with a November report entitled *Unfair Competition by Nonprofit Organizations With Small Business: An Issue for the 1980's.* This report charged that "traditional 'donative' nonprofits, such as the Red Cross and the Salvation Army, which rely primarily on gifts and contributions for their operating revenue, are being replaced by 'commercial nonprofits'... which derive all or nearly all of their income from the sales of goods or services they produce." The report charged some of the nonprofit sector with creating an oversupply of goods, and charging significantly lower than the prevailing market rates as a result of exemptions from laws and regulations. The report concluded:

> *"It is the responsibility of the Congress and the Executive Branch to make a systematic inquiry into whether these exemptions are still justified in light of the emergence of the commercial nonprofit sector."*

Among other recommendations, the report called for:

1. A higher tax or outright prohibition on unrelated business activities by nonprofits

2. Defining the definition of "substantially related" more clearly and narrowly for purposes of what constitutes an unrelated business

3. Establishing a threshold above which a nonprofit engaging in unrelated business activities would lose its tax exemption

4.   Eliminating the "convenience" exception for the payment of unrelated business income taxes.

Soon after the report was released, approximately 20 national business associations, many of which participated in the drafting of the 1983 SBA report, formed the "Coalition for Fair Business Competition" to lobby on behalf of business interests on this issue.

The issue of nonprofit competition with small business was among the most compelling of the issues reported by small business owners at the 1986 White House Conference on Small Business. Conference delegates designated it the number three issue on a list of 40 major concerns culled from a list of 2,232 proposed by small business owners nationwide. Legislation was introduced in several states in response to this conference.

Federal Unrelated Business Income Tax (UBIT)

Federal law provides that nonprofit corporations pay federal taxes on unrelated business income. Corporations with at least $1,000 of such income are required to file a 990-T annually. Income is defined as "unrelated" if it is derived from a trade or business, is regularly carried on, and is substantially unrelated to the exempt purpose of the corporation. Income clearly exempt from UBIT includes that generated from activities performed by volunteers, from selling merchandise received as gifts or contributions, and dividends, interest, royalties, and capital gains. Also exempt is income from business operations conducted for the "convenience" of an organization's members, students, patients, and staff, such as a hospital cafeteria or college bookstore.

The Internal Revenue Service reports that $502 million in UBIT was collected from 50,034 organizations in 1996, and $486 million was collected from 48,563 organizations in 1997.

Both the Congress and the Internal Revenue Service have been skeptical about whether charities should have a broad exemption from paying taxes on business income. The House Ways and Means Committee's Oversight Committee held a series of hearings in June 1987 on the issue of changing federal policy on unrelated business income taxes. The subcommittee followed up on its hearings by issuing a press release on March 31, 1988, describing policy options on changes to UBIT, many of which caused concern in the nonprofit sector. The options included suggestions to narrow the "substantially related" test for exempting organizations from UBIT, repeal the "convenience" exception (which, for example, permits college bookstores and cafeterias to be tax exempt), apply UBIT to fitness/health clubs unless the program is "available to a reasonable cross section of the general public such as by scholarship or by fees based on community affordability," and apply UBIT to advertising income and allow deductions from UBIT only on direct advertising costs (a major concern to exempt nonprofits whose publications accept commercial advertising to defray expenses of the parent organization).

In March 1990, a revised report leaked from the subcommittee entitled *Summary of Main Issues in Possible Modification of Oversight Committee UBIT Options.* The draft proposal eliminated many of the controversial proposals that caused so much concern to nonprofits. While the "substantially related" test was retained in the proposal, the "convenience" exception was repealed. Most indirect and overhead expenses relating to advertising income would be deductible, but such expenses could not reduce net income by more than 80%. The subcommittee membership was unable to reach a consensus on UBIT proposals.

The Internal Revenue Service has aggressively audited some charities focusing on UBIT issues, and has taken charities to court to promote its policy of restricting UBIT exemptions. During the 1990s, the Internal Revenue Service expanded its attention to enforcement of UBIT, and developed policies with respect to some of the gray areas that were problematic to charities. Some cases involving the interpretation of what constitutes unrelated income were litigated. Several relatively recent decisions on generic UBIT issues have been decided in favor of charities. Three examples have been cases involving mailing list rental income, affinity credit card income, and income from bingo games.

Two cases questioning whether mailing list rental income is considered subject to UBIT have resulted in victories for the challenged charity. The first involved the Sierra Club, a case heard by the 9th Circuit Court of Appeals. A subsequent case before United States Tax Court involving the American Academy of Ophthalmology also found that such income was not taxable. Tax Court also rejected the contention of the IRS that payments made to the Mississippi State University Alumni Association by a bank were royalty payments rather than business income, and thus are subject to UBIT. Each of these three cases had fact-specific aspects that may not apply to every case of a charity generating revenues by renting mailing lists or utilizing affinity credit card arrangements, and some caution needs to be taken in generalizing. However, the courts apparently have been reining in the IRS for a generally broad interpretation of what constitutes unrelated business income, and this is a positive trend for charities seeking unconventional methods to generate the revenue they need to provide their services. Another case, involving income from instant pull-tab bingo games, developed when the IRS determined that income from these games conducted by Women of the Motion Picture Industry and other 501(c)(3) and (c)(6) organizations was subject to UBIT. The tax code does provide for UBIT exception for most bingo game income, but the conditions are narrow and do not apply to the instant pull-tab games. Tax Court ruled in favor of the organizations.

A case decided in August 1996 in U.S. District Court involving the American Academy of Family Physicians determined that the organization's income from a group insurance plan offered to its members underwritten by a private insurance carrier was not subject to UBIT. Again, the facts of this case may not be typical of conventional agreements between an insurance carrier and an exempt organization, but the opinion of the court on the issue was a favorable development.

Differences Between Nonprofits and For-Profits

There are clear and fundamental differences between the operations and motivations of nonprofits and for-profits. The buildings of some types of nonprofit charities and their for-profit counterparts may, in some cases, be similar. For-profit and nonprofit hospitals, nursing homes, day care centers, and recreational/youth service facilities may have the same equipment and physical plants, and provide some of the same services. Yet, these similarities often are exaggerated in an effort by some overzealous small business advocates to discredit the tax exemptions of those they perceive as competitors. The YMCAs in a growing number of communities particularly have endured vicious attacks from some private health club owners. In specific cases around the nation, these attacks have been given a credibility unsupported by the facts, and have resulted in the loss of tax-exempt status.

Among the differences between nonprofit charitable organizations and for-profits are the following:

1. A nonprofit charity is driven by its service mission philosophy rather than by the profit motive.

2. A nonprofit charity serves those who cannot afford to pay full costs.

3. Any excess revenue over expenditures is funneled back into the institution to further its exempt purpose.

4. The charitable institution likely will remain in the community even if it suffers financial losses.

5. The nonprofit charity is more accountable to its board for public service.

6. The nonprofit charity often will proactively look for ways to respond to community needs without regard to any profit motive.

7. A nonprofit charity may not compensate its employees higher than "reasonable" rates, as is evident from the successful prosecution of several television religious broadcasters who were paid exorbitant salaries and benefits.

8. A nonprofit charity's board of directors is typically comprised of unpaid community leaders motivated by public service and serving the unmet needs of the community rather than making a profit.

9. A nonprofit charity, because of its legal mission to serve rather than to make profits, often attracts thousands of hours of volunteer time and philanthropic contributions that further its purposes.

Recommendations for Nonprofits with Respect to Competition

1. Nonprofits should not publicly advertise products and services in a manner that underscores price competition with the for-profit sector.

2. Nonprofits should refrain from entering markets that are not substantially related to the mission of the organization, and should be prepared to pay unrelated business income taxes (UBIT) on income derived from activities not "directly" related, should this change in the law be approved.

3. Nonprofits should review their activities that could be construed as commercial, and identify all those that require the filing of a 990-T and payment of UBIT.

4. In exploring options for generating new agency revenue, nonprofits should be sensitive to meeting needs that are unmet by the for-profit sector, rather than relying on undercutting the price of goods and services already being offered in the marketplace.

5. Nonprofits should support efforts to improve disclosure and accountability of the voluntary sector, and cooperate with expanded enforcement of laws governing this sector, so that the few nonprofits that are abusing the law do not stain the reputation of the entire sector.

6. Nonprofits should periodically review their bylaws and tax-exempt status purposes, and update these documents to reflect changing conditions.

Chapter 24
State and Local Tax Exemptions

> Synopsis: Every state authorizes tax exemptions for charitable organizations, although in some jurisdictions, this principle is being challenged. Taxes, payments in-lieu-of taxes, or user charges all have the same effect—draining charities of resources that are better used for providing free and reduced-cost services. The tax exemption for charities is justified, and should continue.

Sales and Use Tax Exemptions

Almost every state levies a sales and use tax or equivalent on purchases of goods and/or services made by the public. With few exceptions, charities are eligible for exemption from paying this tax. Consult the State Directory of this book for more details on which states levy the tax, and the requirements and procedures for exemption.

In many jurisdictions around the nation, exemptions from sales taxes, and local property taxes as well, are under scrutiny by jurisdictions eager to increase revenues at a time when the demand for government services is increasing and revenues are not. Some government entities have sought to impose payments in-lieu-of taxes or user charges on tax-exempt organizations, or have tried to eliminate the exemptions entirely.

Why User Charges May Not Be the Answer

There are no reasonable ways to measure the public services that are directly utilized by charitable nonprofits.

Property taxes, by themselves or disguised as "user charges," neglect the factors by which these institutions have earned their tax exemptions in the first place. They are, for the most part, created to provide benefits to the community. The tax exemption provided to these organizations is a benefit that is returned to the communities many times over.

The amount of financial support accruing to municipalities by taxing charities is generally not believed to be substantial. At least one study done in Wisconsin showed that 67% of the state's tax-exempt property belonged to government, and that an additional 10% was owned by religious organizations. There is no profit that is distributed into private pockets. Thus, the payment of taxes would result in a limited set of options for charitable nonprofits, all of which are injurious.

The first option is that charities can decide that they are unable to continue operations, since the property tax payment required could be substantial in comparison to their total budgets. A second available option is to reduce services. A third option is to increase the cost of their services, but doing so often makes the services inaccessible to those who most need them.

In every one of these cases, the cost of reducing the activities of these charities is eventually borne by the community. That is why these organizations were granted tax-exempt status in the first place—to assure that their total resources are dedicated to meeting community needs.

Even with tax-exempt status, times are tough for these institutions. Government support for many nonprofit charitable activities has substantially declined since 1981. Demographic trends—including the aging of our population; the increase in homelessness, drug abuse, single-parent families, domestic violence, and children living in poverty; and the increasing economic necessity of two parents in the family working in order to make ends meet—have resulted in the demand for more free and subsidized services. Private enterprise has, in recent years, invaded the traditional turf of nonprofit human service agencies. In virtually every case, the for-profit business has marketed its services to garner the most lucrative market segment, siphoning away clients who generated incremental revenue that was used by the nonprofit charities to cross-subsidize services for the needy. By skimming off this market share, private enterprise has placed an additional burden on the charitable nonprofit sector.

Finally, economic instability has had an impact not only on an increase in service demand but a decrease in the revenue depended upon by charities, including fees for service and charitable contributions.

Justification For the Charitable Tax Exemption

The experience of charities with the Colorado ballot question of November 5, 1996, in which an unsuccessful attempt was made to repeal the property tax exemption for many traditionally tax-exempt charities, served as a wake-up call that the charitable exemption may no longer be taken for granted. In Pennsylvania, thousands of charities have had their exemptions challenged as a result of misinterpretation of the state Constitution, and several unfavorable court interpretations. Charities in other states have also been challenged. The principle of exemption for bona fide charities deserves to be protected and continued.

Some of the reasons are:

1.   Charitable nonprofits augment and, in some cases, replace, the role of government in responding to and preventing society's problems. Tax-exempt status is an acknowledgment that these organizations have been deputized to act in the public interest and to improve societal conditions rather than to serve any private interest. As a result, such tax-exempt organizations have a special responsibility to assure that their programs

and activities are consistent with these principles and that the level of accountability is on par with the government's.

2. Non-profit charities have many advantages in responding to societal problems that are not available to government. Among them are:

    a. Non-profit charities can be galvanized to attack a problem much more quickly than can government. Those who disagree with this need only consider how long it took for government to respond to problems such as AIDS, homelessness, and drug abuse compared with individual nonprofit charities. Clearly, nonprofits can respond to problems before a political consensus is developed by either the public at large or a legislative body. Charitable nonprofits can, in many cases, direct resources toward solving the problem without the typical government bureaucracy and lag time between the identification of a problem and the approval of a statute, budget, regulation, request-for-proposal (RFP), and the actual expenditure of funds to solve the problem.

    b. Non-profits can effectively and efficiently respond to and solve problems that are localized in nature. This is a politically difficult task to accomplish under our present governmental system. Our political system often requires that a problem be universal in nature before resources are allocated to it. Also, politics make it more likely that government will be unable to target resources to solve a problem because there is often a cost to obtaining the necessary votes to pass a law.

    c. Non-profits attract volunteers. Volunteers, both on boards and doing the actual work of the agency, include many who would not be attracted to government service and the restraints of government-affiliated organizations.

    d. Non-profits can provide services when government programs, because of a limit on tax revenues, cannot expand. Charitable nonprofits often fill the void between what government provides to those who are destitute and what the for-profit sector provides to those who can afford the market rate for services. These charities provide services to those caught in the middle, who are not "poor enough" for government entitlement programs, but yet would be denied services by the for-profit sector. By charging fees for services on a sliding scale, these nonprofits are able to serve many who would otherwise not be served. This permits government to concentrate on serving only the neediest, while private business serves those who can afford to pay market rates.

The entire public benefits from the improvement of society resulting from the activities of these organizations. The tax exemption provided to charities is a cost to the entire public, but is only a small fraction of the public benefit accruing from these activities. Beyond the monetary benefit of this exemption, which permits these charities to commit *all* of their resources to the mission of the organizations, there is a principle involved. The tax exemption is an acknowledgment that the public values this type of altruistic activity and has foregone the collecting of taxes. It makes a statement that these organizations play an important role in strengthening the safety net that the government cannot offer by itself.

It is in the public interest to promote the health of these charitable organizations, because government could not perform their missions as creatively, efficiently, or as cost-effectively.

Tips:

- **To protect tax-exempt status, serve clients who cannot afford to pay the full costs of services, and make services accessible to some clients who cannot afford to pay anything for services.**

- **Periodically quantify the dollar amount of free and subsidized services provided to the organization's clients and to the public at large.**

- **If state and local tax-exempt status is desired, develop a careful and honest outline of how the organization complies with state and local criteria. If staff feel that compliance with these criteria are problematic, then consider changing operations to reasonably meet them.**

Chapter 25
Property Tax Challenges: How To Respond

> Synopsis: This chapter outlines the steps a nonprofit organization can take to be prepared should its tax-exempt status be challenged.

Recent efforts across the nation to challenge nonprofits' property tax-exempt status have produced a great deal of anxiety within the nonprofit community. Rumors abound; questions are raised; organizations are challenged; exempt status may or may not be retained.

The reasons behind these challenges are many and complex and, thus, are not likely to be addressed easily or quickly. It must be assumed that, for the moment, local governments and school districts will continue their attempts to obtain revenue from the nonprofit community. Nonprofit organizations must be prepared to respond. Organizations may choose from a number of responses: pay the tax bill (accept the loss of property tax-exempt status), negotiate a voluntary payment (retain exempt status) or fight to retain their full exemption. Though there is no single, easy or quick answer that can be offered in response to a challenge to tax-exempt status, there are a number of things organizations can do to ensure that the appropriate response is chosen—whether the choice is to negotiate a settlement or fight the challenge in court. **Each organization must determine for itself how to respond to such a challenge**.

Ultimately the nonprofit organization must be able to articulate its charitable nature through the provision of evidence that leaves no doubt as to its charitable status. Even a choice to negotiate a voluntary contribution is based upon the legitimacy of tax-exempt status. Should the charitable status of the nonprofit organization be overturned, responsibility for the entire tax burden is no longer at issue.

The evidence needed to prove the legitimacy of exempt status can be generated through a process that involves five components: education, planning, documentation, communication, and collaboration. Each will be discussed below. After a brief summary, key questions that must be considered as part of each component are listed.

Education

The first step in preparing an appropriate response to a challenge to property tax-exempt status is to gather the knowledge to make the correct decision. Nonprofit organizations must educate themselves about this issue before a challenge is presented. Through training and discussion, both board and staff must understand the implications of the challenge for their own particular organization. For example, it is no longer enough to assume the mantle of "educational" or "health care" institution. Organizations must be able to articulate for themselves the reason their nonprofit health care organization is different from a for-profit health care organization. Another example might be: Why is a nonprofit day-care center deserving of an exemption when a for-profit day-care center is not?

This process of education is only accomplished through introspection, training and dialogue. Boards of directors and staff must involve themselves in a broad-based conversation in which every member and group understands the issue and its implications. Through this dialogue, the following kinds of questions need to be answered:

1. What has happened in our geographic area regarding tax exemption and nonprofits? What efforts have the taxing authorities initiated? What taxing bodies are actively involved?
2. Which organizations have been formally or informally challenged? How did they respond?
3. What decisions or outcomes have occurred thus far? Are any decisions pending, or in appeal?
4. Why does our organization deserve continued exemption? What is our expressed rationale for tax-exempt status?
5. Is there consensus among the board and staff as to these issues?

Planning

A natural outcome of knowledge is the ability to plan a response. As an organization understands the issues and their implications, decisions can be made as to appropriate strategies. The position of strength for a nonprofit organization is to be prepared for a challenge should one emerge. The goal in a planning process is to have necessary policies and procedures in place so that the normal difficulties associated with a tax challenge will not be exacerbated by indecision, bickering and in-fighting among and between board and staff. To have the time to make reasoned, deliberate decisions is critical; planning allows for this.

Some of the planning questions that need to be answered include:

1. If challenged, what would we do? Would we negotiate? Would we go to court? Who makes this decision?

2. How is the board's position expressed? Is there a policy or stated position?

3. Which board members are involved on a day-to-day basis? At what point does the full board need to be consulted?

4. Which staff would be involved? Who would have direct responsibility for this issue?

5. What legal services would we need? What do we have available?

6. What financial resources would be needed? Where will we get dollars?

Documentation

Critical to any organization's successful response to a property tax challenge is the ability to provide both quantitative and qualitative information as to its charitable nature. It is not enough to simply say, "We serve poor people" or "We do good things for children." Everything an organization says about itself or its services must be proven.

Some of the questions that need to be answered include:

1. Who are our clients? Who is our constituency? How many do we serve?

2. Who uses our services? What are their ages, their incomes?

3. How many donors do we have? Who are they? How much money do they give us?

4. Who are our volunteers? How much time do they give us? What is the dollar value of their time?

5. Are our services responsive to the needs of the community? How do we know this? What information can we provide that shows our organization is responsive to changing needs?

6. Who receives which services? Who uses our programs, our community screenings, our educational programs?

7. If fees are charged, how are levels of payment determined? Is anyone turned away for lack of resources?

8. What levels of subsidy are available? How many people are subsidized? Where do the subsidies come from?

9. What is our policy regarding ability to pay? How do we communicate these policies?

10. If local taxpayers are not the direct receivers of our services, how do they benefit?

11. How is *local* government relieved of a burden?

Communication

Research has revealed the discrepancy between the community's perception of nonprofit organizations and their financial realities. Yet, "perception" can be argued to be "reality" in that what people believe to be true drives behavior and interactions. Therefore, effective communication between the nonprofit organization and its community is critical.

Questions to be considered include:

1. What messages do we, as an organization, communicate to the community?

2. Do our publications and advertising promote an image of inclusivity or exclusivity? Are we communicating, in written form, our charitable nature and mission?

3. Do we communicate issues of reduced fees, subsidies, scholarships? Would members of the community know of these policies?

4. If asked, would the community be able to express the benefits our presence offers? Would they agree that our organization deserves tax exemption? Would they agree that they are the direct or indirect recipients of our services and presence? How do we assess community perception?

Collaboration

The lack of collaboration among nonprofit organizations is viewed as a weakness in potential responses to a property tax challenge. There is tremendous power in the nonprofit sector; choosing to separate oneself from other nonprofit organizations because of some perceived uniqueness can be destructive to that power. This is not to argue that nonprofit organizations should create a single, unified response. Sharing of information and ideas, and efforts to collaborate, however, can be positive for several reasons.

First, collaboration engenders a sense of community across diverse nonprofit organizations. Second, it empowers a group that could easily become fragmented and divisive. Third, it increases knowledge and experience of younger, smaller organizations. Fourth, it communicates to local units of government the strength that can be mustered should nonprofit organizations become united on issues. Fifth, it fosters creativity and innovation within the nonprofit sector. Finally, it creates a knowledge base about this issue. Much of what we know thus far about these challenges to property tax status is anecdotal. More good data is needed to create effective, responsible policy. The nonprofit sector should be proactive in the creation of this data, not reactive. Good information helps to assure a position of power.

Questions to be considered include:

1. What are the issues that unite us across fields of activity, across dimensions of size and geography?

2. What do we as a sector gain through collaboration? What do we lose if we are divided?

3. In what kinds of activities, unrelated to tax exemption, might we collaborate?

4. How can we ensure the adoption of appropriate and effective legislation? What kinds of legislation will strengthen our position as nonprofit organizations?

5. Are there existing structures or organizations in which we can participate and join others on this issue?

Discussion

Many nonprofit organizations will find the questions listed above difficult to answer. Some organizations may find that they are not currently in a position to answer them adequately. For these organizations, this process of self-examination and discussion becomes critical—not only as a means to improve existing services and operations, but also as a means of preparation should exempt status be challenged. Yet, any organization can benefit from this process of self-examination.

In considering *how* to respond to a property tax challenge, the most difficult part may be the removal of "blinders" and acknowledging that, warranted or not, the status of your organization may be challenged. Research has shown that many executives are not really interested in this issue until directly confronted with a tax bill. Chief executives often are surprised and dismayed by a challenge; they wonder how anyone could question their charitable status. Realizing that there are people and groups in your community who do question your charitable status can be a shock. For the smaller, more traditional charities, this may be especially true.

This is a hurdle that must be overcome. Nonprofit organizations and their boards of directors must understand that whether or not they are directly challenged, they will be affected. The manner in which all nonprofit organizations operate in the future will change as a result of these challenges.

To avoid the issue—to *not* plan a response—is the worst tactic an organization can choose. Through a process of discussion and education, planning, effective documentation and communication, and collaboration, a nonprofit organization can be well-prepared for a challenge. It is these organizations that will be in a position of strength when questioned by a local unit of government. It is these organizations that will be successful in defending their exempt status.

Yet, more than being successful in a direct challenge to tax-exempt status, organizations may rediscover the "essence" of the nonprofit sector. Nonprofit sector scholar Jon Van Til (1993) writes,

> ... we might discover that the reason we exist is not to be "nonprofit," but rather to profit our communities and society in ways that families, governments, and corporations cannot. We might, in other words, discover the soul of a sector that has been lost by many contemporary nonprofits, blinded as they are by their quest to be both "business-like" and "tax-free."

Tips:

- **Hire legal counsel with experience handling tax-exemption challenge cases.**

- **If challenged, consider not only appealing the exemption challenge, but appealing the amount of the assessment on the property.**

- **Keep up to date with relevant legislation, case law, and regulations on exempt status, since any judgments involving the feasibility and desirability of making a settlement with a local government will be colored by inaccurate or non-current information.**

NOTE: The strategies suggested in this chapter are based upon conclusions drawn from a research project conducted during the spring of 1994. Information presented here is a slightly modified version of the third chapter of a larger document summarizing this research entitled, *Responding to a Property Tax Challenge: Lessons Learned in Pennsylvania.* Copyright, Pamela J. Leland, Ph.D., ©1994. All rights reserved. Reprinted with permission.

Chapter 26
Mergers and Consolidations

> Synopsis: Mergers involving nonprofit organizations are increasingly common and require planning. There are steps that should be taken when planning for a merger between nonprofit organizations to meet legal requirements and promote a successful transition.

It wasn't too long ago that many nonprofit boards considered liquidation to be a preferable alternative to mergers. Considering the loss of identity was just too painful, and the term "merger" conjured up a vision of a corporate shark gobbling up weaker entities. Since then, mergers and consolidations among nonprofit organizations have become increasingly common, spurred in part by cost-containment pressures that have been affecting the delivery of social services for several decades now, particularly in the healthcare industry.

Managed care, cuts in Medicare and Medicaid, DRG payments, and increased competition have been among the factors that have induced hundreds of nonprofit mergers among hospitals. There are increasing incentives for all nonprofit organizations to improve their efficiency and effectiveness. With the entry of for-profit organizations into providing services historically provided by nonprofits, competition for service dollars has increased. To create new sources of revenue, even staid nonprofits have become entrepreneurial and are offering services that may only be indirectly related to their core mission. Unwittingly, they may be siphoning off revenue from colleague agencies.

Factors That Trigger Merger Consideration

Among the events that trigger consideration of nonprofit mergers are:

- Organizations that deliver similar services recognize economies of scale can be achieved

- Organizations that are struggling financially seek a partner to stave off bankruptcy and liquidation

- National organizations may place restrictions on local affiliates, such as having a minimum asset level, technology capability, and service menu, which cannot be met without combining with another local affiliate

- Two nearby agencies find themselves engaging in destructive competition

- Changes in leadership capability, both of staff and within the board, may trigger a strategic plan that recognizes an organization's inability to continue with the status quo

- Scandal or other ethical challenges in which merger or consolidation is seen as an alternative to liquidation

- Changes in the outside regulatory environment or economic environment (e.g., managed care) that make it more attractive to increase economic power to compete

- A loss of membership that makes it unfeasible to continue

- The agency's mission has been accomplished successfully.

Generally, the reasons for suggesting a merger can be divided into three categories.

Economic reasons: A merger will help the organization become more efficient, take advantage of economies of scale, increase its access to members and/or clients, help it raise more donations and grants, and contain costs. The nonrenewal of a major grant that provided overhead expenses to the agency can threaten its continued existence. There is no longer the cash-flow necessary to continue the operation.

Programmatic reasons: Agencies recognize that there is a duplication of services with an unhealthy competition for the same clients. Or, if there isn't duplication, agencies recognize that combining administration and delivery of services provided to the same population of clients, can promote efficiency.

Strategic reasons: An agency may be in a precarious state either economically or programmatically. Competition from for-profits or other nonprofits is becoming destructive, and funders are complaining. The board might be losing interest. A long-term CEO may be retiring, and there is no one to take his or her place with the vision necessary to lead the organization. The staff is demoralized because of an ineffective CEO who cannot be removed for political reasons. The public or funders have lost confidence in the agency as a result of ethical lapses or a reputation for poor quality, or an agency in the outside environment is identified that, if a merger occurred, would create a strong synergy.

How to Begin

At a 1997 workshop session on nonprofit mergers sponsored by the Pennsylvania Association of Nonprofit Organizations, William Morgan of Performance Industries and Paul Mattaini of Barley, Snyder, Senft & Cohen distributed a list of areas to consider when contemplating a merger.

Among the issues they raised were—

- The importance of infusing key leadership with the view that merging is a viable option

- Whether the CEO will find a way to sabotage the merger because of ego

- Whether the merger will fit into the organization's mission

- Finding the right candidate to merge with, and finding the right staff (such as an attorney, accountant, and consultant)

- Bringing together the two organizational cultures

- Handling the public relations and community relations aspects.

Steps to Merger

1. The participating board should adopt a resolution in favor of the general principle of merging.

2. Each board should appoint a merger committee of board members and staff.

3. An outside, experienced merger consultant should be jointly hired to structure negotiations, with the cost shared by the participating organizations.

4. Meetings should be scheduled among the parties to discuss the goals of the merger, determine whether merging is feasible and makes sense for all parties, and negotiate, over time, the details, such as the change in the mission and values, new name, staffing, logo, merger budget, board selection, bylaws, personnel policies, location, and what happens to staff who are no longer needed.

Budgeting

Mergers cost money. There are likely to be legal fees, consultant fees, audit fees, personnel costs relating to layoffs, moving costs, costs relating to covering the liabilities of the non-surviving corporation (which may be substantial, and responsible for triggering the merger idea in the first place), and even printing new building signs, printing new stationery and business cards, and designing a new logo.

As David La Piana writes in *Nonprofit Mergers: The Board's Responsibility to Consider the Unthinkable,*

> "Although it is unlikely that the financial position of two merging organizations will immediately improve as a result of a merger, well-conceived and –implemented mergers can raise staff morale, better focus the organization's activities, and increase overall energy levels— that will help the new group tackle difficult problems. Thus, a successful merger can offer relief and renewed hope for nonprofit boards, staff, and donors, and, most importantly, benefit clients because of the greater

energy, increased funding, and better management possible with a more stable organization. In contrast, poorly conceived mergers may simply bring together two weak organizations that compound each other's problems."

Obstacles to Merger

Virtually every article about the difficulty of merging two or more organizations refers to the two scourges that often scuttle the best laid plans: "turf" and "ego." Many, if not most, mergers of nonprofit organizations involve a financially strong organization merging with an organization that is merging in order to stave off bankruptcy or liquidation. The surviving organization will have one chief executive, and it is often a traumatic and, at times, potentially humiliating experience for the chief executive of the non-surviving organization to hand over the reins of decision-making. It is not unusual for an otherwise "routine" merger to be derailed by petty squabbling over the name of the combined agency, the logo, or the office space that will be provided to the staff of the non-surviving agency.

Legal Requirements

The legal procedures for mergers and consolidations that involve nonprofit corporations can be found in state law. Obviously, experienced, professional legal advice is necessary to carry out a successful merger.

Chapter 27
Introduction to the Year 2000 (Y2K) Problem

> Synopsis: Nonprofit organizations should take steps to address the Y2K problem, which may affect their internal operations and society in general. There are resources available that will assist nonprofit organizations in responding to Y2K-related problems, and suggestions to minimize disruptions.

Just when you thought you were developing a stable list of donors, the world economy was beginning to recover, and your boss was hinting at a raise as a reward for your successful fundraising and marketing efforts, a looming crisis may keep you and your colleagues burning the midnight oil, literally, come December 31, 1999.

Nonprofit organization leaders are becoming increasingly more skittish about what has become known as the "Y2K problem," also called the "millennium bug" or "Year 2000 problem." There is good reason for this. Compared to their for-profit counterparts, nonprofit organizations are more likely to have older computer hardware and software that is not Y2K-compliant. And nonprofits will be called upon to help clean up any mess caused by disruptions in food supplies, communication, transportation, and health care.

Purveyors of doom predict that some of the consequences of Y2K may be a cataclysmic world-wide depression, riots in the streets, airplanes falling from the skies, electric power shutting down in large cities, food supply disruptions, medical devices implanted into heart patients failing, and nonprofit charities facing public health and safety crises that government has failed to remedy.

Or, Y2K may be the equivalent of the Kohotek comet—all sizzle and no steak. Perhaps the hundreds of consultants who sell Y2K fixes—hardware, software, and protocols to solve the problem—have exaggerated the consequences in order to hype the sales of their products and services.

More likely, it will fall somewhere in between. On March 2, 1999, the Senate's Y2K Committee released a report that suggested that there may be serious disruptions starting January 1, 2000. The Vice Chairman of the Committee, Sen. Christopher Dodd (D-CT), appearing on NBC's *Meet the Press* February 28, 1999. said it would not be unwise "for people to do a little stockpiling" of supplies that would last two to three days.

Some reliably estimate that businesses nationwide will be spending upward of $600 billion to make their computer systems Y2K compliant. And these estimates do not include the billions of dollars worth of lawsuits that will surely follow in the event that individuals and corporations seek to recover damages if they are harmed by third parties as a result of Y2K issues. Estimates of potential Y2K-related lawsuits considered reliable by the Senate Committee have been in the range of $1 trillion.

As people change their behavior to avoid risk—avoiding airline flights and electronic financial transactions, squirreling away cash, stockpiling food and water—these actions may create social and economic ripple effects even if there is not a single *direct* Y2K event.

Nonprofit organizations are routinely receiving forms from those who purchase their products requiring them to certify that Y2K-compliant systems are in place. What is this all about, anyway?

Definition of the Problem

In simple terms, Y2K refers to the issue of what will happen to computer systems and computer data on January 1, 2000. These computers may have an inability to recognize that January 1, 2000 is the day after December 31, 1999, and to process information accordingly. For almost four decades, time was recorded in computerese using just six digits—two digits each for the day, the month, and the year. This made perfect sense back when computer memory was expensive, and saving two digits had measurable cost savings associated with it. Punch cards, the data-entry method of choice thirty years ago, had only limited space to record data, and each space was precious. Even more recently, computer programmers continued to use two digits for the year, expecting that their software would become quickly obsolete and be replaced. Also, it was easier to program in a two-digit year for purposes of printing out next to "19" in preprinted forms.

Some devices will function perfectly well on January 1, 2000, and then crash on February 29, 2000. This emanates from the fact that years divisible by 100 are generally not leap years, unless they are divisible by 400, as is the year 2000. Some software may not account for this fact. Additionally, some software recognizes the number 9999 as a special code rather than a date, so there may be Y2K problems surfacing this year as well.

It was taken for granted that the designation of 82, for example, meant "1982." On January 1, 2000, the computer will record the year as "00" and it is not clear whether this refers to "1900" or "2000."

This problem affects most mainframes and almost all older PCs. Every PC has an internal clock. After midnight on December 31, 1999, some will be set to 1900, some to 1980, some to 1984, and others to some other date.

For most nonprofits that depend on PCs, the extent of the Y2K problem that they can do something about is to test whether their computer's internal clock is Y2K-compliant. This means that the computer will operate correctly when the internal clock is set to every year from 2000 at least through 2009.

Why Nonprofit Organizations Should Be Concerned

Among the reasons are:

1. **Failure of internal computer systems**—Nonprofits using personal computers may have trouble billing delinquent accounts, keeping track of services provided to their clients, calculating personnel benefits due their staff, and a myriad of other tasks performed by PCs that are taken for granted.

2. **Failure of government computer systems**—If government computers fail, nonprofit organizations will experience an overload of clients affected by a failure of government to provide income transfers and health benefits, in addition to potential law enforcement problems that will affect nonprofit service delivery.

3. **Weakness or meltdown in the world-wide economy**—Some predict a shutdown of public services: a failure of utilities to deliver gas, electricity, and water; a general banking system failure, and a cascade of events leading to a world-wide recession or depression. A weak economy usually results in a burgeoning of demand for nonprofit services at a time when people tend to donate less. The U.S. Senate's report expressed many concerns not only in the United States, but also about the lack of mitigation of Y2K-related problems in Africa, Latin America, and Asia, which could slow economic growth. The Senate report concluded that while there was no evidence that the United States would experience social or economic collapse, "some disruptions will occur and in some cases (these disruptions) will be significant." Other technologically advanced countries, such as Germany, also have a lot of work to do to catch up on becoming immune from Y2K chaos.

4. **Failure of logic controllers and programmable logic controllers**—Many electronic devices use semiconductors to manage products such as fax machines, elevators, environmental controls, VCRs, security systems, and even coffee machines. Many of these have date-sensitive codes programmed into their chips. Those machines that have Y2K non-compliant chips may fail, or incorrectly operate.

5. **Failure of financial institution processes**—Some banks are even evaluating credit worthiness based on Y2K compliance in the computer systems of those applying for credit. This also affects other stakeholders of nonprofit organizations, such as the companies that support them and supply them. Accounts receivable may not be paid because a noncompliant computer will not recognize that the bill should be paid. Banks may not be able to process checks or handle other routine transactions.

6. **Fundraising disruption**—Businesses and their leaders may be so focused on Y2K problems that they may not be as able to share their money and time with charities, warns the United Way of America.

What To Do About the Problem

1. Stop buying hardware and software that is not Y2K-compliant.

2. Don't permit organizational staff to install software from home on your organization's computers. This is not only usually illegal because of licensing violations, but may harm your computers as well.

3. Educate your board, staff, and vendors about the Y2K problem, and document what your organization is planning to do to mitigate the potentially bad effects of it.

4. If your agency is large enough, appoint a staff person to have responsibility to deal with the problem, or hire an outside consultant. If your agency is small, purchase reliable, over-the-counter software that will test your computers, and use it, following the directions provided with the software to back up critically needed files.

5. Inventory all equipment and software that may be at risk, and query the manufacturers about whether they are Y2K compliant, and whether there is software that can be obtained to make them compliant, if not. Much of this information may be obtained at the vendor's Web site.

6. Make sure that organizations you use to outsource services (such as payroll, taxes, personnel benefits) are Y2K-compliant.

7. Back up critical data and store it in a safe place in case systems begin to fail. Don't simply back up your data on disk—if your computers fail, you may not be able to access the data on the disk. Store hard copies of critical information as well. Plan how you will respond in the event your organization's computers fail.

Y2K Internet Resources

There are lots of Y2K resources available that can be accessed for free on the World Wide Web, and are targeted to the needs of nonprofit organizations. Among some of the more valuable ones are:

United Way of America
http://www.unitedway.org/year2000/

The United Way of America has prepared a comprehensive document on the Y2K problem, *The Year 2000 Challenge for United Ways*, targeted to its member agencies, but of use to all nonprofit organizations. It contains a solid background about the problem, recommendations on how to deal with it, and an appendix of resources, including manufacturer Web sites and sample staff memos and letters to vendors. The latest version is dated July 1998. It can be downloaded free from the Internet in PDF format (which requires the use of an Acrobat Reader) or in Word 97.

The Cassandra Project
http://cassandraproject.org/home.html

The Cassandra Project is a nonprofit grass-roots advocacy organization founded in 1997 and named after a less-than-optimistic character from Greek mythology whose warnings about the future went unheeded. You can find a bulletin board and a chat room, and sample letters you can write to institutions such as local banks, power companies, hospitals, and local government agencies asking about their Y2K preparations and status of compliance. The group's founder, Paloma O'Riley, is the author of a guide for surviving the worst-case scenarios relating to Y2K, called *Y2K Citizen's Action Guide*. It can be viewed and downloaded free at this site, although there is information as well about purchasing the hard-copy booklet. This is a practical handbook for preparing for any worst-case disruptions attributable to Y2K (and, perhaps, famine, flood, nuclear war, or global depression). It has tips for storing food and water; maintaining supplies; dealing with sanitation, communication, transportation, and power disruptions; handling emergencies and medical problems. It provides advice for engaging in bartering if the financial system is severely disrupted.

CompuMentor
http://www.compumentor.org

Founded in 1987, CompuMentor bills itself as "the largest nonprofit computerization organization in the country." From the home page, click on "Y2K for Nonprofits." You can download the *CompuMentor Year 2000 Workbook for Nonprofits With the Year 2000 Worksheets* at this site. This workbook is described as a "do it yourself manual for people who are at least moderately comfortable with computers to undertake the Y2K Audit." There are also files of general interest about the Y2K problem.

The Nathan Cummings Foundation
http://www.ncf.org/ncf/publications/reports/y2k/intro/intro_contents.html

The Year 2000 Challenge: A Socially Responsive Way to Prepare for Disruptions in Computer-reliant Systems, a working document published October 28, 1998, is available free at this site. It explains the issue from the perspective of foundations—not only what they need to know about Y2K but what they should be doing about it. The document provides nine recommendations for foundation action.

Independent Sector
http://www.indepsec.org/y2k.html

Independent Sector has devoted several useful pages on its site to Y2K. There are articles reprinted from the media, a list of 10 non-technical questions to nonprofit organization leaders should think about (*Preparing for Year 2000: Key Questions Every Philanthropic Leader Should Consider*), links to a database on Y2K product and software compliance information, community group action plans, and to general Y2K information.

Penn State University Y2K Site

ftp://ftp.cac.psu.edu/pub/year2000 and
http://www.psu.edu/Year2000

This site, sponsored by Penn State University, has free software that can be downloaded by FTP and used to test your PC for Y2K compliance. Additional general information files can be found at the University's Web site.

As with any files that you download from the Internet, use common sense when taking any risks relating to viruses or other possibilities for crashing your computer and losing data.

Chapter 28
Quality Issues

Synopsis: Quality is as important, if not more so, to nonprofit organizations as for-profit businesses. Nonprofits need quality programs to compete for donations, clients, board members, workers, and political support.

Introduction

Many who govern and manage nonprofit organizations are increasingly finding their organizations subject to many of the same economic pressures as their for-profit counterparts. Their operations often resemble their for-profit competitors in both organizational structure and corporate culture. They are increasingly led by those trained in business rather than social work, and their mentality and style of administration often reflects this. Stereotypically, they often put the "bottom line" paramount above the needs of clients. One nonprofit CEO I spoke with recognized the inconsistency of trying to run a human service organization and retaining his "humaneness," while at the same time being forced to make rational business decisions that could mean the firing of "nice" people who were hurting the performance of his organization. He commented to me that his management credo was to be "ruthlessly altruistic."

In many cases, the products and services once provided solely by nonprofit, charitable organizations are now being provided by for-profits. One can often find health clubs, hospitals, schools, nursing homes, and day-care centers—both for-profit and nonprofit—competing for clients on an equal basis within communities. When there is this direct competition, particularly in the delivery of human and educational services, cost is just one factor in a customer's decision. Quality of service is often even more important in a decision, and nonprofits that offer high-quality products and services obviously have a competitive edge. Those that can't offer quality may find themselves out of business.

Many thousands of other nonprofit organizations find themselves in a situation where they don't have direct economic competition from others providing the same service. There is only one United Way affiliate in each community, one Arts Council, one Arthritis Foundation, one AARP affiliate, and one Special Olympics affiliate. Except under unusual circumstances, it is unlikely that another organization will sprout up to directly challenge one of these. It would be easy to jump to the conclusion that having a monopoly of this nature would mean that quality and performance are not as important as they are to those with direct, head-to-head competition for providing a particular product or service. That conclusion would be flawed.

Why Quality is Important to Nonprofit Organizations

Quality is important to all nonprofit organizations, and none is immune from the consequences of neglecting quality. Charities rely on loyal customer support. Even if a nonprofit is not involved in direct economic competition, there is substantial competition for things that indirectly affect the viability of organizations. Among them are:

1. **Competition for government and foundation grants.** Most charitable nonprofits depend on grants to supplement any client fees they receive. Foundations are acutely aware of organizations with poor reputations with respect to skimping on service quality. No one wants to be associated with such an organization. It is no wonder that first-class organizations often have little trouble attracting funding, because everyone wants to be associated with them.

2. **Competition for private donations.** Would you make a donation to a charity that had a reputation of treating its clients like animals? Unless that organization is the Society for Prevention of Cruelty to Animals (SPCA), you are more likely to look elsewhere for a charity worthy of your donation.

3. **Competition for board members.** Why would anyone want to serve on a board of a second-class nonprofit and risk being condemned or otherwise embarrassed by the media, the political hierarchy, and clients? There are only so many skilled, committed civic leaders in each community who are willing to donate their time and expertise to serve on nonprofit boards, and it is clearly not attractive to serve on the board of a charity with a reputation for poor quality.

4. **Competition for volunteers.** What can be said for board members goes double for service delivery and other volunteers. No one wants to be associated with an organization with a reputation for poor quality. Many volunteers see their volunteer work as a springboard for a career, and volunteering for a pariah in the community does not serve their interests.

5. **Competition for media.** The media play an important role in helping a nonprofit charity promote its fundraising, encourage clients to utilize its services, and improve employee morale. Poor quality can result in the media ignoring an organization or, worse, highlighting its shortcomings for the entire world to see.

6. **Competition for legislative and other political support.** Nonprofit charities have benefited from the support of political leaders, directly through the provision of government grants, and indirectly through the provision of favors such as cutting government red tape and legislation solving the problems of the agency and those of its clients. Political leaders are certainly not going to be responsive to an organization if they receive letters of complaint about the organization's poor quality.

7. **Competition for qualified employees.** Particularly during the current climate of low unemployment, quality nonprofits have less employee turnover and find it easier to attract employees to fill vacancies and for expansion.

The consequences of having poor quality, or the reputation (public perception) of having poor quality, can result in the board of directors throwing up its hands and deciding to liquidate the organization. Or, in extreme cases, having the government step in and liquidate the organization. Imagine the aftermath of a child care agency that failed to perform a quality background check on an employee who later was found to be a child abuser. Or the hospital that failed to adequately verify whether a staff member it hired was adequately board-certified.

As pointed out by Dr. John McNutt of Boston College's Graduate School of Social Work, most, if not all, states look at the community benefit provided by a nonprofit organization in considering whether it is eligible for nonprofit status in the first place. Quality and community benefit are inextricably linked.

In 1998, a scandal affected international agencies that raise funds for child welfare. Who knows how many millions of dollars will not be contributed to these agencies because some agency official did not feel it was important to inform donor sponsors that their sponsored child had died several years ago? With a public already conditioned as a result of the 1992 United Way of America and the 1995 New Era Foundation scandals to be wary about charities, nonprofits need to be more vigilant about not only quality issues affecting the delivery of direct service, but those that affect fiscal accountability as well.

The Cost of Poor Quality

The cost to organizations that have poor quality standards can be substantial. Read the newspapers, and you can find many examples of the consequences of poor quality in nonprofit organizations. Owners of personal care boarding homes have failed to see the value of installing sprinkler systems and, as a result, have seen the loss of life and of their properties. Doctors have mistakenly removed the wrong kidney from a patient. Hospital maternity ward staff have given the wrong newborn to the wrong parents. The ramifications far exceed the financial loss and loss of prestige to the organization—human suffering for the clients and potentially huge, successful lawsuits against the nonprofit organization as a result of a preventable lapse in quality-related policies.

Quality in the Nonprofit Organizational Context

For the typical nonprofit that doesn't deliver client services, quality should mean much more than the ability to answer the telephone on the first ring. It means having a newsletter without typographical errors. It means having an attractive, periodically updated Web site. It means spelling the names of donors correctly in substantiation letters. It means delivering on promises made to legislators for follow-up materials. It means having conferences at which participants feel that they get their money's worth. It means assuring that each board member has the information necessary and appropriate to make governing decisions. It means that volunteers know in advance what is expected of them.

And for those that deliver direct human services, it means, among other things:

- treating each client with the dignity he or she deserves
- respecting confidentiality
- providing on-time services
- providing timely resolution to legitimate complaints
- providing services in a safe and secure setting
- providing services in a facility that is accessible, clean, and functional
- delivering services provided by competent, trained personnel
- assuring that services provided meet high standards and respond to the clients' needs
- obtaining informed consent from clients before services are provided
- seeking constant feedback from clients to improve the delivery of services
- using advances in technology to improve communication between the organization and its clients.

Chapter 29
Change Management

> Synopsis: Change management strategies, such as Total Quality Management, Business Process Reengineering, Benchmarking, Outcome-Based Management, and Large Group Intervention, are potential ways to improve nonprofit organizational quality and performance.

In the context of this chapter, "change management" does not refer to a prescription of getting rid of the people who run the organization. Rather, it is a menu of management strategies to change the philosophy of management to accomplish an objective or set of objectives such as, for example, improving efficiency and competitiveness, motivating employees and increasing their job satisfaction, or reducing absenteeism. In this sense, "change" is used as a noun rather than a verb.

There is general agreement among scholars, practitioners, and management experts that organizations must adapt to changing conditions to survive. Technology advances, markets change, the requirements and expectations of customers evolve, the needs of workers are altered as a result of demographics, economic conditions, and changes in culture, among other things.

Businesses, both for-profit and nonprofit, go out of business every day. This is attributable to many causes. There may be an organizational scandal that causes the public to lose confidence or the government to take action against it. There may be quality lapses. The services provided by an organization may no longer be needed, or a competitor skims off a lucrative market share. The organization's operations may be too economically inefficient to support it. Government funding priorities or regulatory requirements may shift, leaving an organization in the lurch. The list of possible causes goes on.

For years, the for-profit business community has utilized formal change management strategies to improve operations and keep organizations competitive and vibrant, improve efficiency, generate loyalty, and maintain or expand support from their customers. It has only been recently that the nonprofit community, with health care institutions leading the way, started implementing some of these strategies. The material appearing here is based on my book, *Improving Quality and Performance in Your Non-Profit Organization*, which was published in January 1999. An order form can be found in the back of this book if you want to explore change management in more detail.

Among the most popular change management strategies being considered by nonprofit organizations are Total Quality Management (TQM), Business Process Reengineering (BPR), Benchmarking, Outcome-Based Management (OBM), and Large Group Intervention (LGI).

Total Quality Management

TQM is an innovative, humanistic, general approach to management that seeks to improve quality, reduce costs, and increase customer satisfaction by restructuring traditional management practices. It requires a continuous and systematic approach to gathering, evaluating, and acting on data about what is occurring in an organization. The TQM management philosophy includes the following:

1. It asserts that the primary objective of an organization is to meet the needs of its "customers" by providing quality goods and services, and to continually improve them. In the nonprofit organization context, customers include not only the direct recipients of services, such as clients, but the organization's board, elected and appointed government officials, the media, and the general public.

2. It instills in all organization members an *esprit de corps* that assures them that *having quality* as the number one goal is an important tenet. *All* organizational members are responsible for quality, even if it is related to an issue beyond the scope of his or her job. Eliminating the "It's not my job" mentality becomes an achievable organizational objective.

3. It continuously searches for ways to improve every activity, program, and process. It does so by constantly seeking feedback from its customers, and promoting suggestions from all sources, both external and internal, on how to improve.

4. It rewards quality, not only internally, but from its suppliers. It recognizes that poor quality from its collaborators, be they suppliers or other organizations, affects the organization's quality.

5. It recognizes that staff must receive continuous training to improve their work performance.

6. It encourages all components of the organization to work as a team to solve problems and meet customer needs rather than compete against each other.

7. It empowers workers at every level, and permits them to be actively engaged in decisions that affect the organization and to constantly look for ways to improve it.

8. It permits employees the opportunity to have pride in what they produce for the organization and to see the fruits of their labor measured in the quality of the service they provide rather than just having a paycheck.

9. It promotes a planning process geared toward continuously improving quality in *everything* the organization does.

In 1992, the United Way of America developed an award for nonprofit human service agencies, recognizing that quality improvement is just as important, if not more so, in charities as in private business. Known as the Excellence in Service Quality Award (ESQA), 501(c)(3) charities are eligible for four levels of recognition. Judging and criteria are patterned after the Baldrige Award competed for by private corporations.

TQM principles are finding their way into nonprofit settings other than healthcare, such as community centers, arts organizations, and human services agencies. Focusing on the needs of the "customer" rather than on the "bottom line" is a value that the nonprofit sector should feel comfortable with compared with its for-profit counterparts. When a nonprofit organization's leadership becomes excited about TQM, it can become contagious, provided that the behaviors of the leaders are consistent with their words. When it "happens," those in a TQM environment notice the difference, whether they work there or benefit from the organization's services. Workers feel empowered. Clients notice a positive difference in staff attitudes. Everyone associated with the organization feels good about it.

Business Process Reengineering

If your heart stops beating and you keel over breathlessly, a professionally-trained medical professional often can revive you by administering CPR. But if it's your *organization's* heart that fails, BPR, administered by professionally trained consultants or by those within an organization, is increasingly becoming the TLA ("three-letter acronym") of choice for cutting-edge managers. BPR is a successor to TQM as the latest management bromide for reviving comatose organizations.

Business Process Reengineering is defined by Michael Hammer, BPR's leading guru, as "the fundamental rethinking and radical redesign of business processes to achieve dramatic improvements in critical measures of performance (cost, quality, capital, service and speed)."

Fanatical interest in Total Quality Management peaked in the 1980s, but its once-pervasive influence seems to have waned in recent years. One of the reasons often given for its apparent decline in the United States is that the philosophy of slow, incremental, and continuous improvement is generally inconsistent with American culture. Perhaps this is so; American organizational leaders are perceived as more impatient to see tangible results of their business management interventions compared with their Asian, African, and European counterparts. They want to see quantum leaps of measurable improvement rather than the tortoise-paced improvement promised by TQM advocates. The tenure of many organizational leaders is short; several CEOs may come and go before TQM is fully implemented and shows results.

A major strategy involved with BPR efforts is to look at a business process that has many tasks that have been performed by several specialists. Then, the specialists are replaced with generalists (or the specialists are retrained to become generalists) who can handle all of the tasks of the process and have access to all of the information they need to perform *all* of the tasks.

BPR requires a new way of thinking. Unlike TQM, which requires the involvement of everyone in the organization, BPR is necessarily implemented from the top. It is the zero-based budgeting of business processes, contending that, at least theoretically, the past should have no bearing on what is planned for the future. It makes the assumption that organizations have evolved incrementally, reflecting a history of culture, tradition, technology, and customer needs that may not be particularly relevant today. BPR suggests that managers step out of the constraints of their current physical plant, work processes, organizational charts, and procedures and rules, and look at how the work would be performed if they were starting from scratch.

BPR requires an organizational leader to step back and answer the question: If I were building this organization today from scratch, knew what I know now, had the technology and human resources that I have now, and the customer needs that I have now, would I still be doing things the same way? More often than not, the answer is a resounding "no!" In the nonprofit environment, this might mean redesigning data collection and reporting, client intake, billing, purchasing, and every other process.

In many cases, new technology is available that will enable efficiencies. For example, a human service agency may receive a telephone call from a client requesting even a minimal change in service as a result of some change in circumstances. The person answering the telephone may have to put the person on hold and call the client's caseworker, who has the client's case file. The caseworker may have to put the person on hold and check with the supervisor for a decision on whether to waive a rule, and the supervisor may have to meet with the caseworker to make the decision.

Following BPR, the person answering the telephone for the agency may be able to pull up the case file on a computer screen and be preauthorized to approve a change in services within a constraint programmed into the computer by the agency. Or the person answering the telephone may be able to give the caller technical advice on how to solve a problem by searching a "frequently asked questions" file on a computer screen that previously was routinely transferred to a technical specialist.

Another way of looking at this is that everyone in the organization is conventionally functioning solely as his or her part of a process rather than on the objective of the organization. The receptionist answers the telephone. The case manager holds the file for a particular set of clients. The supervisor makes decisions authorizing variances from agency rules. BPR permits a work process to change so that the true objective of the process—responding to the client's needs—does not require the intervention of several people in the organization. The revolutionary advances in information technology permit this.

With the use of networked computers and an educated labor force, it is possible for a single person to process and troubleshoot an entire order that previously may have required being passed serially from person to person in the organization, taking many days to complete. And the probability of an error under the old method multiplies, the more hands are involved.

Among the major principles of BPR are:

1. Use modern technology to redesign work processes rather than work tasks, concentrating on permitting a single person to achieve a desired outcome/objective.

2. Let the worker who uses the output of a process also perform the process. For example, instead of having a purchasing department make purchases of pencils and paper clips for the accounting department and other departments, the accounting department orders its own pencils and paper clips and other "inexpensive and nonstrategic" purchases.

3. Let those in the organization who collect information be the ones who process it. For example, when the public relations department wants to send out its newsletter to a mailing list, it should be able to generate the mailing labels itself rather than having to make a request to a data processing department.

4. Treat decentralized organizational resources as centralized, utilizing information technology to bring them together. A college with several satellite campuses, for example, could link its bursars so that a student making a payment at either the main office or a satellite campus would have the payment show up in the records of the registrars of all of the campuses.

5. Electronically link disparate parts of an organization to promote coordination.

6. Let those who perform the work make the decisions, thereby flattening the pyramidal management layers and eliminating the bureaucracy and delay that slow down a decision-making process.

7. Use relational databases and other technology to collect and store information only once, eliminating both redundancy and error.

Generally, BPR often enables a single person to perform all of the steps in a process by using information technology. One byproduct of BPR is that the need for many employees may be eliminated. This saves a lot of money for organizations. One downside is that it may have the consequence of terrorizing a work force.

Benchmarking

Benchmarking refers to studying how similar organizations to yours perform their business processes, and learning how to adapt those that are most efficient, innovative, and successful. Obviously, no two organizations are alike, and there is no guarantee that copying something from another organization will automatically work well in your own. But certainly there is value in exploring how other organizations are performing some of the tasks your organization does, and discussing what efficiencies they may have found that would improve your business operations. For-profit organizations have been doing this in a formalized way for many years. Nonprofit organizations are only recently recognizing the value of benchmarking.

There are two types of benchmarking that nonprofit organizations might wish to consider. The first, internal benchmarking, looks at your organization and projects future goals, including a process by which employees are encouraged to meet performance targets. External benchmarking, on the other hand, tries to determine the "best practices" of similar organizations. Rather than reinventing the wheel, external benchmarking permits you to allocate minimal resources to finding how others have solved a problem, or have exponentially increased productivity with respect to some process, rather than having to discover that on your own. Many nonprofit organizations are not only willing to share this information, but are quite proud to do so. The fact that competition among nonprofit organizations is almost always either friendly or nonexistent promotes benchmarking in a manner that avoids some of the troublesome potential conflicts and ethical dilemmas in the for-profit context.

Jason Saul, writing in a chapter on benchmarking in *Improving Quality and Performance in Your Non-Profit Organization*, says that nonprofits should typically consider benchmarking in three general categories: A **process** (such as screening job applicants or organizing inventory in a food bank), a **policy** (such as a salary structure or incentive plan), or a **program** (such as welfare-to-work or educational incentives).

The approaches taken to benchmarking include:

- *technical approach* (using computer models, statistics, spreadsheets, and other quantitative methods),

- *committee approach* (bringing in a team of experts from outside of your organization to gather data and make judgments about what changes would be beneficial to the organization), and the

- *survey approach* (combining the above two models by creating a team of individuals from within the organization to identify which processes should be benchmarked, define the measures and organizational performance, obtain the "best practices" information, and implement these practices).

Saul, who is the author of a 1999 book on the subject (*Benchmarking Workbook for Nonprofit Organizations*, published by Wilder Foundation Publishing), recommends a seven-step process for benchmarking. It includes self-assessment, measuring performance, assembling the team, data collection, evaluating practices, translating best practices, and continuously repeating the process.

Outcome-Based Management

To improve quality in a larger organization, simply adopting a progressive management philosophy such as TQM or BPR is not going to be enough in today's modern competitive business climate. As an organization grows, there are more pressures for accountability, not only internally from a board of directors, but externally from elected officials, government funders, foundation funders, individual donors and volunteers, and the public. Leaders of large organizations generally do not have the ability to visualize every aspect of their organization's operations and assess what is going on just by looking out their office windows, or by engaging in informal conversations with their staff and clients. The proverbial "one-minute manager" is an ideal construct that is not particularly well-suited to crystallizing the information a CEO needs to make judgments on how to allocate precious resources.

To accomplish the important task of assessing what is really going on within a large organization, most organizations have a Management Information System (MIS) that permits the aggregation of data in a form that can be analyzed by a manager, enabling him or her to see trouble spots and make adjustments in operations and to generate reports required by the government, funders, auditors, and the board of directors.

For many larger nonprofits, particularly those that depend on government and foundation grants rather than private donations, the objective of "meeting clients' needs" has become a more formalized process. Times have changed within just the last decade or so. Traditionally, measures of organizational performance for human service organizations were based on a model more appropriate for industrial processes, where raw materials were turned into finished products. In the language of industrial systems analysis, inputs (the raw material) were processed into outputs (the finished product). In adopting an analogous frame of reference to industry, the conventional thinking was that human service agencies took in unserved clients (input), provided services (process), and changed them into served clients (output). In this way of thinking, organizations improved their output by increasing the number of clients served.

An exciting new way of looking at the output of an agency is called outcome-based management (OBM) or "results-oriented accountability" (ROA). Most recently, results-oriented management and accountability (ROMA) has become the buzzword describing this general tool. OBM focuses on program outcomes rather than simply quantifying services delivered. Program outcomes can be defined as "benefits or changes for participants during or after their involvement with a program" (from *Measuring Program Outcomes: A Practical Approach, United Way of America*). For example, an organization dealing with reducing drug abuse may have a stellar record of attracting clients through a flashy outreach program. It may be exemplary in convincing doctors in the community to donate thousands of hours of free services to the program, thereby reducing unit costs per client. It may have few complaints from the clients, who feel the staff are competent and treat them with dignity. An analysis of conventional data might indicate that there is little room for improvement. But, perhaps, no data is collected on whether those treated for drug abuse by the organization are successfully able to become independent, avoid future interactions with the criminal justice system, and rid themselves of the scourge of drug dependence for an extended period of time—all measurable outcomes for a successful substance abuse program. If most of these clients are back on the street and drug-dependent, is that organization providing successful treatment, even if drug abuse services are being provided? Are funders and taxpayers getting a fair return on their investment?

In the outcome-based management model, the number of clients served is an input. The output is considered to be measurements concerning the change in the condition of the clients after receiving the services. For example, if thousands of clients are served, but the conditions of the clients have not improved, then the outcome is zero, even if the services were provided 100% on time, every client received a satisfactory number of hours of services, and there were no client complaints. It no longer is indicative of the effectiveness and value of an organization to only collect data on how many clients sought services, how many of these were accepted into the client stream rather than being referred or turned down, how many hours of service were provided, and how much each service cost and was reimbursed. Outcome data together with the above process data is needed to measure the effectiveness and value of an organization.

In addition to a significant change in attitude about the accountability of the private nonprofit sector, the passage in 1993 of the *Government Performance and Results Act,* PL 103-62, changed the way federal agencies plan, budget, evaluate, and account for federal spending. The intent of the act is to improve public confidence in federal agency performance by holding agencies accountable for program results and improving congressional decision-making. It seeks to accomplish this by clarifying and stating program performance goals, measures, and costs "up front." These changes were implemented beginning in September 1997.

For some organizations, the shift to outcome-based management will have modest cost implications. It may mean more data being collected from clients during intake. It may mean follow-up surveys to see what happens to clients after they have availed themselves of the organization's services. When this information is available, it is of extraordinary value to those who design, administer, and deliver those services.

What makes outcome-based management an easy sell to the human services sector is that it is common sense. What is the point of investing thousands, if not millions, of dollars of an agency's resources if the end result is not accomplishing what is intended by the investment—improving the lives of the agency's clients? Our human service organizations have been established to make people's lives better. When our organizations change their focus to concentrating on doing what it takes to make people's lives better, compared with simply providing human services, then it is much more likely that this worthy goal can be accomplished successfully. This is compatible with the values of most in the sector, who often make financial sacrifices to make a difference in the lives of those who need human services.

In cases where the data show that an agency is successfully providing services, but those services are not having the intended effect on the clients, then the agency leadership should be the first to recognize that it is wasteful to continue business as usual. Outcome-based management is a powerful tool that allows organizations to allocate their precious resources to do the most good. If successfully implemented, it also can provide the ammunition to fight the increasing public cynicism about what is often perceived to be a poor return on investment of tax dollars, and provide a competitive edge to organizations that adopt it.

Large Group Intervention

Large Group Intervention (LGI) is the generic name given to a family of formal change management strategies that involve placing large parts of an organization, or even the entire organization, in simultaneous contact with one another to plan how the organization is going to change. Proponents and users of LGIs believe these methods are particularly well suited for organizations that are seeking to establish a shared vision of their future and to build a road to get there. Some LGI models are designed specifically for organizations that are seeking to change the way their work is done (e.g., through reengineering or business process redesign).

Although many different LGI models have been developed and are in current use, they generally have common origins and are rooted in similar principles. Among these principles are getting the "whole system" into interactive discussion, using a carefully designed mixture of communication elements and processes designed to make effective use of participants' emotions as well as thoughts, and facilitating effective dialogue while validating differing perspectives.

Large Group Interventions are usually staged in a setting away from the workplace, where participants can focus on the objective at hand without the distractions of the normal work environment. Artificial boundaries within organizations, such as functional departments, are routinely and intentionally fractured to facilitate communication and participation. These boundaries often get in the way of addressing important needs of organizations. Strategies such as TQM and BPR, as well as strategic planning itself, demand that each member of the organization think about the needs of the entire organization rather than his or her piece of it. "Democratic," participatory efforts by organizations may facilitate their members to see beyond the borders of their individual organizational niche, and develop the spirit required to make TQM not simply a "program" but a working philosophy.

The general philosophy inherent in planning change is to recognize that there is resistance to change within organizations, and change is more likely to be success-fully implemented when people affected can participate in the process, influence the process, and prepare for its consequences.

Much more than a device for overcoming psychological resistance, LGI is an effective approach to substantially improve the planned change and achieve more desirable results for the organization. One dimension of additional benefits is more effective communication about the changes planned. Plans become far less distorted when everyone affected is hearing the same message at the same time, rather than having it communicated through the grapevine, through regular hierarchical chan-nels, or not at all.

Another advantage of LGI is that those affected by the changes can provide invaluable input. It is rare that a few layers of management (or a subset of the full breadth of functions) within an organization can have an adequately detailed grasp of the whole. In most change management strategies, those at the bottom of the hierarchy, who are usually the most aware of the "nuts and bolts" of current reality, are often frozen out of the planning process. Most LGI models bring in a broad base of stakeholders to brainstorm together and to weed out problems and unintended consequences that often are otherwise built into initial designs for change, because they are invisible to the traditionally unrepresentative group of staff involved in planning.

A third advantage of LGI is that it builds a diverse and broad base of support for planned changes. Useful in all cases, this advantage becomes particularly powerful when circumstances alter, planned changes need to be modified, and time is of the essence. Circumstances that otherwise could be expected to derail well-laid plans can be addressed by a robust and already engaged subset of the organization. Plans are far more open to effective alteration midstream when developed via an LGI approach.

LGIs tend to bring together people from various hierarchical levels within the organization, who otherwise may have minimal direct interaction. Many organizational development experts believe that bringing large groups of organizational members together pays an additional dividend of creating positive social linkages among organizational members that would not otherwise have been created. Large Group Interventions create a new and different organizational bonding, which increases networks of informal communication within an organization and makes for more robust capabilities.

All of this can occur in a three-day period, significantly curtailing the process time of conventional change management planning.

Permitting workers affected by planning to participate in the planning process is one strategy to erode resistance to organizational change, in addition to generating fresh ideas from people who have expertise as a result of doing their job every day. They may have shied away from making valid, responsible suggestions, not only because "no one ever asked us," but because they may feel that their views are not important, or that management does not have an interest in listening to them.

Among the most popular models for LGIs are The Search Conference, Future Search Conference, and Real-Time Strategic Change. For additional details about these interventions, consult the book *Improving Quality and Performance in Your Non-Profit Organization.*

Chapter 30
Recent Nonprofit Sector Developments

Since the last edition of the *Nonprofit Handbook* published in April 1997, there have been major developments affecting the nonprofit sector in the United States. The purpose of this chapter is to provide a convenient summary of them.

1. Taxpayer Bill of Rights 2—Intermediate Sanctions

The Taxpayer Bill of Rights 2 was signed into law by President Clinton on July 30, 1996. The principal purpose of this law is to punish individuals affiliated with charities and social welfare organizations who are participating in financial abuses, and to provide the government with a sanction other than simply revoking the charity's exemption status. The law also includes expanded public disclosure requirements for organizational annual federal tax returns.

Previous law required charities to make their 990 tax returns available for public inspection, but did not require that copies be provided. The law was changed to require that if a person requests a copy of the 990 in person, it must be immediately provided for a reasonable fee for copying. If the request is made in writing, it must be provided for a reasonable copying and postage fee within 30 days. Organizations that make these documents "widely available," such as posting them on the Internet, are exempt, although they still must make the document available for public inspection. The law expands the disclosure that must be made on the 990, adding information about excess expenditures to influence legislation, any political expenditures, any disqualified lobbying expenditures, and amounts of "excess benefit" transactions.

The law increases the fine for failure to file a timely 990 from $10 per day to $20 per day, with a maximum of $10,000. Higher fines apply to organizations with gross receipts over $1 million.

Both state and federal law have prohibitions against "private inurement"—permitting a charity's income to benefit a private shareholder or individual. Legislation at the federal level to define what constitutes a prevalent form of private inurement and to refine the definition of a private shareholder was enacted to respond to alleged financial abuses by some organizations that were perceived as providing unreasonable compensation to organizational "insiders."

To curb financial abuses, the law authorizes the IRS to impose an excise tax, 25% in most cases, on certain improper financial transactions by 501(c)(3) and 501(c)(4) organizations. The tax applies on transactions that benefit a "disqualified person," defined as people in positions to exercise substantial influence over the organization, their family members, or other organizations controlled by those persons. Disqualified persons include voting members of the board, the president or chair, the CEO, the chief operating officer, the chief financial officer, and the treasurer, among potential other officers and staff. The benefit to the disqualified person must exceed the value that the organization receives in order to be subject to the tax. To avoid problems, tax experts are advising organizations to treat every benefit to a director or staff person as compensation, and reflect these benefits in W-2s, 1099s, and in their budget documents. Seemingly innocent benefits, such as paying for the travel and lodging expenses for a spouse attending a board retreat or a health club membership for an executive director, may trigger questions about excess benefit. Luxury travel could be considered an excess benefit.

Compensation is considered reasonable if it is in an amount that would ordinarily be paid for similar services by similar organizations in similar circumstances. The term "compensation" is defined broadly, and includes severance payments, insurance, and deferred compensation. The draft regulations provide that a charity with less than $1 million in annual receipts can use salary data from five comparable charities in the same community as evidence that the compensation that charity provides is reasonable.

Most of the provisions relating to intermediate sanctions apply retroactively to September 14, 1995, the date the legislation was first introduced. Steep additional excise tax penalties, up to 200% of the excess benefit plus the initial 25% excise tax, apply to excess benefit transactions that are not corrected in a reasonable amount of time. An excise tax may also be applied to organizational managers (a term that is meant to include an officer, director, or trustee) who approve the excess benefit transaction in an amount of 10% of the excess benefit, up to $10,000 maximum per transaction.

Although these excise taxes apply to individuals and not to the organizations themselves, there is nothing in this law that prohibits organizations from paying the tax or purchasing insurance to cover an individual's liability for the tax penalty. However, if the organization does purchase this insurance, the premium must be considered compensation to the individual. This insurance could become the basis for an excess benefit if total compensation to the individual, including this insurance, exceeds the fair market value that the person provides to the organization in exchange for the total compensation that person receives from the organization. It makes sense to consult an attorney knowledgeable about the *Taxpayer Bill of Rights 2* if there are any questions that would make an organization's directors and staff vulnerable to an IRS audit.

The Internal Revenue Service published draft regulations on this section of the Revenue Code in the *Federal Register* on August 4, 1998. The IRS intended to promulgate final regulations early in 1999, but announced a delay in these regulations until late 1999 or early 2000. The draft regulations can be viewed at the following web site:

http://www.access.gpo.gov/su_docs/fedreg/a980804c.html

The Taxpayer Bill of Rights 2 was signed into law on July 30, 1996. The principal purpose of this law is to punish individuals affiliated with charities and social welfare organizations who are participating in financial abuses. It provides the government with a sanction other than simply revoking the charity's exemption status. The law also includes expanded public-disclosure requirements for annual federal tax returns.

2. Volunteer Protection Act

In July of 1997, President Clinton signed into law the *Volunteer Protection Act*, legislation designed to provide volunteers for nonprofits and governmental entities with a decreased standard of liability.

The law now provides a volunteer whose efforts on behalf of the organization resulted in harming others with a defense against civil lawsuits, unless that harm resulted from the volunteer's "willful or criminal misconduct, gross negligence, reckless misconduct, or a conscious, flagrant indifference to the rights or safety of the individual harmed by the volunteer." The decrease in the liability standard does not apply to volunteers causing harm while under the influence of drugs or alcohol, or while operating a motor vehicle.

The version signed into law differs from previous versions in that it lowers the standard of immunity for volunteers rather than for the charitable organizations providing the volunteer services. This law permits states to enact laws opting out of this new tort standard, although it is not likely that states will choose to do so. Proponents of the legislation pointed to a survey that indicated that one in six potential volunteers refused to participate in volunteer work because of the fear of being sued.

3. U.S. Postal Service Support of Philanthropy

Forty-thousand suggestions for new stamps arrive each year on the doorstep of the Postal Service's Citizens' Stamp Advisory Committee, and only about 30 of these are approved each year. In October 1998, the Postal Service issued a 32-cent stamp honoring philanthropy, with the line "Giving and Sharing: An American Tradition." In April 1998, the Postal Service announced that it would issue a 40-cent, first-class "Semipostal Stamp," in accordance with legislation passed by the Congress in 1997. Up to $60 million of the proceeds from sales of the stamp, after costs for postage, designing, and marketing are deducted, will be contributed to the National Institutes of Health and the Defense Department for breast cancer research. The sale of the stamp is expected to continue for at least two years and, if the experiment is successful, other charities will be petitioning for stamps supporting their causes.

4. IRS Form 990 Disclosure Regulations

Final regulations promulgated by the Internal Revenue Service published April 9,1999 in the Federal Register provide guidance to nonprofit organizations seeking to comply with the 1996 Taxpayer Bill of Rights 2 provision of law regarding public accessibility of Form 990. The full text appears in the *Federal Register*, Vol. 64, No. 68, pp. 17279-17291, and has been posted on several Internet sites, including Independent Sector's (point your browser to *http://www.indepsec.org/programs/* and click on Form 990.pdf). Previous IRS policy required the three most recent 990s and tax exemption application (1023, for 501(c)(3)s) to be available for public inspection at the charity's principal place of business. The final regulations require copies to be provided upon request. Charities may charge a "reasonable fee" for this service, limited to $1 for the first page, 15 cents for each additional page, plus postage. If the request is made in writing, charities have 30 days to send the copy, beginning from the time that payment is received. If the request is made in person, the copies must be provided the same day, unless an "unusual circumstance," such as the temporary absence of staff, does not permit this accommodation. One exception to these rules is that if the organization provides access to its 990 and 1023 by posting them on the Internet, it is excused from the requirement to provide copies. However, it still must make these documents available for public inspection. Another exception has been made if the requests for copies are considered by the IRS to be a part of a harassment campaign against your organization, although you must apply to the IRS for relief. The fine for "willful failure" to allow inspection or provide copies is $5,000, plus $20 for each day that the organization is out of compliance, up to $10,000. There are several national organizations that are willing to post your 990 form for free to facilitate compliance with these regulations for those organizations that do not have their own Web site.

5. Philanthropysearch.com Nonprofit Search Engine Launched

In April 1999, an Internet search engine was created that is intended to provide user sites related solely to the nonprofit sector, reducing irrelevant results. The site, located at: *http://philanthropysearch.com*, is expected to assist nonprofits to find resources of interest about charitable giving, volunteering, advocacy, management, and other issues. The site was founded by Leann Garms, president of the Wentworth Group, a public relations and nonprofit consulting firm. Organizations can post information about their Web sites instantaneously by submitting their Web site addresses to: *http://philanthropysearch.com/submit.html*

Directory of State and National Organizations and Publications of Interest

State Organizations

ALABAMA
Nonprofit Resource Center of Alabama
3324 Independence Dr., Suite 100
Birmingham, AL 35209
Phone: (205) 879-4712, Fax: (205) 879-4724
E-mail: resource@wwisp.com
Web Site: http://www.nonprofit-al.org

ALASKA
Association of Nonprofit Corporations
420 Kayak Drive
Anchorage, AK 99515
Phone: (907) 274-1880, Fax: (907) 345-6714

ARKANSAS
Nonprofit Resources, Inc.
500 Broadway, Suite 403
Little Rock, AR 72201-3342
Phone: (501) 374-8515, Fax: (501) 374-6548
E-mail: nonprofit@aristotle.net
Web Site: http://www.nonprofitresources-ar.org

CALIFORNIA
California Association of Nonprofits
315 West 9th Street, Suite 705
Los Angeles, CA 90015
Phone: (213) 347-2070, Fax: (213) 347-2080
E-mail: info@CAnonprofits.org
Web Site: http://www.CAnonprofits.org

COLORADO
Colorado Association of Nonprofit Organizations
225 E. 16th Avenue, Suite 1060
Denver, CO 80203
Phone: (303) 832-5710, Fax: (303) 894-0161
E-mail: canpo@canpo.org
Web Site: http://www.canpo.org

CONNECTICUT
Connecticut Association of Nonprofits
90 Brainard Road
Hartford, CT 06114
Phone: (860) 525-5080, Fax: (860) 525-5088
E-mail: rcretaro@ctnonprofits.org
Web Site: http://www.CTnonprofits.org

Connecticut Nonprofit Cabinet
c/o CT Association of Human Services
110 Bartholomew Avenue, Suite 4030
Hartford, CT 06106
Phone: (860) 951-2212, Fax: (860) 951-6511
E-mail: pgionfriddo@cahs.org
Web Site: http://www.cahs.org

DELAWARE
Delaware Association of Nonprofit Agencies
100 West 10th Street, Suite 102
Wilmington, DE 19801
Phone: (302) 777-5500, Fax: (302) 777-5386
E-mail: dana@diamond.net.udel.edu
Web Site: http://www.delawarenonprofit.org

DISTRICT OF COLUMBIA
Washington Council of Agencies
1001 Connecticut Avenue, NW, Suite 925
Washington, DC 20036
Phone: (202) 457-0540, Fax: (202) 457-0549
E-mail: wca@wcanonprofits.org

FLORIDA
Florida Association of Nonprofit Organizations
7480 Fairway Drive, #206
Miami Lakes, FL 33014
Phone: (305) 557-1764, Fax: (305) 821-5528
E-mail: (under construction)
Web Site: (under construction)

GEORGIA
Nonprofit Resource Center
The Hurt Building, 50 Hurt Plaza, Suite 220
Atlanta, GA 30303
Phone: (404) 688-4845, Fax: (404) 521-0487
E-mail: nonprofitga@mindspring.com
Web Site: http://www.nonprofitgeorgia.org

ILLINOIS
Donors Forum of Chicago
208 South LaSalle Street, Suite 740
Chicago, IL 60604
Phone: (312) 578-0090, Fax: (312) 578-0103
E-mail: info@donorsforum.org
Web Site: http://www.donorsforum.org

INDIANA
Indiana Association of Nonprofit Organizations
4451 Central Avenue
Indianapolis, IN 46205
Phone: (317) 283-5886, Fax: (317) 283-5887
E-mail: omer01@aol.com

KANSAS
Kansas Nonprofit Association
P.O. Box 47054
Topeka, KS 66647
Phone: (785) 266-6422, Fax: (785) 266-2113
E-mail: mainstrm@inlandnet.net

KENTUCKY
Kentucky Association of Nonprofit Organizations
1623 Foxhaven Drive
Richmond, KY 40476
Phone: (606) 624-2046, Fax: (606) 624-2049
E-mail: awoodman@mis.net
Web Site: http://www.kyriverfoothills.org

LOUISIANA
Louisiana Association of Nonprofit Organizations
P.O. Box 4308
Baton Rouge, LA 70821
Phone: (225) 343-5266, Fax: (225) 343-5363
E-mail: contactus@lano.org
Web Site: http://www.lano.org

MAINE
Maine Association of Nonprofits
565 Congress Street, Suite 301
Portland, ME 04101
Phone: (207) 871-1885, Fax: (207) 780-0346
E-mail: manp@nonprofitmaine.org
Web Site: http://www.nonprofitmaine.org

MARYLAND
Maryland Association of Nonprofit Organizations
Main Office
190 West Ostend Street, Suite 201
Baltimore, MD 21230
Phone: (410) 727-6367, Fax: (410) 727-1914

Silver Spring Office
8720 Georgia Ave., Suite 303
Silver Spring, MD 20910
Phone: (301) 565-0505, Fax: (301) 565-0606
E-mail: mdnp@mdnonprofit.org
Web Site: http://www.mdnonprofit.org

MASSACHUSETTS
Massachusetts Council of Human Service Providers
250 Summer Street, 1st Floor
Boston, MA 02210
Phone: (617) 428-3637, Fax: (617) 428-1533
E-mail: naomi@providers.org
Web Site: http://www.providers.org

MICHIGAN
Michigan Nonprofit Association
29 Kellogg Center
East Lansing, MI 48824-1022
Phone: (888) 242-7075, Fax: (517) 355-3302
E-mail: singhsam@pilot.msu.edu
Web Site: http://www.mna.msu.edu

Michigan League for Human Services
300 North Washington Square, Suite 401
Lansing, MI 48933
Phone: (517) 487-5436, Fax: (517) 371-4546
E-mail: hn0809@handsnet.org
Web Site: http://www.msu.edu/user/mlhs/

MINNESOTA
Minnesota Council of Nonprofits
2700 University Avenue West, #250
St. Paul, MN 55108
Phone: (651) 642-1904, Fax: (651) 642-1517
E-mail: MCN@mncn.org
Web Site: http://www.mncn.org

MISSISSIPPI
Mississippi Center for Nonprofits
612 North State Street, Suite B
Jackson, MS 39202
Phone: (601) 968-0061, Fax: (601) 352-8820
E-mail: jennifer@netdoor.com
Web Site: http://www.msnonprofits.org

NEW HAMPSHIRE
Granite State Association of Nonprofits
6 Loudon Road, Suite 404
Concord, NH 03301-5327
Phone: (603) 225-1947, Fax: (603) 228-5574
E-mail: gsan@chi.tds.net
Web Site: http://www.nhnonprofits.org

NEW JERSEY
Center for Non-Profit Corporations
1501 Livingston Avenue
North Brunswick, NJ 08902
Phone: (732) 227-0800, Fax: (732) 227-0087
E-mail: center@njnonprofits.org
Web Site: http://www.njnonprofits.org

NEW YORK
Council of Community Services of New York State
200 Henry Johnson Boulevard, Box 17
Albany, NY 12210
Phone: (518) 434-9194, Fax: (518) 434-0392
E-mail: HN4284@handsnet.org

Nonprofit Coordinating Committee of New York
1350 Broadway, Suite 1801
New York, NY 10018
Phone: (212) 502-4191, Fax: (212) 502-4189
E-mail: pswords@npccny.org
Web Site: http://www.npccny.org

NORTH CAROLINA
North Carolina Center for Nonprofits
1110 Navaho Drive, Suite 200
Raleigh, NC 27609-7322
Phone: (919) 790-1555, Fax: (919) 790-5307
E-mail: nccenter@aol.com
Web Site: http://www.ncnonprofits.org

NORTH DAKOTA
North Dakota Association of Nonprofit Organizations
Plaza Center Office Building
1025 North Third Street
Bismark, ND 58501
Phone: (701) 258-9101, Fax: (701) 222-8257
E-mail: ndano@ncdc.com
Web Site: http://www.ncna.org/ND

OHIO
Ohio Association of Nonprofit Organizations
P.O. Box 164353
Columbus, OH 43216-4353
Phone: (614) 280-0233, Fax: (614) 280-0657
E-mail: lonestar@iwaynet.net

OREGON
Oregon Nonprofit Coalition Coordinating Council
1903 SE Ankeny
Portland, OR 97214
Phone: (503) 239-4001, Fax: (503) 236-8313
E-mail: info@tacs.org
Web Site: http://www.tacs.org

PENNSYLVANIA
Pennsylvania Association of Nonprofit Organizations
132 State Street
Harrisburg, PA 17101
Phone: (717) 236-8584, Fax: (717) 236-8767
E-mail: jgeiger528@aol.com
Web Site: http://www.pano.org

RHODE ISLAND
Nonprofit Resources of Southern New England
176 Broad Street
Providence, RI 02903
Phone: (401) 861-1920, Fax: (401) 861-8198
E-mail: craigk@intap.net
Web Site: http://www.ncna.org/RI

SOUTH CAROLINA
South Carolina Association of Nonprofit Organizations
P.O. Box 11252
Columbia, SC 29211
Phone: (803) 929-0890, Fax: (803) 929-0173
E-mail: ephardwick@aol.com
Web Site: http://www.ncna.org/SC

TENNESSEE
Tennessee Nonprofit Association
2012 21st Avenue, South
Nashville, TN 37212
Phone: (615) 385-2221, Fax: (615) 385-2157
E-mail: kfranklin@ccs1.org

TEXAS
Texas Association of Nonprofit Organizations
P.O. Box 12963
Austin, TX 78711
Phone: (512) 627-8266, Fax: (888) 467-4238, Fax: (512) 478-5014
E-mail: pbrownlie@austin.rr.com
Web Site: http://www.tano.org

UTAH
Utah Nonprofits Association
1901 E. South Campus Drive, Room 2120
Salt Lake City, UT 84112
Phone: (801) 581-4883, Fax: (801) 585-5489
E-mail: jrandall@cppa.utah.edu
Web Site: http://www.nonprofit.utah.org/UNA

VERMONT
The Vermont Alliance of Nonprofit Organizations
P.O. Box 8345
Burlington, VT 05402
Phone: (802) 862-0292, Fax: (803) 862-0292
E-mail: VTNONPROF@aol.com

WASHINGTON
The Evergreen State Society
PO Box 20682
Seattle, WA 98102-0682
Phone: (206) 329-5640, Fax: (206) 322-8348
E-mail: info@tess.org
Web Site: http://www.tess.org

Northwest Nonprofit Resources
525 East Mission Avenue
Spokane, WA 99202
Phone: (509) 484-6733, Fax: (509) 483-0345
E-mail: sgill@iea.com
Web Site: http://www.indra.com/nnr

National Organizations

American Society of Association Executives
1575 I Street, NW
Washington, D.C. 20005-1168
phone: (202) 626-2723; fax: (202) 371-8825
E-mail: membersvcs@asaenet.org
Web Site: http://www.asaenet.org

The Foundation Center
79 Fifth Avenue
New York, NY 10003-3076
phone: (212) 620-4230; fax: (212) 691-1828
E-mail: feedback@fdncenter.org
Web Site: http://fdncenter.org

Independent Sector
1848 L Street, NW
Washington, D.C. 20036
phone: (202) 659-2729; fax: (202) 575-2666
http://www.indepsec.org

Mandel Center for Nonprofit Organizations
Case Western Reserve University
10900 Euclid Avenue
Cleveland, OH 44106
phone: (216) 368-1690; fax: (216) 368-1690
Web Site: http://www.cwru.edu/msass/mandelcenter/

National Council of Nonprofit Associations
1900 L Street, NW
Suite 605
Washington, D.C. 20036-5024
phone: (202) 467-6262; fax: (202) 467-6261
E-mail: ncna@ncna.org
Web Site: http://www.ncna.org

National Center for Nonprofit Boards
1828 L Street, NW
Suite 900
Washington, D.C. 20036
phone: (202) 452-6262; fax: (202) 452-6299
E-mail: ncnb@ncnb.org
Web Site: http://www.ncnb.org

National Society of Fund Raising Executives
1101 King Street
Suite 700
Alexandria, VA 22314
phone: (703) 684-0410; fax: (703) 684-0540
E-mail: nsfre@nsfre.org
Web Site: http://www.nsfre.org

The Union Institute
Office for Social Responsibility
1710 Rhode Island Avenue, NW
Suite 1100
Washington, D.C. 20036
phone: (202) 496-1630; fax: (202) 496-1635
Web Site: http://www.tui.edu

Publications of Interest

Nonprofit Issues (monthly)
PO Box 482
Dresher, PA 19025-0482
phone: (215) 542-7547; fax: (215) 542-7548
E-Mail: info@nonprofitissues.com
Web Site: http://www.nonprofitissues.com

Nonprofit Times (monthly)
Circulation Department
240 Cedar Knoll Road
Suite 318
Cedar Knolls, NJ 07927
phone: (201) 734-1700; fax: (973) 734-1777
Web Site: http://www.nptimes.com

Chronicle of Philanthropy (biweekly)
PO Box 1989
Marion, OH 43306-4089
phone: 1-800-728-2819; fax: (202) 223-6292
E-Mail: subscriptions@philanthropy.com
Web Site: http://www.philanthropy.com

Nonprofit and Voluntary Sector Quarterly
Sage Publications, Inc.
2455 Teller Road
Thousand Oaks, CA 91320
phone: (805) 499-0721; fax: (805) 499-0871
E-mail: order@sagepub.com
Web Site: http://www.sagepub.com

State Directory

How to Use this State Directory

The following pages provide state-specific, summary information on incorporation procedures, lobbying registration, tax-exemption eligibility, and charitable solicitation qualification for all 50 states and the District of Columbia.

The information included in this directory is a summary culled from several sources. in preparation for the first edition of this book, the author wrote to each office requesting forms, statutes, instruction booklets, and policies relating to the four general issues. Most responded, although some of the responses were incomplete. The information provided was edited to fit the format for this directory. It was supplemented by information provided by the actual state statutes, which was obtained by research at the State Law Library of Pennsylvania and the Law Library of the Widener School of Law. Additional information was obtained through Internet searches and telephone calls to many of the offices that administer the laws described in the directory. In December 1998, each office received a copy of what appeared in the first edition with a request to make corrections and update it. Again, most, but not all responded. A followup survey was sent in April to those that did not respond. Again, information obtained in law libraries supplemented the material provided by each office,or to fill in missing data.

First, a word of caution. The information concerning these laws and procedures changes frequently. Fees for filing documents often increase annually. State legislatures pass new laws. Courts sometimes rule that some laws are unconstitutional. It is not recommended that you rely solely on the information in this directory. Always consult the contact office whose name, address, and telephone number are included. If for some reason this information has changed, try the switchboard telephone number included at the top of each state page.

Almost all of this information will change over time; telephone numbers change, offices move, governmental reorganization gives and takes away administrative responsibility. And well-meaning government officials sometimes give out wrong information. An effort was made to make the information in this directory as correct and as current as possible.

A second word of caution. The information included in this directory is a condensed and edited summary. For example, a statement in the directory that corporate names "may not be the same as or deceptively similar to another without written consent" may be shorthand for what the law actually states, such as—

> *(2) Except as authorized by subsection (3) of this section, a corporate name shall be distinguishable upon the records of the secretary of state from:*
>
> > *(a) The corporate name of a corporation incorporated or authorized to transact business in the state;*
> > *(b) A corporate name reserved or registered under KRS 271B.1-300;*
> > *(c) The fictitious name adopted by a foreign corporation authorized to trans-*

act business in this state because its real name is unavailable;
(d) The corporate name of a not-for-profit corporation incorporated or authorized to transact business in this state; and
(e) A name filed with the secretary of state under KRS Chapter 362 or 365.

(3) A corporation may apply to the secretary of state for authorization to use a name that is not distinguishable upon his records from one (1) or more of the names described in subsection (2) of this section. The secretary of state shall authorize use of the name applied for if:

(a) The other corporation consents to the use in writing and submits an undertaking in a form satisfactory to the secretary of state to change its name to a name that is distinguishable upon the records of the secretary of state from the name of the applying corporation; or
(b) The applicant delivers to the secretary of state a certified copy of the final judgment of a court of competent jurisdiction establishing the applicant's right to use the name applied for in this state.

(excerpt from 273.177 of the Kentucky Revised Statutes)

A third word of caution. In an undertaking of the magnitude of this book, some mistakes are inevitable. Misunderstandings from reading a statute, typographical errors, and misinformation obtained from direct interviews all potentially create mistakes. Again, the purpose of this directory is to provide a summary guide to issues which you will find useful when you consider these issues. Don't rely on this information as the final word. Even if there is not a single mistake in this Directory, which is unlikely, the information changes over time.

Finally, some assumptions are made, and some information does not explicitly appear in the directory. You can assume that only one incorporator is required unless this is explicitly contradicted. If there is no provision relating to renewability of a name reservation, you can assume that it is renewable (although the statute may be silent on this issue). Almost every state provided forms required for lobbying registration and charitable solicitation registration. Many states provided blank forms for incorporation. Some states have publications concerning these four issues which, for one reason or another, were not provided to me, but may be available upon request. There are commercial publishing firms, such as West Publishing (1-800-328-9352), which, for a fee, will provide the entire corporations code for an individual state.

Let me know if the format and content was useful to you in starting your organization, or if you have a suggestion for a future edition. Contact me by e-mail at: Gary.Grobman@paonline.com or write to me c/o the publisher.

Alabama

Central Switchboard: (334) 242-8000
State Web Home Page: http://www.state.al.us/

INCORPORATION

Contact:

> Office of the Secretary of State
> Corporation Division
> P.O. Box 5616
> Montgomery, AL 36103-5616
> (334) 242-5324

Citation: *Alabama Non-Profit Corporation Act,* Title 10, Chapter 3A, Code of Alabama.

Publications Available: A sample Articles of Incorporation form is provided by the contact office; corporate forms may be downloaded at the web site.

General Requirements: One or more persons, partnerships or corporations may act as incorporators. Articles of Incorporation must set forth the name of the corporation; duration; purposes; a statement as to whether the corporation will have members; the street address of the registered office and the name of the registered agent at that office; the names and addresses of directors (must have at least three directors); the name and address of each incorporator; and any provision for the regulation of the internal affairs of the corporation, including a provision for distribution of assets on dissolution or final liquidation.

Corporate Name: Shall not contain a word or phrase which indicates or implies that it is organized for one or more purposes other than permitted by the articles; shall not be the same as, or deceptively similar to another; shall be transliterated into letters of the English language if it is not in English.

Name reservation: Not permitted.

How to File: The original and two copies of the Articles of Incorporation must be filed in the county where the corporation's registered office is located. The Judge of Probate's filing fee is

$25 and the Secretary of State's filing fee is $20.

Other Filings/reports: None required.

LOBBYING

Contact:

> Secretary of the Senate
> Alabama State House
> 11 S. Union Street
> Montgomery, AL 36130-4600
> (334) 242-7803
>
> Ethics Commission
> RSA Union
> 100 N. Union; Suite 104
> Montgomery, AL 36104
> (334) 242-2997

Citation: § 36-25-16 et seq.

Publications: *The Ethics Law* is provided by the contact office.

Registration required: Registration is required by the House and Senate each calendar year. The form discloses general information, including name, address, business name and address, and areas of interest. There is no fee to register with the General Assembly. All lobbyists must register with the Ethics Commission no later than January 31, or within 10 days of qualifying as a lobbyist. There is a $100 annual fee. Registration statement discloses general information, information about clients, the subject matter which is the target of lobbying, and a statement signed by each client authorizing lobbying on their behalf.

Forms to use: *Lobbyist Registration Form.*

Reporting requirements: Quarterly expense reports are due January 31, April 30, July 31, and October 31 covering the preceding quarter. The reports disclose certain expenses valued at more than $250 that are expended within a 24-hour period on a public official, public employee and members of his or her respective household, with the name of the beneficiary of the expense; the nature and date of financial transactions between the lobbyist and public officials or candidates valued in excess of $500 per quarter (not including campaign contributions); information about loans given to or promised to such persons; and a statement of any direct business relationships with such persons or members of their households.

TAX EXEMPTIONS

Contact:

> Alabama Department of Revenue
> Corporate Income Tax Section
> PO Box 327430
> Montgomery, AL 36132
> (334) 242-1200 (income tax information)
> (334) 242-1490 (sales tax information)

Citation: §40-18-32—Corporate Income taxes; §40-23-5—Sales and Use taxes.

Requirements: Certain organizations are explicitly exempt from sales and use taxes, including Goodwill Industries, Elks Club, Diabetes Trust Fund, some veterans organizations, rescue service organizations, and volunteer nonprofit rescue units. Most nonprofits are exempt from corporate income taxes other than unrelated business income taxes.

Application Procedure: No forms are required for sales tax exemptions; show vendor the reference in the statute. No return is required for exemption from corporate income tax; send the Department a copy of the IRS determination letter.

CHARITABLE SOLICITATION

Contact:

> Office of the Attorney General
> Alabama State House
> 11 South Union Street
> Montgomery, AL 36130
> (334) 242-7300

Citation: Alabama Charitable Solicitations Act, Code of Alabama, 13A-9-70 —13A-9-76.

Publications: Copies of the law and forms are provided by the contact office.

Initial Registration: Non-exempt organizations which intend to solicit charitable contributions in excess of $25,000 for each fiscal year or which pay fundraisers, must file a *Charitable Organization Registration Statement* with the contact office. The statement discloses general information about the organization. The statement must be accompanied by a copy of the organizational charter; Articles of Incorporation and bylaws; and a statement setting forth where and when the organization was legally established, the form of the organization, and its tax exemption status. The federal or state tax exemption determination letters must be attached. A fee of $25 payable to the Office of the Attorney General must be paid at the time of registration.

Annual Reports: Within 90 days of the close of the organization's fiscal year ending after the date on which it files its initial registration, it must file an annual written report. The report must include a financial statement covering the fiscal year setting forth gross income, expenses and net income; a balance sheet; a schedule of activities; and the amounts expended for those activities. An IRS 990 may be submitted in lieu of this report.

Organization Solicitation Disclosure Requirements: See below.

Paid Solicitor Requirements: Professional fundraisers must register, pay an annual fee of $100, and post a bond of at least $10,000. Those employed by professional fundraisers as professional solicitors must also register and pay an annual filing fee of $25. The registration expires on September 30 each year. Professional fundraisers must disclose their names, that they are professional fundraisers, and the percentage of funds going to the charity.

Fundraising Counsel Requirements: None.

Alaska

Central Switchboard: (907) 465-2111
State Web Home Page: http://www.state.ak.us/

INCORPORATION

Contact:

Alaska Department of Commerce
Corporations Section
PO Box 110808
Juneau, AK 99811-0808
(907) 465-2530

Citation: AS Title 10, 10.20 et seq.

Publications Available: A sample Articles of Incorporation form is provided by the contact office.

General Requirements: Three or more natural persons at least 19 years of age may act as incorporators. The Articles must include the corporate name; the period of duration; the purpose(s); provisions relating to the internal regulation of the corporation including provisions for distribution of assets upon disolution or final liquidation; the physical address of its initial registered office and the name of its initial registered agent; the number of directors constituting the initial board of directors; their names and addresses (must be at least three); and the name and address of each incorporator. Issues relating to whether the corporation has members shall be set forth in either the Articles or the bylaws.

Corporate Name: May not contain a word or phrase implying that the corporation is a municipality; may not imply that it is organized for a purpose other than one or more purposes contained in the Articles of Incorporation.

Name reservation: A $25 fee is charged for reservation of corporate name. The reservation is valid for 120 days, is nonrenewable, but is transferable.

How to File: Submit the original and an exact copy of the Articles of Incorporation along with a $50 filing fee. Fax filings of all documents are accepted at (907) 465-3257.

Other Filings/reports: Biennial corporate reports must be filed with the Division. There is a filing fee of $15. The report is due every other year from the year of incorporation. Report forms are mailed out by the Division at least 30 days in advance of the due date, and are due on July 2.

LOBBYING

Contact:

Alaska Public Offices Commission
PO Box 110222
Juneau, AK 99811
(907) 465-4864

Citation: Regulation of Lobbying Law, AS 24.45.

Publications: Manual of Instructions for Lobbyists and Employers of Lobbyists and forms are available from the contact office.

Registration: Registration is required before engaging in lobbying activities. All lobbyists must register; those that receive a fee or salary must also pay a $100 lobbyist registration fee. If a registration is filed under a firm name, the $100 fee must be paid for each individual within the firm who is designated to lobby. Registrations must be renewed annually and expire at the end of each calendar year. Those who employ lobbyists must certify the lobbyist registration authorizing the activity.

Forms to use: APOC Form 24-1, Lobbyist Registration Statement for Lobbyists; APOC Form 24-4 for employers of lobbyists.

Reporting requirements: Paid lobbyists are required to submit monthly reports when the legislature is in session, and quarterly reports after adjournment. Reports must be submitted even if there is no reportable activity. Monthly reports are due on or before the last day of the month after the month which is the subject of the report; quarterly reports are due on or before the last day of the month which succeeds the quarter which is the subject of the report. The Commission sends a reminder two weeks before each report due date. Disclosure on the reports includes itemizations of any gifts made to public officials valued at more than $100; an exchange of more than $100 in value of money, goods or services with any public official or member of a public official's immediate family, or an exchange of more than $100 in value with a business entity that is owned or controlled by a public official. Schedule A is a summary of income and expenditure activity. Employers of lobbyists must file APOC Form 24-4 quarterly, due on or before the last day of the month which succeeds the quarter which is the subject of the report. The reports disclose the amounts of payments made to influence administrative and legislative action and the date and nature of any gift exceeding $100 in value to a public official, as well as in-house lobbying costs.

TAX EXEMPTIONS

Contact:
> Alaska Department of Revenue
> State Office Building
> PO Box 110420
> Juneau, AK 99411-0400
> (907) 465-2320 (Juneau)
> (907) 269-6620 (Anchorage)

Citation: §10.06.845(c).

Requirements: There is no state sales tax. An exempt organization is required to file a return using federal form 990. If the organization files a federal 990T, an Alaska return (form 04-611) accompanied by a copy of the 990T must be filed.

Application Procedure: Send a copy of the organization's 990 and 990T (if applicable) to the Department of Revenue.

CHARITABLE SOLICITATION

Contact:
> Alaska Department of Law
> Attorney General's Office
> 1031 W. 4th Avenue
> Suite 200
> Anchorage, AK 99501-1994
> (907) 276-3550

Citation: Chapter 68, Sec. 45.68 et seq.

Publications: Copies of the statute and forms are provided by the contact office.

Initial Registration: All organizations soliciting charitable contributions in excess of $5,000 during a fiscal year must register with the Department of Law. There is no registration fee.

Annual Reports: Registration is annual, and expires on September 1 each year. Registration discloses general information about the organization; its purpose; a summary of its programs and activities; how a citizen can verify and observe these activities; names and titles of three officers or employees receiving the greatest compensation from the organization; names, addresses and telephone numbers of paid solicitors; and information about federal tax exempt status. Copies of the most recent Form 990 and/or audited financial report must be provided, or financial information must be provided on the form.

Organization Solicitation Disclosure Requirements: See below.

Paid Solicitor Requirements: Must register with the Department; must have a bond of $10,000 if less than 60% of the amount raised goes to the charity; must have a written contract with the charity in an approved form. Before a solicitation, a paid solicitor shall clearly and conspicuously disclose the true name of the person making the solicitation; the true name of the charity; the true name of the paid solicitor; the name of the person who is employing and compensating the person making the solicitation; whether the person making the solicitation is being paid or is an unpaid volunteer; the name and address of the principal headquarters of the charity; a description of how the donation will be used; and that a financial statement of the charity, and a copy of the paid solicitor's contract, will be provided upon request.

Fundraising Counsel Requirements: None.

Arizona

Central Switchboard: (602) 542-4900
State Web Home Page: http://www.state.az.us/

INCORPORATION

Contact:

>Arizona Corporation Commission
>1300 West Washington
>Phoenix, AZ 85007-2929
>(602) 542-3135

Citation: Arizona Revised Statutes, Title 10, Chapter 24, 10-3101 et seq. (complete text can be viewed at: http://www.azleg.state.az.us).

General Requirements: Articles of Incorporation shall set forth the corporate name, a brief statement of the affairs which the corporation initially intends to conduct, the name and address of the initial statutory agent, the names and addresses of the initial board of directors, a statement whether or not the corporation will have members, the name and address of each incorporator, optional provisions relating to director liability, and other optional provisions.

Corporate Name: Shall not contain a word or phrase which indicates or implies that it is organized for one or more purposes other than permitted by the Articles; and is distinguishable from another if it is not so identical to a name that in the judgment of the Commission the corporate name is likely to mislead the public.

Name reservation: May be reserved for 120 days for a fee of $10.

How to File: Check availability of corporate name with the Commission, sign and date a Certificate of Disclosure, and deliver the original and one copy of the Articles of Incorporation to the contact office with the $40 filing fee. A copy will be returned when all requirements are satisfied. Advise the Commission in writing of the fiscal year end date adopted by the corporation, publish in three consecutive issues an approved copy of the Articles in a newspaper of general circulation in the home county within 60 days, and file an affidavit evidencing this publication.

Other Filings/reports: An annual report is due on or before the date assigned by the Commission. There is a $10 fee. The report discloses general information; a statement of the character of the corporation's affairs; a statement that all corporate income tax returns have been filed; a statement of financial conditions; whether or not the corporation has members; and a certificate of disclosure relating to any criminal misconduct by the organization's officers, directors, trustees and incorporators.

LOBBYING

Contact:

>Office of the Secretary of State
>1700 West Washington
>7th Floor
>Phoenix, AZ 85007-2808
>(602) 542-8683

Citation: Title 41, Chapter 7, Article 8.1.

Publications: "Lobbyist Handbook" is available from the contact office.

Registration required: Organizations which employ lobbyists must register within five business days after any lobbying activity. Registration must be renewed in November of even-numbered years unless the organization no longer engages a lobbyist. Lobbyists must register within 30 days of being listed on a principal (client) registration form, and re-register in odd-numbered years. The registration fee is $25 for each principal and is valid for a two-year period.

Forms to use: For principal registration, use form PRG-1; for lobbyist registration, use form LRG-1; for Principal Annual Report, use Form PAR-1.1; for lobbyist quarterly report, use Form LQER-1.3.

Reporting requirements: Lobbyists must itemize expenditures of more than $20 according to date, amount, name of state officer or employee, nature of expenditure, and name of lobbyist or other person making the expenditure on the principal annual report. Gifts greater than $10 to a state officer or employee are prohibited. Expenditure reporting is grouped by the categories of food or beverages, entertainment, travel and lodging, flowers, and other expenditures.

TAX EXEMPTIONS

Contact:

Arizona Department of Revenue
1600 West Monroe
Phoenix, AZ 85007-2650
(602) 255-2060 (in Phoenix or outside Arizona)
(520) 628-6421 (in Tucson)
(800) 843-7196 (elsewhere in Arizona)

Citation: Arizona Revised Statutes titles 42 and 43, §43-1201; Arizona Administrative Code R15-5-182.

Publications: *Non-Profit Organizations* (publication 501) and *Arizona Sales Tax, Organizations Exempt from Sales Tax* (publication 500) are available from the contact office.

Requirements: Organizations with federal tax exemptions are generally exempt from state income tax. 501(c)(3) organizations are exempt from the transaction privilege tax (sales tax) on sales of retail items but may not be exempt from taxes on some activities such as commercial rentals, transporting, amusements, and personal property rentals.

Nonprofit organizations are generally not exempt in making purchases from retailers other than hospitals, rehabilitation programs for the mentally and/or physically handicapped, or qualifying health care organizations. Such organizations must obtain written approval for exemption on an annual basis.

Application Procedure: For sales tax exemptions, submit the request to the Arizona Dept. of Revenue by December 1 for succeeding year exemptions. Include a copy of the IRS determination letter. Exemptions may be granted retroactively for up to four prior years.

CHARITABLE SOLICITATION

Contact:

Office of the Secretary of State
1700 West Washington—7th Fl.
Phoenix, AZ 85007-2808
(602) 542-4286

Citation: A.R.S. § 44-6551 et seq.

Publications: A copy of the statute and forms are available from the contact office.

Initial Registration: All organizations which solicit at least $25,000 in charitable contributions annually must register with the Secretary of State. The statement, filed on form CS-1, includes general information about the charity; its officers and directors; any paid solicitors; a general description of the methods, locations, types and amounts of solicitations; the duration of its solicitation period; financial information (which may include a form 990); information about previous misconduct by any contracted fundraiser; and a description of the purpose of the charitable organization. Organizations established and operated in Arizona exclusively for a charitable purpose with unpaid board members, and whose solicitations are conducted by unpaid volunteers or paid employees of the charitable organization, are also exempt. There is no registration fee.

Annual Reports: Registration is required to be repeated each January.

Organization Solicitation Disclosure Requirements: See below.

Paid Solicitor Requirements: Must register by using form CS-3, pay a $25 registration fee, and post a $25,000 bond. Registration is valid for one year and may be renewed with the application and registration fee. Contracted fundraising solicitors must disclose, at any time during the solicitation, the name of the charity and the name of the contracted fundraiser. For oral solicitations, the solicitor must provide a written confirmation within five days which includes the name of the charity, the name of the contracted fundraiser, that information relating to the charity is available for public inspection, and the toll-free number of the Secretary of State. Written solicitations must include all of the above.

Fundraising Counsel Requirements: None.

Arkansas

Central Switchboard: (501) 682-3000
State Web Home Page: http://www.state.ar.us/

INCORPORATION

Contact:

> Secretary of State
> Corporations Division
> Aegon Building, Suite 310
> 501 Woodlane
> Little Rock, AR 72201-1010
> (501) 682-3409

Citation: *Arkansas Non-Profit Act* (Act 1147 of 1993), Title 4, §4-33-101 et seq.

Publications Available: An Articles of Incorporation sample form is available from the contact office.

General Requirements: One or more persons may act as incorporators. Articles of Incorporation must set forth the corporate name, the type of nonprofit corporation (public benefit, mutual benefit, or religious corporation), whether the corporation will have members, how assets will be distributed upon dissolution, the street address of the corporation's initial registered office, the name of its initial registered agent at that office, and the signatures and addresses of each incorporator.

Corporate Name: Shall not contain a word or phrase which indicates or implies that it is organized for one or more purposes other than permitted by the Articles; must be distinguishable from another without written consent.

Name reservation: May be reserved for a non-renewable period of 120 days by filing an application with a $25 fee.

How to File: File Articles of Incorporation in duplicate with the Secretary of State along with a $50 filing fee. A filed-stamped duplicate is returned. Submit the filed-stamped copy to the county circuit court.

Other Filings/reports: None.

LOBBYING

Contact:

> Secretary of State
> Elections Department
> State Capitol
> Little Rock, AR 72201-1094
> (501) 682-3476

Citation: *The Disclosure Act for Lobbyists and State and Local Officials*, 21-8-401 et seq.

Publications: A copy of the statute and forms are provided by the contact office.

Registration required: Lobbyists who either receive more than $250 per quarter for lobbying, or who spend more than $250 per quarter for lobbying, must register within five days of beginning to lobby using the *Lobbyist Registration* form. There is no fee for registration. Lobbyists must submit this form to the Secretary of State. The one-page form discloses information about the nature or kind of business represented by the lobbyist, the branch of government lobbied, and the address where the lobbyist's records may be inspected. Annual registration is renewed by January 15.

Reporting requirements: Lobbyists must file a monthly activity report if the legislature is in session and all lobbyists must file a quarterly report. The reports itemize expenditures for food, entertainment, living accommodations, advertising, printing, postage, travel, telephone, office expenses, other expenses, and other services for each lobbying client. Gifts of $100 or more to public servants must also be reported as well as spending on any individual public servant in excess of $25. Lobbyists must also report details concerning any direct business association with public servants they lobby.

TAX EXEMPTIONS

Contact:

Department of Finance and Administration
7th and Wolfe
PO Box 1272
Little Rock, AR 72203
(501) 682-4775 (income tax information)
(501) 682-7104 (sales tax information)

Citation: 26-54-102 et seq.; 26-51-303 (income tax).

Requirements: Nonprofit corporations and those exempt from federal income tax are generally exempt from the annual corporate franchise tax. Generally, organizations with 501(c)(3) and (c)(4) federal exemptions, as well as certain fraternal organizations, cemeteries, nonprofit business leagues, and certain agricultural, labor and horticultural organizations are exempt from the corporate income tax. There are limited exemptions from the sales tax for named organizations, such as the Boy Scouts, Girl Scouts, and boys and girls clubs.

Application Procedure: Organizations with an IRS determination letter should file a copy of that letter, a copy of pages one and two of their form 1023 or 1024, and a statement declaring Arkansas Code exemption. Organizations without an IRS determination letter should submit an Arkansas Form AR1023CT; a copy of their Articles of Incorporation, Articles of Association, or copy of Trust Indenture or Agreement; and a copy of their bylaws. Those exempt from sales tax must present a copy of the regulation to the vendor.

CHARITABLE SOLICITATION

Contact:

Office of the Attorney General
200 Tower Building
323 Center Street
Little Rock, AK 72201
(501) 682-6150

Citation: Act 1177 of 1991.

Publications: *A Synopsis of Act 1177 of 1991* is provided by the contact office.

Initial Registration: Before engaging in fundraising activities, charitable organizations must register with the Attorney General, unless they raise less than $10,000 each year and conduct their promotions solely by volunteers without any inurement to any officer or member. Some organizations, such as hospitals and volunteer fire companies, are exempt from registration and reporting requirements but must maintain and make available information which they would otherwise be required to report.

Annual Reports: Organizations that do not file a 990 but have received contributions in excess of $10,000 during the previous calendar year must report the gross amount of contributions pledged, the amount allocated and dedicated to the charitable purpose represented in each promotion, the aggregate amount paid for each promotion including overhead; and the aggregate amount paid to, and to be paid to, professional fundraisers and solicitors. Organizations that do file a 990 must submit a copy of it. Reports or 990s must be filed on or before May 15 of each year.

Organization Solicitation Disclosure Requirements: If asked, a solicitor must disclose what percentage of funds raised go to the charitable purpose and what percentage goes to the solicitor; before accepting funds, the solicitor must disclose the identity of the person responsible for the solicitation and whether the solicitor is being paid for his or her efforts.

Paid Solicitor Requirements: Every solicitor must register within 72 hours after accepting employment with a professional fundraiser. There is a $10 annual fee. Fundraisers must register, pay a $100 annual fee, and post a $10,000 bond. All contracts, scripts, pamphlets, handouts and other materials used by professional fundraisers and solicitors must be in writing and kept on file in the office of both the professional fundraiser and the charitable organization. Every contract between a professional fundraiser and a solicitor must be filed with the Attorney General within 3 days of the beginning of the solicitation.

Fundraising Counsel Requirements: Must register, pay a $100 fee and post a $10,000 bond.

California

Central Switchboard: (916) 322-9900
State Web Home Page: http://www.state.ca.us/s

INCORPORATION

Contact:

> Secretary of State
> Document Support Filing Unit
> 1500-11th Street
> Sacramento, CA 95814
> (916) 657-5448

Citation: California Corporations Code sections 5000 to 13356 and sections 14500-14551.

Publications Available: *Organization of California Nonprofit, Nonstock Corporations* is available from the contact office.

General Requirements: The Articles of Incorporation must set forth the corporate name; the required purpose statement (religious, public benefit, or mutual benefit, corporation sole or consumer cooperative); the specific purpose, if applicable; the name and address of the corporation's initial agent for service of process; and the typed or printed name and signature of each incorporator.

Corporate Name: May not have "bank," "trust," "trustee," or related words appear unless a certificate of approval of the Superintendent of Banks is attached; shall not set forth a name which is likely to mislead the public or which is the same as, or resembles so closely as to tend to deceive, the name of another.

Name reservation: May be reserved for a period of 60 days for a fee of $10, but not for two or more consecutive 60-day periods.

How to File: Submit the original Articles of Incorporation, four copies, a $30 Secretary of State filing fee, an *Application for Exemption* from the annual minimum franchise tax, and a $25 processing fee relating to this exemption. Without such tax exemption, there is a $300 or $800 minimum annual franchise tax applicable (see sections 23153 and 23221 of the Revenue and Taxation Code).

Other Filings/reports: Must file a statement of officers within 90 days of incorporation, and annually by the anniversary month of incorpora-

tion. A preprinted form (Form SO-100) is mailed to the organization at the time of initial filing of the Articles, and automatically mailed each year prior to the annual due date.

LOBBYING

Contact:

> Secretary of State, Political Reform Division
> 1500 11th Street
> PO Box 1467
> 1500 11th Street
> Sacramento, CA 95814-1467
> (916) 653-6224

Citation: *Political Reform Act of 1974*, as amended, Government Code §81000-91015.

Publications: *Lobbying Disclosure Information Manual* and forms are available from the contact office.

Registration required: Lobbyists who receive $2,000 or more in any calendar month to lobby, or whose principal duties as an employee are to communicate directly or through his or her agents with any elective state official, agency official, or legislative official for the purpose of influencing legislative or administrative action, must file a *Lobbyist Certification Statement* (Form 604) with the Political Reform Division within 10 days of qualifying as a lobbyist; lobbying firms must register (form 601) no later than 10 days after qualifying as a lobbying firm. The registration form must include a recent head and shoulders-only photo of each lobbyist. Lobbyist employers/lobbying coalitions must register within 10 days after a partner, owner, officer, or employee qualifies as an in-house lobbyist (form 603). Lobbyist employers and lobbying coalitions which only contract with a lobbying firm are not required to register, but must complete a Form 602 authorizing the firm to lobby. Persons who do not employ an in-house lobbyist or contract with a lobbyist, but who spend more than $5,000 in any calendar quarter to influence legislation or administrative actions are not required to register but must file disclosure reports. Lobbying firms, lobbyists, and lobbyist employers must renew registration for each regular session of the State Legislature. Lobbyists pay a $25 fee.

Reporting requirements: All lobbyists (form 615), lobbying firms (form 625), lobbyist employers and lobbying coalitions (form 635) must file a report for each calendar quarter regardless of activities or whether expenditures have been made. The reports are due on the last day of the month following the three months which are being reported. The reports cover "activity expenses" (which include gifts, honoraria, consulting fees, salaries, and other forms of compensation which benefits public officials or their immediate families) and campaign contributions of $100 or more. Lobbying firms have more extensive reporting requirements. Lobbyists are required to attend an orientation course conducted by the Legislature.

TAX EXEMPTIONS

Contact:

> *Franchise Tax Board*
> *PO Box 942840*
> *Sacramento, CA 94279-0040*
> *1-800-852-5711*

For information about sales and use tax exemptions, contact:

> *Board of Equalization*
> *450 N Street*
> *PO Box 942879*
> *Sacramento, CA 94279-0001*
> *1-800-400-7115*

Citation: California Revenue and Taxation Code, § 23701 et seq.

Publications: An FTB 3500 form and instruction booklet are provided by the contact office or http://www.ftb.ca.gov

Requirements: An organization must be organized and operated for purposes described in sections of the Revenue and Taxation Code which parallel many federal 501(c) categories. To avoid paying a substantial franchise tax, file Articles of Incorporation and exemption application together through the Office of Secretary of State rather than the contact office. The statute has explicit exemptions for named charitable organizations; consult the statute or the contact office for more information.

Application Procedure: File form FTB 3500, *Exemption Application*; Articles of Incorporation, bylaws, and sample publications; along with a $25 application fee.

CHARITABLE SOLICITATION

Contact:

> *Office of the Attorney General*
> *Registry of Charitable Trusts*
> *PO Box 903447*
> *Sacramento, CA 94203-4470*
> *(916) 445-2021*

Citation: §17510.1 et seq. of the Business and Prof. Code, and §12580 et seq. of the Government Code.

Reporting Requirements: Charities that collect more than 50% of their annual income and more than $1 million from California donors during the previous calendar year and spend more than 25% of their annual income on non-program activities must provide three copies of a 1-page report to the contact office. The report discloses general information, total revenue and contributions, total salaries, fundraising administration costs, travel expenses, overhead and other administrative expenses, salaries of the five highest-paid employes, and dollar amount and percentage of total revenue and charitable contributions allocated to programs.

Organization Solicitation Disclosure Requirements: Prior to any solicitation, the solicitor must exhibit a "Solicitation or Sale for Charitable Purposes Card." It discloses the name and address of the soliciting organization, the name of the person who signed the card, and the name and business address of the solicitor. In lieu of exhibiting the card, information must be included in the solicitor's brochure which includes, in at least 10-point type, the name and address of the organization; how the money collected will be used (if there is no organization or fund); that an audited financial statement is available; that the organization is not tax-exempt if that is the case; and information about membership and references used to certain law enforcement agencies and veterans organizations, if it makes such references.

Paid Solicitor Requirements: Must pay a $200 registration fee by certified check and post a $25,000 bond or make a $25,000 cash deposit. Annual financial reports are also required to be filed. Paid solicitors must disclose prior to solicitation that the solicitation is conducted by a professional fundraiser, and the name as registered with the Attorney General. They must also disclose, if asked, information about their employer, whether the contributions are tax-deductible, and the percentage of total fundraising expense.

Fundraising Counsel Requirements: If they have gross compensation of more than $25,000, must register annually with the contact office by January 15th, and certify that they have written contracts with their clients with a clear statement of fees. The registration fee is $200.

Colorado

Central Switchboard: (303) 866-5000
State Web Home Page: http://www.state.co.us/

INCORPORATION

Contact:

> Secretary of State
> Commercial Recording Division
> 1560 Broadway, Suite 200
> Denver, CO 80202
> (303) 894-2251

Citation: *Colorado Nonprofit Corporation Act.* 7-20-101 et seq.

Publications Available: *Nonprofit Corporation Guide* (1996) and Articles of Incorporation form are provided by the contact office.

General Requirements: One or more natural persons may establish a nonprofit corporation. Articles must set forth the corporate name; address of the initial registered office and the name of the registered agent at that address; whether the corporation will have members; provisions regarding the distribution of assets upon dissolution; the number of initial directors; and the name, address, and signature of each incorporator.

Corporate Name: Shall not contain any word or phrase which indicates or implies that it is organized for one or more purposes other than permitted by the Articles; shall not be the same as, or deceptively similar to, another without written consent. Shall be transliterated into letters of the English alphabet if it is not in English; if comprised of initials, the initials shall be separated by a full typewriter space of one letter, or each initial shall be followed by a period.

Name reservation: May be reserved for a period of 120 days for a fee of $10. Consecutive reservations are not permitted.

How to File: Articles of Incorporation form must be typed and filed in duplicate with a $50 filing fee. Include a self-addressed envelope.

Other Filings/reports: A biennial report is required which is due between January 1 and May 1 every two years. Corporations incorporated in even-numbered years file each even-numbered year; corporations incorporated in odd-numbered years file each odd-numbered year. The contact office mails reports out on the first of the month in which a corporation was incorporated. The reports are due no later than the end of the second month following the mailing. The report discloses general information, including the names and addresses of directors; and a brief statement on the character of the business.

LOBBYING

Contact:

> Secretary of State
> Lobbyist Section
> 1560 Broadway
> Suite 200
> Denver, CO 80202
> (303) 894-2680; press "2"

Citation: *Colorado Sunshine Law, Regulation of Lobbyists* (Title 24, Article 6, Part 3); Rule 36, Joint Rules of the Senate and House of Representatives.

Publications: *Lobbying Instruction Manual for Professional Lobbyists* is available from the contact office. *How a Citizen Can Testify Before a House Legislative Committee* is available from the Colorado House of Representatives.

Registration required: All lobbyists must register prior to lobbying. Certificates of registration are processed within 24 hours of receipt. Registration expires on January 15 each year. Professional lobbyists register with the Secretary of State's lobbyist section; volunteer lobbyists register with the Clerk of the House of Representatives. There is no fee to register.

Forms to use: *Registration Statement for Professional Lobbyist; Professional Lobbyist Monthly*

Disclosure Statement; volunteer lobbyists use a simple, 1-page registration form.

Reporting requirements: Professional lobbyists disclose information itemizing income and expenditures, gifts, media expenses and the subject matter lobbied.

TAX EXEMPTIONS

Contact:

> Department of Revenue
> 1375 Sherman Street
> Denver, CO 80261
> (303) 232-2446—income tax
> (303) 232-2416—sales tax

Citation: §39-26-114(1)(a)(II)C.R.S.—sales tax; §39-22-304(1)—corporate income tax.

Publications: *Sales Tax Exempt Status for Charitable Organizations: Application Requirements* is available from the contact office.

Requirements: Organizations which have federal 501(c)(3) tax exemptions are generally exempt from state-collected sales tax for purchases made in the conduct of their regular charitable functions and activities, but application must be made to, and approved by, the Department. Charitable organizations with both 501(c)(3) status and a Colorado exemption certificate may also be exempt from collecting sales tax during fundraising events if sales occur for 12 days or less during a calendar year and total sales do not exceed $25,000. Corporations exempt from federal income tax are exempt from the state corporate income tax.

Application Procedure: Apply by filing an *Application for Sales Tax Exemption* for Colorado Organizations (DR 0715).

CHARITABLE SOLICITATION

Contact:

> Office of the Secretary of State
> Licensing Section
> 1560 Broadway, Suite 200
> Denver, CO 80202
> (303) 894-2680

Citation: *Colorado Charitable Solicitations Act,* C.R.S. 6-16-101 et seq.

Publications: A copy of the statute may be obtained from the *Office of Revisor of Statutes, State Capitol, Room 091, Denver, CO, 80203.*

Initial Registration: Prior to any solicitation campaign (which must last one year or less or be newly registered annually), charities employing professional solicitors, and some that do not employ solicitors but do not have 501(c)(3) tax-exemption status, must file a *Solicitation Notice* with the contact office. The notice must include a copy of the contract between the paid solicitor and the charitable organization; the solicitor's full legal name and address and telephone number; when the solicitation campaign will begin and end; the nature of the campaign; address where records are kept; and the charitable purposes for which the campaign is being carried out. The registration fee is $62.50, including a 25% legislative surcharge.

Annual Reports: Professional solicitors or the charity itself must file a *Solicitation Campaign Financial Report* within 90 days after a fundraising campaign has concluded with financial information about the campaign including gross proceeds and the amount actually paid to the charity. The filing fee is $12.50, including a 25% legislative surcharge. The report must be signed by both the paid solicitor and an officer of the charity.

Organization Solicitation Disclosure Requirements: None.

Paid Solicitor Requirements: Must disclose information about their employers; must disclose information about the tax-deductibility of contributions, and that the solicitor is being paid.

Fundraising Counsel Requirements: None.

Connecticut

Central Switchboard: (860) 566-2211
State Web Home Page: http://www.state.ct.us/

INCORPORATION

Contact:

Office of the Secretary of State
Commercial Recording Division
30 Trinity Street
PO Box 150470
Hartford, CT 06115-0470
(860) 509-6001

Citation: *Nonstock Corporation Act,* Conn. Gen. Stat.

General Requirements: The Certificate of Incorporation must set forth the name; nature of activities conducted or the purposes; a statement that it is nonprofit and shall not have or issue shares of stock or pay dividends; whether it is to have members, and, if it does, provisions relating to them; the period of duration; and optional provisions relating to internal regulation and management.

Corporate Name: Shall contain the word "corporation" or "company" or "incorporated" or shall contain the abbreviation "corp." or "co." or "inc." The initial letter may be a capital letter and shall be written in English letters or numbers; shall not describe corporate powers, purposes or authority which the corporation does not possess; shall be distinguishable from other corporations.

Name reservation: May be reserved for a period of 120 days for a $30 fee.

How to File: File Articles of Incorporation with the Secretary of State with a $10 filing fee and the mimimum franchise tax of $30.

Other Filings/reports: An annual report must be filed annually along with a $25 filing fee.

LOBBYING

Contact:

State Ethics Commission
20 Trinity Street
Hartford, CT 06106-1660
(860) 566-4472

Citation: Chapter 10, Part II, Connecticut General Statutes.

Publications: *Lobbyist Code Information for Individual and Business Organization Communicator Lobbyists; Procedures Manual for Lobbyist Recordkeeping and Audit* are provided by the contact office.

Registration required: Individuals or organizations which receive or spend, or agree to spend, more than $2,000 in a calendar year for lobbying activities must register. Registration must occur on or before January 15 or prior to the commencement of lobbying, whichever is later. Registration filed in 1997 covers both 1997 and 1998, unless terminated. The fee is $150, which covers a two-year period. Communicator lobbyists (those engaged in the business of lobbying on behalf of others) must disclose the terms of their compensation including dollar amounts and the issues on which they expect to lobby as well as unreimbursed expenditures for the benefit of a public official. Clients of lobbyists must disclose detailed expenditure information on a periodic basis as well.

Forms to use: Form ETH-1a, *Communicators Biennial Lobbyist Registration;* Form ETH-1b, *Client/In-House Communicator(s) Biennial Lobbyist Registration;* Form ETH-2D, *Lobbyist Financial Report for Use by Client;* Form ETH-2B, *Communicator Lobbyist Report of Contract Terms, Unreimbursed Expenditures;* Form ETH-2A, *Communicator Lobbyist Report of Annual Compensation, Sales Tax and Reimbursement.*

Reporting requirements: Lobbyists must report expenditures; reimbursements for expenditures or gifts made for the benefit of a state employee, public official, candidate for public office, or a member of such person's staff or immediate family; and other lobbying-related payments.

Within the first 10 days of the calendar year, communicator lobbyists must file Form ETH-2A, an annual report of compensation, sales tax and reimbursement received from each client during the previous calendar year. Within 30 days, lobbyists must file Form ETH-NX reporting unreimbursed expenditures of $10 or more for necessary expenses incurred by a public official or state employee. Lobbyists must also file Form ETH-2B to report contract terms and unreimbursed expenditures for each client which must be filed within 10 days after the end of a month in which the General Assembly is in session, and if there was an expenditure or change in a contract to report. If there was not a regular session during that month, the report is due between the first and tenth days of the next April, July or January, whichever is earliest. Client of lobbyists must also file detailed spending reports, using form ETH-2D.

TAX EXEMPTIONS

Contact:
> Department of Revenue Services
> Taxpayer Services Division
> Twenty-Five Sigourney Street
> Hartford, CT 06106
> (860) 297-5962

Citation: Conn. Gen. Stat. §12-412(8), as amended by 1995 Conn. Pub. Acts 359, §2 —sales tax; § 12-710—corporate income tax.

Publications: 1995 Legislative Changes Affecting Exempt Purchases by Exempt Organizations leaflet is available from the contact office.

Requirements: Corporations which are exempt from federal income tax are generally exempt from Connecticut corporate income tax as well, but not until a determination letter is issued.

Sales tax: The Department no longer issues exemption certificates. A new procedure was implemented effective for sales occurring on or after October 1, 1995. Organizations issued exemption permits before July 1, 1995 can continue making purchases exempt from sales and use taxes after July 1, 1995 even if the organization does not qualify under the new exemption criteria. When making an exempt purchase on or after October 1, 1995, the organization must issue to retailers a completed CERT-119, Certificate for Purchase of Tangible Personal Property and Services by Exempt Organizations along with a copy of its exemption permit. If the organization was not issued an exemption certificate by the Department before July 1, 1995, the organization must have a federal determination letter for 501(c)(3) or (c)(13) exemption.

Application Procedure: On Form REG-1, Application for Tax Registration Number, check the appropriate box indicating federal income tax exemption, and provide a copy of the federal determination letter.

CHARITABLE SOLICITATION

Contact:
> Department of Consumer Protection
> Public Charities Unit
> c/o Office of the Attorney General
> 55 Elm Street
> Hartford, CT 06106
> (860) 566-5836

Citation: Solicitation of Charitable Funds Act, Chapter 419d, Section 21a-175 et seq.

Publications: Information for Charitable Organizations on the Connecticut Solicitation of Charitable Funds Act, a copy of the statute, and forms are available from the contact office.

Initial Registration: Organizations soliciting contributions, which normally receive more than $25,000 in contributions annually or which compensate any person primarily to conduct solicitations must register prior to beginning solicitation. Religious institutions, nonprofit hospitals, and government entities are generally exempt from registration. Organizations register by filing a form CPC-63, Charitable Organization Registration Statement along with a $20 filing fee. Registration is effective as soon as it is received by the Department.

Annual Reports: Within five months after the close of each fiscal year, organizations must file a Form CPC-60 (Annual Report Face Sheet); a copy of the organization's IRS Form 990 (and must complete one for the state even if it is exempt from filing it with the IRS) and an audit report if the organization's gross receipts exceed $100,000.

Organization Solicitation Disclosure Requirements: See below.

Paid Solicitor Requirements: Must register annually, pay a fee of $120, and post a bond of $20,000. Contracts must be in writing. Paid solicitors must, for oral solicitations, send a written confirmation within five days to each person who has pledged to contribute. The confirmation shall disclose the name of the solicitor, the fact that the solicitor is being paid, and the percentage of the gross proceeds that the charity will receive. Written solicitations must include the same information. Paid solicitors must file financial reports no more than 90 days after each campaign.

Fundraising Counsel Requirements: Contracts with organizations must be in writing and filed with the Department at least 15 days before services begin.

Delaware

Central Switchboard: (302) 739-4000
State Web Home Page: http://www.state.de.us/

INCORPORATION

Contact:

> Department of State
> Division of Corporations
> PO Box 898
> Dover, DE 19903
> (302) 739-3073

Citation: DCA Title 8, 101 et seq.

Publications Available: A packet entitled *Incorporate in Delaware* is available from the contact office.

General Requirements: Articles of Incorporation must set forth the corporate name; registered office; the registered agent; that the corporation shall be a nonprofit corporation; that it shall not have any capital stock; conditions for membership, if any; and the name and mailing address of each incorporator.

Corporate Name: Must include one of the following words: Association, Company, Corporation, Club, Foundation, Fund, Incorporated, Institute, Society, Union, Syndicate, or Limited, or one of the abbreviations: Co., Corp., Inc., or Ltd.; must be distinguishable from the names of others without written consent; must be in English or transliterated into letters of the English alphabet.

Name reservation: May be reserved for a renewable, 30-day period for a fee of $10.

How to File: Documents must be suitable for scanning (e.g., black ink, 8.5" by 11" with large margins). The filing fee includes $10 for one certified copy. The fee is $50 plus the recorder's fee. The recorder's fee is $24 for the first page plus $9 for each additional page.

Other Filings/reports: An annual report is required. The due date is March 1.

LOBBYING

Contact:

> State Public Integrity Commission
> Tatnall Building, Ground Floor
> 150 William Penn Street, STE 4
> Dover, DE 19901
> (302) 739-2399

Citation: 29 Del. C. §5831 et seq.

Registration required: Lobbyists must register with the Commission before lobbying activity occurs. Registration statement discloses general information, length of employment, and subject matter. Clients of lobbyists must provide to the lobbyist a written authorization to act in their behalf which is filed by the lobbyist. There is no fee for registration.

Forms to use: *Lobbyist Registration Statement; Employer's Authorization; Lobbyist Quarterly Report Form.*

Reporting requirements: On or before the 20th day of the month following each calendar quarter, a report must be filed covering the preceding quarter itemizing total expenditures by food and refreshment, entertainment, lodging expenses, travel, recreation expenses, and gifts and contributions (excluding political contributions). The report must also disclose information about specific expenditures of more than $50 per day which benefitted a member of the General Assembly, or for employees or members of any state agency.

TAX EXEMPTIONS

Contact:

> Department of Finance
> Division of Revenue
> 820 French Street
> Wilmington, DE 19801
> (302) 577-8783

Citation: Title 30, § 1902.

Requirements: Most 501(c)(3)s and (c)(4)s, fraternal benefit societies, business leagues, fire companies, civic leagues, clubs organized and operated exclusively for pleasure, recreation and other nonprofit purposes are exempt from income taxes. The state has no sales tax.

Application Procedure: Send a copy of the organization's IRS determination letter to the Division.

CHARITABLE SOLICITATION

Contact:

> Department of Justice
> Carvel State Building
> 820 N. French Street
> Wilmington, DE 19801
> (302) 577-2500

Citation: Chapter 25, Title 6, Subchapter IX, §2591 et seq.

Delaware has no statute requiring registration of charitable organizations or fundraisers, but such legislation has been proposed. Legislation was enacted in 1996 to protect the public against those who fraudulently solicit contributions. The act also prohibits solicitations after 9 p.m. and before 8 a.m.

Initial Registration: None.

Annual Reports: None.

Organization Solicitation Disclosure Requirements: None.

Paid Solicitor Requirements: The law also requires every professional solicitor to keep accurate fiscal records concerning its charitable/fraternal solicitations in Delaware, and to have written contracts with charities that clearly state their obligations and compensation terms. Professional solicitors must dis-close their identities and that the solicitor is a paid solicitor. They must, upon request, disclose the amount/percentage of the contribution which will be turned over to the charity or a good faith estimate if that amount is not known.

Fundraising Counsel Requirements: None.

District of Columbia

Central Switchboard: (202) 727-1000
Web Home Page: http://www.ci.washington.dc.us

INCORPORATION

Contact:

> Department of Consumer and Regulatory
> Affairs
> Corporate Division
> 941 N. Capitol Street, NE
> Washington, DC 20002
> (202) 442-4430

Citation: *District of Columbia Nonprofit Corporation Act,* § 29-501.

General Requirements: Three or more incorporators over the age of 21 are required for incorporation. Articles of Incorporation must set forth the name of corporation; duration; purpose(s); a statement as to whether the corporation will have members; provisions relating to membership if it will have members; how directors will be elected or appointed (or that this will be provided for in the bylaws); optional provisions relating to the internal management and regulation of the corporation, including any provisions for the distribution of assets upon dissolution or final liquidation; address of the initial registered office and name of the registered agent at that office; the names and addresses of directors (must have at least three directors); the number of directors constituting the initial board of directors and their names and addresses; and the name, address and signature of each incorporator.

Corporate Name: Shall not contain a word or phrase which indicates or implies that it is organized for any purpose other than permitted by the Articles of Incorporation; shall not be the same as, or deceptively similar to another; shall be transliterated into letters of the English language if it is not in English; and shall not indicate that the corporation is organized under an act of Congress.

Name reservation: May be reserved for a 60-day period for a fee of $25; may be renewed once, and may be renewed for an extended reasonable period after "good cause" is shown.

How to File: File an original and one copy of the Articles of Incorporation with the contact office with a fee of $30.

Other Filings/reports: A five-year report is required to be filed along with a $100 filing fee. The report discloses general information, including the names and addresses of directors and officers, and a brief statement of the character of the affairs that the corporation is actually conducting.

LOBBYING

Contact:

> Office of Campaign Finance
> District of Columbia Board of Elections and
> Ethics
> 441 4th Street, NW
> Suite 250N
> Washington, DC 20001
> (202) 727-2525

Citation: §1-1451.

Registration required: Lobbyists must register with the Director of Campaign Finance if they receive compensation or expend $250 or more in any three consecutive calendar month period for lobbying. The registration form must be filed for each person from whom the lobbyist receives compensation. The form discloses general information, information about clients, the nature of the client's business, and information about the matters which are the target of lobbying.

Reporting requirements: Semi-annual reports are due between July 1 and July 10 and in January covering the previous six-month period. The report discloses information on the registration form, expenses itemized by office expenses, advertising and publication, compensation to others, personal sustenance, lodging and travel, and other. Expenditures of $50 or more must be itemized by name and address of the recipient as well as political expenditures, loans, gifts, and honoraria; and information about who has been the target of lobbying activity.

TAX EXEMPTIONS

Contact:
> Department of Finance and Revenue
> Audit Division
> PO Box 556
> Washington, DC 20044
> (202) 727-6070

Citation: Titles 47, §1802, 47-2005 and 47-1508 of the D.C. Code.

Requirements: Nonprofit organizations located in the District of Columbia which provide benefits to D.C. residents may be exempt from the corporation franchise tax, sales and use taxes, and personal property taxes. There is no exemption from unrelated business taxes. A prerequisite for exemption is an IRS exemption from federal taxes. Other provisions apply as well.

Application Procedure: Submit an FR 164 form and the following documents: the organization's IRS tax exemption determination letter; a statement about the type of activities carried on; a copy of the Articles of Incorporation or other governing document; a copy of the bylaws; a complete, detailed statement of assets and liabilities as of the end of the latest annual accounting period; a detailed statement of receipts and expenditures; and a representative sample of publications or literature.

CHARITABLE SOLICITATION

Contact:
> Department of Consumer and Regulatory Affairs
> 614 H Street, NW
> Washington, DC 20001
> (202) 727-7089

Citation: §2-702.

Initial Registration: Charities must register with the Department and pay an $80 registration fee.

Annual Reports: Financial reports are due within 30 days after the end of each licensing period. The Department issues solicitation cards that must be presented to each prospective donor. The report discloses the amount of contributions, expenses, and how the funds were used.

Organization Solicitation Disclosure Requirements:. Solicitors must exhibit a solicitor information card and read or present it to the person being solicited.

Paid Solicitor Requirements: See above.

Fundraising Counsel Requirements: None.

Florida

Central Switchboard: (850) 488-1234
State Web Home Page: http://fcn.state.fl.us/gsd/

INCORPORATION

Contact:
>Secretary of State
>Division of Corporations
>PO Box 6327
>Tallahassee, FL 32314
>(850) 488-9000

Citation: *Florida Not-for-Profit Corporation Act;* Chapter 617, Florida Statutes, 617.01011 et seq.

Publications Available: *Florida Not-For-Profit Corporation Act* which includes forms, laws, and instruction booklets, and other useful state and federal information, is available from the contact office.

General Requirements: Three or more directors are required. Articles of Incorporation must set forth the corporate name; principal place of business and mailing address; purposes; manner of election of directors; limitation of corporate powers; initial registered agent and street address; and the names, addresses, and signatures of each incorporator.

Corporate Name: Must contain the word "corporation" or "incorporated" or the abbreviation "corp." or "inc." or words or abbreviations of like import in language as will clearly indicate that it is a corporation. May not contain the word "company" or its abbreviation "co."; may contain the word "cooperative" or "co-op" only if the resulting name is distinguishable from the name of any corporation, agricultural cooperative marketing association, or nonprofit cooperative association existing or doing business in the state; may not contain language stating or implying that it is organized for a purpose other than permitted by law or by its Articles of Incorporation; may not contain language stating or implying that it is connected with a state or federal government agency or corporation chartered under the laws of the U.S.; must be distinguishable from the names of all other entities.

Name reservation: None.

How to File: Send completed Articles of Incorporation to the Division of Corporations with a filing fee payable to the Dept. of State of $35 plus a fee of $35 to designate the registered agent, plus optional fees of $8.75 for a certified copy of the Articles or an optional fee of $8.75 for a certificate of status.

Other Filings/reports: An annual report must be filed by May 1 with the Secretary of State which discloses general information, including names and addresses of its directors and principal officers; the federal ID number; and other information required by the Department.

LOBBYING

Contact:
>Lobbyist Registration Office
>Claude Pepper Building
>111 West Madison St.; Room G-68
>Tallahassee, FL 32399-1425
>(904) 922-4990

Citation: *Executive Branch Lobbying Registration Act,* Section 11.044-11.062 and 112.3213-3217, Florida Statutes; Joint Rule 1 of the Florida Senate and House of Representatives; Senate Rule 9; House Rule 13.

Publications: *Guide to Legislative Lobbyist Registration and Reporting* is provided by the contact office.

Registration required: Registration for those who lobby the executive branch is separate from registration for those who lobby the legislature; the contact office administers both registrations. All lobbyists must register annually for each client represented; a separate form is required for each client. Registration reports disclose lobbyist's area of legislative interest, name of one principal, and any direct business association or partnership with any member of the Legislature. The fee is $30 for each House for each client and $10 additional for each House for each additional client.

Forms to use: The *Florida Legislature Lobbyist Registration Form; Lobbyist's Expenditure Report for the Florida Legislature; Authorization to Represent the Principal; Executive Branch Lobbyist Registration.*

Reporting requirements: Lobbyists must file reporting statements not later than 45 days after the end of a reporting period. The first report covers January 1 through the date of adjournment of the regular session. The second report covers the remainder of the calendar year. When there is a special session, a separate, supplemental report is required, disclosing expenditures incurred since the last report through adjournment of the special session. Each report provides itemized expenditures for four general categories of expenditures: those made directly by the lobbyist, those made directly by the client, those initiated or expended by the lobbyist and paid by the client, and those initiated or expended by the client and paid for by the lobbyist. These categories are subdivided into itemized expenses for food and beverage, entertainment, research, communication, media advertising, publications, travel, lodging, special events, and other.

TAX EXEMPTIONS

Contact:

> Florida Department of Revenue
> 5050 West Tennessee Street
> Tallahassee, FL 32399-0100
> 1-800-352-3671 (calls originating inside Fl)
> (850) 488-6800 (calls originating outside Fl)

Citation: Chapter 220, Florida Statutes—corporate income tax; Chapter 212, Florida Statutes—sales and use tax.

Publications: A version of the *Florida Tax Guide* is available online at: http://sun6.dms.state.fl.us/dor/

Requirements: Organizations exempt from federal income taxes are generally exempt from state corporate income tax. Most charitable organizations are exempt from sales and use tax.

Application Procedure: Nonprofit organizations which are federally exempt must file Form F-1120 Florida Corporate Income/Franchise and Emergency Excise Tax Return on or before the 1st day of the 4th month following the close of the tax year or the 15th day following the due date of the federal tax return, whichever is later. They must attach a copy of the IRS determination letter for the first year they qualify as an exempt organization or the first year they are subject to the Florida Income Tax Code. Additional returns are not required so long as these organizations continue to qualify for federal exemption. Exempt organizations which have unrelated trade or business income must file Form F-1120 annually and pay Florida Corporate Income Tax. For sales tax exemption, file Form DR-5, *Application for Consumer's Certificate of Exemption* along with a copy of the organization's 501(c)(3) determination letter; Articles of Incorporation; a detailed list of all services and activities currently being provided by the organization; and a detailed, complete statement of income and expenses for the most recent fiscal year. Charitable organizations without a financial history may qualify for a temporary certificate of exemption if they also include a projected one-year budget and an estimate of the organization's expenditures which would be taxable without receiving the exemption.

CHARITABLE SOLICITATION

Contact:

> Florida Department of Agriculture and Consumer Services
> Division of Consumer Services
> Solicitation of Contribution Section
> Second Floor, Mayo Building
> Tallahassee, FL 32399-0800
> 1-800-HELPFLA
> (850) 413-0840

Citation: Chapter 496, Florida Statutes, 496.401 et seq.

Publications: A copy of the statute and forms are provided by the contact office.

Initial Registration: All organizations are required to register with the Department prior to engaging in solicitation activities. The registration fee ranges from $10 (for those with less than $5,000 in contributions annually) to $400 (for those with more than $10 million annually). The registration statement must include the charity's financial report on a form prescribed by the Department or Federal 990 or, for those that are newly formed, a budget for the current fiscal year. Also included must be the name of the charity; the purpose for which it is organized; the purposes for which the contributions will be used; whether there has been certain types of misconduct by those associated with the charity; the tax-exempt status of the charity along with a copy of its IRS determination letter; and information about professional solicitors and fundraising consultants, including the terms of their compensation.

Annual Reports: Annual renewal statements are required which include updates to the information required on the initial registration statement.

Organization Solicitation Disclosure Requirements: Solicitations must disclose the name of the charity; a description of the purposes for which the solicitation is being made; upon request, the name, address, or telephone number to whom inquiries can be made; the amount of the contribution which may be deducted as a charitable contribution under federal law; and the source from which a financial statement may be obtained. The written financial report must be provided within 14 days of the request. Every printed solicitation, written confirmation, receipt or reminder about a contribution must have a disclaimer conspicuously displayed in capital letters:

A COPY OF THE OFFICIAL REGISTRATION AND FINANCIAL INFORMATION MAY BE OBTAINED FROM THE DIVISION OF CONSUMER SERVICES BY CALLING TOLL-FREE WITHIN THE STATE 1-800-HELP-FLA. REGISTRATION DOES NOT IMPLY ENDORSEMENT, APPROVAL, OR RECOMMENDATION BY THE STATE."

Paid Solicitor Requirements: Similar disclosure constraints to those detailed above apply to professional solicitors. Professional solicitors must register with the Department, pay a $300 fee, and post a $50,000 bond. Not less than 15 days before commencing a fundraising campaign, professional solicitors must file a solicitation notice, which includes detailed information, including a copy of the contract with the charity. A financial report of campaign must be filed within 90 days of the conclusion of a campaign or the one-year anniversary of the campaign.

Fundraising Counsel Requirements: Must register and pay a $300 registration fee; no bond is required.

Georgia

Central Switchboard: (404) 656-2000
State Web Home Page: http://www.state.ga.us/

INCORPORATION

Contact:

Secretary of State
315 West Tower
#2 Martin Luther King Jr. Drive
Atlanta, GA 30334
(404) 656-2817 (Corporations Division)

Citation: O.C.G.A. §14-3-202, Georgia Nonprofit Corporation Code.

Publications Available: *Corporation Filing Procedures, Georgia Profit or Nonprofit Corporations* (includes sample Articles of Incorporation) is available from the contact office. Instructions for filing Articles and a sample format may be downloaded from the web site.

General Requirements: Articles must set forth the corporate name; that the corporation is organized as a nonprofit; the street address of the initial registered office (must be in the state) and the initial registered agent at that address; the name and address of each incorporator; whether the corporation will have members; and the mailing address of the initial principal office. Other items required by the IRS code regarding tax exempt status and internal regulation provisions are optional.

Corporate Name: Must contain the word "corporation," "incorporated," "company," or "limited," or the abbreviation "Corp.," "Inc.," "Co.," or "Ltd." or words or abbreviations of like import in a language other than English. May not contain anything, within the reasonable judgment of the Secretary of State, that is obscene; shall not exceed 80 characters excluding spaces and punctuation; must be distinguishable from other corporations or reserved names without written permission from the other entity.

Name reservation: Required prior to incorporation; accomplished by calling the contact office; is valid for 90 days and is not renewable. There is no fee. The name may be reserved online at the office's web site: http://www.sos.state.ga.us

How to File: Reserve the corporate name; file BSR Form 227 (Transmittal Form) with the corporate name reservation number and Articles of Incorporation, and the filing fee of $60. Arrange for newspaper advertisement in the home county of the registered agent's address. The fee for this is $40. The advertisement must appear weekly for two consecutive weeks in a format provided by the Georgia law.

Other Filings/reports: An annual report must be filed with the Secretary of State with general information, including the names and addresses of the CEO, chief financial officer and Secretary. The first report is due 90 days after incorporation, and then between January 1 and April 1 of each year.

LOBBYING

Contact:

State Ethics Commission
8440 Courthouse Square East
Douglasville, GA 30134
(770) 920-4385

Citation: O.C.G.A. 21-5-70 et seq, *The Public Officials Conduct and Lobbyist Disclosure Act of 1992.*

Publications: *Lobbyist Guide* is available from the contact office.

Registration required: All lobbyists must register with the Commission before lobbying activity occurs. All registrations expire on December 31. Registration application must contain name; address; telephone number; the person or agency which employs, appoints, or authorizes the applicant to lobby on its behalf; a statement of the general business purpose of those the applicant represents; and a signed authorization statement by that person or agency. There is no fee for registration.

Forms to use: *Lobbyist Registration Form; Lobbyist Report Form.*

Reporting requirements: Lobbyists registered to lobby the General Assembly or Governor must file a disclosure report within five days following the close of a month that the General Assembly is in session; on or before the fifth day of August covering the period April 1-July 31; and the fifth day of January covering the period August 1-September 31. Reports must be filed whether or not expenditures were made. The reports provide for the name of the public officer for which an expenditure was made; the amount; date of expenditure; description of the expense; and the number of the bill, resolution or regulation that was the target of the expense. The report also requires a listing of any member of a public officer's immediate family employed by, or whose professional services were paid for by, a lobbyist during the reporting period, and their relationship to the public officer.

TAX EXEMPTIONS

Contact:

Georgia Income Tax Division
Tax Exempt Organizations
PO Box 38467
Atlanta, GA 30334
(404) 656-4191

Sales tax:

Sales and Use Tax Division
Trinity-Washington Building
Room 310
Atlanta, GA 30334
(404) 656-4060

Citation: §48-7-25 —income taxes; §48-8-3 — Sales and Use Tax.

Publications: Forms are provided by the contact office.

Requirements: Organizations with federal income tax exemptions are generally exempt from income tax other than unrelated business income tax. Exemption takes effect when the Commissioner grants an exemption using a determination letter. Certain 501(c)(3)s, including many hospitals, nursing homes, and certain educational institutions, are exempt from sales and use tax as provided by the statute. Consult the contact office or the statute for details.

Application Procedure: For income tax exemption, file form 3605 and attach a copy of the Articles of Incorporation or equivalent, bylaws, determination letter, and a copy of the certificate of registration with the Secretary of State (if a corporation). Application requires a narrative description of activities.

CHARITABLE SOLICITATION

Contact:

Secretary of State
Division of Securities and Business Regulation
Suite 802, West Tower
2 Martin Luther King Jr. Drive
Atlanta, GA 30334
(404) 656-4910

Citation: *Georgia Charitable Solicitations Act of 1988,* as amended, O.C.G.A. §43-17-5.

Initial Registration: All organizations and individuals who solicit contributions for charitable purposes must register with the Secretary of State using form C100. The initial registration fee is $25. Registration must be renewed annually or 12 months from the effective date of the current registration using Form C101. Charitable organizations with total gross revenues of under $25,000 in a calendar year are exempt.

Annual Reports: Renewal registrations must include a financial statement, form C101, and a $10 renewal fee. Renewal applications are sent by the Department prior to the expiration date.

Organization Solicitation Disclosure Requirements: Upon solicitation, the organization must disclose its name and location and state that a full description and financial statement or summary of the organization is available upon request.

Paid Solicitor Requirements: Charitable organization registration requires disclosure of the terms of remuneration of paid solicitors and fundraising counsel; contracts must be in writing; must pay a $250 fee and post a $10,000 bond and provide notice prior to campaign.

Fundraising Counsel Requirements: None.

Hawaii

Central Switchboard: (808) 586-2211
State Web Home Page: http://www.state.hi.us

INCORPORATION

Contact:

> Dept. of Commerce and Consumer Affairs
> Business Registration Division
> 1010 Richards Street, 2nd Floor
> PO Box 40
> Honolulu, HI 96810
> (808) 586-2727

Citation: Section 415B, Hawaii Revised Statutes.

Publications Available: *Instructions for Filing Articles of Incorporation* and sample form are available from the contact office.

General Requirements: Articles must set forth the corporate name; street address of the corporation's initial office (PO Box is acceptable only if there is no street address); period of duration; purposes; number of directors (must be at least three); name; title; and residence street address of initial officers and directors; whether the corporation will have members; a statement that the corporation is nonprofit, no stock will be authorized, and that there will be no part of the corporation's income or profit distributed to its members, directors, or officers, except for services actually rendered and except upon liquidation of its property in the case of corporate dissolution.

Corporate Name: Shall not be the same as, or substantially identical to, another without written consent.

Name reservation: May be reserved for a 120-day period for a $20 fee.

How to File: Articles must be typewritten or printed in black ink; signatures must be in black ink; one original should be filed with the contact office along with a $50 filing fee. Include an additional fee of $10 plus 25 cents/page for a certified copy.

Other Filings/reports: Annual reports must be filed with the Director between January 1 and March 31. The first report is due in the year following the year of incorporation; information includes disclosure of general information and a brief statement of the character of the affairs which the corporation is conducting.

LOBBYING

Contact:

> Hawaii State Ethics Commission
> Bishop Square
> 1001 Bishop Street
> Pacific Tower 970
> Honolulu, HI 96813
> (808) 587-0460

Citation: *The "Lobbyists" Law*—Chapter 97, Hawaii Revised Statutes.

Publications Available: *Lobbying Registration and Reporting Manual* is available from the contact office.

Registration required: Lobbyists who receive compensation are required to register with the Commission, provided they either spend more than $750 for lobbying in any reporting period or spend more than five hours lobbying in any month of any reporting period. The registration period is from January 1 of each odd-numbered year to the following December 31 of each even-numbered year. Re-registration is required within 10 days of the opening of the odd-numbered year's legislative session. Registration forms are not automatically mailed out by the Commission. Separate registration is required for each person, organization, or business for which the lobbyist renders services.

The registration provides an authorization section from the client represented, and a menu of subjects on which the lobbyist indicates a lobbying interest. There is no fee for registration.

Forms to use: *Lobbyist Registration Form.*

Reporting requirements: Lobbyists, those who employ or contract for lobbyists, and those who spend $750 or more in any six-month period for lobbying must file a *Statement of Expenditures* form with the Commission. Itemizations include preparation and distribution of lobbying materials; media advertising; telephone, telegraph, and other forms of telecommunication; compensation; fees; entertainment; food and beverages; gifts; loans; and other expenditures. The forms are due on January 31, March 31 and May 31 of each year. The January report covers the period of May 1-December 31 of the preceding calendar year. The March 31 report covers the period of January-February, and the May 31 report covers the period March 1-April 30. Lobbyists report only the expenditures made which were not reimbursed by the client.

TAX EXEMPTIONS

Contact:
>Department of Taxation
>830 Punchbowl Street
>Honolulu, HI 96813-5045
>(808) 586-2596
>1-800-222-3229

Citation: HRS §235-2.3 —corporate income tax; HRS §237-23.

Publications: *How to Start a Business in the State of Hawaii* is available from the Department of Business & Economic Development & Tourism, Business Information Service, Hemmeter Center, 4th Floor, 250 South Hotel St., Honolulu, HI 96813-3210; tel: (808) 586-2600. *An Introduction to the General Excise Tax, Tax Facts,* and various leaflets explaining exemptions available to nonprofit organizations are available from the contact office.

Requirements: All organizations exempt from federal income tax are exempt from the state corporate income tax, other than those with 501(c)(12), (15), and (16) status. The state has no general sales tax. However, any taxpayer conducting business in the state is subject to the general excise tax, a tax on gross receipts. Certain nonprofit organizations may be exempt from the general excise tax on income which they receive, but other businesses will pass this tax on to customers, including exempt organizations.

Application Procedure: No application is required to obtain exemption from state income tax. File Form G-6, *Application for Exemption From the Payment of General Excise Taxes* along with a copy of bylaws and Charter of Incorporation, IRS determination letter, and a $20 registration fee to apply for exemption from the state general excise tax.

CHARITABLE SOLICITATION

Contact:
>Department of Commerce and Consumer Affairs
>Business Registration Division
>1010 Richards Street, 2nd Floor
>PO Box 40
>Honolulu, HI 96810
>(808) 586-2727

Citation: Chapter 467B, Hawaii Revised Statutes; Act 120 (enacted 6/17/96) —repealed organization registration requirements.

Publications: *Solicitation of Funds From Public* may be obtained from the Department of Commerce and Consumer Affairs, Attention: Cashier; PO Box 541; Honolulu, HI; 96809 for 75 cents.

Initial Registration: None (repealed by a 1996 law).

Annual Reports: Charities must file financial reports if requested.

Organization Solicitation Disclosure Requirements: None.

Paid Solicitor Requirements: Must register with the Department, post bond in the amount of $5,000, and pay a $60 fee (comprised of a $50 filing fee and a $10 Compliance Resolution Fund fee).

Fundraising Counsel Requirements: Must register, pay a $60 fee (comprised of a $50 filing fee and a $10 Compliance Resolution Fund fee) and post a $5,000 bond.

Idaho

Central Switchboard: (208) 334-2411
State Web Home Page: http://www.state.id.us/

INCORPORATION

Contact:

> Secretary of State
> PO Box 83720
> Boise, ID 83720-0080
> (208) 334-2301

Citation: *Idaho Nonprofit Corporation Act,* Title 30, §30-3-1 et seq.

Publications Available: *Idaho Nonprofit Corporation Act* is available from the contact office.

General Requirements: Articles of Incorporation must set forth the corporate name; purpose(s); names and addresses of initial directors; street address of the initial registered office and name of initial registered agent at that office; name and address of each incorporator; mailing address of the corporation; whether the corporation will have members; and provisions not inconsistent with law regarding the distribution of assets upon dissolution. The Articles may provide for provisions for managing and regulating the affairs of the corporation; defining, limiting or regulating the powers of the corporation and its board of directors or members; provisions relating to each class of members; and provisions required or permitted by state law to be set forth in the bylaws.

Corporate Name: Shall contain the word "corporation," "incorporated" or "limited," or shall contain an abbreviation of one of such words, provided however, that if the word "company" or its abbreviation is used, it shall not be immediately preceded by the word "and" or by an abbreviation or symbol representing the word "and"; shall not contain a word or phrase which indicates or implies that it is organized for any purpose other than what is contained in its Articles; shall be distinguishable upon the records of the Secretary of State.

Name reservation: May be reserved for four months for a fee of $20.

How to File: File Articles of Incorporation with the contact office along with the filing fee of $30 ($50 if expedited service is requested).

Other Filings/reports: An annual report must be filed with the Secretary of State. The report is mailed from the Secretary of State's office directly to the mailing address indicated in the Articles of Incorporation. The annual report is due each year on the last day of the anniversary month the Articles were filed in the Office of the Secretary of State.

LOBBYING

Contact:

> Secretary of State
> PO Box 83720
> Boise, ID 83720-0080
> (208) 334-2852

Citation: *The Sunshine Law for Political Funds and Lobbyist Activity Disclosure,* Title 67, Idaho Code, Chapter 66, 67-6617 et seq.

Publications: *The Sunshine Law for Political Funds and Lobbyist Law Disclosure; Reporting Manual for Registered Lobbyists* are available from the contact office.

Registration required: Prior to engaging in lobbying or within 30 days after being employed as a lobbyist, lobbyists must register with the Secretary of State if they receive compensation in excess of $250 during any calendar quarter for lobbying. A $10 fee is required. The registration statement discloses the lobbyist's name, permanent business address, any temporary residential and business address during the legislative session; the name, address and general nature of the occupation or business of the lobbyist's employer; whether those who pay the lobbyist employ him or her solely as a lobbyist or include other duties; the general subject(s) of legislative interest; and the name and address of the person who will have custody of the lobbyist's records. A separate notice of representation is required of the lobbyist for each client with an additional $10 fee for each.

Forms to use: L-1 for Lobbyist Registration; L-2 for annual reports; L-3 for monthly reports.

Reporting requirements: Annual reports are due January 31. While the legislature is in session, interim monthly periodic reports are required for each month or portion thereof that the legislature is in session. These interim reports are due by the 10th day after the end of the month that the report covers. The annual and monthly reports must contain itemized expenditures categorized by entertainment/food, living accommodations, advertising, travel, telephone, office expenses and other expenses/services; the totals of each expenditure of more than $50 for a legislator or other public official; contributions made to any legislator or on behalf of any legislator; and the subject matter, including bill numbers, which was supported or opposed by the lobbyist.

TAX EXEMPTIONS

Contact:

Idaho State Tax Commission
Taxpayer Service
800 Park Boulevard, Plaza IV
PO Box 36
Boise, ID 83722-2610
(208) 334-7660

Citation: §63-3025B —corporate income tax; §63-3622o —sales tax.

Publications: *Nonprofit Groups and Churches, An Educational Guide to Sales Tax in the State of Idaho; Retailers & Wholesalers: Making Exempt Sales* are available from the contact office.

Requirements: 501(c)(3)s, fraternal benefit societies, and certain agricultural organizations are exempt from income taxes other than unrelated business income taxes; sales tax exemptions on sales to, or purchases by, nonprofit hospitals, educational institutions, the Idaho Food Bank Warehouse, and certain other health-related entities are specifically exempt by law. However, sales to most religious, charitable and nonprofit organizations are taxable. Sales by nonprofit, charitable, and religious organizations are usually taxable but some incidental sales by religious organizations are exempt by law.

Application Procedure: Provide the vendor with a completed ST-101 form if exempt.

CHARITABLE SOLICITATION

Contact:

Office of the Attorney General
Consumer Protection Unit
Len B. Jordan Building, Lower Level
PO Box 83720
Boise, ID 83720-0010
(800) 432-3545 (in Idaho)
(208) 334-2424

Citation: *Idaho Charitable Solicitation Act,* Chapter 12, 48-1201 et seq.

Publications: A copy of the statute is provided by the contact office.

Initial Registration: None.

Annual Reports: None.

Organization Solicitation Disclosure Requirements: It is unlawful to utilize unfair, false, deceptive, misleading or unconscionable acts or practices.

Paid Solicitor Requirements: None.

Fundraising Counsel Requirements: None.

ILLINOIS

Central Switchboard: (217) 782-2000
State Web Home Page: http://www.state.il.us/

INCORPORATION

Contact:

Secretary of State
Business Services Department
Corporation Division
Howlett Building, Third Floor
Springfield, IL 62756
(217) 782-6961

Citation: *Illinois General Not-For-Profit Corporation Act of 1986* (Public Act 88-691).

General Requirements: Articles of Incorporation must set forth corporate name; purposes; address; name and address of each incorporator; and the names and addresses of first board of directors (must have at least three members).

Corporate Name: Must be distinguishable from existing Illinois corporations; may not imply that it is organized for a purpose other than what is set forth in its Articles of Incorporation; must not contain a name of an established political party without permission of that party; and must be written in English letters with Arabic or Roman numerals.

Name Check/name reservation: Verify that a name is available by telephoning (217) 782-9520. Names may be reserved for a $25 fee for a period of 90 days by written request or by filing a form NP-104.10.

How to File: Deliver two copies of the Articles of Incorporation (using form NP-102.10), one of which must be the original copy with a certified check, money order, or cashiers check to the Secretary of State. Articles of Incorporation and certificate from the Secretary of State must be filed with the county Recorder of Deeds in the home county of the organization within 15 days after receiving them.

Other filings/reports: An annual report must be filed with the Secretary of State before the first day of the corporation's anniversary month on forms provided by the Secretary of State 60 days before the due date. The report discloses general information, including information about officers and directors, and a brief description of the affairs that the corporation is conducting in the state.

LOBBYING

Contact:

Secretary of State
Department of Index
111 East Monroe Street
Springfield, IL 62756
(217) 782-0705

Citation: *The Lobbyist Registration Act, 25 ILCS §170/1 et seq.*

Registration required: All lobbyists who for compensation or otherwise undertake to influence executive, legislative or administrative action, and those who employ such persons, must register on or before January 31 every year or before lobbying activity occurs. Registrations expire on December 31 each year. There is a $50 annual fee for each lobbyist and/or each employer employing a lobbyist.

Forms to use: *Entity Registration Statement* and *Exclusive Lobbyist Information Statement.*

Reporting requirements: Registered entities must file semi-annual and annual reports of expenses; includes schedules for itemized and non-itemized reporting forms for large gatherings of officials, gifts or honoraria; travel, meals and entertainment; a separate form is required for reporting grass-roots lobbying activities.

Publications: *A Guide to Lobbyist Registration* is available from the contact office.

TAX EXEMPTIONS

Contact:

Illinois Department of Revenue
Income Tax Division
101 W. Jefferson Street
Springfield, Il 62794
(800) 732-8866

Citation: 35 ILCS 5/ §205(a)— corporate income tax; 86 Ill. Admin. Code Section 130.2007(b)—Illinois Retailers' Occupation Tax.

Requirements: Organizations exempt from federal income tax are exempt from state corporate income tax, other than unrelated business income tax. The Retailers' Occupation Tax exemption extends to tangible personal property sold to a "governmental body, to a corporation, society, association, foundation, or institution organized and operated exclusively for charitable, religious, or educational purposes, or to a not-for-profit corporation, society, association, foundation, institution, or organization that has no compensated officers or employees and that is organized and operated primarily for the recreation of persons 55 years of age or older." Exemption also exists for various other entities, including property sold to a "not-for-profit music or dramatic arts organization that establishes, by proof required by the Department by rule, that it has received an exemption under Section 501(c)(3) of the Internal Revenue Code and that it is organized and operated for the presentation of live public performances of musical or theatrical works on a regular basis." More details about exemptions can be found in Section 120/2-5 of Title 35 of the ILCS.

Application: No special petition is required for exemption from the state income tax. For exemption from the Illinois Retailers' Occupation Tax, submit request by letter to the Illinois Department of Revenue; include copy of Articles of Incorporation, constitution; bylaws; a narrative explaining purposes, functions and activities; the IRS determination letter, if available; most recent financial statement (other than for religious organizations); and other relevant information.

CHARITABLE SOLICITATION

Contact:

Office of the Illinois Attorney General
Charitable Trusts Bureau
100 W. Randolph Street
12th Floor
Chicago, IL 60601
(312) 814-2595

Citation: The Illinois Charitable Trust Act (Ill. Rev. Stat. 1992, ch 14, pars. 51-69) and the Solicitation for Charity Act (Ill. Rev. Stat. 1992, ch. 23, pars. 5101-5121).

Initial Registration: Organizations which solicit, or intend to solicit, must file a registration statement (Form CO-1) with the Attorney General. If the organization has been in operation for less than one year, it must also file a financial information form (CO-2).

Annual Reports: Organizations which receive more than $100,000 in contributions in a calendar or fiscal year, or which utilize paid professional fundraisers, must file an audit report in addition to Form AG 990-76 and federal tax information.

Solicitation Disclosure Requirements: None.

Paid Solicitor requirements: Must register and post a $10,000 bond.

Fundraising Counsel requirements: Must register every two years.

Indiana

Central Switchboard: (317) 232-3140
State Web Home Page: http://www.state.in.us/

INCORPORATION

Contact:

> Secretary of State
> Business Services Division
> 302 W. Washington Street
> Room E018
> Indianapolis, IN 46204
> (317) 232-6576

Citation: *Indiana Nonprofit Corporation Act of 1991,* IC 23-17-1.

Publications Available: Forms and *Indiana Entrepreneur's Guide* are available from the contact office.

General Requirements: Articles of Incorporation must set forth the corporate name; that the corporation is either a public benefit corporation, mutual benefit corporation, or a religious corporation; the street address of the corporation's initial registered office and the name of the initial registered agent at that office (must be either a person who resides in Indiana or a corporation with an office in the state); the registered office address (may not be a post office box); the name, address, and original signature of each incorporator; whether the corporation will have members; provisions relating to distribution of assets upon dissolution; and optional information, which may include purposes, names and addresses of the initial board of directors, and internal regulating provisions.

Corporate Name: Must include the word "corporation," "incorporated," "company," or "limited," or the abbreviation "corp.," "inc.," "co.," or ltd." Must be distinguishable from any other domestic corporation or have written consent from the other corporation.

Name Check/name reservation: Call (317) 232-6576 to check corporate name availability; May be reserved for a 120-day period for a fee of $20.

How to File: File Articles of Incorporation along with a filing fee of $30.

Other Filings/reports: An annual report must be submitted to the Secretary of State each year which includes a brief description of the corporation's activities. The due date is the last day of the month in which the corporation was originally incorporated. The filing fee is $10.

LOBBYING

Contact:

> Indiana Lobby Registration Commission
> National City Center
> 115 W. Washington Street
> Suite 1375 South
> Indianapolis IN 46204-3420
> (317) 232-9860

Citation: IC-2-7; Acts 1981, PL 9 as amended.

Publications: *Indiana Lobbyist Handbook* is available from the contact office.

Registration required: Lobbyists who receive or spend at least $500 in any registration year must register with the Commission. Separate registrations are required for employer lobbyists (those that compensate others to lobby on their behalf) and compensated lobbyists. Registration statements must be filed within 15 days of becoming a lobbyist or no later than January 15, whichever is later. Registrations terminate on December 31. There is a fee of $100 for each lobbyist registration statement; $50 for 501(c)(3) or (c)(4)s, or an employee who performs lobbying services for the employer as part of the employee's salaried responsibilities.

Forms to use: Employer Lobbyists file the *Employer Lobbyist Registration Statement;* others file *Compensated Lobbyist Registration Statement; Report on Employer Lobbyist Activities; Report on Compensated Lobbyist Activities.*

Reporting requirements: Employer lobbyists and compensated lobbyists file semi-annual reports on or before July 31 and on or before January 31 for activities for the six-month periods of January 1-June 30 and July 1-

December 31. The January 31 report includes totals for the full year. Expenses are itemized by compensation to others (employer lobbyists only), reimbursement to others (employer lobbyists only), receptions, entertainment, lobby registration and penalty fees, and other expenses. Gifts and the subject of lobbying activity must also be reported. A lobbyist must file a written report with both the Commission and with the relevant member of the General Assembly within 30 days of gifts worth in excess of $100 or more (or aggregating more than $250) and certain purchases valued at more than $100 from a member of the General Assembly, or more than $1,000 from a partner of a General Assembly member.

TAX EXEMPTIONS

Contact:

Indiana Department of Revenue
Not-for-Profit Section
IN Government Center North-Room N203
100 North Senate Avenue
Indianapolis, IN 46204-2253
(317) 232-2188

Citation: Indiana Code 16-2.1-3.

Publications: *Income Tax Information Bulletin #17, Taxation and Filing Requirements of Not-for-Profit Organizations and Sales Tax Information Bulletin #10, Application of Sales Tax for Not-for-Profit Organizations* are available from the contact office.

Requirements: Amounts received by institutions, trusts, groups and bodies organized and operated exclusively for religious, charitable, scientific, fraternal, education, social and/or civic purposes and not for private benefit are exempt from the Gross Income Tax. Generally, 501(c)(3)-type organizations, business leagues, cemetery associations, churches, labor unions, hospitals, and most schools are exempt from paying sales tax. Organizations that conduct selling activities on fundraising events during 31 or more days in a calendar year may be required to register as a retail merchant for the collection and remittance of sales tax to the Department.

Application Procedure: File form IT-35A, *Application to File as a Not-for-Profit Organization* with a copy of Articles of Incorporation and bylaws, and a copy of the IRS determination letter. If not incorporated, include a copy of the

Constitution and/or bylaws, Articles of Association, Declaration of Trust, and copies of amendments.

CHARITABLE SOLICITATION

Contact:

Office of the Attorney General
Consumer Protection Division
Indiana Government Center South, Fifth Fl.
402 West Washington Street
Indianapolis, IN 46204-2770
(317) 232-6201

Citation: Indiana Code 23-7-8-1 et seq.

Publications: A copy of the statute and forms are available from the contact office.

Initial Registration: None.

Annual Reports: None.

Paid Solicitor Requirements: Must register with the Division and pay an initial $1,000 registration fee. Renewals are annual (before July 2) and have a fee of $50. Must have a contract filed with the Division which specifies the gross contributions to be received by the charity; must file a solicitation notice with the Division specifying the projected dates of the campaign, the location and telephone number where solicitation will be conducted, the names and address of each person responsible for supervising the campaign, and a certification from the charity that the information is correct to the best of its knowledge. At time of solicitation, professional solicitors must disclose before the donor agrees to making a contribution the name of the charity, and if requested, the charity's address; the fact that the solicitor is being compensated; the name of the solicitor and a number to call for the donor to confirm information; the charitable purpose for which the funds are being raised; the name of the professional solicitation company; the name of the solicitor; the phone number and address of the location from which the call is being made; and the percentage of charitable contribution that will be expended for charitable purposes after administrative costs and the costs of the solicitation.

Fundraising Counsel Requirements: Must register ($1,000 initial fee and $50 renewal) and comply with most provisions that apply to professional solicitors.

Iowa

Central Switchboard: (515) 281-5011
State Web Home Page: http://www.state.ia.us/

INCORPORATION

Contact:
>Secretary of State
>Corporations Division
>Hoover Building
>2nd Floor
>Des Moines, IA 50319
>(515) 281-5204

Citation: *Iowa Nonprofit Corporation Act,* 504 A.1. et seq.

Publications Available: *Guidelines Under Federal Revenue Law; Iowa Nonprofit Corporation Act Application for Certificate of Authority (Nonprofit)* forms are available from the contact office.

General Requirements: Articles of Incorporation must set forth the name of the corporation; the period of duration if it is for a limited time; the purposes; provisions relating to the distribution of assets on dissolution; the address of its initial registered office; the county where the registered office is located; the name of its initial registered agent(s); the number of directors constituting the initial board of directors and their names and addresses; provisions limiting the powers granted to the corporation's directors described in Iowa law; the date on which corporation existence begins; and the name, address, and signature of each incorporator.

Corporate Name: May not imply a purpose different from that which is in the Articles of Incorporation; must not be identical or similar to another; must have letters in the English alphabet.

Name reservation: May be reserved for a non-renewable 120-day period by filing an application with the contact office along with a $10 fee.

How to File: File the original of the Articles of Incorporation with the Secretary of State with a $25 filing fee.

Other Filings/reports: A biennial report must be filed with the Secretary of State each odd-numbered year, due March 31st. The report discloses general information. Forms are provided by the Secretary of State automatically. There is no fee.

LOBBYING

Contact:
>Chief Clerk of the House
>Statehouse
>Des Moines, IA 50319
>(515) 281-5381
>(515) 281-5403 (Secretary of the Senate)

For lobbying the executive branch:

>Iowa Ethics and Campaign Disclosure Board
>514 E. Locust Street
>Des Moines, IA 50309-1912
>(515) 281-4028

Citation: Iowa Code section 68B.2, subsection 13, paragraphs a and b (definitions); section 68B.36 (registration procedures).

Publications: *General Information for Persons Lobbying Before the Iowa General Assembly; Overview of Lobbying the Legislature; House Rules Governing Lobbyists; and Senate Rules Governing Lobbyists* are available from the contact office.

Registration required: Lobbyists must file at the beginning of each calendar year. House and Senate rules require each registered lobbyist to file a statement with the chief clerk on the general subjects of legislation of interest, the file number of the bills that will be the target of lobbying, whether the lobbyist intends to lobby for or against the bills, and on whose behalf the lobbyist is lobbying. There is no fee.

Forms to use: *Iowa General Assembly Lobbyist Registration Statement; Iowa General Assembly Lobbyist Report; Iowa General Assembly Lobbyist Client Report; House and Senate Lobbying Declarations.*

Reporting requirements: Reports are due not later than 25 days following any month the General Assembly is in session and on or before July 31, October 31, and January 31 for months when not in session. Reports must contain a list of the lobbyist's clients, information on campaign contributions made by the lobbyist, and expenditures. Lobbyists' clients are required to file semi-annual reports on salaries, fees and retainers paid to lobbyists for lobbying purposes.

Lobbyist clients must file no later than January 31 and July 31 each year and disclose all salaries, fees and retainers paid by the lobbyist's client to the lobbyist during the preceding six calendar months. The January 31 report provides a cumulative total for the preceding year.

TAX EXEMPTIONS

Contact:

> Taxpayer Services
> Iowa Department of Revenue and Finance
> PO Box 10457
> Des Moines, IA 50306-0457
> (515) 281-3114
> 1-800-367-3388 (in Iowa only)

Citation: § 422.34 —corporate income tax exemption; § 422.45 —sales tax exemption.

Publications: *Iowa Tax Guide for Non-Profit Entities* is available from the contact office.

Requirements: Organizations with federal tax-exempt status are automatically exempt from Iowa corporation tax other than unrelated business income; they must file form IA 1120 to report unrelated business income; they may be subject to the alternative minimum tax (requires filing of form IA 4626). Charities are treated the same as other businesses when purchasing goods and taxable services at retail—they pay sales taxes on goods and taxable services, except when the goods or services are for resale. Only organizations explicitly named in Iowa law are exempt from sales tax. These include the following: American Red Cross; Navy Relief Society; USO; governmental units; federal corporations created by the federal government which are exempt under federal law; private nonprofit educational institutions located in Iowa; community health centers; migrant health centers; certain residential care, ICF, and group homes for the mentally retarded and mentally ill; foster care residential facilities; rehabilitation facilities for the disabled; adult day care facilities; community mental health centers; nonprofit legal aid organizations; nonprofit private museums; nonprofit organizations which lend property to the general public for nonprofit purposes (such as libraries); statewide nonprofit organ procurement organizations; and sales of tangible personal property and services made to nonprofit hospitals.

Application Procedure: Organizations qualify for income tax exemption automatically upon receiving their IRS determination letters certifying federal exemption.

CHARITABLE SOLICITATION

Contact:

> Department of Justice
> Consumer Protection Division
> Hoover Building
> Des Moines, IA 50319
> (515) 281-5926

Citation: §13C.1 et seq., Iowa Code.

Publications: A copy of the solicitation law and the application for registration permit are available from the contact office.

Initial Registration: Registration applies only to professional commercial fundraisers. There is a $10 registration fee. Charitable organizations are not required to register.

Annual Reports: None.

Organization Solicitation Disclosure Requirements: Must disclose upon request, and without cost, financial disclosure information concerning contributions received and disbursements for the organization's last complete fiscal year, or for the current year if the organization has not completed an entire fiscal year. This information must be provided within five days of the request. Charitable organizations may not solicit contributions by claiming that all or a portion of the proceeds will be given to another charity in Iowa without permission from that other charity.

Paid Solicitor Requirements: Must register and pay a $10 registration fee.

Fundraising Counsel Requirements: None.

Kansas

Central Switchboard: (785) 296-0111
State Web Home Page: http://www.state.ks.us/

INCORPORATION

Contact:
> Secretary of State
> 2nd Floor, State Capitol
> 300 SW 10th Avenue
> Topeka, KS 66612-1594
> (785) 296-4564

Citation: Kansas General Corporation Code, K.S.A. 17 §6001 et seq.

Publications Available: *Filing Suggestions for Not-for-Profit Corporations* is available from the contact office.

General Requirements: Articles of Incorporation must set forth the corporate name; name and address of registered office and agent at that address; the purpose(s); whether the corporation is authorized to issue capital stock; if there are members and the conditions for membership; the names and addresses of incorporators (only 1 required); the names and addresses of directors if the powers of incorporators end upon filing; the term of existence of the corporation; and other lawful provisions.

Corporate Name: Must include one of the words of incorporation such as "association," "company," "Church," "corporation," "Club," "foundation," "fund," "incorporated," "institute," "society," "union," "syndicate," or "limited," or one of the abbreviations "co.," "corp.," "inc.," "ltd.," or words or abbreviations of like import in other languages. Must be distinguishable from other names without written consent.

Name Check/name reservation: May be reserved for a period of 120 days for a $20 fee.

How to File: File an original and one copy of the Articles of Incorporation with a $20 filing fee. A certified copy is returned.

Other Filings/reports: An annual report must be filed with the Secretary of State with a $20 privilege fee. The first report is not required until the corporation is six months old; blank annual reports are provided by the contact office. The report is due on the 15th day of the 6th month following the close of the taxable year.

LOBBYING

Contact:
> Kansas Governmental Ethics Commission
> 109 West Ninth
> Topeka, KS 66612-1287
> (785) 296-4219

Citation: K.S.A. 46-215 et seq. and administrative regulations K.A.R. 19-60-1 through 19-63-6.

Publications: *Handbook for Legislative Lobbyists* is available from the contact office.

Registration required: Lobbyists must register with the Secretary of State prior to engaging in lobbying activity. Registration expires annually on December 31. Registration for succeeding calendar years may begin on or after October 1. There is a $30 registration fee if spending $1,000 or less in the registration year; $250 if spending more than $1,000; $300 fee if an employee of a lobbying group or firm and not an owner or partner.

Forms to use: *Lobbyist Registration Statement.*

Reporting requirements: Expenditure reports must be filed on the 10th of the month following each of the six reporting periods (January, February, March, April, May-August; September-December). The report includes lobbying expenditures itemized for food and beverages; entertainment, gifts or payments; mass media communications; recreation; communications; and other. No itemization is required if expenditures did not exceed $100.

TAX EXEMPTIONS

Contact:

Division of Taxation
Kansas Dept. of Revenue
915 SW Harrison Street
Topeka, KS 66625
(785) 296-2461

Citation: § 79-32, 113.

Requirements: Organizations exempt from federal income taxes are exempt from Kansas corporate income taxes. Some organizations are explicitly exempt under Kansas law from the sales and use tax including YMCAs; YWCAs; the Salvation Army; church entities; nonprofit educational institutions; nonprofit hospitals; nonprofit blood tissue and organ banks; non-profit historical societies and museums that are 501(c)(3)s; and non-commercial, educational TV and radio stations. Other organizations should write to the Division's Office of Policy and Research (2nd Floor, Docking State Office Building, Topeka, KS 66625) and request a private letter ruling. Applicants may call the office (785-296-3081) in advance of the written request to informally explore whether their activities qualify the organization for exempt status.

CHARITABLE SOLICITATION

Contact:

Secretary of State
2nd Floor, State Capitol
300 SW 10th Avenue
Topeka, KS 66612
(785) 296-4564 or
(785) 296-4565

Citation: Charitable Organizations and Solicitations Act, K. S. A. 17-1759 et seq.

Publications: Forms and a copy of the statute are available from the contact office.

Initial Registration: Charitable organizations which raise more than $10,000 or which have paid fundraisers must file a Form SC registration statement with a $20 registration fee, or may instead file a Uniform Registration Statement (URS).

Annual Reports: Registrations expire on the last day of the sixth month following the month in which the fiscal year of the charitable organization ends, and must be renewed each year. A financial statement must be enclosed with each registration (IRS annual returns are accepted). If the organization received contributions exceeding $100,000, it must also file an audited financial statement. The registration statement, in addition to general information, requires a calculation of total costs as a percentage of contributions received.

Organization Solicitation Disclosure Requirements: See below.

Paid Solicitor Requirements: Must register annually and post a $5,000 bond. Registrations expire on June 30. All solicitations by professional solicitors must disclose the name, address and telephone number of the charity; the registration number for the charity; the solicitor's registration number; and that an annual financial report for the preceding fiscal year is on file with the Secretary of State.

Fundraising Counsel Requirements: If counsel meets the definition of a professional fundraiser, then he/she must register as one.

Kentucky

Central Switchboard: (502) 564-3130
State Web Home Page: http://www.state.ky.us/

INCORPORATION

Contact:

> *Office of the Secretary of State*
> *Business Filings*
> *State Capitol Building—Room 154*
> *700 Capitol Avenue*
> *Frankfort, KY 40601*
> *(502) 564-2848*

Citation: Title XXIII, Private Corporations and Associations, § 273 (Religious, Charitable and Educational Societies—Nonstock, Nonprofit Corporations).

Publications Available: Kentucky Business Organizations Law and Rules (1996-97 edition) is provided for a fee by calling 1-800-562-1197.

General Requirements: Articles of Incorporation must set forth the corporate name, purposes, provisions for distribution of assets or dissolution or liquidation, street address, name of the initial registered agent, mailing address, number of directors constituting the initial board of directors and their names and addresses, and the name and address of each incorporator. At least three directors are required.

Corporate Name: Shall include the word "corporation" or "incorporated" or the abbreviation "Inc.," or the word "company" or the abbreviation "Co." If the word "company" or the abbreviation "Co." is used, it may not be immediately preceded by the word "and" or the abbreviation "&." This does not apply to corporations existing on June 13, 1968. Must be distinguishable upon the records from other business names in Kentucky. Shall not imply that the corporation is organized for purposes not permitted by law.

Name reservation: May be reserved for a nonrenewable period of 120 days for a $15 fee.

How to File: File one original and two copies of the Articles of Incorporation with the Secretary of State with an $8 fee. Two copies are returned; one copy must be filed with the county clerk of the county in which the registered office is located.

Other Filings/reports: An annual report must be filed with the Secretary of State with general information, including the names and business addresses of the directors and principal officers. The first report is due between January 1 and June 30 after the year following the calendar year of incorporation. Subsequent reports are due between January 1 and June 30. There is a $4 filing fee.

LOBBYING

Contact:

> *Kentucky Legislative Ethics Commission*
> *22 Mill Creek Park*
> *Frankfort, KY 40601*
> *(502) 573-2863*

Citation: KRS 6.611; KRS 6.807.

Publications: *Kentucky Legislative Ethics Code*, statutes, relevant forms, and legal opinions are provided by the contact office.

Registration required: All lobbyists must register with the Commission. There is a two-year registration period, expiring on December 31 of each odd-numbered year. A $250 fee is required to be paid by the employer and covers one or more lobbyists. Registration requires the name of the lobbyist, employer, and a description of the bill or legislative action which is to be the target of the lobbying activity.

Expense Reporting: Required to be filed on the 15th day of January, February, March, April May and September of even-numbered years and January, May and September of odd-numbered years.

TAX EXEMPTIONS

Contact:

Department of Tax Administration
Division of Compliance and Taxpayer
  Assistance
200 Fair Oaks Lane
Frankfort, KY 40620
(502) 564-5170 (sales and use tax)

Citation: §136.010—income tax exemption;
§ 139.010 et seq. —sales and use tax exemption.

Publications: Forms and instructions for applying for sales and use tax exemption are provided by the contact office.

Requirements: Organizations with federal 501(c) tax exemptions such as religious, educational, charitable or like corporations not organized or conducted for pecuniary profit are exempt from income tax. All 501(c)(3)s are exempt from paying tax on the sales of tangible personal property or services to them, provided the property or services are used solely for the educational, charitable, or religious function. Most sales by such organizations are taxable. All nonprofits not engaged in the business of selling are exempt on the first $1,000 of sales made in any calendar year.

Application Procedure: Submit a 51A125 *Application for Purchase Exemption, Sales and Use Tax* to the contact office along with Articles of Incorporation, a detailed schedule of receipts and disbursements, and the IRS determination letter.

CHARITABLE SOLICITATION

Contact:

Consumer Protection Division
Office of the Attorney General
Suite 200
1024 Capital Center Drive
Frankfort, KY 40601-8204
(502) 696-5389

Citation: *Kentucky Charitable Solicitations Act,* KRS 367.650, et seq.; *Telephone Solicitations Act,* KRS 367.46951.

Publications: Both statutes and relevant forms are provided by the contact office.

Registration requirements: All charitable organizations that are required to file a federal 990 with the Internal Revenue Service are required to register.

Initial Registration: Prior to solicitation, the organization must file its latest federal 990 or, if newly formed, a notice of intent to solicit on a *Uniform Registration Statement* (see Chapter 14).

Annual Reports: Charitable organizations must file a copy of their federal 990s each year.

Organization Solicitation Disclosure Requirements: If solicitation is by telephone, the organization must disclose immediately the name of the solicitor, name of the charity, telephone number or address where the charity is located, and the town from which the solicitor is physically located. The solicitor must immediately discontinue the solicitation "if the consumer responds in the negative."

Paid Solicitor Requirements: There is a $300 annual registration fee and $25,000 bonding requirement ($50,000 bonding for telephone solicitors); must undergo a background check by the Attorney General's Office paid for by the solicitor ($5 fee for "Request for Conviction Record").

Fundraising Consultant Requirements: Must pay a $50 annual fee plus the costs of a background check.

Louisiana

Central Switchboard: (225) 342-6600
State Web Home Page: http://www.state.la.us/

INCORPORATION

Contact:

> Secretary of State
> Corporation Division
> PO Box 94125
> Baton Rouge, LA 70804
> (225) 925-4704

Citation: *Nonprofit Corporation Law*, R.S. 12 § 201 et seq.

General Requirements: One or more natural or artificial persons capable of contracting may form a nonprofit corporation. Articles must be notarized and must set forth corporate name; purpose(s), in general terms; duration if other than perpetual; that it is a nonprofit corporation; location and street address of the registered office and name and address of each registered agent; name, address, and signature of each incorporator; names, addresses, and terms of office of each initial director; whether it is organized on a stock basis, nonstock basis, or both, and information about shares if it is organized, in whole or in part, on a stock basis; qualifications of members if it has members; its tax ID number (optional); and optional provisions relating to the rights of shareholders and members. Filing must include a notarized affidavit of any registered agent accepting his or her appointment.

Corporate Name: Must be expressed in English letters or characters; shall not imply that it is an administrative agency of any parish, the state, or the U.S.; shall not contain the words "bank," "banking," "savings," "trust," "deposit," "insurance," "mutual," "assurance," "indemnity," "casualty," "fiduciary," "homestead," "building and loan," "surety," "security," "guarantee," "cooperative," "state," "parish," "redevelopment corporation," "electric cooperative," or "credit union." Shall be distinguishable from others without written consent.

Name reservation: May be reserved for a 60-day period for a fee of $20. May be renewed for two 30-day periods.

How to File: File Articles of Incorporation with the Secretary of State with a $60 filing fee. A certified copy is returned along with a certificate of incorporation. File the certified copy and a copy of the certificate with the Office of the Recorder of Mortgages of the parish in which the registered office is located, within 30 days of filing with the Secretary of State.

Other Filings/reports: An annual report must be filed with the Secretary of State on or before May 15 each year disclosing general information and tax I.D. number. There is a $5 filing fee (which does not apply to churches).

LOBBYING

Contact:

> Louisiana Board of Ethics
> 8401 United Plaza Blvd.; Suite 200
> Baton Rouge, LA 70809
> (225) 922-1400

Citation: *Lobbyist Disclosure Act*, R.S. 24:50 et seq.

Publications: *Summary of Lobbyist Disclosure Act* is available from the contact office.

Registration required: Lobbyists who are compensated and who make expenditures of $200 or more in a calendar year for lobbying purposes must register with the Board. Certain other lobbyists may also have to register. Registration must occur within five days of employment as a lobbyist or within five days after the first action requiring registration as a lobbyist. The registration form includes general information, the name of the employer/client, a 2-inch by 2-inch photograph, and a $10 registration fee. Registrations expire on January 31 of each year.

Forms to use: *Lobbying Registration Form*; *Lobbying Expenditure Report*.

Reporting requirements: Expenditures on a legislator exceeding $50 on any one occasion or totaling more than $250 in a six-month reporting period require listing the legislator's name and the total expenditures made on the legislator. Lobbyists must also disclose expenditures for receptions or social gatherings to which the entire legislature or committees or delegations thereof are invited. Reports must be filed semi-annually. Reports are due by August 15 for the period January 1-June 30 and by February 15 for the period July 1-December 31.

TAX EXEMPTIONS

Contact:

Department of Revenue and Taxation
330 Ardenwood Drive
PO Box 201
Baton Rouge, LA 70821
(225) 925-4611

Citation: R.S. 47 §287.501; R.S. 47:301(8)(d);(10)(q).

Requirements: Most organizations exempt from federal income taxes are exempt from state income taxes. Purchases of songbooks, bibles, and literature for classroom instruction by nonprofit religious organizations are exempt from sales/use tax. Approved nonprofit private and parochial schools that have been certified by the Department of Education as having complied with the Dodd-Brumfield decision may purchase books, workbooks, computers, computer software, films, videos, and audiotapes for classroom instruction exempt from the sales/use tax, provided Department approval of the exemption is obtained prior to its being claimed.

CHARITABLE SOLICITATION

Contact:

Department of Justice
Public Protection Division
PO Box 94095
Baton Rouge, LA 70804-9095
(225) 342-2752

Citation: Act 1053, 1995 Regular Session, R.S. 51:§1901 et seq.

Publications: Governor's Consumer Protection Division, Rules and Regulations is available from the contact office.

Initial Registration: At least 10 days prior to soliciting for contributions, charities utilizing professional solicitors must file a Charitable Solicitations Questionnaire with the Consumer Protection Section. The questionnaire includes general information; whether the organization is federally tax-exempt (a copy of the IRS determination letter must be attached, if so); how funds will be raised; information about professional solicitors used; and financial information (must attach a copy of a certified financial statement or current budget or annual report).

Charities that utilize a professional solicitor must register. There is a $25 filing fee. Charities must include a copy of their Articles of Incorporation and bylaws, IRS determination letter, copy of current financial statements and/or annual reports, copy of all contracts with professional solicitors, and a list of other states in which the organization is registered.

Annual Reports: Registration must be renewed annually.

Organization Solicitation Disclosure Requirements: Any charitable organization solicitor, upon request to a donor, must provide information substantiating the claims of the charity that it is a bona-fide charity or that the organization delivers certain goods or services; its disclosure statement; the names and residential addresses of incorporators, shareholders, directors, officers, sales persons, and employees; and any information or documentation required under the Louisiana Unfair Trade Practices and Consumer Protection Law.

Paid Solicitor Requirements: Not less than 10 days prior to doing business in the state, professional solicitors must register with the Department by filing an application, application fee, and bond. The fee is $150; the bond is $25,000. Registration is valid for one year. Professional solicitors must, prior to an oral solicitation or at the same time a written solicitation is made, disclose a clear and conspicuous statement that the solicitation is being performed by a for-profit fundraising firm; the identity of that firm; and the specific charitable purpose for which the solicitation is being conducted. Upon request, they must provide the percentage of funds that go to the charity, the percentage of funds that go to the for-profit fundraising firm, and the percentage of funds to the charitable organization that is used for a charitable purpose.

Fundraising Counsel Requirements: None.

Maine

Central Switchboard: (207) 624-9494
State Web Home Page: http://www.state.me.us/

INCORPORATION

Contact:

Secretary of State
Bureau of Corporations, Elections and
Commissions
101 State House Station
Augusta, ME 04333-0101
(207) 287-4195

Citation: Maine Law on Nonprofit Corporations,
Title 13-B, §401 et seq.

Publications Available: Maine Law on Nonprofit
Corporations is available for a fee from the
contact office.

General requirements: Articles of Incorporation must set forth the corporate name;
purpose(s); name of registered agent (must be a
Maine resident or another corporation other
than your own) and address of the registered
office; number of directors (must be at least 3);
minimum and maximum number of directors;
whether the corporation will have members;
whether no substantial part of the activities of
the corporation shall be the carrying on of
propaganda, or otherwise attempting to influence legislation and whether the corporation
will be prohibited from intervening in any
political campaign on behalf of any candidate
for public office (consistent with 501(c)(3)
status); provisions relating to corporate dissolution and private inurement; other provisions
relating to regulation of the internal affairs;
the names, addresses, and signatures of each
incorporator (only one required); and the
signature of the registered agent.

Corporate Name: Shall not contain any word or
phrase which indicates or implies that it is
organized for any purpose for which a corporation may not be organized under the Non-Profit
Act; may not use the same or deceptively
similar name of a corporation or limited partnership, limited liability company, or limited
liability partnership without written permission; may not be the same as, or deceptively

similar to, any registered mark under Title 10
without permission; and may not be the same
as, or deceptively similar to, the name of any
department, bureau or other agency of the
state.

Name reservation: May be reserved for 120
days for a $5 fee.

How to File: File Articles of Incorporation using
form MNPCA-6 with a $20 filing fee.

Other Filings/reports: An annual report must
be filed with the Secretary of State disclosing
general information, including the names and
addresses of the president, treasurer, registered agent, secretary or clerk, and directors.
Reports are due no later than June 1 of the
following year for each corporation on file as of
December 31 in any year. The fee for filing an
annual report is $20.

LOBBYING

Contact:

Commission on Governmental Ethics &
Election Practices
#135 State House Station
Augusta, ME 04333
(207) 287-6221

Citation: 3 M.R.S.A. Chapter 15 §311 et seq.

Publications: Lobbyist Disclosure Procedures is
available from the contact office.

Registration required: Lobbyists who lobby at
least eight hours in any calendar month must
register with the Commission. The fee is $200
for each lobbyist and $100 for each "lobbyist
associate" (partners, associates or employees of
a lobbyist who lobby on behalf of the employer
named on the lobbyist registration and lobby
more than eight hours in any calendar month).

Forms to use: Lobbyist/Employer Joint Registration form. Must be filed no later than 15 business
days after a lobbyist is required to register.

Reporting requirements: Monthly reports are required to be filed, due by 5 p.m. on the 15th day following the month that is the subject of the report, or the next business day when the 15th day is on a weekend or holiday. The report specifies the dollar amount of compensation received for lobbying, preparation of documents and research; the dollar amount of lobbying expenditures; and the legislative action taken by bill number or topic. Each registered lobbyist and employer must file an annual disclosure report by 5 p.m. on December 30 following the year which is the subject of the report. Itemization includes expenses made on behalf of any official in the legislative branch or a member of that person's immediate family totaling $25 or more in any calendar month.

TAX EXEMPTIONS

Contact:

> Maine Revenue Services
> 24 State House Station
> Augusta, ME 04333-0024
> (207) 287-2076

Citation: 36 M.R.S.A., Section 1760; Rule No. 302 (08-125 CMR 302).

Publications: *Government Agencies, Exempt Organizations and Sales Thereto; General Information Bulletin* are available from the contact office.

Requirements: Must be eligible for exemption under Section 1760 of the Sales and Use Tax Law. That section lists the types of organizations eligible for exemption, which include hospitals, schools, libraries, community action agencies, and more than three dozen other types of organizations. Organizations exempt from federal income taxes are exempt from state income tax.

Application Procedure: Apply for an exemption certificate from the Maine Revenue Services; include a copy of the IRS determination letter.

CHARITABLE SOLICITATION

Contact:

> Department of Professional and Financial Regulation
> Division of Licensing and Enforcement
> 35 State House Station
> Augusta, ME 04333
> (207) 624-8603

Citation: Title 9, Chapter 385 §5001 et seq.

Publications Available: Forms and a copy of the statute are available from the contact office.

General Requirements: Charitable organizations that raise more than $10,000 during a calendar year must register with the Department at least 30 days prior to solicitation. File *State of Maine Charitable Organization Registration.* Initial and renewal registration fees are $40. Registration statements include general information, purposes for which the contributions will be used, the total amount of money received during the preceding fiscal year, and the estimated percentage of each dollar contribution which will be expended in Maine.

Annual Reports: See above. At the same time as renewal of registration, organizations must file a financial report covering the most recent audited fiscal year if gross contributions from the public are over $30,000. There is a $50 fee for filing financial reports. A federal 990 may be acceptable in lieu of a financial report.

Organization Solicitation Disclosure Requirements: See below.

Paid Solicitor Requirements: Must pay a $200 registration fee, post a $10,000 bond, and pay a $50 application fee. Solicitors must disclose prior to a request for contributions the name and address of the charitable organization; professional solicitors, fundraising counsel or commercial coventurers must fully disclose prior to the request for contributions their name and address, and the following statement "(Insert name of professional fundraising counsel, professional solicitor or commercial coventurer) is a professional charitable fundraiser."

Fundraising Counsel Requirements: Must pay a $200 registration fee, post a $10,000 bond, and pay a $50 application fee. See above.

Maryland

Central Switchboard: (410) 841-3000
State Web Home Page: http://www.mec.state.md.us/

INCORPORATION

Contact:

> State Department of Assessments and
> Taxation
> Corporate Charter Division
> 301 West Preston Street
> Baltimore, MD 21201
> (410) 767-1340

Citation: Annotated Code of Maryland, Section 2-101 et seq.

Publications Available: *The Business Corporation Laws of Maryland and the District of Columbia* is available for $16 from Prentice-Hall Legal and Financial Services, 15 Columbus Circle, NY, NY 10023-7808; *Information Guide For: Forming a Corporation in Maryland* and *Guidelines for Drafting Articles of Incorporation for a "Nonstock Corporation"* are available from the contact office.

General Requirements: Articles must set forth the names and addresses of incorporators (minimum of one; must be at least 18); corporate name; description of the business; address of the principal place of business (cannot be a PO Box); name and address of registered agent (must be in Maryland and cannot be a PO Box); that the corporation has no authority to issue capital stock; the number and names of initial directors; and provisions which are optional, such as IRS required language for tax-exempt status.

Corporate Name: Must contain the word "company," (if it is not preceded by the word "and" or a symbol for "and"), "Corporation," "Incorporated," "Limited," "Inc.," "Corp.," or "Ltd." Cannot be misleadingly similar to a name already on record in Maryland. May not contain any word or phrase that indicates or implies that it is organized for any purpose not contained in its charter.

Name Check/name reservation: Call (410) 767-1330 for a non-binding check on name availability. May be reserved for a period of 30 days for a fee of $7.

How to File: File Articles of Incorporation using sample form or original form of the organization plus a $40 filing fee.

Other Filings/reports: Every corporation is required to file an annual personal property return each calendar year following the year in which it was incorporated. These forms are provided automatically by the Department and are due by April 15.

LOBBYING

Contact:

> State Ethics Commission
> 300 E. Joppa Road
> Suite 301
> Towson, MD 21286
> (410) 321-3636

Citation: *Maryland Public Ethics Law*, Section 15-701 et seq.

Publications: *Maryland Public Ethics Law— Lobbying Law Requirements* is available from the contact office.

Registration required: Legislative Lobbyists who incur more than $100 in lobbying-related expenses during a reporting period or receive $500 or more as compensation for lobbying must register. Similar expense-related registration requirements apply to those who lobby the executive branch. There is a $20 registration fee; those who expend $2,000 or more for grass-roots lobbying in a reporting period must also register. The registration form consists of general information disclosure, the matters which will be subject of lobbying, and employer identification. Registration expires on October 31.

Forms to use: Ethics Commission Form No. 3.

Reporting requirements: Lobbyists must file a *General Lobbying Activity Report* (Form No. 4) by May 31 for activities during the period November 1-April 30; and by November 30 for activities May 1 through October 31. These reports cover itemized expenses of compensation, meals, special events, meetings, gifts, office expenses, professional and technical research, publications, witness fees, and other expenses. Gifts of more than $75 must be disclosed on a separate reporting schedule; gifts of tickets, meals and beverages to a legislator or member of a legislator's immediate family worth more than $15 must be reported on a separate form.

TAX EXEMPTIONS

Contact:

> Legal Unit
> Comptroller of the Treasury
> Revenue Administration Division
> PO Box 1829
> Annapolis, MD 21404-1829
> (410) 260-7292

Citation: §10-104—income tax exemption; § 11-204— sales and use tax exemption.

Requirements: 501(c)(3) organizations are exempt from the corporate income tax; Sales and Use Tax exemptions are codified in Section 11-204 of the Tax General Article. Consult the statute or the contact office for more details.

Application Procedure: File an application for an exemption certificate with the Comptroller; include a copy of the IRS determination letter.

CHARITABLE SOLICITATION

Contact:

> Office of the Secretary of State
> State House
> Annapolis, MD 21401
> (410) 974-5534

Citation: *Maryland Charitable Solicitations Act,* Business Regulation Article §6-101 et seq.

Publications: *Giving Wisely,* a copy of the statute and forms, and a *Registration Instructions and Check List* sheet are available from the contact office.

Initial Registration: Every charitable organization must submit a registration statement to the Secretary of State before contributions are solicited if it collects $25,000 or more in a year or uses a professional solicitor. Organizations receiving less than $25,000 in contributions are required to submit a one-page annual "Exempt Organization Fund-Raising Notice." The registration fees vary with contributions collected ($50 for $50,000 or less; $200 for at least $100,001). An annual fee of $50 is required for charitable organizations that collect less than $25,000 but that use the services of a professional solicitor. In addition to general information, the registration requires a copy of the IRS determination letter and Articles of Incorporation; a copy of the federal 990 or financial information in a form required by the Secretary; an audit of gross contributions if they are at least $200,000, or a review if gross income from contributions is between $100,000 and $200,000; and a copy of any contracts with fundraising counsel or professional solicitors.

Annual Reports: Charitable organizations must submit annual reports within 6 months after the end of each fiscal year containing financial information and supporting audit/review and any changes to the previous annual report or registration statement.

Organization Solicitation Disclosure Requirements: Written solicitations must provide a disclosure statement that information filed can be obtained from the Secretary of State.

Paid Solicitor Requirements: Must register by filing an SS-PS-0001 form, pay a $300 fee, and post a $25,000 bond or irrevocable letter of credit. Written agreements are required with the charity. Copies of these agreements must be provided to the Secretary of State.

Fundraising Counsel Requirements: Must register and pay a $200 registration fee. Written agreements are required with the charity. Copies of these agreements must be provided to the Secretary of State.

Massachusetts

Central Switchboard: (617) 727-2121
State Web Home Page: http://www.state.ma.us/

INCORPORATION

Contact:

*Corporations Division
Secretary of the Commonwealth
One Ashburton Place; Room 1717
Boston, MA 02108
(617) 727-9640*

Citation: General Laws, Chapter 180.

Publications Available: *Organizing a Non-Profit Corporation* and sample Articles of Incorporation form are available from the contact office; *Massachusetts Corporate Laws*, a compilation of state laws relating to corporations, is available for $15 plus $3.05 shipping & handling from: The State Bookstore, Secretary of the Commonwealth, State House, Room 116, Boston, MA 02133.

General Requirements: Articles must set forth the corporate name; purpose; information about its members if it chooses to have members (or may be included in the bylaws); provisions relating to conduct and regulation of the business, voluntary dissolution, and limiting or defining powers of the corporation, its members or directors; that the bylaws have been duly adopted by the board and its officers and initial directors have been duly elected; the effective date of the incorporation; the street address of the principal office (not a PO Box); the name, residential address and post office address of each director and officer; the fiscal year of the corporation; the name and business address of the resident agent; and signatures of incorporators (may be another corporation represented with the signature of someone with authority).

It must include one of the following words: Limited (Ltd.), Incorporated (Inc.), or Corporation (Corp.) unless it is a religious organization. The name must not be the same as, or similar to, another entity operating or having recently operated in the Commonwealth.

Name Check/name reservation: May be reserved for 30 days, renewable once for an additional 30 days, in writing, by paying $15. Name check is available by calling (617) 727-9640.

How to File: File Articles (blue form) with a $35 fee. A copy will be returned approximately one month after approval by the Secretary.

Other Filings/reports: An annual report must be filed with the Secretary of the Commonwealth's Corporations Division. This report is due November 1. The fee is $15.

LOBBYING

Contact:

*Secretary of the Commonwealth
Public Records Division
Lobbyist Section
One Ashburton Place
Room 1719
Boston, MA 02108
(617) 727-2832*

Citation: Chapter 80, the acts of 1995.

Publications: *Lobbying In Massachusetts* is available from the contact office.

Registration required: All lobbyists and employers of lobbyists must register annually, using a Form 43A, *Employer Authorization for Executive or Legislative Agent*, and provide three passport size photographs (or have them taken at the registration office). The registration fee for initial annual registration with photo service is $65, or $50 without photo service; each subsequent registration is $25. Registration and photos expire at the end of each legislative session for that year. Registration is permitted by mail for lobbyists located outside the 508 or 617 area code, but they must provide three passport-size photographs.

Reporting requirements: Financial disclosure reports must be filed semi-annually covering the periods of January 1- June 30 (due July 15) and July 1-December 31 (due January 15). The reports must include the total amount of lobbying expenses, and must be itemized when the amount during a single day is $35 or more. Itemization categories include information about the amount, date, to whom the expenditure was paid, purpose, bill number, and campaign contributions (to be reported on Form 43C). If the expenditure was made for meals, entertainment or transportation, all persons participating must be listed.

TAX EXEMPTIONS

Contact:

> Department of Revenue
> Bureau of Desk Audit
> 200 Arlington Street; Room 4300
> Chelsea, MA 02150
> (617) 887-6970

Citation: AP 301.2 —corporate excise—G.L. c. 63, § 30, 1 and 2; AP 101—sales and use tax.

Publications: *A Guide to Sales and Use Tax* booklet and *Massachusetts Trustee Tax Form TA-1, Application for Registration and Instructions* are available from the contact office.

Requirements: Generally, 501(c)(3) organizations are exempt from paying sales/use tax and all 501(c) organizations are exempt from paying corporate excise tax, other than unrelated business income tax.

Application Procedure: All businesses file TA-1 forms. There are lines on the form that indicate application for tax-exempt status which require an attached copy of the IRS determination letter. An organization that has a 501(c)(3) determination by the IRS pending may apply for a temporary certificate of exemption from sales and use tax by submitting a Form TA-1, a copy of its submitted IRS Form 1023, a copy of its Articles of Incorporation, and bylaws. If issued, the certificate is effective for two years or until 30 days after a determination by the IRS is provided.

CHARITABLE SOLICITATION

Contact:

> Division of Public Charities
> Office of the Attorney General
> Room 1413
> One Ashburton Place
> Boston, MA 02108-1698
> (617) 727-2200

Citation: G.L. c. 68, §§ 18-35 and G.L. c. 12 §§ 8 et seq.

Publications: *Attorney General's Question and Answer Guide for Professional Fundraisers* is available from the contact office.

Initial Registration: Must register annually and pay a $35-$250 license fee.

Annual Reports: Financial statements must be filed within 4½ months of the end of the fiscal year; audited financial statements must be included if the organization receives $250,000 or more.

Organization Solicitation Disclosure Requirements: See below.

Paid Solicitor Requirements: Must register, post $10,000 bond and pay a $300 fee; must file Form 11-A solicitation campaign reports by February 28 of the year after a campaign takes place; must file Form 10-A and a copy of the contract with the charity for each solicitation campaign; professional solicitors must state that they are paid fundraisers; the potential donor must be given the name, address, and telephone number of the charitable organization; when selling advertising space for a publication, the solicitor must tell the potential donor how many copies will be published and where the copies will be distributed; they may not solicit for organizations that are not themselves registered and in compliance; they must tell a potential donor how much is going to the charity if asked.

Fundraising Counsel Requirements: Must pay a $200 fee. Commercial coventurers must post a $10,000 bond and pay a $50 registration fee.

Michigan

Central Switchboard: (517) 373-1837
State Web Home Page: http://www.migov.state.mi.us/

INCORPORATION

Contact:

>Michigan Department of Consumer &
>Industry Services
>Corporation, Securities and Land Development Bureau
>Corporation Division
>PO Box 30054
>Lansing, MI 48909-7554
>(517) 334-6302

Citation: M.S.A. 21.101 et seq.

Publications Available: *Business Corporation Act-Nonprofit Corporation Act and Related Statutes,* a compilation of law, is available from the Michigan Department of Consumer and Industry Services; Corporation, Securities and Land Development Bureau; 6546 Mercantile Way; PO Box 30054; Lansing, MI 48909; (517) 334-6302 or (517) 334-7561 for $6. Sample Articles of Incorporation form and *State of Michigan Entrepreneur's Guide* are provided by the contact office. Forms are also available on disk or at the web site: http://www.cis.state.mi.us/corp/

General Requirements: Articles of Incorporation must set forth the corporate name; purpose(s) (it is not sufficient to state that the corporation may engage in any activity within the purposes for which corporations may be organized under the Act); whether organized on a stock or non-stock basis; description of real property assets; address of the registered office; name of the resident agent at that office; name, address, and signature of each incorporator; and additional provisions that are optional.

Corporate Name: May not contain a word or phrase implying a purpose different than permitted by the Articles; shall not be the same as, or confusingly similar to, another entity of the state; shall not contain a word or phrase or abbreviation or derivative thereof that is prohibited or restricted by any other statute unless that restriction has been complied with.

Name reservation: May be reserved for four calendar months following the calendar month which contains the date the reservation was made for a fee of $10; up to two extensions of two months may be granted.

How to File: File one legible original form C&S 502 Articles of Incorporation with $20 filing and Franchise fee. The document must be signed in ink by each incorporator, but incorporators may, by resolution, designate one incorporator to sign on their behalf, provided a copy of that resolution is attached.

Other Filings/reports: An annual report is required to be filed with the administrator on or before October 1 each year after the year of formation containing general information about the corporation; the nature and kind of business that the corporation has engaged in during the year covered by the report; and the names of officers and directors.

LOBBYING

Contact:

>Michigan Department of State
>Bureau of Elections
>PO Box 20126
>Lansing, MI 48901-0726
>(517) 373-8558

Citation: *The Michigan Lobby Registration Act,* Public Act 472 of 1978, MCL 4.411 et seq.

Publications: A copy and summary of the statute and forms are available from the contact office.

Registration required: Lobbyists who make expenditures of more than $1,675 to lobby a number of public officials, or spend at least $425 to lobby a single public official in any 12-month period, must register within 15 calendar days after exceeding these thresholds. Lobbyist agents (those who receive compensation or reimbursement of more than $425 for lobbying on behalf of employers or clients during any 12-month period) must register within three calendar days of exceeding the threshold. These thresholds are adjusted annually based on the Detroit Consumer Price Index (the amounts quoted are for 1998).

Forms to use: LR-1, *Lobbyist Registration*; LR-2, *Lobbyist Agent Registration.*

Reporting requirements: Lobbyists must submit a financial report on August 31 (covering the period January 1-July 31) and January 31 (covering the period August 1-December 31) each year detailing activities and expenditures. They must submit a list of persons compensated or reimbursed in excess of $17 for lobbying on their behalf. Expenditures are categorized by food and beverage for public officials; mass mailings and advertising; and all other lobbying expenses.

TAX EXEMPTIONS

Contact:

> Department of the Treasury
> Treasury Building
> 430 West Alleganst St.
> Lansing, MI 48922
> (517) 373-3190 (sales, use, and withholding taxes division)
> 800-487-7000 (income tax division)

Citation: §7.525 —sales tax; §7.557 (1201) —income tax.

Publications: *Revenue Administrative Bulletin 1995-3, Sales and Use Tax— Nonprofit Entities* is available from the contact office.

Requirements: Organizations exempt from federal income taxes are exempt from state income tax, other than unrelated business income tax; some 501(c)(3) and 501(c)(4) organizations are statutorily exempt from Michigan sales and use taxes. Consult the contact office for more information.

Application Procedure: A 1994 law eliminated the application process for sales and use tax exemptions. For exemption, the vendor should be presented with a copy of the IRS determination letter and a "certificate of exemption" form that is available from the contact office.

CHARITABLE SOLICITATION

Contact:

> Department of Attorney General
> Charitable Trust Division
> PO Box 30214
> Lansing, MI 48909
> (517) 373-1152

Citation: *Charitable Organizations and Solicitations Act,* 1975 PA 169, as amended, MCL 400.271, et seq.

Publications: A copy of the statute is available from the contact office.

Initial Registration: All those who request or receive charitable contributions in excess of $8,000, or intend to receive more than $8,000 annually or who pay or compensate persons for fundraising services, with some statutory exemptions, must obtain a license prior to solicitation, and file financial statements with the Attorney General before solicitations. The license application must include general and detailed financial information about the charitable organization, all methods by which solicitations will be made, and copies of contracts between the organization and professional fundraisers. Copies of solicitation materials must be supplied upon request of the Attorney General. The license expires six months after the close of each fiscal year. There is no registration fee.

Annual Reports: See above.

Organization Solicitation Disclosure Requirements: None.

Paid Solicitor Requirements: Must post $10,000 bond and be licensed annually (using form DAG 009-007). The application form must include the surety bond; Articles of Incorporation (if incorporated); copies of all contracts with organizations which solicit contributions; the *Registration of Professional Solicitor* form; and campaign financial statements for certain campaigns and special events.

Fundraising Counsel Requirements: Same requirements as paid solicitors.

Minnesota

Central Switchboard: (651) 296-6013
State Web Home Page: http://www.state.mn.us/

INCORPORATION

Contact:

> Secretary of State
> Business Services Division
> 180 State Office Building
> 100 Constitution Avenue
> Saint Paul, MN 55155-1299
> (651) 296-2803

Citation: *Minnesota Nonprofit Corporation Act,* Minnesota Statute Chapter §317A.001 et seq.

Publications Available: A blank form is provided by the contact office, and all forms are available at: http://www.sos.state.mn.us

General Requirements: One or more adult natural persons may act as incorporators. Articles of Incorporation must include corporate name; street address for the registered office (PO Box not acceptable); number of shares which the corporation is authorized to issue (nonprofit corporations may issue shares); name, address, and signature of each incorporator (only one required); and a contact name and telephone number.

Corporate Name: A corporate designation is not required; must be in the English language or expressed in English letters or characters; shall not contain a word or phrase that shows or implies that it may not be incorporated under Minnesota law; must be distinguishable from others or, if not distinguishable, must obtain written permission to use the name.

Name reservation: May be reserved for 12-month periods for a fee of $35 through the mail or $55 if made in person; renewals of name reservations are permitted.

How to File: File form *State of Minnesota Secretary of State Articles of Incorporation, Business and Nonprofit Corporations* along with a $70 filing fee ($90 if filed in person). Incorporators may file their own form of Articles if the standard form does not meet their needs and requirements.

Other Filings/reports: An annual registration is required on forms provided by the Secretary of State. The report is due on or before December 31. There is no fee for annual registration, unless the corporation is not in good standing.

LOBBYING

Contact:

> Campaign Finance and Public
> Disclosure Board
> 1st Floor South, Centennial Building
> St. Paul, MN 55155
> (651) 296-5148

Citation: Minn. Stat. § 10A. and Minn. Rules 4501, 4511 and 4525.

Publications: *Handbook for Lobbyists and Lobbyist Principals* is available from the contact office.

Registration required: All lobbyists must register within five days of meeting the criteria for registration. Lobbyists file a Lobbyist Registration Form (ET-6) with the Board. The registration threshold is spending more than five hours in any month if paid or more than $250 in any calendar year for lobbying, including grass-roots lobbying. Registration is permanent until a termination report (ET-7) is filed.

Reporting requirements: Lobbyists must provide reports due April 15 (for January 1-March 31 reporting period); July 15 (for April 1-June 30 reporting period); and January 15 (for July 1-December 31 reporting period). Reports must be filed even if there are no reportable receipts of disbursements. Reports of those who employ lobbyists are due March 15 for the calendar year reporting period.

TAX EXEMPTIONS

Contact:

Minnesota Department of Revenue
600 North Robert Street
St. Paul, MN 55146
(651) 297-5199 (Twin Cities)
1-800-657-3619, ext. 7-5199 (elsewhere in MN)
(651) 296-6181 (sales tax)

Citation: M.S.A. §290.05— corporate income taxes; M.S.A. §297A.01 and M.S.A. 297A.25— sales tax.

Requirements: Organizations that are exempt from federal income tax are exempt from the corporate income tax, but must pay taxes on unrelated business income. The statute provides limited exemptions from the sales tax for certain nonprofits, including 501(c)(3)-type organizations, senior citizens groups, and YMCA/YWCA membership.

Application Procedure: File form ST-16 for sales tax exemption. Veterans organizations and their auxiliaries file form ST-18. Form instructions explain supporting documents and information that must be included.

CHARITABLE SOLICITATION

Contact:

Office of the Attorney General
Charities Division
Suite 1200, NCL Tower
445 Minnesota Street
St. Paul, MN 55101-2130
(651) 297-4613

Citation: The *Social and Charitable Organizations Act,* Minnesota Statutes §§ 309.50 et. seq.

Publications: *Fiduciary Duties of Directors of Charitable Organizations* booklet; *A Guide to Minnesota's Charities Laws* booklet; and a copy of the registration forms are available from the contact office.

Initial Registration: Organizations must register with the Attorney General's Office before they solicit contributions, unless they do not have paid staff or professional fundraisers and receive or plan to receive less than $25,000 in total contributions during an accounting year. The registration statement must include a financial statement using a form provided by the Attorney

General, IRS 990, or an audited financial statement. There is a $25 registration fee. The Articles of Incorporation and IRS determination letter should also be attached.

Annual Reports: Charities must file an annual report within six months of the close of their fiscal year. The report must include a balance sheet, a statement of income and expense and a statement of functional expenses; a list of its five highest paid directors, officers and employees that receive total compensation of more than $50,000 together with total compensation paid to each; and a list of the five highest paid directors, officers, and employees of any related organization if that organization receives funds from the charity. Registered charities with total revenue in excess of $350,000 must provide an audited financial statement. There is a $25 fee to file the annual report.

Organization Solicitation Disclosure Requirements: Along with a written request or prior to an oral request for contributions, organizations and professional fundraisers must disclose the name and location by city and state of the charity; the tax deductibility of the contribution; a description of the program for which the solicitation is being carried out and, if different, a description of the programs and activities of the organization generally.

Paid Solicitor Requirements: Must register annually, pay a $200 fee, and post a $20,000 bond if the fundraiser will have custody or access to the contributions at any time; must provide a copy of the contract between themselves and the charity that, among other things, discloses the percentage or reasonable estimate of the amount raised that will go to the charity; must provide a completed "solicitation notice" providing information about the fundraising campaign, and a post-solicitation campaign financial report within 90 days after a campaign. Professional fundraisers must disclose their name during solicitations and that the solicitation is being conducted by a "professional fundraiser."

Fundraising Counsel Requirements: Must register and pay a $200 fee.

Note: The contact office specifically requested a statement that those interested in these requirements refer to the statute for specific definitions and requirements.

Mississippi

Central Switchboard: (601) 359-1000
State Web Home Page: http://www.state.ms.us/

INCORPORATION

Contact:
> Office of the Mississippi Secretary of State
> PO Box 136
> Jackson, MS 39205-0136
> (601) 359-1633
> 1-800-256-3494

Citation: *Mississippi Nonprofit Corporation Act*, Section 79-11-101 et seq. of the Mississippi Code of 1972.

Publications Available: All forms are available at the website: http://www.sos.state.ms.us

General Requirements: Articles of Incorporation must set forth whether the corporation is profit or nonprofit; the corporate name; the future effective date (if applicable); the period of duration; the name and street address of the registered agent and registered office; the name, address, and signature of each incorporator; and other optional provisions.

Corporate Name: Nonprofit organizations are not required to provide a corporate name ending. No language shall be included that implies a purpose other than permitted by law or its Articles; must be distinguishable from others on the record.

Name reservation: May be reserved for a 180-day period for a non-refundable fee of $25.

How to File: File Articles on bar-coded form F0001 along with a $50 filing fee; forms must be completed suitable for scanning by a computer.

Other Filings/reports: Any amendment, agent changes, mergers or corrections can be filed upon the completion of the proper bar-coded application and submission of the appropriate filing fees. At the preference of the Secretary of State, a status report shall be filed by each nonprofit corporation every five years.

LOBBYING

Contact:
> Mississippi Secretary of State
> Lobbyist Registration and Reporting
> 401 Mississippi Street
> PO Box 136
> Jackson, MS 39205-0136
> (601) 359-6359

Citation: *Lobbying Law Reform Act of 1994*, Miss. Code Ann. §5-8.

Publications: *Lobbying in Mississippi*, forms, and a copy of the statute are provided by the contact office.

Registration required: Lobbyists must register by January 1 or within five days of becoming employed as a lobbyist. The lobbying cycle extends from January 1 through December 31, and registration is required on a calendar year basis. The registration form discloses general information about the lobbyist and the lobbyist's client and the specific issues to be lobbied. The fee is $25 per registration. Clients may employ more than one lobbyist, and lobbyists may represent more than one client. A numbered certificate is issued for each registration.

Forms to use: SS95LL2, *Registration Form*.

Reporting requirements: Lobbyists are required to file two legislative expenditure reports (Form E) and an annual report (Form A) for each registration. Additionally, the lobbyist's client is required to file one annual report (Form C). The first legislative report period is from the legislative convening date through February 25. The report is due February 25. The second legislative report covers February 26 through *sine die* adjournment, and is due 10 days after *sine die*. The form requires itemized disclosure of each reportable expenditure made or promised to a public official or employee. The report also discloses the provider's name, the value of the payment, the object that was given or promised, the date, and the place given or promised. Lobbyists must file a separate annual report for each registration. A notarized original and two copies must be filed by January 30 of the year following registration. The lobbyist's annual report (Form A) is used to disclose all lobbying expenses and receipts during the calendar year. Lobbyist's clients must also file an annual report (Form C) disclosing all lobbying expenses during the calendar year. A notarized original and two copies must be filed by January 30 of the year following registration. Clients file a single annual report for all registrations.

TAX EXEMPTIONS

Contact:

Mississippi State Tax Commission
PO Box 1033
Jackson, MS 39215-3338
(601) 923-7015 (sales tax)
(601) 923-7099 (corporate income tax)

Citation: § 27-7-29 —corporate income tax; § 27-13-63 —corporate franchise tax; §27-65-111 —sales tax exemption.

Requirements: Most corporations exempt from the federal income tax are also exempt from the state corporation income tax and corporation franchise tax. Limited exemptions are provided from the sales tax for certain named organizations. Consult the contact office or the statute for more information.

Application Procedure: Write a letter to the Department requesting the exemption; the Department will respond with an exemption determination letter. While none is required, most vendors request to see the determination letter from the Department certifying that the exemption is legitimate.

CHARITABLE SOLICITATION

Contact:

Secretary of State
202 North Congress Street; Suite 601
PO Box 136
Jackson, MS 39205-0136
(601) 359-1633
1-888-236-6167

Citation: Miss. Code Ann. §§79-11-501 et seq. (Supp. 1992).

Publications: A copy of the statute is available from the contact office.

Initial Registration: Prior to solicitation, charitable organizations must register with the Secretary of State. There is a $50 nonrefundable registration fee. Registration is accomplished by using the Unified Registration Statement (URS), along with the Mississippi Supplement to the URS. The form discloses general information about the organization, its officials and professional fundraisers, if any. Copies of any and all IRS forms must be filed. An audited financial statement for the most recently completed fiscal year must be filed if contributions are over $100,000 and/or a professional fundraiser is used. If a professional fundraiser is used, copies of contracts between the organization and the fundraiser must be filed. With the initial registration only, the organization must file a copy of its Articles of Incorporation, bylaws, and IRS determination letter. Registration remains in effect for one year.

Annual reports: Registration must be renewed annually before the expiration date of the current registration using the Unified Registration Statement, Mississippi Supplement to this statement, and the Annual Financial Report Form (Form FS).

Organization Solicitation Disclosure requirements: All solicitations must be compliant with §79-11-523. The charity may not use registration to imply endorsement by the state.

Paid Solicitor Requirements: Must register annually, pay a $250 registration fee and post a $10,000 bond. A Solicitation Campaign Notice must be filed prior to beginning a campaign and a Campaign Finance Report must be filed at the end of a campaign. Prior to orally requesting a contribution or contemporaneously with written requests for a contribution, the solicitor/fundraiser must disclose the name of the fundraiser on file with the Secretary of State, that the solicitation is being conducted by a professional fundraiser, the name of the charity on file, and a description of how the contribution will be used for charitable purposes. Each written solicitation or confirmation must state: "The official registration and financial information of (Charity's legal registered name) may be obtained from the Mississippi Secretary of State's office by calling 1-888-236-6167. Registration does not imply endorsement by the Secretary of State."

Fundraising Counsel Requirements: Must register and pay a $250 nonrefundable registration fee, and file copies of contracts. Registration expires on June 30 of each year.

Missouri

Central Switchboard: (573) 751-2000
State Web Home Page: http://www.state.mo.us/

INCORPORATION

Contact:

> Secretary of State
> Corporation Division
> PO Box 778
> Jefferson City, MO 65102
> (573) 751-4153

Citation: Chapter 355 RSMo.

Publications Available: *Corporation Laws Handbook* and a sample form are provided by the contact office.

General Requirements: Each corporation must have at least a president and/or chairman, secretary, and treasurer. The same person may hold more than one office simultaneously. Articles of Incorporation must set forth the corporate name; whether the corporation is a public or mutual benefit corporation; the period of duration; the name and street address of the registered agent and registered office; the name, address, and signature of each incorporator; whether the corporation has members; provisions relating to the distribution of assets on dissolution; the corporate purposes; and the effective date of the document if other than when filed.

Corporate Name: Must contain the word "corporation," "company," "incorporated," or "limited," or end with an abbreviation of one of those words; must be distinguishable from other corporations, limited liability companies, limited partnerships, limited liability partnerships, and limited liability limited partnerships.

Name Check/name reservation: May be reserved for a period of 60 days for a $25 fee; name check may be made by telephone, but this does not guarantee availability of the name.

How to File: File Corp. #52 *Articles of Incorporation of a Nonprofit Corporation* form in duplicate with original signatures and a $25 filing fee.

Other Filings/reports: An annual report must be filed each year with the Secretary of State listing officers and directors. This report is due August 31 for other than new corporations.

LOBBYING

Contact:

> Missouri Ethics Commission
> PO Box 1370
> 221 Metro Drive
> Jefferson City, MO 65102
> (573) 751-2020
> 1-800-392-8660

Citation: Section 105.470 RSMo.

Publications: *Should I be Registered as a Lobbyist?* booklet and a copy of the statute are available from the contact office.

Registration required: There are three types of lobbyists under the act—executive lobbyist, legislative lobbyist, and judicial lobbyist. Lobbyists must register annually with the Commission if they have $50 or more in lobbying expenditures in any 12-month reporting period. Registration must occur within five days of beginning lobbying activity. The names and addresses of persons employed by the lobbyist for lobbying purposes and the names and addresses of the clients of the lobbyist or his/her employer must also be disclosed. There is a $10 fee for registration.

Forms to use: MO 300-0972 *Lobbyist Registration and Updating Sheet*; MO 300-0536 *Lobbyist Semi-Annual Expenditures Report.*

Reporting requirements: Lobbyists must file monthly expenditure reports with the Commission. On March 15 and May 30 each day, every lobbyist principal must file a report with a general description of the legislation that is the subject of lobbying and whether the principal supported or opposed the legislation or executive action.

TAX EXEMPTIONS

Contact:
> Department of Revenue
> Tax Administration Bureau
> PO Box 840
> Jefferson City, MO 65105-0700
> (573) 751-2836

Citation: §143.441 —corporate income tax; §144.030(19) and (20) —sales tax.

Requirements: All nonprofits that file federal 990s are not required to file a Missouri corporation income tax return unless the organization files a 990T (unrelated business income) and at least $100 of gross income is from Missouri sources. Nonprofits are exempt from the Missouri franchise tax. All sales made to religious and charitable organizations and institutions in their religious, charitable or educational functions and activities, not-for-profit civic, social service or fraternal organizations; not-for-profit public and private institutions of higher education; eleemosynary and penal institutions; benevolent, scientific and educational associations formed to foster, encourage and promote the progress and improvement in the science of agriculture and in the raising and breeding of animals, and nonprofit summer theatres are eligible for exemption from the sales and use tax. Certain sales made by these organizations are also eligible for exemption. Consult the contact office or Regulation 12 CSR 10-3.870 for details.

Application Procedure: Use Form DOR-1746 and the *Missouri Sales/Use Tax Exemption Application Affidavit* (Form DOR-1922). Include a copy of the Articles of Incorporation, bylaws, or both; a copy of the IRS determination letter; a copy of the tax exemption ruling issued by the assessing officers in each county in which the applicant's property is or will be located; financial statements for the previous three years indicating sources of revenue and a breakdown of disbursements, or, if just beginning the organization, an estimated budget for one year; and a letter of explanation if any of these documents are not being provided.

CHARITABLE SOLICITATION

Contact:
> Attorney General's Office
> Consumer Protection Division
> P.O. Box 899
> Jefferson City, MO 65102
> (573) 751-3321

Citation: *Charitable Organizations and Solicitations Law*, § 407.450, Missouri Revised Statutes.

Initial Registration: All charities must register before soliciting in the state. The registration fee is $15.

Annual reports: Must file an annual report within 75 days after the end of the fiscal year. There is a $15 filing fee.

Organization Solicitation Disclosure requirements: If a professional fundraising organization is used, a charity, upon request, must disclose the percentage of funds spent on the costs of fundraising in the last 12-month period for which an annual report was filed; fundraising literature must state that a portion of funds contributed pay marketing expenses, if this is the case.

Paid Solicitor Requirements: All solicitors for a professional fundraising organization must register at the time they are initially employed. There is no fee for solicitor registration. A solicitor must disclose the fact that he/she is a paid solicitor for a professional fundraising organization.

Fundraising Counsel Requirements: Fundraising counsels are exempt from registration, but must contact the Attorney General's Office in writing with exemption information.

Montana

Central Switchboard: (406) 444-2511
State Web Home Page: http://www.mt.us/

INCORPORATION

Contact:
>Secretary of State
>Business Services Bureau
>PO Box 202801
>Helena, MT 59620-2801
>(406) 444-3665

Citation: Montana Code Annotated, Title 35, Chapter 2.

Publications Available: A sample Articles of Incorporation form is available from the contact office.

General Requirements: Articles of Incorporation must set forth the corporate name; a statement that it is a public benefit, mutual benefit, or religious corporation; the street address of the initial registered office, and, if different, the mailing address; the name of the initial registered agent at that address; the name, address, and signature of each incorporator; whether the corporation will have members; provisions consistent with law regarding the distribution of assets upon dissolution; optional provisions relating to the purpose(s), names and addresses of the initial directors; provisions relating to the internal management and regulation of the corporation; liability provisions; and the powers of members and directors. If directors are named in the articles, then these directors must sign as well.

Corporate Name: Must consist of English letters or Arabic or Roman numerals; may not contain language stating or implying that it is organized for a purpose other than permitted by its Articles; must be distinguishable from other corporate names in the state unless it has consent; may not be the same as, or identical to, another.

Name reservation: May be reserved for a non-renewable, 120-day period.

How to File: File an original and a duplicate Articles of Incorporation form and a $20 filing fee with the Secretary of State. Form DN-1 may be used, but is not required.

Other Filings/reports: Each corporation must file an annual report with the Secretary of State providing the name of the corporation, address of its registered office and registered agent at that address, address of its principal office, the names and business or residence addresses of its directors and principal officers, a brief description of the nature of its activities, and whether or not it has members. The first annual report is due between January 1 and April 15 of the year following the calendar year of incorporation; subsequent annual reports are due between January 1 and April 15.

LOBBYING

Contact:
>Commissioner of Political Practices
>1205 Eighth Avenue
>PO Box 202401
>Helena, MT 59620-2401
>(406) 444-2942

Citation: §5-7-101 et seq.

Publications: *Lobbying* booklet of forms and the statute are available from the contact office.

Registration required: Lobbyists and those who hire lobbyists must register with the Commissioner. Licenses expire on December 31 of each even-numbered year. There is a $50 license fee. Disclosure consists of general information and the name, address and telephone number of each client and specific subjects of legislation for each client. Clients must disclose the subjects on which they authorize the lobbyist to represent them, and provide an authorization statement authorizing their lobbyist.

Forms to use: Lobbyists file Form L-1; Clients file Form L-2; both filings are required for the lobbyist to receive a license; L-5 (see below).

Reporting requirements: Lobbyists' clients must file L-5 reports listing each lobbyist to which they have made payments of more than $25 to the benefit of any public official; payments of more than $100 to the benefit of more than one public official; contributions or membership fees of $250 or more paid to the client for lobbying expense; and the issue, if any, for which the payment was earmarked; an itemized list of lobbying expenses categorized by printing, advertising, postage, travel expenses, salaries and fees, entertainment, telephone and telegraph, and other office expenses.

TAX EXEMPTIONS

Contact:

Department of Revenue
Natural Resource and Corporation Tax
Division
PO Box 202701
Helena, MT 59620-2701
(406) 444-2441

Citation: Montana Code Annotated §15-31-102(1).

Publications: A copy of the exemption statute is provided by the contact office.

Requirements: Nonprofit corporations may be exempt from the Montana Corporation License Tax. There is no sales and use tax in Montana. Once an organization has qualified for tax-exempt status from the Department, it is not required, in most cases, to file a return other than when it has unrelated business income tax liability exceeding $100. Those that do have this liability must file a copy of their federal 990T with the Department.

Application Procedure: Provide an affidavit showing the character of the organization, the purpose for which it was organized, its actual activities, the sources and disposition of its income, and whether or not any of its income may inure to the benefit of any private shareholder or individual. Attach a copy of the Articles of Incorporation; a copy of the bylaws;

copies of the latest financial statements showing the assets, liabilities, receipts and disbursements; and, if applicable, a certified copy of the IRS tax exemption determination letter.

CHARITABLE SOLICITATION

There is no statute governing charitable solicitation activities.

Nebraska

Central Switchboard: (402) 471-2311
State Web Home Page: http://www.state.ne.us/

INCORPORATION

Contact:

> Secretary of State
> Corporation Division
> Suite 1305
> PO Box 94608
> Lincoln, NE 68509-4608
> (402) 471-4079

Citation: § 21-1901 et seq., revised Statutes of Nebraska.

Publications Available: None provided.

General Requirements: Articles of Incorporation must set forth corporate name; period of duration; purpose(s); optional provisions relating to the internal management and regulation of the organization; street address of the initial registered office; name of the initial registered agent at that office; the number of directors constituting the initial board of directors (optional); and the names, addresses, and signatures of each incorporator.

Corporate Name: Shall not contain any word or phrase which indicates or implies that it is organized for any purpose other than the one or more purposes contained in its Articles of Incorporation; shall not be the same as, or deceptively similar to, another; shall be transliterated into letters of the English alphabet if it is not in English; and must be distinguishable.

Name reservation: May be reserved for a non-renewable, 120-day period for a fee of $30.

How to File: File an original and a copy of the Articles with the Secretary of State. The fee is $10 plus $5 per page.

Other Filings/reports: A biennial report must be filed with general information on forms provided by the Secretary of State. The reports are due on or before April 1 every odd-numbered year. The first report is due April 1 of the odd numbered year next succeeding the year of incorporation. There is a $20 filing fee.

LOBBYING

Contact:

> Nebraska Accountability and Disclosure Commission
> 11th Floor, State Capitol Building
> PO Box 95086
> Lincoln, NE 68509
> (402) 471-2522

Citation: *The Nebraska Political Accountability and Disclosure Act*, 49-1401 et seq.

Publications: *Lobbying Guidelines: Rules and Regulations* booklet is available from the contact office.

Registration required: All lobbyists, whether compensated or not, must file an *Application for Registration* with the Clerk of the Legislature prior to lobbying. The registration is valid through the end of the calendar year. The registration fee is $100 for lobbyists who receive compensation for lobbying and $15 for those who do not. Employees who lobby are considered lobbyists for compensation.

Forms to use: NADC Form A, *Application for Registration as a Lobbyist*; NADC Form B, *Nebraska Registered Lobbyist Quarterly Report*; NADC Form C, *Nebraska Principal Quarterly Report*; Form D, *Nebraska Lobbyist Statement of Activity*.

Reporting requirements: Each lobbyist and client must file quarterly reports disclosing itemized expenditures categorized by miscellaneous, entertainment, lodging, travel, lobbyist fees, and receipts. Special monthly reports are required for expenditures of more than $5,000 for lobbying purposes during any calendar month in which the Legislature is in session, due 15 days after the end of that month (does not apply to fees for lobbying services previously disclosed on the registration statement). There are gift limitations and gift-reporting provisions as well. The registration form includes general information, compensation given or planned to be given to the lobbyist, and identification of matters on which the client or lobbyist expects to lobby. The form is in triplicate; two are filed and one is a lobbyist copy.

TAX EXEMPTIONS

Contact:

> Department of Revenue
> 301 Centennial Mall South
> PO Box 94818
> Lincoln, NE 68509-4818
> (402) 471-2971

Citation: §77-2704.12—sales and use tax; §77-2714 —income tax.

Requirements: Sales and use taxes are not imposed on the gross receipts from the sale, lease, or rental of, and the storage, use, or other consumption of, purchases by the following: any organization created exclusively for religious purposes, any nonprofit organization providing services exclusively to the blind, any private educational institution established under certain specified statutes, any private college or university established under certain specified statutes, any hospital, any health clinic when two or more hospitals or the parent corporations of the hospitals own or control the health clinic for the purpose of reducing the cost of health services or when the health clinic receives funds under certain federal programs, skilled nursing facilities, intermediate care facilities, or nursing facilities licensed under certain statutes and organized not for profit, any nonprofit organization providing services primarily for home health care purposes, any licensed child-caring agency, and any licensed child placement agency.

Organizations which are exempt from federal income tax are generally exempt from the corporate income tax, but this does not include those required to file federal 990T unrelated business income tax returns.

Application Procedure: File Form 4, *Nebraska Exemption Application* with the Department. The statute and regulation provides enumerated exemptions by type of organization purchasing and type of organization selling. Form 4 discloses general information; requires disclosure of the social security numbers, names, and addresses of corporate officers; and the basis for exemption which includes religious organizations, educational institutions, hospitals, ICF or nursing facilities; child care agencies; child-placing agencies; nonprofit organizations providing services to the blind; home health care agencies; and certain nonprofit health clinics. A copy of the organization's bylaws, Articles of Incorporation, or current license may be required to be provided.

CHARITABLE SOLICITATION

Contact:

> Secretary of State
> Suite 2300 Capitol Building
> Lincoln, NE 68509-4608
> (402) 471-2554

Citation: As of March 1, 1996, the Nebraska Charitable Solicitor registration laws have been repealed as a result of a ruling by the Nebraska Supreme Court.

Nevada

Central Switchboard: (775) 687-5000
State Web Home Page: http://www.state.nv.us/

INCORPORATION

Contact:

> Secretary of State
> Customer Service Division
> Capitol Complex
> 101 N. Carson Street, Suite 3
> Carson City, NV 89701-4786
> (775) 684-5708

Citation: NRS Chapter 82, §82.006-82.541;
Nonprofit Corporations.

Publications Available: A compilation of
applicable law and forms is available from the
contact office. Forms are also available at:
http://sos.state.nv.us or by faxback service (1-
800 583-9486).

General Requirements: Articles of Incorporation must set forth the corporate name; name
and address of the resident agent; that the
corporation is a nonprofit corporation; the
nature of the business or objects, or purposes;
whether the members of the governing board
are styled directors or trustees and their
number, names, and addresses with provisions
relating to the right to change the number of
directors; the name, address, and signature of
each incorporator; and optional provisions
relating to dissolution, voting, and internal
management.

Corporate Name: Must be distinguishable from
the names of all other artificial persons
formed, organized or registered under Title 7 of
NRS and on file in the office of the Secretary of
State, unless accompanied by written consent
from the holder of the name. May not be a
name appearing to be that of a natural person
and containing a given name or initials except
with an additional word or words such as
"Incorporated," "Inc.," "Limited," "Ltd.," "Company," "Co.," "Corporation," "Corp." or other word
which identifies it as not being a natural
person. It must not be the same as another

corporation, or deceptively similar without
permission of the other corporation, partnership, or limited liability company. May not
contain the words "bank," "trust," engineer,"
"engineered," "engineering," "professional
engineer," "licensed engineer" or "insurance."

Name reservation: May be reserved for a
renewable period of 90 days for a fee of $20.

How to File: File original Articles of Incorporation with the Secretary of State with a $25
filing fee.

Other Filings/reports: An annual list of offic-
ers/directors must be filed within 60 days prior
to the anniversary date of incorporation.

LOBBYING

Contact:

> Legislative Counsel Bureau
> 401 S. Carson Street
> Carson City, NV 89701-4747
> (775) 687-6800

Citation: Nevada Lobbying Disclosure Act,
§218.900 et seq.

Registration required: Every lobbyist, within
two days after lobbying activity begins, must
file a registration statement with the director
of the Legislative Counsel Bureau. The form
discloses general information, a list of lobbyist
clients, a list of direct business associations
and partnerships with any member of the
Legislature, a description of the principal areas
of interest, and a statement that compensation
is not contingent upon the production of any
legislative action. Fees are $15 for unpaid
lobbyists, and $95 plus $1 for each additional
client for paid lobbyists.

Forms to use: NVLOB97, Declaration of Registrant; Lobbyist's Report.

Reporting requirements: Each lobbyist must
file an itemized final expense report within 30

days after the close of each legislative session, and interim reports within 10 days following the close of each month during sessions. Expenses are itemized by entertainment, parties, gifts and loans, and other. Lobbyists must wear identification badges when lobbying.

TAX EXEMPTIONS

Contact:

Nevada Department of Taxation
1550 E. College Parkway STE 115
Carson City, NV 89706-7921
(702) 687-4820

Citation: Nevada Revised Statutes, Chapter 372, Sales and Use Taxes, §372.326 and §372.3261.

Requirements: There is no corporate income tax. Qualifying organizations created for religious, charitable, or education purposes may be exempt from sales tax on sales of tangible personal property to and/or by the organization upon application review and approval.

Application Procedure: Complete a *Sales and Use Tax Exemption for Religious, Charitable and Educational Organizations* form (available at: http://www.state.nv.us/taxation/eforms) with the Department, with bylaws, Articles of Incorporation, IRS determination letter, financial statements, and other relevant information, such as pamphlets, brochures and fact sheets. If the application is for a charitable organization, an outline of charitable activities, fundraisers, goals, and a copy of the business plan must be attached. If the application is approved, the organization is issued a sales tax exemption letter. Exemption letters must be renewed by reapplication every five years. Copies of the letter are given to vendors in order to not be charged sales tax.

CHARITABLE SOLICITATION

There is no law regulating charitable solicitation.

New Hampshire

Central Switchboard: (603) 271-1110
State Web Home Page: http://www.state.nh.us/

INCORPORATION

Contact:

> Secretary of State
> Corporation Division
> State House
> Room 204
> 107 North Main Street
> Concord, NH 03301-4989
> (603) 271-3244

Citation: RSA Chapter 292, 292:1 et seq.

Publications Available: *New Hampshire Non-profit Corporations* booklet is available from the contact office.

General Requirements: At least five or more individuals of lawful age are required to form a nonprofit corporation. Articles of Agreement must set forth the corporate name; object for which the corporation is established; provisions for establishing membership and participation in the corporation; provisions relating to distribution of assets upon dissolution; address where business will be carried on; amount of capital stock, if any; provisions limiting liability of directors and/or officers (optional); and the signature and post office address of each of the persons forming the corporation.

Corporate Name: May not be the same or deceptively similar to an existing corporation name, reserved or registered name, New Hampshire investment trust, partnership or trade name, limited liability company or limited liability partnership without written consent of the other entity.

Name Reservation: Nonprofit corporation names may not be reserved.

How to File: Articles of Agreement must first be filed with the clerk of the city or town in which the business of the corporation will be carried out and then with the Corporation Division. The fee for filing locally is $5; the fee

for filing with the state is $25. File form NP 1, *Articles of Agreement of A New Hampshire Nonprofit Corporation*.

Other Filings/reports: Corporations must file a "return" during the calendar year 2000 and every five years thereafter. The return fee is $25. The forms for returns are provided by the Department. The return includes the corporation's principal address and the names and addresses of all of the officers and directors.

LOBBYING

Contact:

> Department of State
> State House
> Room 204
> Concord, NH 03301
> (603) 271-3242

Citation: RSA 15 15:1 et seq.

Publications: A copy of the statute is available from the contact office.

Registration required: Must be done in person; all lobbyists (legislative counsel) must register with the Secretary of State; all registrations expire each year on December 31; the fee is $50 for each lobbyist and $50 for each client. Lobbyists must wear a clearly visible name tag when lobbying in the state house or the legislative office building. The badge shall have white lettering on a hunter orange background and shall be at least 2.5 inches high and 2.5 inches long with their first and last name and the word "lobbyist" at least .25 inches high.

Reporting requirements: Lobbyists must file itemized statements on April 15, August 15, and December 15 covering the periods of registration March 31, April 1-July 31, and August 1-December 1 respectively. The form requires disclosure of lobbyist fees and other compensation; expenditures made directly by the lobbyist; and lobbyist expenditures charged by the lobbyist to the client. All disclosures are itemized by date received, who paid, and the amount of expenditure.

TAX EXEMPTIONS

Contact:

Department of Revenue Administrator
45 Chenell Drive
PO Box 457
Concord, NH 03302-0637
(603) 271-2186

Citation: 77-A:1—Business Profits Tax.

Requirements: Corporations exempt from the federal income tax are exempt from the state business profits tax. There is no corporate sales tax. Nonprofit corporations other than 501(c)(3)s are subject to the Business Enterprise Tax.

CHARITABLE SOLICITATION

Contact:

Department of Justice
Office of the Attorney General
Charitable Trusts Unit
33 Capitol Street
Concord, NH 03301-6397
(603) 271-3591

Citation: RSA 7:19 et seq.

Publications: A copy of the statute is available from the contact office and from the web site: http://www.state.nh.us/oag/char.html

Initial Registration: Charitable organizations must register with the Register of Charitable Trusts one time only. There is a fee of $25. Registration discloses general information about the charity. Charitable corporations must attach Articles of Incorporation and bylaws; other types of organizations must attach a copy of Articles of Agreement or other governing document; names and home addresses, telephone numbers and titles of at least five trustees/directors and officers; a copy of the most recent balance sheet or financial information (copy of checkbook register and/or savings passbook account if newly formed and without a balance sheet); a copy of the organization's conflict of interest policy; whether the organization has applied to the IRS for a tax exemp-

tion and a copy of the IRS determination letter if applicable; and disclose the month the fiscal year ends. Every charitable organization must adopt a conflict-of-interest policy, pursuant to RSA 19 II.

Annual reports: Must file financial reports (or federal 990 form) within 4 months and 15 days after the end of each fiscal year along with a $50 filing fee.

Organization Solicitation Disclosure requirements: see below.

Paid Solicitor Requirements: Must register, pay a $200 filing fee and post a $20,000 bond. Contracts with charities must be in writing. Paid solicitors must clearly and conspicuously disclose prior to orally requesting a contribution, or contemporaneously with a written request, the name of the paid solicitor, that the solicitation is being conducted by a paid fundraiser, and that the charity shall receive a fixed percentage of the gross revenue, or the reasonable estimate, which is included in the contract between the solicitor and the charity. There are restrictions on solicitations involving tickets to events as well.

Fundraising Counsel Requirements: Must register, pay a $75 fee and post a $10,000 bond. Within 90 days after a solicitation campaign, and on the anniversary of a campaign lasting more than one year, a fundraising counsel shall account to the charitable trust for all contributions collected and expenses paid, in writing. Each contribution collected shall within five days of receipt be deposited at a bank or other federally insured financial institution in the name of the charity. The charity shall have sole authority to make withdrawals.

New Jersey

Central Switchboard: (609) 292-2121
State Web Home Page: http://www.state.nj.us/

INCORPORATION

Contact:

New Jersey Division of Revenue
Corporate Filing Unit
225 West State Street
PO Box 308
Trenton, NJ 08625-0308
(609) 530-6412

Citation: *New Jersey Nonprofit Corporation Act;*
N.J.S.A. 15A:1-1 et seq.

Publications Available: Forms and instructions are available from the contact office.

General Requirements: One or more individuals at least 18 years of age or corporations may act as incorporators (10 or more persons are required to serve as incorporators of volunteer fire companies). Certificate of Incorporation must set forth the corporate name; purpose(s); if it will have members; the qualifications and rights of membership if there will be members; the method for electing trustees (or a statement that this will be in the bylaws); optional provisions relating to the internal regulation and management of the corporation; the address of the initial registered office; the name of the initial registered agent at that address; the number of trustees of the first board of directors (may not be less than three); their names and addresses; the name, address and signature of each incorporator; the duration (if other than perpetual); the method for the distribution of assets upon dissolution (or that this is described in the bylaws); and optional limitations on liability for directors and officers.

Corporate Name: Shall contain one of the following: "a New Jersey nonprofit corporation," "incorporated," "corporation," "inc." or "corp;" shall not contain any word or phrase, or abbreviation or derivation thereof, which indicates or implies that it is organized for any purpose other than permitted by its Certificate of Incorporation; shall not be the same as, or confusingly similar to, another without written permission; shall not contain any word or phrase, abbreviation or derivation thereof, the use of which is prohibited by any other statute.

Name Check/name reservation: Call (609) 530-8312 for name search. There is a charge for expedited telephone name search (credit cards accepted). The name may be reserved for 120 days for a $50 fee.

How to File: File Form C-101 in triplicate along with a filing fee of $50 plus $15 for each certified copy requested. Enclose a self-addressed, stamped envelope to receive a filed copy.

Other Filings/reports: An annual report must be filed along with a $15 filing fee. The report discloses general information, including the names and addresses of trustees and officers, on forms provided by the contact office. The contact office notifies each corporation within 60 days prior to the due date, and the report must be filed during the anniversary month of the organization's initial incorporation.

LOBBYING

Contact:

Election Law Enforcement Commission
CN-185
Trenton, NJ 08625-0185
(609) 292-8700

Citation: 52:13C-18 et seq.

Registration required: Lobbyists must register with the Commission before lobbying, or within 30 days of being hired as a lobbyist. The registration form discloses general information, information about clients, a description of lobbying interest, whether the lobbyist is a paid lobbyist, and the legislation or regulation of interest.

Reporting requirements: Quarterly reports on lobbying activity must be filed describing the target of lobbying activity that was actively promoted or opposed. These reports are due between the first and tenth days of each calendar quarter covering activity during the preceding calendar quarter. If receipts or expenditures exceed $2,500 in any calendar year, an annual report of financial activity is required to be filed.

TAX EXEMPTIONS

Contact:

Department of Treasury
Division of Taxation—Tax Services Branch
50 Barrack Street
PO Box-269
Trenton, NJ 08646-0269
(609) 292-5995

Citation: 54 §10A-3, Exempt Corporations—corporate income taxes; 54 § 32B-9—sales and use taxes.

Publications: *Exempt Organization Certificate* form and information booklet are available from the contact office.

Requirements: Nonprofit corporations are exempt from the Corporation Business Tax Act. Certain nonprofit organizations, churches, scientific, and charitable organizations with 501(c)(3) status may apply for sales tax exemption status.

Application Procedure: To apply for exemption from the Corporation Business Tax, file an affidavit, signed by an officer of the corporation and sworn before a notary public, indicating that the corporation is not operated to make a profit, without regard as to whether there is a profit or loss for any particular year; is organized without capital stock; is incorporated under the provisions of Title 15, Title 15A, 16, or 17 of the Revised Statutes of New Jersey or under a special charter or similar general or special law; and is not conducted for the pecuniary profit or benefit of any shareholder or individual. Include a copy of the Certificate of Incorporation and bylaws containing a dissolution clause with respect to how assets will be distributed upon dissolution. To apply for sales and use tax exemption, submit an *Application for Exempt Organization Permit* (Form ST-5B) with an *Application for Registration* (Form REG-1), Articles of Incorporation, bylaws, IRS determination letter, and a REG-1E application form.

CHARITABLE SOLICITATION

Contact:

NJ Dept. of Law & Public Safety
Charities Registration Section
124 Halsey Street
PO Box 45021
Newark, NJ 07101
(201) 504-6262
(201) 504-6215 (Charities Hotline)

Citation: *Charitable Registration and Investigation Act*, New Jersey Statutes Annotated Title 45, Subtitle 2, Chapter 17A 45:17A-18 et seq.

Publications: *Charitable Registration and Investigation* booklet is available from the contact office.

Initial Registration: Annual registration is accomplished by using the long form (150I) or short form (CRI-200, for those that did not receive more than $25,000 in gross contributions during the preceding year and fundraising was conducted entirely by volunteers). Fees range from $30 to $250 depending upon contributions raised (minimum $60 fee for those filing the long form). Generally, organizations must submit audited financial reports and IRS 990s, IRS determination letters, information about paid fundraisers and solicitors, and information about organizational misconduct. If a charity has gross revenue over $100,000, a certified audit is required.

Annual reports: Charities must file *Renewal Statements* each year. The report is due within six months of the end of the charity's fiscal year along with an annual fee ranging from $60 to $250 based on amount raised. The statement provides for itemized receipt and expenditure disclosures, conflict of interest disclosures, information about how contributions were used, information about paid fundraisers, and general information.

Organization Solicitation Disclosure requirements: Solicitation materials must contain a disclaimer "Information filed with the attorney general concerning this charitable solicitation may be obtained from the attorney general of the state of New Jersey by calling (973) 504-6215. Registration with the attorney general does not imply endorsement." Upon request of the donor, written confirmation, receipts, or written reminders must be sent.

Paid Solicitor Requirements: Must register annually and pay a $250 fee and post a $20,000 bond. There is also a $15 fee for persons working with a paid solicitor. Renewal of registration for solicitors is $15. At least 10 days prior to initiating a solicitation campaign the solicitor must send the contract with a $30 fee to the Attorney General describing the nature, purpose, and the proposed dates and location of the solicitations.

Fundraising Counsel Requirements: Must register; pay a $250 fee and, if applicable, post a $20,000 bond if they have access to the charity's funds at any time. Contracts with a charity must be in writing and must be filed along with a form CRI-500 to assure that the contract meets the requirements of the law.

New Mexico

Central Switchboard: (505) 827-9632
State Web Home Page: http://www.state.nm.us/

INCORPORATION

Contact:

New Mexico Public Regulation Commission
1120 Paseo de Peralta
PO Box 1269
Santa Fe, NM 87504-1269
(505) 827-4084

Citation: New Mexico Nonprofit Corporation Act, NMSA 53-8-1 et seq.

Publications Available: Requirements for Incorporating a New Mexico Corporation for Nonprofit and forms and instructions are available from the contact office.

General Requirements: One or more persons may serve as incorporators. The Articles of Incorporation must set forth the corporate name; period of duration; purpose(s); provisions relating to the distribution of assets upon dissolution; provisions relating to internal regulation; the address of the initial registered office and the name of the registered agent at that address; the number of directors constituting the initial board of directors (must be at least three), their names, and addresses; and the name and address of each incorporator.

Corporate Name: Shall not contain any word or phrase that indicates or implies that it is organized for any purpose other than contained in its Articles of Incorporation; shall not be the same as, or confusingly similar to, another.

Name reservation: May be reserved for 120 days for a $10 fee.

How to File: File duplicate originals of the Articles of Incorporation along with a $25 filing fee with the contact office. There is an additional fee of $10 if a certified copy is requested plus a copying fee of $1/page, minimum $5, if provided by the Commission. The initial registered agent must submit an affidavit accepting appointment as that agent.

Other Filings/reports: An annual report is required to be filed disclosing general information, including the names and addresses of its directors and officers, and a brief statement of the character of the affairs the corporation is actually conducting in the state. Forms for the report are sent out at least 30 days before the due date by the contact office.

LOBBYING

Contact:

Office of the Secretary of State
Ethics Administration
State Capitol Room 420
Santa Fe, NM 87503
(505) 476-0354

Citation: Lobbyist Regulation Act, Chapter 2, Article 11 2-11-1 et. seq. NMSA 1978.

Publications: Am I A Lobbyist?, the occasional newsletter Lobbyist Letter, Highlights of the Lobbyist Regulation Act, and a copy of the statute are available on the web site: http://www.sos.state.nm.us/

Registration required: Lobbyists must register with the Secretary of State. Lobbyists must also pay a $25 fee for each employer for which compensation is received. If no compensation is provided, then no fee is required. Each lobbyist must also file a lobbyist authorization form for each client/employer.

Forms to use: LOB-REG-Lobbyist Registration Form; Lobbyist Authorization Form; Lobbyist Report of Expenditures and Contributions.

Reporting requirements: Reports of expenditures and contributions are due by January 15 (January 18 for the year 2000) for all expenditures and political contributions made/incurred during the preceding year and not previously reported; within 48 hours, expenditures of $500 or more must be reported; reports are due May 1 for all previously unreported expenditures and political contributions made or incurred since the January filing.

The reports are divided as follows: *Lobbyist Reporting Form A* is a general overview of the entire report; *Lobbyist Reporting Form B* itemizes expenditures; *Lobbyist Reporting Form C* provides for disclosure concerning special events; *Lobbyist Reporting Form D* discloses information about political contributions; and *Lobbyist Reporting Form E* discloses information about bundling of political contributions.

Itemized expenditures are categorized by meal and beverage, entertainment, gift, other, special events, and political contributions.

TAX EXEMPTIONS

Contact:

Taxation and Revenue Department
Tax Information/Policy Office
PO Box 630
Santa Fe, NM 87504-0630
(505) 827-0939

Citation: §7-2-4.

Publications: *Information for Non-Profit Organizations* booklet is available from the contact office.

Requirements: 501(c)(3)s are generally exempt from gross receipts tax on their sales and can make tax-free purchases of tangibles (but not services or leasing) if they furnish a *Nontaxable Transaction Certificate* (NTTC). Federally exempt organizations are generally exempt from the income and franchise tax.

Application Procedure: File a *Combined Reporting System* (CRS) which consists of a tax form relating to the gross receipts tax, withholding tax, and compensating tax.

CHARITABLE SOLICITATION

Contact:

Attorney General
Consumer Protection Division
PO Drawer 1508
Santa Fe, NM 87504-1508
(505) 827-6693
1-800 678-1508 (in NM)

Citation: *Charitable Organizations and Solicitations Act*, Section 57-22-1, et seq., NMSA 1978.

Publications: A copy of the statute and *Registration and Annual Reporting Requirements* leaflet are available from the contact office.

Initial Registration: All 501(c)(3) charities or those that have applied for such status must register with the Registrar of Charitable Organizations prior to solicitation of funds. Charities must submit a copy of the Articles of Incorporation and Certificate of Incorporation, a copy of their IRS tax exemption determination letter or, if the status has not been granted, a copy of the completed *Request for Exemption* (form 1023); a copy of the most recent IRS Form 990 or, if not required to file it, a completed *Annual Report Form* provided by the Attorney General. Charities which raise $2,500 or less annually, educational institutions, and religious organizations are among those exempt from registering.

Annual reports: A charity must file its federal 990 each year, due 75 days after the close of the charity's fiscal year. Because the state's filing date precedes the date the 990s are due to the IRS, organizations filing the 990 or 990-EZ are granted an extension of time up to the IRS 990 filing deadline.

Organization Solicitation Disclosure requirements: Upon request, all charities must disclose the percentage of funds solicited which are spent on the costs of fundraising.

Paid Solicitor Requirements: Professional fundraisers must disclose that they are such to prospective contributors.

Fundraising Counsel Requirements: None.

New York

Central Switchboard: (518) 474-2121
State Web Home Page: http://www.state.ny.us/

INCORPORATION

Contact:

Department of State
Bureau of Corporations
41 State Street
Albany, NY 12231-0001
(518) 473-2492

Citation: *Not-for-Profit Corporation Law*, Chapter 35, Articles 1-15, Sec. 101 et seq. of the Consolidated Laws.

Publications Available: Excerpts from the *Not-for-Profit Corporation Law* are provided by the contact office.

General Requirements: Articles of Incorporation must set forth the name, address and signature of each incorporator; corporate name; purpose(s); the county where the corporation will be located; the names and addresses of initial directors (Type A, B & C only—see below); the duration; the corporation's agent; the name and address of any registered agent; statements required for special not-for-profit corporations; and provisions relating to internal regulation.

Type A: corporations formed for any lawful non-business purpose or purposes, including, but not limited to, any one or more of the following non-pecuniary purposes: civic, patriotic, political, social, fraternal, athletic, agricultural, horticultural, animal husbandry, and for a professional, commercial, industrial, trade or service association.

Type B: corporations formed for any one or more of the following non-business purposes: charitable, educational, religious, scientific, literary, cultural or for the prevention of cruelty to children or animals.

Type C: corporations formed for any lawful business purpose to achieve a lawful public or quasi-public objective.

Type D: corporations formed when such formation is authorized by any other corporate law of this state for any business or non-business, or pecuniary or non-pecuniary, purpose or purposes specified by such other law, whether such purpose or purposes are also within types A, B, C above or otherwise.
If a corporation is formed for purposes which are both type A and B, it is type B. If a corporation has among its purposes any purpose which is within type C, it is type C.

Corporate Name: Shall contain the word "corporation," "incorporated," or "limited," or an abbreviation, unless it is formed for charitable or religious purposes; shall not be the same as or so similar to any such name as to tend to confuse or deceive; may not be indecent or obscene or ridicule or degrade any person, group, belief, business or agency of government or indicate or imply any unlawful activity; may not contain any word or phrase that indicates or implies that it is authorized for a purpose other than that is permitted; may not contain certain words that are financially related, or words such as "doctor" or "lawyer," unless the organization is composed exclusively of doctors or lawyers, as the case may be.

Name Check/name reservation: May be done in writing; telephone inquiries are not accepted; the fee for the name search is $5 for each name. To reserve a name, file DOS-635 form *Application for Reservation of Name*. The fee is $10; the name will be reserved for 60 days with two extensions permitted.

How to File: Forms for filing Articles of Incorporation are available for purchase from NY State legal stationery stores. Forms may also be drafted by the filer following the requirements in the law. Each document must contain a separate page that sets forth the title of the document being submitted and the name and address of the individual to which the receipt for the filing of the document should be mailed. The filing fee is $75.

Other Filings/reports: An annual report must be filed with the appropriate office showing assets and liabilities, changes thereto, revenues, expenses, number of members, and a statement of their increase or decrease.

LOBBYING

Contact:

New York State Commission on Lobbying
Two Empire State Plaza
Suite 1701
Albany, NY 12223-1254
(518) 474-7126

Citation: *Lobbying Act*, (L. 1981, Chapter 1040 of the Consolidated Laws of New York, as amended by chapter 435, Laws of 1997).

Publications: A copy of the statute and *Guidelines* are available from the contact office or through its web site (www.nylobby.state.ny.us).

Registration required: Lobbyists, public corporations, and clients of lobbyists must register annually if they expend or receive more than $2,000 of combined reportable compensation and expenses for lobbying activities. Registration discloses general information about the lobbyist and client. Written lobbying contracts must be attached or a summary of any oral agreement. The dollar amount of compensation must be included. The general subject of lobbying must be disclosed as well as the nature of the client's business.

Forms to use: *New York State Lobbyist Statement of Registration for (current year)*.

Reporting requirements: Four itemized spending reports are required disclosing compensation and expenditures for the periods ending March 31 (due April 15), May 31 (due June 15), August 31 (due September 15), and an annual report for the year (due January 15). Client annual report forms and instruction booklets are mailed out each December. Any lobbying expense in excess of $75 must be fully identified. Clients must also file annual reports.

TAX EXEMPTIONS

Contact:
> NY State Department of Taxation and Finance
> Taxpayer Assistance Bureau
> WA Harriman Campus
> Albany, NY 12227
> 1-800-972-1233

Citation: §§209.9-Article 9A—Business Corporations —corporation tax; §1116 —sales and use tax.

Requirements: Organizations exempt from federal income tax are exempt from state corporation income taxes, other than unrelated business income tax. Generally, 501(c)(3) organizations are exempt from sales and use tax.

Application Procedure: File form CT-247 for corporate franchise tax exemption. Present form ST-119.1 to each vendor for sales tax exemption. To claim tax-exempt status, use form ST-119.2 to apply for an Exempt Organization Certificate, which will permit tax-exempt purchases and sales. However, if an organization makes sales through a shop, store, restaurant, tavern or similar establishment, they must register as a vendor and collect and pay sales tax.

CHARITABLE SOLICITATION

Contact:
> New York State Department of Law
> Charities Bureau
> 120 Broadway
> New York, NY 10271
> (212) 416-8400

Citation: Article 7-A of the Executive Law.

Publications: *Summary of Registration and Filing Requirements for Charitable Organizations Soliciting Charitable Contributions in New York State* is available from the contact office.

Initial Registration: Charitable organizations must register with the Attorney General prior to soliciting contributions if they solicit or receive contributions in excess of $25,000 annually or pay anyone other than an employee of the charity for fundraising functions. Charities register by filing a Form CHAR 410 *Charities Registration Statement* or the Unified Registration Statement (URS) and paying a one-time $25 fee. The registration form includes general information; a list of professional fundraisers and fundraising counsel; the purposes of the organization; the purposes for which contributions are solicited; the names, addresses, titles and terms of directors, trustees and officers; other entities which share in the revenues raised; names of banks, addresses, and account numbers; and information about previous organizational misconduct. Charities must enclose their Certificate of Incorporation, IRS tax exemption determination letter, and previous year's financial report.

Annual reports: Charities must file CHAR 497, *Annual Financial Report*, and IRS 990 if they have one. The fee ranges from $10 to $25 based on contributions received. The CHAR 497 provides a financial summary of support, revenue and expenses; a balance sheet; itemizations of public support and government grants; descriptions of campaigns; and information about professional fundraisers, fundraising counsel and commercial coventurers. An accountant's review is required of organizations with income between $75,000 and $150,000 and an audit is required of organizations with income over $150,000. The organization's 990 must be attached. The report is due within 4½ months following the close of the fiscal year.

Organization Solicitation Disclosure requirements: Must include the statement: "A copy of the latest annual report may be obtained from the organization or from the Attorney General, 120 Broadway, NY, NY 10271."

Professional Fundraiser Requirements: Registration is required, along with payment of an annual fee of $800 and the posting of a $10,000 bond. There is an $80 registration fee for individuals employed by a professional fundraiser.

Fundraising Counsel Requirements: Annual registration is required along with an $800 fee.

North Carolina

Central Switchboard: (919) 733-1110
State Web Home Page: http://www.state.nc.us/

INCORPORATION

Contact:
> Corporations Division
> Department of Secretary of State
> 300 North Salisbury Street
> Raleigh, NC 27603-5909
> (919) 733-4201

Citation: *North Carolina Nonprofit Corporation Act*, N.C. Gen. Stat. (paragraph) 55A.

Publications Available: *North Carolina Nonprofit Corporation Guidelines* is available from the contact office.

General Requirements: Must have at least one director. Articles of Incorporation must set forth the corporate name, designation as a charitable or religious corporation if applicable; the name and address of its registered agent who must be a resident of the state; the address of a registered office and the county where it is located; the name and address of at least one incorporator; a statement that the corporation has or does not have members; provision for the distribution of assets upon dissolution and termination; and the address of its principal office. The Articles may also, but are not required to, contain a statement of the corporation's purposes; the names and addresses of the initial directors; provisions relating to the corporation's management and regulation; provisions defining, limiting, or regulating the powers of the corporation, its members, or directors; provisions relating to the qualifications, rights, and responsibilities of members; and provisions relating to personal liability of directors.

Corporate Name: May not imply a purpose other than a purpose that is lawful and permitted by its Articles of Incorporation; must be distinguishable from names of other corporations authorized to transact business in North Carolina.

Name Check/name reservation: May check with the Office of the Secretary of State to see whether a proposed name is available; may be reserved for a 120-day period for a $10 fee, but is not renewable.

How to File: One original and one exact or conformed copy of the Articles of Incorporation must be submitted to the Office of the Secretary of State by mail or in person with a $50 filing fee.

Other Filings/reports: None.

LOBBYING

Contact:
> Lobbyist Registration
> Department of the Secretary of State
> 300 North Salisbury Street
> Raleigh, NC 27603-5909
> (919) 733-5181

Citation: Article 9A, Chapter 120, General Statutes of North Carolina.

Publications: A copy of the statute and *Lobbying Guidelines—General Information* sheet (Form LR-GI) and relevant forms are available from the contact office.

Registration required: Lobbyists must register with the Department of Secretary of State before lobbying; registration is effective from date of filing to January 1 of the following odd-numbered year; filing fee is $75 for each lobbyist's client/employer (the entity on whose behalf the lobbying is performed); a written authorization must be filed by each lobbyist client/employer within 10 days of registration that the lobbyist is authorized to lobby for the client.

Forms to use: LR-1 for Lobbyist Registration; LR-2 for Authorization statements; LR-3 for Lobbyist Expense Reports; LR-4 for Principal Expense Reports.

Reporting requirements: Expense reports are filed with respect to each client/employer within 60 days after the last day of the regular legislative session. These reports are divided into the following categories: transportation, lodging, entertainment, food items with a cash equivalent of greater than $25, and contributions. Supplemental reports must be filed for the period after the legislative session ends but by February 28th of the following year.

TAX EXEMPTIONS

Contact:

> North Carolina Department of Revenue
> PO Box 25000
> Raleigh, NC 27640
> (919) 733-4668

Citation: G.S. Subchapter 5b —Franchise Tax; 5c— Corporate Income Tax; 105-125, 105-130.11, 105-130.12.

Publications: *Franchise Tax and Corporate Income Tax, Rules and Bulletins* are available from the contact office.

Requirements: Upon incorporation, the Department of State sends a notice to the Department of Revenue. The Department of Revenue sends a letter of notification to the corporation with a five-part questionnaire that is used to determine tax-exempt status. The fact that a corporation is exempt from federal income taxes is a factor in state exemption.

Application Procedure: The corporation should submit the questionnaire along with its Articles of Incorporation, bylaws and, if applicable, any tax-exempt organization provisions. The Department notifies the corporation by mail as to whether it is exempt from franchise and income taxes.

CHARITABLE SOLICITATION

Contact:

> Department of the Secretary of State
> Solicitation Licensing Branch
> PO Box 29622
> Raleigh, NC 27626-0525
> (919) 733-4510

Citation: Charitable Solicitations Act; N.C. Gen. Stat. (PP)131F-1-131F-33.

Publications: A copy of the statute, regulations, and forms are available from the contact office.

Initial Registration: Applies only to organizations that receive more than $25,000 in contributions in any calendar year and do not provide compensation to any officer, trustee, organizer, incorporator, fundraiser, or solicitor. Many types of organizations, such as hospitals, volunteer fire and rescue squads, educational institutions, non-commercial radio and TV stations, and YMCA/YWCAs are exempt. Registration must disclose general information; the purpose for which the contributions will be used; the date when the fiscal year ends; a list or description of major program activities; the names of individuals in charge of solicitation activities; a financial report which includes a balance sheet; a statement of support, revenue and expenses and any changes in the fund balance; a statement of program, management and general, and fundraising expenses (or a copy of its federal 990 and schedule A); a budget for the current year if it does not have a financial history; a statement including whether it is authorized by any other state to solicit contributions; whether any of its officers, directors, trustees, or paid staff have engaged in unlawful practices relating to solicitation or otherwise have been implicated in unlawful solicitation practices; the names, addresses and telephone numbers and compensation/terms of reimbursement for expenses of any solicitor, fundraising consultant, or coventurer; a copy of any IRS tax determination letter; and when/where the organization was established (for initial registration only). Fees for registration are $50 for contributions received during the previous fiscal year of under $100,000, $100 if $100,000-$199,999, and $200 if $200,000 or more in contributions.

Annual reports: see above.

Organization Solicitation Disclosure Requirements: Must display in at least 9-point type a statement that *"Financial information about this organization and a copy of its license are available from the State Solicitation Licensing Branch at (919-733-4510). The license is not an endorsement by the State."* The statement must be made conspicuous by either underlining, a border, or bold type.

Paid Solicitor Requirements: A $200 registration fee is required for both initial and renewal licenses; license expires on March 31 of each year. A bond of $20,000 is required if contributions received for the last fiscal year were less than $100,000; $30,000 if at least $100,000 and less than $200,000; and $50,000 if at least $200,000.

Fundraising Counsel Requirements: Same as above.

North Dakota

Central Switchboard: (701) 328-2000
State Web Home Page: http://www.state.nd.us/

INCORPORATION

Contact:

> Secretary of State
> Business Division
> Department 108
> 600 East Boulevard Avenue
> Bismarck, ND 58505-0500
> (701) 328-4284

Citation: *ND Nonprofit Corporation Act*, North Dakota Century Code, Chapter 10-33.

Publications Available: A copy of the *ND Nonprofit Corporation Act* is available from the contact office for a fee.

General Requirements: Articles of Incorporation must set forth the corporate name; that it is organized under Chapter 10-33 of the North Dakota Century Code; the address of the registered office; the name of the initial registered agent at that office; the effective date of the corporation; and the names, addresses, and signatures of the incorporators (at least one required).

Corporate Name: May not contain any word or phrase which indicates or implies that it is organized for any purpose other than a legal purpose for which a nonprofit corporation may be organized; may not be the same as, or deceptively similar to, another without written consent; must be transliterated into letters of the English language if it is not in English.

Name reservation: May be reserved for a renewable period of one year for a $10 fee.

How to File: Submit to the Secretary of State an original of the Articles of Incorporation, a signed consent of the registered agent form, a filing fee of $30 for the Articles of Incorporation and $10 for the consent form.

Other Filings/reports: An annual report must be filed disclosing general information, a brief statement describing the purpose that is actually pursued in the state, the names and addresses of officers and directors, and federal tax exemption information. The report, submitted on forms provided by the Secretary of State, is due on or before February 1 each year; the first report is due February 1 of the year following the year of incorporation. There is a $10 filing fee.

LOBBYING

Contact:

> Secretary of State
> Licensing Division
> 600 East Boulevard Avenue
> 1st Floor, Capitol Building
> Bismarck, ND 58505-0500
> (701) 328-3665

Citation: North Dakota Century Code, Chapter 54-05.1- 01 et seq.

Publications: A copy of the statute is available from the contact office.

Registration required: All lobbyists must register with the Secretary before engaging in lobbying. Registration includes general information, the code of primary activities of the entity, and a letter of authorization from each entity represented. The fees is $20 for the first entity represented and $5 for each additional one.

Forms to use: SFN 11106 *Lobbyist Registration;* NDCC 54-05.1 *Authorization Letter for Lobbyist.*

Reporting requirements: A detailed report is required to be submitted on or before August 1 each year of expenditures of $25 or more during the legislative session for lobbying.

TAX EXEMPTIONS

Contact:

> North Dakota Office of State Tax Commissioner
> 600 E. Boulevard Avenue
> Bismarck, ND 58505-0599
> income tax: (701) 328-2046
> sales tax: (701) 328-3470

Citation: §57-38-09 —state income tax; §57-39.2-04 —sales tax.

Requirements: Organizations exempt from paying federal income tax are exempt from the state income tax. There are limited exemptions provided under the sales tax law. Consult the statute or the contact office.

CHARITABLE SOLICITATION

Contact:

> Secretary of State
> 600 East Boulevard Avenue
> Bismarck, ND 58505-3665
> (701) 328-3665

Citation: North Dakota Century Code, Section 50-22-01 et seq.

Publications: A copy of the statute is provided by the contact office.

Initial Registration: All charitable organizations must obtain an annual license to solicit before soliciting; licenses expire on September 1. If an initial license is issued in July or August, the license is valid until September 1 of the following year. The license fee is $25 for the initial license and $10 for subsequent licenses. The license application requires disclosure of general information, information about officers and the organization's auditor, names of professional fundraiser/solicitor, copies of the agreement between them, and information about organizational misconduct. Registration form must disclose the gross amount of contributions pledged or collected, the amount given to the charitable purpose, the amount paid for fundraising expenses, and the amount paid to professional fundraisers and solicitors.

Annual reports: See above.

Organization Solicitation Disclosure requirements: None.

Paid Solicitor Requirements: Must apply for a license and pay a $100 annual fee.

Fundraising Counsel Requirements: Must apply for a license and pay a $100 annual fee.

Ohio

Central Switchboard: (614) 466-2000
State Web Home Page: http://www.state.oh.us/

INCORPORATION

Contact:
> Secretary of State
> Business Services
> 30 East Broad Street
> 14th Floor
> Columbus, OH 43266-0418
> (614) 466-3623

Citation: *Nonprofit Corporation Law,* §1702.01 et seq.

Publications Available: *Legal Handbook for Nonprofit Organizations* is available from the contact office.

General Requirements: Any person, without regard to residence, may act as an incorporator. Articles of Incorporation must set forth purpose(s) (must not be too general), the names and street addresses of at least three natural persons who will serve as initial trustees, and the corporate name and location of the principal office. The articles must be signed by the incorporators.

Corporate Name: Is not required to end in "Incorporated" or "Inc.;" must be distinguishable from others without written permission.

Name reservation: May be reserved for 60 days for a fee of $5.

How to File: File Articles of Incorporation with the Secretary of State. The filing fee is $25.

Other Filings/reports: A statement of continued existence must be filed within five years from the date of incorporation or previous corporate filing. The Secretary of State provides the form and notice. The fee is $5.

LOBBYING

Contact:
> Office of the Legislative Inspector General
> Joint Legislative Ethics Committee
> 50 W. Broad Street
> Suite 1308
> Columbus, OH 43215-3365
> (614) 728-5100

Citation: Section 101.70 et seq., Ohio Revised Code; Section 121.60 et seq., Ohio Revised Code.

Publications: *Ohio Lobbying Handbook; Scenarios and Reporting Requirements for Legislative Agents and Employers,* and a copy of the statute and rules are provided by the contact office.

Registration required: Every lobbyist and employer, within 10 days after hiring a lobbyist, must file an initial registration statement with the Committee disclosing general information, a brief description of the type of legislation being lobbied, and the category of the principal business or activity of the employer. There is a $10 filing fee, which is waived for state employees. Lobbyists and employers of lobbyists must file an updated registration statement by the last day of January, May, and September, covering four-month periods ending in the month prior to the month in which the report is filed. There is no fee for that filing. The updated registration reports provide for itemized expenditure reporting. For-profit business arrangements between lobbyists or their employers (including immediate family) and members of the general assembly and certain other public officials, including staff, also require disclosure.

Forms to use: *Legislative Agent/Employer Initial Registration Statement; Legislative Agent Updated Registration Statement; Employer of Legislative Agent Updated Registration Statement*

Reporting requirements: See above.

TAX EXEMPTIONS

Contact:

> Taxation Department
> Corporate Income Tax Division
> 30 E. Broad Street; 22nd Floor
> PO Box 182857
> Columbus, OH 43218-2857
> 1-888-405-4039

Citation: §5739.02 —sales tax; §5747.01 et seq. —corporate income tax.

Publications: *Business Tax Guide* is available by calling 614-466-3960 or from the web site at http://state.oh.us/tax/

Requirements: Organizations with federal tax-exempt status are generally exempt from corporate income taxes as well, with the exception of unrelated business income taxes. Nonprofits are exempt from the Ohio franchise tax. Religious organizations and charities are generally exempt from paying Ohio sales or use tax on their purchases. Most sales by exempt organizations require the collection of sales/use tax.

Application Procedure: There is no application process for sales tax exemption. 501(c)(3)s present vendors with a certificate of exemption which is purchased from print shops, not supplied by the Department.

CHARITABLE SOLICITATION

Contact:

> Attorney General
> 101 East Town Street
> Columbus, OH 43215-5148
> (614) 466-3180

Citation: Chapter 1716, Section 1716.01 et seq.

Publications: A copy of the statute is available from the contact office.

Initial Registration: Most charitable organizations that compensate those primarily to solicit contributions or which raise more than $25,000 during their most recent fiscal year must register with the Attorney General. Initial registration must include a copy of the Articles of Incorporation or other organizational charter, bylaws, a copy of the IRS determination letter, and general information. The filing fee ranges from $50 ($5,000-$25,000 in contributions) to $200 (more than $50,000 in contributions) for the last calendar or fiscal year, received from persons within Ohio. Renewals also include general information; information about organizational misconduct; names and addresses of all officers, directors, trustees, and executive personnel; and specific financial arrangements with outside fundraisers.

Annual reports: Registration statements must be refiled on or before the 15th day of the fifth calendar month after the close of each fiscal year. The fees apply to renewal registrations as well. Charities that are required to register must file annual financial reports that include a balance sheet; a statement of support, revenue, expenses, and changes in the fund balance; the names and addresses of fundraising counsel, professional solicitors, and commercial coventurers used and the amounts received from each; a statement of functional expenses itemized by categories of program, management/general and fundraising; and a financial statement, report or IRS 990 tax return.

Organization Solicitation Disclosure requirements: Whether or not required to register by the law, every charitable organization must make disclosures at the point of solicitation of the name of the charity and the city of the principal place of business of the charity. The particular charitable purpose to be advanced with the funds raised if no 501(c)(3) determination letter has been received and is currently in effect must also be disclosed.

Paid Solicitor Requirements: Must register, pay a $200 fee and post bond in the amount of $25,000. Prior to the beginning of a solicitation campaign, professional solicitors must file a Solicitation Notice with the Attorney General. The Notice includes a copy of the contract with the charity, a certification statement by the charity, and general information about the campaign. Not later than 90 days after the campaign has been completed or on the first anniversary of the campaign, the solicitor must file a financial report.

Fundraising Counsel Requirements: Those with custody of contributions at any time must register, post a $25,000 bond, and pay a $200 fee.

Oklahoma

Central Switchboard: (405) 521-2011
State Web Home Page: http://www.state.ok.us/

INCORPORATION

Contact:

>Secretary of State
>101 State Capitol
>2300 N. Lincoln Boulevard
>Oklahoma City, OK 73105-4897
>(405) 521-3911 (forms)
>(405) 522-4560 (information)

Citation: Title 18, *Oklahoma General Corporation Act, 18 § 1001 et seq.*

Publications Available: *Title 18-Oklahoma Corporation Act* is available from the contact office; Forms and *Procedures for Organizing an Oklahoma Business Corporation* are available from the contact office.

General Requirements: A minimum of three incorporators are required. Any person (without regard to residence), partnership or corporation may act as an incorporator; must set forth the name; address of registered office; the name of the registered agent at that office; the nature of the business or purposes; the name, addresses, and signatures of each incorporator; that the corporation does not afford pecuniary gain, incidentally or otherwise, to its members; the name and mailing address of each trustee or director and the number to be elected at the first meeting; optional provisions relating to the internal regulation and management; and the duration, unless it is perpetual.

Corporate Name: Must contain one of the following words: association, company, corporation, club, foundation, fund, incorporated, institute, society, union, syndicate, or limited, or one of the abbreviations "co.," "corp.," "inc.," "ltd.," or words or abbreviations of like import in other languages provided that such abbreviations are written in Roman characters or letters. The name must be distinguishable from other corporations, limited partnerships, or limited liability companies or reserved names, including those that existed at any time during the preceding three years.

Name Check/name reservation: May be reserved for 60 days for a $10 fee by filing a name reservation application; may be checked by telephone or in person by calling (405) 522-4560.

How to File: File Articles of Incorporation in duplicate with the Secretary of State with a $25 fee.

Other Filings/reports: None.

LOBBYING

Contact:

>Ethics Commission
>B-5 State Capitol
>Oklahoma City, OK 73105
>(405) 521-3451

Citation: 74 § 4249 et seq; 74 CH 62 App., §257:23-1-1 et seq.; § 257:1-1-2.

Publications: *Constitutional and Statutory Provisions and Constitutional Ethics Rules governing the Ethical Conduct of State Officers and Employers and Campaigns for State Office or State Issues* and *1999-2000 Lobbyist Registration and Regulation* are available from the contact office.

Registration required: Lobbyists who are employed or retained by another for compensation to perform services that include lobbying must register with the Commission. Registration must occur within five days after engaging in lobbying for a new client, or during the month of January of each odd-numbered year. The form requires general information and the names and addresses of the lobbyist's clients.

Forms to use: L-1, *Lobbyist Registration;* L-2 *Lobbyist or Other Person Gift Report.*

Reporting requirements: All lobbyists and those who give things to state officers or state employees with a value of more than $50 in the aggregate during any six-month period (January 1-June 30 and July 1-December 31) must submit an L-2 report.

TAX EXEMPTIONS

Contact:
Oklahoma Tax Commission
Taxpayer Assistance Division
2501 Lincoln Blvd.
Oklahoma City, OK 73194
(405) 521-3160

Citation: 68 § 2359— income tax; 68 § 1356— sales tax.

Requirements: Organizations that are exempt from paying federal income tax are exempt from paying state income taxes other than on unrelated business income. There are limited exemptions provided to charities and educational institutions provided in the statute, such as churches, council organizations of the Boy Scouts and Girl Scouts, and the Camp Fire Girls. Consult the contact office or the statute for more information.

Application Procedure: File an annual form 512-E with the Commission.

CHARITABLE SOLICITATION

Contact:
Oklahoma Secretary of State
2300 N. Lincoln Boulevard
State Capitol Building
Room 101
Oklahoma City, OK 73105-4897
(405) 521-3911

Citation: Oklahoma Solicitation of Charitable Contributions Act, 18 §552.1 et seq.

Initial Registration: All charitable organizations must register with the Secretary of State using the Uniform Registration Statement— Charitable Organization form. The statement discloses general information, information about organizational misconduct, information about use of outside professional fundraisers and amounts paid to them during the previous year, total contributions in the previous year, total fundraising costs in the previous year, and information about methods of solicitation. Charities must attach any brochures used for solicitation, a $15 check, a copy of their federal form 990, a photocopy of the driver's license of

the executive director or one member of the executive board, and the birth date and social security number of one or the other.

Annual reports: Every charity which has received contributions during the previous calendar year must file an annual report on or before March 31 of the following year, or 90 days after the end of the fiscal year. This report provides financial information, how contributions were used, and a copy of contracts with professional fundraisers. The federal 990 and annual statement or audit report must be attached. A year-end financial statement of revenues and expenses must be sent if the organization does not file a 990.

Organization Solicitation Disclosure requirements: None.

Paid Solicitor Requirements: Must register, pay a $50 fee and post a $2,500 bond.

Fundraising Counsel Requirements: None.

Oregon

Central Switchboard: (503) 378-6500
State Web Home Page: http://www.state.or.us/

INCORPORATION

Contact:
> Secretary of State
> Corporation Division
> 255 Capitol St. NE; Suite 151
> Salem, OR 97310-1327
> (503) 986-2200

Citation: Chapter 65 ORS65.001 et seq.

Publications Available: A copy of Chapter 65, Nonprofit Corporations law, is available from the Legislative Counsel (503-986-1243). The Business Information Center (503-986-2222) provides an information packet that includes Articles of Incorporation forms and the *Oregon Business Guide.*

General Requirements: Articles of Incorporation must set forth corporate name; a statement that the corporation is a public benefit corporation, a mutual benefit corporation, or a religious corporation; the address of the corporation's initial registered office and the name of its initial registered agent at that location; the name and address of each incorporator; an alternative corporate mailing address until the principal office has been designated in the annual report; whether the corporation will have members; provisions regarding distribution of assets upon dissolution; and optional provisions.

Corporate Name: May not contain language stating or implying that it is organized for a purpose other than permitted by law or its articles; shall not contain the word "cooperative" or the phrase "limited partnership." Shall be written in the alphabet used for the English language, but may include Arabic and Roman numerals and incidental punctuation; and shall be distinguishable from others.

Name reservation: May be reserved for a renewable 120-day period for a fee of $10.

How to File: File one original with the Secretary of State with a $20 filing fee. Documents can be faxed in with a Visa or MasterCard number. The fax number is on the form; faxed documents will be filed in 2-3 business days.

Other Filings/reports: An annual report with a $10 filing fee must be filed with the Secretary of State with general information, a brief description of the nature of the activities, and the names and addresses of the president and secretary. Forms are mailed by the Secretary of State in advance of the due date, but failure to receive the form does not relieve the corporation of its duty to file the report.

LOBBYING

Contact:
> Oregon Government Standards and Practices Commission
> 100 High Street, SE, Suite 220
> Salem, OR 97310
> (503) 378-5105

Citation: ORS 171.725 et seq.

Publications: *Guide to Lobbying in Oregon* is available from the contact office.

Registration required: All lobbyists who spend more than 24 hours excluding travel time lobbying in any calendar quarter, or spend more than $100 (excluding personal travel, meals, and lodging) for lobbying in a calendar quarter must register, within three days of achieving these thresholds. There is no registration fee.

Forms to use: *Lobbyist Registration Statement; Lobbyist Expenditure Report; Entity Expenditure Report.*

Reporting requirements: All lobbyists must submit quarterly or semi-annual itemized expenditure reports. Employers of lobbyists must submit annual itemized expenditure reports. Lobbyist reports are due on January 31 and July 31 of each even-numbered year and January 31, April 30, and July 31 of each odd-numbered year. Employer reports are due January 31 each year. Expenditure categories for lobbyists include food and refreshment; entertainment; printing, postage and telephone; advertising and public relations; education and research; and miscellaneous. Itemization of expenditures of more than $62 (for 1999) is required if on behalf of an individual legislator or executive official. This threshold is adjusted annually based on the Portland area CPI.

TAX EXEMPTIONS

Contact:

> Oregon Department of Revenue
> 955 Center Street, NE
> Salem, OR 97310
> (503) 378-4988
> 1-800-356-4222 (January -April)

Citation: Chapter 317.080, Oregon Revised Statutes —corporate income tax.

Requirements: Organizations with federal tax-exempt status are automatically exempt from state corporate excise taxes/income taxes other than unrelated business taxable income. If organizations have unrelated taxable income, they need to file a Form 20 (Oregon Corporate Excise Tax Return) and attach a copy of their federal 990T.

Application Procedure: Organizations qualify for exemption automatically upon receiving their IRS determination letters certifying federal exemption.

CHARITABLE SOLICITATION

Contact:

> Department of Justice
> Civil Enforcement Division
> Charitable Activities Section
> 1515 SW 5th Avenue, Suite 410
> Portland, OR 97201
> (503) 229-5725

Citation: Charitable Trust and Corporation Act, ORS 128.610 et seq.; Oregon Administrative Rules, Chapter 137, Section 10-005 et seq.

Publications: Forms and a copy of the statute are available from the contact office.

Initial Registration: Charitable corporations and trusts must register with the Department of Justice. Corporations must include Articles of Incorporation; bylaws; IRS determination letter; printed brochures, reports and newsletters; and a list of directors. Charitable trusts must include a trust agreement or will, the IRS determination letter (if applicable), and a list of trust officers. The registration form discloses general information, and a brief description of the mission and activities of the organization. Organizational publications may substitute for a specific narrative statement. There is no fee for the initial registration, which is accomplished by filing the Registration of Charitable Corporation or Charitable Trust form.

Annual reports: An annual financial report must be submitted on either a calendar year or fiscal year basis, and is due four months and 15 days after the close of accounting year. Forms are mailed at the end of each accounting year. A filing fee ranges from $10 (less than $25,000 in income and receipts) to $200 (for more than $1 million in income and receipts), plus an additional fee of .1% of the fund balance up to $10 million. No fee based on fund balance is required if the fund balance is less than $50,000.

Organization Solicitation Disclosure Requirements: None.

Paid Solicitor Requirements: Must register and pay an annual registration fee of $250; must file a fundraising notice with the Attorney General and a written financial plan with the charity. Solicitors must disclose that the solicitor is operating under the direction and control of a named professional fundraising firm. Must submit a financial report to the Attorney General within 90 days after a solicitation campaign is completed.

Fundraising Counsel Requirements: Must register and pay a $250 fee if they have access to contributions.

Pennsylvania

Central Switchboard: (717) 787-2121
State Web Home Page: http://www.state.pa.us/

INCORPORATION

Contact:

> Department of State
> Corporation Bureau
> 308 North Office Building
> Harrisburg, PA 17120-0029
> (717) 787-1057

Citation: Title 15, 5101 et seq.

Publications Available: *The Pennsylvania Nonprofit Handbook, 5th Edition* is available for $31.45 including S&H (PA residents please add $1.89 sales tax) from White Hat Communications, PO Box 5390, Harrisburg, PA 17110-0390.

General Requirements: One or more natural persons of full age are required to incorporate. Articles of Incorporation must set forth the corporate name; address of the initial registered office (PO Box is not allowed); name of its commercial registered office provider; purpose(s); that the corporation does not contemplate pecuniary gain or profit, incidental or otherwise; that it is organized on a nonstock basis; whether the corporation will have members; whether the incorporators constitute a majority of the members of the committee authorized to incorporate; the name, address, and signatures of each incorporator; the effective date; and additional optional provisions.

Corporate Name: Corporate designation is not required. May not contain the word "cooperative" or its abbreviation. Must be in the English language or letters; may not contain a blasphemy; may not contain language that the corporation is organized for a purpose other than those stated in the Articles or that it is a government agency of Pennsylvania or the U.S., a bank or savings institution, a trust company, insurance company, or a public utility. May not be the same or similar to another corporation or any other reserved or registered name.

Name Check/name reservation: Telephone (717) 787-1057 for a name search at no charge; name check will be provided in writing for a $12 fee. Names may be reserved for a renewable 120-day period for a fee of $52.

How to File: Provide the $100 filing fee, one original of the Articles of Incorporation and three copies of docketing statement form DSCB:15-134A. The docketing statement asks 16 questions, including whether the association solicited or intends to solicit contributions in Pennsylvania. Incorporators must advertise their intention to file or the corporation shall advertise the filing of the Articles. The advertisement must appear in both a general circulation newspaper in the home county of the corporation, and a legal journal.

Other Filings/reports: Most nonprofit corporations must annually notify the Corporation Bureau of any changes in officers, using the DSCB:15-5110 form. There is no fee for this report.

LOBBYING

Contact:

> State Ethics Commission
> 309 Finance Building
> PO Box 11470
> Harrisburg, PA 17108-1470
> (717) 783-1610

Citation: *Lobbying Disclosure Act of 1998 (Act 93).*

Publications: Required forms are available from the contact office and on the web site (see below).

Registration required: All lobbyists and principals must register within 10 days of acting as a lobbyist or principal. Lobbyists must disclose general information, the names of clients and their addresses, affiliated political action committees, and provide a recent photo. A separate registration is required for every principal of the lobbyist. There is a biennial fee of $100 for lobbyists and principals.

Forms to use: The forms are curently under development by the Ethics Commission, but will be available at its web site at: http://www.ethics.state.pa.us/PA_Exec/Ethics/

Reporting requirements: Lobbyists and principals must file quarterly reports with the Commission. The reports include by whom the lobbying was conducted; the subject matter/issue; good faith estimates of the amount spent for personnel and office expenses related to lobbying; and estimates of spending for direct communication, gifts, entertainment, meals, transportation, lodging and receptions, indirect communication, and itemization of gifts of value made to state officials, employees, or their immediate families.

TAX EXEMPTIONS

Contact:

Department of Revenue
Taxpayer Inquiry Unit
10th Floor
Strawberry Square
Harrisburg, PA 17128
(717) 787-8210

Citation: 72 P.S. §7204(1)—corporate income tax 61 Pa. Code §§32.1 and 32.21—sales and use tax.

Requirements: All nonstock, nonprofit corporations are exempt from the corporate income tax. For sales and use tax exemption, organizations must demonstrate that they meet a five-part test (advance a charitable purpose; donate or render gratuitously a substantial portion of its services; relieve government of some of its burden; serve a substantial, indefinite class of persons who are legitimate subjects of charity; and operate entirely free from private profit motive) emanating from a 1985 Pennsylvania Supreme Court decision.

Application Procedure: Submit PA-100 combined form along with REV-72 form.

CHARITABLE SOLICITATION

Contact:

Department of State
Bureau of Charitable Organizations
124 Pine Street, 3rd Floor
Harrisburg, PA 17101
(717) 783-1720
1-800-732-0999

Citation: Act 90-202, *Solicitation of Funds for Charitable Purposes Act*, 10 P.S. § 162.1 et seq.

Publications: A copy of the statute and required forms are available from the contact office.

Initial registration: Every charitable organization which raises $25,000 or more, or which uses paid solicitors, must register with the Bureau within 10 working days prior to conducting a solicitation. Registration fees range from $15 (organizations filing the BCO-400 short form, or those with $25,000 or less in gross contributions annually) to $250 (for organizations with more than $500,000 in gross contributions). The long form is BCO-100.

Annual reports: Renewal registrations are due within 135 days after the close of the organization's fiscal year. Reports vary with amount of gross contributions:

$0-$25,000 in gross contributions (or $100,000 or less in contributions for certain organizations which are exempt from registration requirements, such as nursing homes, libraries, senior citizen centers, and volunteer fire organizations): financial statements, Form BCO-23; and federal 990 (for those required to file it with the IRS).

More than $25,000-$100,000 in gross contributions: financial statements subjected to a review or audit; Form BCO-23; federal 990 (for those required to file it with the IRS).

More than $100,000 in gross contributions: audited financial statements, Form BCO-23; and federal 990.

The BCO-23, *Pennsylvania Public Disclosure-Long Form,* discloses information about contributions; receipts; contributions received from federated fundraising organizations; gross contributions; program service revenues; government grants and contracts; administrative expense; membership dues receipts; fundraising expenses; fund balances; and other fiscal information. Long-form registrants must submit detailed financial statements. Some organizations qualify for submission of short form, BCO-20.

Organization Solicitation Disclosure requirements: Every written confirmation, receipt or reminder of a contribution shall conspicuously state:

"The official registration and financial information of (insert legal name of the charity registered with the Department) may be obtained from the Pennsylvania Department of State by calling toll free, within Pennsylvania, 1 (800) 732-0999. Registration does not imply endorsement."

Paid Solicitor Requirements: Must register, pay a $250 fee, and post a $25,000 bond; must file a copy of the contract with the charity with a solicitation notice, which has a $25 fee.

Fundraising Counsel Requirements: Must register and pay a $250 annual fee.

Rhode Island

Central Switchboard: (401) 222-2000
State Web Home Page: http://www.state.ri.us/

INCORPORATION

Contact:
>Secretary of State
>Corporations
>100 North Main Street
>Providence, RI 02903
>(401) 222-3040

Citation: *Rhode Island Nonprofit Corporation Act,* Chapter 7-6-1 et seq. of the General Laws of Rhode Island.

Publications Available: The blank forms are provided by the contact office.

General Requirements: Articles of Incorporation must set forth the corporate name; period of duration; purpose(s)(must be specific); provisions, if any, not inconsistent with the law, which the incorporators elect to set forth in the Articles for the regulation of the internal affairs of the corporation; address of the initial registered office and the name of the initial registered agent at that address; the number of directors constituting the initial board of directors; their names and addresses; the name, address, and signature of each incorporator; and the date when the corporate existence is to begin. This date cannot be more than 30 days after the Articles are filed.

Corporate Name: Shall not contain any word or phrase which indicates or implies that it is organized for any purpose other than one or more purposes contained in its Articles of Incorporation; shall not be the same as, or deceptively similar to, the name of another; shall be transliterated into letters of the English alphabet if it is not in English.

Name Check: May be checked by telephoning the contact office.

How to File: File original Articles of Incorporation in duplicate on forms provided by the contact office with a $35 filing fee.

Other Filings/reports: Annual reports must be filed in June; annual reports are mailed by the contact office prior to the due date. There is a $20 filing fee.

LOBBYING

Contact:
>Department of State
>Lobbyist Registrar
>Room 38
>State House
>Providence, RI 02903
>(401) 222-3983

Citation: 22 §10-1 et seq., General Laws of Rhode Island.

Publications: *Guide to Rhode Island Lobbying Laws* is provided by the contact office.

Registration required: Lobbyists must register with the Department of State within seven days of employment as a lobbyist; disclosure includes general information and the legislation by bill number or subject matter that is the target of lobbying. Those who hire a lobbyist must have the name of their lobbyist entered into the lobbyist register of the Secretary of State. Lobbyists must wear identification badges.

Reporting requirements: Lobbyists and those who hire lobbyists must file updated expense reports on the first Monday of each month from March to final adjournment of the General Assembly, and a final report no later than 30 days after adjournment. The reports disclose compensation paid to the lobbyist, itemizations of expenditures, and gifts and honoraria in excess of $25.

TAX EXEMPTIONS

Contact:

Department of Administration
Division of Taxation
One Capitol Hill
Providence, RI 02908-5800
(401) 277-3053

Citation: §44-18-30.1 —sales and use tax; §44-11-1(iv) —business corporation tax.

Requirements: Organizations with federal tax exemption status are not required to file corporate or franchise tax returns unless they have a filing requirement with the IRS (such as unrelated business income taxes). Organizations exempt from RI Sales and Use tax are: nonprofit hospitals, educational institutions, churches, orphanages, institutions operated exclusively for religious or charitable purposes, nonprofit interest-free loan associations, nonprofit youth sporting leagues and bands for youth under 19, PTAs, state chapters of certain vocational student organizations, and certain senior citizens organizations.

Application Procedure: File an *Application for Certification of Exemption for an Exempt Organization From the Rhode Island Sales and Use Tax*, and include a $25 application fee.

CHARITABLE SOLICITATION

Contact:

Department of Business Regulation
Securities Division
233 Richmond Street, Suite 232
Providence, RI 02903-4232
(401) 277-3048

Citation: §5-53-1 et seq. Note: An amended Charitable Solicitation Law is pending in the Rhode Island General Assembly.

Initial Registration: Charities that do not intend to receive or do not receive more than $3,000 in contributions during a calendar year are exempt, as well as 12 other categories of organizations. File *Application for Exemption or Registration as a Charitable Organization in Rhode Island* (one or the other); the filing fee is $75 for annual registration; the form discloses general information; IRS status; the percent-age of contributions received that is spent on fundraising and administration; and information about officers, directors, trustees and CEO. Submit an audited financial report (unaudited report acceptable if annual budget is less than $100,000); a description of solicitation methods; purposes of contributions; and names, addresses and amounts of compensation for those who receive annual compensation in excess of $12,500. Other disclosure is required. Renewal forms are sent automatically each year by the Department.

Annual reports: Same as registration (see above).

Organization Solicitation Disclosure Requirements: None.

Paid Solicitor Requirements: Must pay a $200 registration fee and post a $10,000 bond.

Fundraising Counsel Requirements: Must pay a $200 annual registration fee and post a $10,000 bond.

South Carolina

Central Switchboard: (803) 734-1000
State Web Home Page: http://www.state.sc.us/

INCORPORATION

Contact:
> Secretary of State
> PO Box 11350
> Columbia, SC 29211
> (803) 734-2158

Citation: *South Carolina Nonprofit Corporation Act,* §33-31-101 et seq.

Publications Available: A sample Articles of Incorporation form is provided by the contact office.

General Requirements: Articles must set forth corporate name; that it is either a public benefit, mutual benefit, or religious corporation; the address of the initial registered office; the name of the initial registered agent at that office; the name, address, and signature of each incorporator; whether it will have members; provisions relating to the distribution of assets upon dissolution; the address of the principal office; and optional provisions relating to the internal regulation and management, directors, and rights of members.

Corporate Name: Must contain the word "corporation," "incorporated," "company," or "limited," the abbreviation "corp.," "inc.," "co.," or "ltd.," or words or abbreviations of like import in another language. May not contain language stating or implying that it is organized for a purpose other than that permitted by law or its Articles of Incorporation. Must be distinguishable from others without written permission.

Name reservation: Names may be reserved for a non-renewable 120-day period for a $10 fee.

How to File: File with the Secretary of State two copies of the Articles of Incorporation (the original and either a duplicate original or a conformed copy) and a $25 filing fee.

Other Filings/reports: An annual report may be required to be filed with the South Carolina Department of Revenue.

LOBBYING

Contact:
> State Ethics Commission
> 5000 Thurmond Mall
> Suite 250
> PO Box 11926
> Columbia, SC 29211
> (803) 253-4192

Citation: *Lobbyists Registration Act,* §2-17-10, Code of Laws of South Carolina.

Registration required: Lobbyists must register with the Commission and pay a $50 fee. The form discloses general information about the lobbyist and client(s) and the legislative, agency, or gubernatorial action to which the lobbying relates. Clients must also register with the Commission and pay a $50 fee. Registration is on an annual basis and must be done prior to January 5 of each year.

Forms to use: SEC—L1A.2 *Lobbyist Registration* (green form); SEC—L4A *Lobbyist Disclosure Statement*; SEC—L2A.2 *Lobbyist's Principal Registration;* and SEC—L5A.2 *Lobbyist's Principal Disclosure Statement.*

Reporting requirements: Lobbyists and their clients/employers must file itemized income and expenditure reports prior to April 10 and October 10, and also prior to December 31 if contributions or expenditures were incurred after September 30. The report discloses all income and expenses related to lobbying, categorized by supplies, rent, utilities, compensation of support personnel, and other expenditures.

TAX EXEMPTIONS

Contact:

> Department of Revenue
> 301 Gervais Street
> PO Box 125
> Columbia, SC 29214
> (803) 737-5000

Citation: Code Section 12-36-2120(41)—sales tax; §12-6-540 and §12-20-110—income tax.

Requirements: Corporations exempt from federal income tax pursuant to IRC Section 501 are exempt from the state license on capital (franchise tax) and income tax. Sales tax exemption covers only items sold by certain exempt charitable organizations, if used for exempt purposes with no inurement to any individual.

Application Procedure: File form ST-387, *Application for Sales Tax Exemption Under Code Section 12-36-2120(41), "Exempt Organizations."* Include charter and bylaws, most recent income statement and balance sheet, IRS determination letter, a copy of property tax exemption letter (if applied for and granted), and disclose general information.

CHARITABLE SOLICITATION

Contact:

> Secretary of State
> PO Box 11350
> Columbia, SC 29211
> (803) 734-1790

Citation: *South Carolina Solicitation of Charitable Funds Act of 1994*, Title 33, 33-56-10 et seq.

Publications: A copy of the statute and forms are available from the contact office.

Initial Registration: Charities that raise $20,000 or more in a calendar year or have paid staff or do not have an IRS exemption letter must register with the Division annually. The filing fee is $50. The uniform registration statement discloses general information, purposes, information about organizational misconduct, outside professionals used for fundraising, the amount paid to them in the previous year, total contributions during the previous year, and total fundraising costs during the previous year.

Annual reports: Each charity must submit an annual financial report, but may submit its federal 990 or 990-EZ in lieu of the form provided by the Secretary of State's Office. Attached schedules itemize contributions, and information about contracts with professional fundraising solicitors, fundraising counsels, and commercial coventurers.

Organization Solicitation Disclosure requirements: See below.

Paid Solicitor Requirements: Must register annually, pay a $50 filing fee, and post a $15,000 bond. They must deliver information about the charity, purpose of contributions, and financial statements upon request of a solicited party; must disclose his/her status as a professional solicitor, the name of the fundraising organization, and the charity represented at the initial time of solicitation.

Fundraising Counsel Requirements: Must register and pay a $50 annual filing fee.

South Dakota

Central Switchboard: (605) 773-3011
State Web Home Page: http://www.state.sd.us/

INCORPORATION

Contact:

> Secretary of State
> State Capitol
> 500 E. Capitol
> Pierre, SD 57501-5077
> (605) 773-4845

Citation: *South Dakota Nonprofit Corporation Act,* SDCL 47-22,

Publications Available: A copy of the statute and sample incorporation forms are available from the contact office.

General Requirements: Three or more natural persons of legal age are required to act as incorporators. Articles must set forth the corporate name; period of existence; purposes; whether the corporation will have members and provisions relating to members; how directors will be elected or appointed if not elected or appointed by members; provisions relating to internal affairs and provision for the distribution of assets upon dissolution; street address of the initial registered office (or a statement that there is no street address); the name of the initial registered agent at that address; the number of directors and their names and addresses; and the name, address, and signature of each incorporator. A consent of appointment must also be provided by the registered agent.

Corporate Name: Shall not contain a word or phrase which indicates or implies that it is organized for a purpose other than permitted in the Articles; may not be the same or deceptively similar to another corporation without written permission; shall be transliterated into letters of the English alphabet if not in English.

Name reservation: May be reserved for a non-renewable period of 120 days for a $10 fee.

How to File: Send an original and one exact or conformed copy of the Articles with a $20 filing fee.

Other Filings/reports: Every domestic non-profit corporation must file a corporate report every three years. The form is mailed by the Secretary of State's Office as a reminder to the registered agent listed with the office. The report is due the anniversary month of the original filing of the incorporation. An additional penalty fee is assessed if the report is not filed by the last day of the month following the anniversary month.

LOBBYING

Contact:

> Secretary of State
> State Capitol, Suite 204
> 500 East Capitol Avenue
> Pierre, SD 57501-5070
> (605) 773-3537

Citation: Chapter 2-12, 2-12-1 et seq.

Publications: A copy of the statute and forms are available from the contact office.

Registration required: Lobbyists must register with the Secretary of State and pay a $25 fee. The registration form discloses general information, employer, and subject of interest. All lobbyists must file the lobbyist employer's written authorization with the Secretary of State within 10 days after registration.

Forms to use: SOS form *Lobbyist Registration; Lobbyist Expense Report Form; Lobbyist Employer Expense Report form:* There is also a form to authorize lobbying on behalf of a client/employer. Lobbyists and their employers, on separate forms, must report the date, amount, and purpose of each lobbying expense; lobbyists must wear lobbyist badges.

Reporting requirements:, Expense reports must be filed by lobbyists and their employers on or before July 1 each year. The compensation to the lobbyist is not required to be reported.

TAX EXEMPTIONS

Contact:

> Department of Revenue
> 445 East Capitol Avenue
> Pierre, SD 57501-3185
> (605) 773-3311

Citation:§10-45-13; 10-45-14.

Requirements: Charities must submit an application form to the Department for exempt status. For exemption from sales tax, the organization must be organized and conducted solely for the benefit of the general public and for the relief of public burden, may not turn away someone in need of the agency's service if not able to pay for it, may not provide for gain or profit for any private member of the agency, and must be recognized as a 501(c)(3).

There is no corporate income tax or personal income tax in the state.

Application Procedure: Submit ST-130 form with bylaws, Articles of Incorporation, constitution and IRS determination letter. Exemption must be renewed every five years.

CHARITABLE SOLICITATION

Contact:

> Office of the Attorney General
> Division of Consumer Protection
> 500 East Capitol
> Pierre, SD 57501-5070
> (605) 773-4400

Citation: Chapter 37-30, 37-30-1 et seq.

Publications: A copy of the telephone solicitation statute is available from the contact office.

Initial Registration: None.

Annual reports: None.

Organization Solicitation Disclosure requirements: None.

Paid Solicitor Requirements: Paid solicitors must register no less than 30 days before conducting any solicitation. Registration is annual. A bond of $10,000 is required if the applicant solicits contributions but does not have physical access to contributions, and a $20,000 bond is required if physical access is available. Must file solicitation notices with the Department; contracts between solicitor and charity must be in writing and shall state the minimum amount the charity will receive as a percentage of gross revenue and may not include expenses of the solicitor paid by the charity. Financial reports must be filed by the solicitor within 90 days after a solicitation campaign has been completed or on the anniversary of the commencement of a campaign that lasts more than one year.

Fundraising Counsel Requirements: None.

Tennessee

Central Switchboard: (615) 741-3011
State Web Home Page: http://www.state.tn.us/

INCORPORATION

Contact:

> Department of State
> Corporations Section
> James K. Polk Building
> Nashville, TN 37243-0306
> (615) 741-0537

Citation: *Tennessee Nonprofit Corporation Act,* Tennessee Code Annotated Section 48-51-101 et seq.

Publications Available: A *Non-Profit Filing Guide* and all forms are available from the contact office, and can be accessed at: http://www.state.tn.us/sos

General Requirements: Charter must set forth the corporate name; whether it is a public benefit, mutual benefit, or religious corporation; the address of the initial registered office and the name of the initial registered agent at that office; the name, address, and signature of each incorporator; the address of the principal office; that the corporation is a nonprofit corporation; that the corporation will or will not have members; provisions regarding the distribution of assets upon dissolution; and optional provisions.

Corporate Name: May not contain language stating or implying that it is organized for a purpose other than permitted by law or its charter; or organized as, or affiliated with, or sponsored by, any fraternal, veterans', religious, charitable or professional organization unless it is certified by those organizations in writing; must be distinguishable from others without written permission; must not state or imply that it is or is affiliated with an agency or instrumentality of a government agency unless if such is true and is certified in writing.

Name reservation: May be reserved for a renewable four-month period upon payment of a $20 fee.

How to File: File the original with the Secretary of State with a $100 filing fee.

Other Filings/reports: An annual report is required to be filed disclosing general information. The report is due the first day of the fourth month following the close of the corporation's fiscal year.

LOBBYING

Contact:

> Registry of Election Finance
> 404 James Robertson Parkway
> Suite 1614
> Nashville, TN 37243-1360
> (615) 741-7959

Citation: *Tennessee Lobbyist Registration and Disclosure Act of 1975,* 3-6-101 et seq.

Publications: *Campaign Financial Disclosure Guidelines* (includes lobbying information) is available from the contact office.

Registration required: All lobbyists must register with the Registry of Election Finance within 5 days after becoming a lobbyist. There is a $25 registration fee. Registration is annual and expires on December 31. Disclosure includes general information and a listing of general subject matter which is the target of lobbying activity.

Reporting requirements: Reports are required to be filed no later than 30 days after the end of the annual General Assembly session or July 30, whichever is later, and December 31. The reports disclose information on business arrangements with public officials or candidates; and an itemized list of political contributions in excess of $100.

TAX EXEMPTIONS

Contact:

> Department of Revenue
> Taxpayer Services Division
> Andrew Jackson State Office Building
> Nashville, TN 37242
> (615) 741-2594

Citation: T.C.A. Section 67-6-322 —sales tax; §67-2-104 —income tax on stocks and bonds.

Publications: An excerpt of the statute is provided by the contact office.

Requirements: Exemptions from sales and use tax are provided by statute to churches, temples, synagogues, and mosques; colleges and universities; schools; orphanages; institutions for homeless and foster children; homes for the aged; hospitals; girls' and boys' clubs; community health councils; volunteer fire departments; organ banks; organizations such as the USO; property owned by the state and operated by the historical commission; non-profit community blood banks; senior citizen centers; nonprofit beauty contest organizations; and 501(c)(3)s, (c)(5)s and (c)(19)s. Exempt organizations are exempt on items they buy, not items they sell.

Organizations exempt from federal income taxes are generally exempt from the corporate franchise and excise tax.

Application Procedure: Submit an RV-0462 form to the Department.

CHARITABLE SOLICITATION

Contact:

> Department of State
> Division of Charitable Solicitations
> Suite 1700, James K. Polk Building
> Nashville, TN 37243-0308
> (615) 741-2555

Citation: *Tennessee Charitable Solicitations Act,* Tennessee Code Annotated 48-101-501 et seq.

Publications: A copy of the statute and forms are available from the contact office or from the web site at: http://www.state.tn.us/sos

Initial Registration: Charitable organizations that raise or intend to raise more than $30,000 annually must register annually with the Division. There is a $50 filing fee for initial registrations. Registrants must disclose the birthdate and 10-year employment history of the charity's key employees; information about the charity's most recent fiscal year; and must provide an audited financial report if they received more than $250,000 in gross revenue. All registering organizations must submit their federal 990. New organizations must submit their corporate charter and bylaws, and a copy of their IRS determination letter.

Annual reports: Registration renewal statements must be accompanied by a renewal fee ranging from $100 for organizations that have gross revenues of less than $49,000 annually to $300 for those with gross revenues of more than $500,000. All registrations expire on the anniversary date of the organization (the last day of the sixth month following the month in which the fiscal year of the organization ends). During the first year of operation, charities must submit quarterly financial reports due within 30 days of the end of each quarter, disclosing gross amounts of contributions; amount of contributions disbursed; aggregate amounts paid to any professional solicitor or fundraising counsel; and the amounts spent for overhead, expenses, commissions, and similar purposes. For subsequent years, reports must be filed annually, within six months after the close of the fiscal year.

Organization Solicitation Disclosure requirements: Every solicitor, paid or otherwise, must furnish identification indicating that the solicitor is authorized by the organization to solicit.

Paid Solicitor Requirements: Must register annually, pay an $800 fee and post a $25,000 bond. Prior to an oral solicitation and at the same time as a written one, professional solicitors must disclose their names, the names of their employers, and that they are professional solicitors who will receive as costs, expenses and fees a portion of the solicited funds. For written solicitations, the disclosure must be in at least 12-point type.

Fundraising Counsel Requirements: Must register annually, pay a $250 fee, and post a $25,000 bond.

Texas

Central Switchboard: (512) 463-4630
State Web Home Page: http://www.state.tx.us/

INCORPORATION

Contact:

> Secretary of State
> Statutory Filings Division, Corporation Sec.
> PO Box 13697
> Austin, TX 78711-3697
> (512) 463-5555

Citation: *Texas Non-Profit Corporation Act,* Title 32, Article 1396-1.01 et seq.

Publications Available: *Filing Guide for Business Organizations and Nonprofit Organizations* is available for $35 from the contact office.

General Requirements: Must set forth corporate name; a statement that it is nonprofit; period of duration; purpose(s); a statement that it will have no members, if such is the case; optional provisions relating to internal regulation and management; the street address of its initial registered office; the name of the initial registered agent at that office; the number of directors or trustees of the initial board and their names and addresses; and the name, address, and signature of each incorporator.

Corporate Name: Shall not contain any word or phrase that indicates that it is organized for any purpose other than authorized by its Articles of Incorporation; shall not be the same as, or deceptively similar to, another without written consent; may not contain the word "lottery."

Name reservation: May be reserved for a renewable period of 120 days for a fee of $40.

How to File: File an original and a copy of the Articles of Incorporation with the Secretary of State along with a $25 fee.

Other Filings/reports: A report is required to be filed every four years disclosing general information, including the names and addresses of directors and officers. The report is due within 30 days of receiving a notice from the Secretary of State that the report needs to be filed.

LOBBYING

Contact:

> Texas Ethics Commission
> PO Box 12070
> Austin, TX 78711-2070
> (512) 463-5800

Citation: § 305.001 et seq.

Publications: *Guide to Lobbying In Texas* available at: http://www.ethics.state.tx.us/guides/lobby.htm

Registration required: All lobbyists who spend $500 or more in a calendar quarter on lobbying or who receive at least $1,000 per quarter in compensation for lobbying must register with the Commission. The fee is $300. The fee is reduced to $100 for lobbyists employed by 501(c)(3) and 501(c)(4) organizations. Registration discloses general information, names of clients, subject matter/docket number, and amount of compensation.

Reporting requirements: Itemized expenditure reports are required to be filed with the Commission. Itemized spending categories include transportation and lodging; food and beverages; entertainment; gifts; awards and momentos; expenditures made to attend fundraisers and charity events; and certain mass media expenditures. Reports are due between the first and tenth days of each month.

TAX EXEMPTIONS

Contact:

> Comptroller of Public Accounts
> Exempt Organizations Section
> PO Box 13528
> Austin, TX 78711-3528
> 1-800-252-5555 (sales tax)
> 1-800-252-1381 (franchise tax)

Citation: V.T.C.A. §151.310 —sales, excise and use taxes; §171.051-171.087—franchise tax.

Publications: *Texas Sales Tax Exemptions for Nonprofit Organizations (Pub. 96-122)* and *Franchise Tax Subchapter B. Exemptions* (Pub. 96-212), Sales Tax Rule 3.322, and Franchise Tax Rule 3.541 are available from the contact office.

Requirements: While the general details are in the statutes and rules, religious, charitable, educational and organizations granted a federal exemption under 501(c)(3), (4),(8),(10), and (19) are some of the organizations that qualify for sales tax exemptions. The exemption is on purchases made by the organization for its own use, provided the item is not used for the personal benefit of a private stockholder or individual. Religious, charitable, educational, and organizations granted a federal exemption under certain sections of the Internal Revenue Code are among the corporations that qualify for exemption from the franchise tax. There is no corporate income tax.

Application Procedure: Organizations must write to the contact office for exemption. The request must include a detailed description of the activities conducted; Articles of Incorporation if a corporation; bylaws, constitution, or articles of association if the organization is not a corporation; services performed by the organization; a report of all income, assets and liabilities; and/or the IRS determination letter. The details about the criteria for determining the exemption can be found in the statutes and rules.

CHARITABLE SOLICITATION

Contact:

> *Secretary of State*
> *Statutory Documents Section*
> *PO Box 12887*
> *Austin, TX 78711-2887*
> *(512) 475-0775*

Citation: Tex. Rev.Civ. Stat. Ann. art. 9023b for veterans organizations; Tax. Rev. Civ. Ann. art. 9023C for public safety organizations; Title 4, Texas Bus. & Comm. Code, Chapter 38.

Publications: Copies of the statutes are available from the contact office.

Initial Registration: Veterans' and public safety organizations must register with the Secretary of State before beginning solicitations. The registration fee is $150 for veterans' and $250 for public safety organizations. Bond must be posted of either $1,000, $5,000, $10,000, or $25,000 depending upon the geographical range of the solicitation. The organization may not use a professional solicitor unless the organization has membership of at least 500 veterans, or have a membership consisting of at least 90% who are veterans. The organization must provide a copy of its most recently filed federal 990 and a statement of how the contributions will be used. Registration statements are effective for one year after their effective date, and may be renewed annually along with the filing fee. Registration is also required for telephone solicitation, but all 501(c)(3)s are exempt.

Annual reports: Each veterans' organization which received more than $500 in solicited funds during the previous calendar year must submit a report to the Secretary before January 15, along with a $50 filing fee. The report must disclose administrative; travel; gifts to veterans and veterans organizations; gifts to non-veterans; payments for the purchase, rental or lease of, and repairs to, facilities; and other expenditures.

Organization Solicitation Disclosure requirements: See below. Note: changes in the telephone solicitation statute are expected in 1999.

Paid Solicitor Requirements: Paid solicitors must register, provide disclosure statements, pay a $500 registration fee, and post a bond in an amount equal to the organizations (see above). The solicitor, at the time each solicitation is made, must disclose the following: "The Secretary of State has on file important information about persons that seek contributions in the name of veterans, and the number to call about that information is the Solicitation Information Hotline 1-800-648-9642." At the end of each calendar quarter, solicitors who raise more than $5,000 for a veterans' organization must file a financial disclosure report and pay a $50 filing fee. Solicitors must disclose the county or counties actually served by the organization if soliciting outside of the area served; solicitors for public safety organizations must disclose on their literature information about the hotline as well as the name of the solicitor and how the net funds will be used, and post a $10,000 bond.

Fundraising Counsel Requirements: None.

Utah

Central Switchboard: (801) 538-3000
State Web Home Page: http://www.state.ut.us/

INCORPORATION

Contact:

> Department of Commerce
> Division of Corporations and Commercial
> Code
> Heber M. Wells Building
> 160 East 300 South
> PO Box 45802
> Salt Lake City, UT 84145-0802
> (801) 530-4849

Citation: *Utah Revised Business Corporation Act,* Chapter 10A; 16-10-a-201 et seq.

Publications Available: *Revised Business Corporation Act; Commentary to Utah Revised Business Corporation Act; Doing Business in Utah—A Guide to Business Information; Business Licensing Guide; Why Register Your Business?* are available from the contact office (a fee is charged for some of these publications, but they are free if accessed at the web site: http://www.state.ut.us).

General Requirements: Articles of Incorporation must set forth the corporate name; term of the corporation's existence (may be perpetual); purposes for which it is being formed; a statement that it is organized as a nonprofit corporation; whether the corporation will have members; the names and street addresses of the board of trustees (must be at least 3); the name, address, and signature of each incorporator; the Utah address of the corporation's registered office and the name of its registered agent at that address; and a statement in the Articles or an attachment signed by the registered agent acknowledging acceptance as such.

Corporate Name: Must contain the word "corporation," "incorporated," or "company," or the abbreviation "corp.," "inc.," or "co." or words or abbreviations of like import in another language; may not contain language stating or implying that the corporation is organized for a purpose other than permitted by law or its Articles of Incorporation; may not, without the

written consent of the US Olympic Committee, contain the word "Olympic," "Olympiad," or "Citius Altius Fortius." Must be distinguishable from other corporations unless it has consent from the other corporation.

Name reservation: May be reserved for 120 days for a fee of $20; the reservation may be renewed for an additional 120 days.

How to File: No form is required; send Articles of Incorporation in duplicate with original signatures on one copy with the $20 filing fee. Forms may be faxed (801-530-6438) if valid Visa/MasterCard information is provided.

Other Filings/reports: Each corporation must file an annual report on an approved form that includes the corporate name, state or country under which it is incorporated; street address of its registered office; name of its registered agent at that office; street address of its principal office; name and addresses of its directors and principal officers; and a brief description of the nature of its business.

LOBBYING

Contact:

> Lt. Governor's Office
> Elections Division
> 116 State Capitol Building
> Salt Lake City, UT 84114
> (801) 538-1041

Citation: *Lobbyist Disclosure and Regulation Act,* Utah Code 36-11-101-106.

Publications: *Utah Election Laws* and *Information Pamphlet for Lobbyists* are available from the contact office.

Registration required: Lobbyists must register with the Lt. Governor's Office prior to lobbying. There is a $25 fee for a lobbyist license. The license expires on December 31 of even-numbered years.

Forms to use: *Lobbyist Registration* form; *Lobbyist Disclosure Report* with attached schedules.

Reporting requirements: Any lobbyist, client, or government officer who makes expenditures to benefit public officials or members of their immediate families in any calendar quarter of the calendar year must file a financial disclosure report. Lobbyists who have spent $50 or more during a reporting period or any calendar quarter must file an interim report.

TAX EXEMPTIONS

Contact:

> Utah State Tax Commission
> 210 North 1950 West
> Salt Lake City, UT 84134
> (801) 297-3257

Citation: Utah Code Ann. Section 59-7-102; 59-12-104.1.

Requirements: Corporations that have federal exempt status under Section 501(c) are exempt from the Utah corporation franchise tax.

Sales and Use tax: Exemption is limited to those with 501(c)(3) tax exempt status; sales tax must be collected on any sales income arising from unrelated trades or businesses unless the sales are otherwise exempt by law.

Application Procedure: Corporate franchise tax: Send a letter to the contact office requesting exemption, along with a copy of the federal IRS determination letter. For sales and use tax exemption, apply using form TC-160.

CHARITABLE SOLICITATION

Contact:

> Department of Commerce
> Division of Consumer Protection
> 160 East 300 South
> PO Box 146704
> Salt Lake City, UT 84114
> (801) 530-6601

Citation: *Charitable Solicitations Act*, UCA §13-22-1—13-22-21.

Publications: The text of the statute and forms are provided by the contact office.

Initial Registration: Must include a $100 application fee; bylaws; Articles of Incorporation; IRS tax exemption determination letter; most recent federal 990 or financial audit; telephone scripts (if applicable); copy of contractual agreement with parent foundation (if applicable); copy of contracts with professional fundraisers, counsel, or consultants; and an acknowledgment that fundraising in Utah will not begin until the organization, its parents, professional fundraiser, counsel, or consultant are registered and in compliance with the law. The permit card must have a disclaimer statement:

"THE STATE OF UTAH DOES NOT WARRANT THAT THE INFORMATION CONTAINED ON THIS CARD IS TRUE."

Annual reports: Must report annually; newly registered organizations must file quarterly financial reports during their first year, due within 30 days after the end of each quarter. Each report must disclose the gross amount of contributions; amount of contributions disbursed; aggregate amounts paid to any professional fundraiser, amount spent on overhead, expenses, commissions, and similar purposes; and the name and address of any paid solicitors.

Organization Solicitation Disclosure requirements: See below.

Paid Solicitor Requirements: Must include a $250 application fee; post a surety bond of $25,000; provide a copy of the contractual agreement with each charitable organization; provide a copy of the telephone script (if applicable); and an acknowledgment that fundraising in Utah will not begin until the professional fundraiser or professional fundraising counsel, or consultant, and the charity, its parent foundation (if any) are registered and in compliance with the law. The permit card must have a disclaimer statement:

"THE STATE OF UTAH DOES NOT WARRANT THAT THE INFORMATION CONTAINED ON THIS CARD IS TRUE."

Fundraising Counsel Requirements: Same requirements as paid solicitors.

Vermont

Central Switchboard: (802) 828-1110
State Web Home Page: http://www.cit.state.vt.us/

INCORPORATION

Contact:

> Secretary of State
> Division of Corporations
> 109 State Street
> Montpelier, VT 05609-1104
> (802) 828-2386

Citation: Title 11B, Vermont Statutes Annotated.

Publications Available: None.

General Requirements: Nonprofit organizations file Articles of Incorporation that require one or more persons who are at least 18. Articles must set forth the corporate name; duration; purpose; whether public or mutual benefit; provisions relating to internal regulation (optional); the address of the registered office; name and address of its registered agent; names and addresses of initial board of directors (must be at least three); and the name and address of each incorporator.

Corporate Name: May not be the same as, or deceptively similar to, another registered or reserved name; may not contain any word or phrase that implies a purpose other than contained in the Articles; must be transliterated into the English alphabet if it is not in English.

Name reservation: May be reserved for a 120-day period for a fee of $20; may be renewed up to two additional times.

How to File: Mail Articles of Incorporation form in duplicate to: Vermont Secretary of State; 109 State Street; Montpelier, VT 05609-1104 with a $75 filing fee.

Other Filings/reports: A report is due between January 1 and April 1 every two years. Forms are mailed by the contact office.

LOBBYING

Contact:

> Secretary of State
> Attention: Elections
> 26 Terrace St.; Drawer 09
> Montpelier, VT 05609-1101
> (802) 828-2464

Citation: § 261 et seq., Vermont Statutes Annotated.

Registration required: Lobbyists who are paid more than $500 annually to lobby or who expend more than $500 in any calendar year on lobbying activities must register with the Secretary of State within 48 hours after commencing lobbying activity. Registration discloses general information, a description of the matters for which lobbying has been engaged, and a signed registration form from the client/employer authorizing the lobbying. Registration is valid for two years and expires on December 31 of every even-numbered year. Every employer and every lobbyist must pay an initial registration fee of $25. An employer pays a fee of $5 for each lobbyist engaged. A lobbyist pays a $5 fee for each employer represented.

Reporting requirements: Every lobbyist and employer of a lobbyist must file expense reports. The reports are due March 25 covering January and February; July 25 covering March-June; and January 25 covering July-December. Employers must disclose the total of all lobbying expenditures to the nearest $200, the amount of compensation paid to lobbyists to the nearest $200, and provide an itemized list of every gift valued at more than $5. Lobbyists must disclose the total of all lobbying expenditures to the nearest $200, and provide an itemized list of every gift valued at more than $5.

TAX EXEMPTIONS

Contact:

Department of Taxes
Agency of Administration
Pavilion Office Building
Montpelier, VT 05602
(802) 828-2551

Citation: 32 § 9743 —sales taxes; § 5811 — income taxes.

Requirements: Generally, most organizations exempt from federal income taxes are exempt from state income taxes; 501(c)(3)s are exempt from sales and use taxes; 501(c)(4)s are exempt if they provide their net income to 501(c)(3)s.

Application Procedure: For exemption from sales and use taxes, corporations must obtain an exemption certificate from the Commissioner. File a Vermont Business Account Number application, along with the IRS determination letter, Articles of Incorporation, and bylaws.

CHARITABLE SOLICITATION

Contact:

Office of the Attorney General
109 State Street
Montpelier, VT 05609-1001
(802) 828-5507

Citation: T.9, Chapter 63, Subchapter 2, § 2471 et seq.

Publications: A copy of the statute is available from the contact office and accessed at the web site: http://www.state.vt.us/atg/ consumerprotectionstatutes.htm

Initial Registration: None.

Annual reports: See below.

Organization Solicitation Disclosure requirements: None.

Paid Solicitor Requirements: All paid fundraisers must file a *Notice of Charitable Solicitation* at least 10 days prior to the start of a fundraising campaign; must post a $20,000 bond; must file a financial report no later than 90 days after the campaign has been completed or no more than 90 days after the anniversary of a campaign that lasts more than one year.

Fundraising Counsel Requirements: None.

Virginia

Central Switchboard: (804) 786-0000
State Web Home Page: http://www.state.va.us/

INCORPORATION

Contact:

> Clerk's Information Office
> State Corporation Commission
> Tyler Building
> 1300 East Main Street
> PO Box 1197
> Richmond, VA 23218-1197
> (804) 371-9733

Citation: Chapter 10 of Title 13.1 of the Code of Virginia.

Publications Available: *Business Registration Guide* is available from the contact office. It includes the Articles of Incorporation form for nonstock corporations.

General Requirements: Articles of Incorporation must set forth the corporate name; whether the corporation will have members and provisions relating to members; how directors will be elected or appointed; the address of the initial registered office; the name of the initial registered agent and whether that agent is either an initial director, a member of the Virginia State Bar, or a professional corporation or professional limited liability company of attorneys; optional provisions; the names and addresses of initial directors; and the signature of each incorporator.

Corporate Name: Shall not contain any word or phrase that indicates or implies that it is organized for a purpose other than for what it is authorized to conduct; must be distinguishable from other corporations without written permission.

Name reservation: May be reserved for up to 120 days and may be renewed for successive 120-day periods for a fee of $10.

How to File: File the original Articles of Incorporation along with a filing fee of $75 with the Clerk of the State Corporation Commission at the contact office.

Other Filings/reports: An annual report must be filed with the Commission disclosing general information including the names and addresses of the corporation's directors and principal officers on forms provided by the Commission. The report is due between January 1 and April 1 each year following the year of incorporation.

LOBBYING

Contact:

> Secretary of the Commonwealth
> Post Office Box 2454
> Richmond, VA 23218-2454
> (804) 786-2441

Citation: *Lobbying Disclosure and Regulation Act,* Chapter 49, § 2.1-779 et seq.

Publications: A copy of the statute is available from the contact office.

Registration required: All lobbyists who receive more than $500 for compensation and reimbursements in a calendar year or who spend more than $500 in a calendar year for lobbying must register with the Department prior to engaging in lobbying. If the lobbying occurs entirely outside of Richmond, the lobbyist has 15 days to register after commencing the lobbying activity. Registrations expire annually on May 1. There is a $50 registration fee. Disclosure includes general information, an identification of the subject matter, and information about the client.

Forms to use: *Lobbyist's Registration* form.

Reporting requirements: Annual expenditure reports are due July 1 covering the preceding 12 months ending April 30. The report includes a list of executive and legislative actions lobbied for and a description of the activities conducted; expenses itemized by entertainment, gifts, office expenses, communications, personal living and travel expenses, compensation of lobbyists, honoraria, registration costs, and other; and the dollar amount of the lobbyist's compensation.

TAX EXEMPTIONS

Contact:

> Department of Taxation
> Registration Unit
> PO Box 1411
> Richmond, VA 23212-1411
> (804) 367-8057

Citation: § 58.1-401 —corporate income tax; § 58.1-608 —retail sales and use tax.

Publications: *Business Registration Guide.*

Requirements: Nonprofit corporations with federal income tax exemptions are exempt from the state corporation income tax, other than unrelated business income tax; certain 501(c)(3) organizations are statutorily exempt; consult the statute or the contact office.

Application Procedure: All companies doing business in Virginia must register with the Department of Taxation by completing and filing a Form R-1, *Combined Registration Application Form.* Request a *Tax Exempt Questionnaire Form* from the contact office, which will be used by the Department to determine eligibility for tax-exempt status.

CHARITABLE SOLICITATION

Contact:

> Department of Agriculture
> Division of Consumer Protection
> Office of Consumer Affairs
> PO Box 526
> Richmond, VA 23218-0526
> (804) 786-1343

Citation: *Virginia Solicitation of Contributions Law,* §§ 57-48 et seq. of the Code of Virginia, as amended.

Publications: A copy of the statute and rule are available from the contact office.

Initial Registration: Every charitable organization must register annually with the contact office and file an initial registration statement, using Form 102. The initial statement must include a balance sheet and income and expense statement with the opinion of an independent public accountant, complete information on fundraising activities and expenses (organizations with gross revenue of less than $25,000 may submit a balance sheet and income and expense statement verified under oath or affirmation by the Treasurer), the general purpose(s) for which funds will be used, the names of those who will have final responsibility for the custody of the funds and how they will be distributed, information about previous misconduct, and a copy of governing documents. Annual fee ranges from $30 (for not more than $25,000 in contributions during the preceding year) to $325 (for contributions in excess of $1 million annually). The initial registration fee is $100 plus the registration fee above. Less stringent notification requirements apply to organizations that raise (or intend to raise) less than $5,000 annually, and 11 classes of organizations that may request exemption from registration.

Annual reports: Annual registration renewals on Form 102 are due on the 15th day of the fifth month following the end of the fiscal year. The renewal must include a copy of the federal 990 (or a certified treasurer's report, if annual income is under $25,000), updates to information provided in the initial registration, and much of the information required by the registration.

Organization Solicitation Disclosure requirements: Registered organizations must disclose that a copy of their financial statements are available from the contact office.

Paid Solicitor Requirements: Must register annually using Form 104, pay a $500 fee annually; and post a $20,000 bond; and must file a copy of an authorization, *Consent to Solicit* form, from two officers of the charity. In the course of each solicitation, they must identify themselves by disclosing their own real first name and surname, disclose that they are paid solicitors, disclose the primary name under which they are registered, identify their employing charitable or civic organization and file an accounting report not later than 90 days following a fundraising campaign or 90 days after the anniversary of the beginning of a campaign. A *Notice of Solicitation* form must be filed with each contract. There is a late registration fee of $250 for paid solicitors who begin fundraising before registering.

Fundraising Counsel Requirements: Must register and pay a $100 fee, and provide a copy of all contracts.

Washington

Central Switchboard: (360) 753-5000
State Web Home Page: http://access.wa.gov

INCORPORATION

Contact:

Office of the Secretary of State
Corporations Division
PO Box 40234
Olympia, WA 98504-0234
(360) 753-7115

Citation: *Washington Nonprofit Corporation Act*, RCW 24.03 et seq.

Publications Available: A form for filing Articles of Incorporation is available from the contact office or on the web site: http://www.secstate.wa.gov

General Requirements: Shall set forth corporate name; period of duration; purpose(s); provisions relating to the internal regulation and management including the distribution of assets upon dissolution; the address of the initial registered office and the name of the initial registered agent at that office; the number of directors of the initial board of directors and their names and addresses; and the name, address, and signature of each incorporator.

Corporate Name: Cannot contain a corporate designation such as "Incorporated," "Company," "Ltd.," "Corporation," "Partnership," "Limited Partnership," "limited liability company," "Ltd," "L.L.C.,"or an abbreviation thereof. Shall not contain any word or phrase that indicates or implies that it is organized for any purpose other than contained in its Articles of Incorporation; shall not be the same as, or deceptively similar to, another; shall be transliterated into letters of the English alphabet if it is not in English; may not include the term "public benefit" unless designated as such by the Secretary.

Name reservation: May be reserved for a non-renewable period of 180 days for a fee of $20.

How to File: File an original and one copy of the Articles with the Secretary of State along with a $30 filing fee. To receive expedited service (processing within 24 hours of receipt), enclose $20 per entity and write "EXPEDITE" on the outside envelope.

Other Filings/reports: An annual report is required to be filed before the last day of the corporation's annual renewal month along with a $10 filing fee. The report discloses general information including the names and addresses of directors and officers, and a brief statement of the character of the affairs that the corporation is actually conducting.

LOBBYING

Contact:

Public Disclosure Commission
711 Capitol Way
Room 403
PO Box 40908
Olympia, WA 98504-0908
(360) 753-1111

Citation: Chapter 42.17 RCW, *The Public Disclosure Law.*

Publications: *Employers of Lobbyists*; and *Lobbyist Reporting* booklets and forms are available from the contact office.

Registration required: All lobbyists must register within 30 days of being employed as a lobbyist or before doing any lobbying, whichever comes first. Registrations are valid until the second Monday of each odd-numbered year. Anyone who attempts to influence legislation or the rulemaking action of state agencies is a lobbyist. Persons who receive some form of compensation to lobby must register and file monthly expenditure reports.

Forms to use: PDC Form L-1. Lobbyists must provide a brief biographical sketch and a 2" x 2" glossy photo taken within the last 12 months.

Reporting requirements: Lobbyists must submit PDC Form L-2 *Monthly Expense* reports. These reports are due the 15th of each month and cover activity of the previous calendar month. "Zero" reports may be filed if there is nothing to report. The reports itemize compensation; some personal expenses; entertainment, gifts, and travel; contributions to elected officials; advertising, printing, and informational literature; and other expenses. The report must describe the subject matter lobbied for each client. Employers of lobbyists must file PDC Form L-3 annual comprehensive expense reports that are due by the last day of February covering the previous year's compensation and expenditures for lobbying during the previous year.

TAX EXEMPTIONS

Contact:

> Department of Revenue
> PO Box 47478
> Olympia, WA 98504-7478
> (360) 786-6100
> 1-(800) 647-7706 (Telephone Information Center)

Citation: Chapter 82.04 RCW —Business and Occupation Tax; Chapter 82.08 RCW —Retail Sales Tax.

Requirements: There is no corporate income or franchise tax. Nonprofit corporations are generally liable for the same sales taxes as their for-profit counterparts. There are some limited exemptions for qualifying nonprofit organizations relating to fundraising activities, childcare resource and referral activities, and emergency lodging.

CHARITABLE SOLICITATION

Contact:

> Secretary of State
> Charities Program
> 505 E. Union Avenue
> PO Box 40234
> Olympia, WA 98504-0234
> (360) 753-0863 (select option "5")

Citation: Chapter 19.09 RCW, *Washington State Charitable Solicitations Act.*

Publications: A copy of the statute and summary of the statute are available from the

contact office or from the web site at: http://www.secstate.wa.gov/charities

Initial Registration: All charities that raise at least $25,000 in an accounting year, or which use paid fundraisers, must register annually unless otherwise exempted. The fee for new registrations is $20; fee for renewals is $10. Renewals are due no later than the 15th day of the fifth month after the end of the fiscal year.

Annual reports: See above. Financial reporting includes total revenue, total expenses and expenses applied to charitable purpose, information about paid fundraisers, types of solicitations and how conducted, and the names and addresses of officers.

Organization Solicitation Disclosure requirements: Must disclose the name of the person making the solicitation, the identity of the charity, the city of the principal place of business, and the published number of the secretary for the donor to obtain financial disclosure information filed with the secretary. Some types of solicitation require the published number of the Secretary to be included in the solicitation materials.

Paid Solicitor Requirements: Commercial fundraisers must register, pay an initial filing fee of $250 ($175 for renewals), and post a $15,000 bond. They must disclose at the point of solicitation the name of the person making the solicitation, the employer of the paid fundraiser, and the published number of the secretary (see above). Mass media advertising or mass distribution solicitation must disclose that the solicitation is being conducted by a paid fundraiser if it is; that the notice of solicitation is on file with the secretary, and that financial disclosure information may be obtained at the published number of the secretary. Those that contract for fundraising services must submit a *Fundraising Service Contract* with a copy of the contract and a $10 fee prior to the start of any fundraising campaign.

Fundraising Counsel Requirements: None. The contact office requests that charities provide the name of their fundraising counsel.

West Virginia

Central Switchboard: (304) 558-3456
State Web Home Page: http://www.state.wv.us/

INCORPORATION

Contact:

> Secretary of State
> Corporations Division
> State Capitol, W-139
> 1900 Kanawha Blvd. East
> Charleston, WV 25305-0770
> (304) 558-8000

Citation: *West Virginia Corporation Act*, W. Va. Code 31-1-136 et seq.

Publications Available: A copy of the form is available from the contact office.

General Requirements: Articles of Incorporation must set forth the corporate name; principal office (may be in another state); the address of the principal place of business in the state; the name of the "agent of process" (registered agent); that the corporation is organized as a nonprofit; the purposes (may not be general); whether the provisions regulating the internal affairs of the corporation are set forth in the bylaws or in the Articles (and attached if the latter); the names and addresses of incorporators; the number of directors constituting the initial board of directors; and their names and addresses; and the number of pages attached.

Corporate Name: Must include the term "corporation," "company," "incorporated," "limited," or an abbreviation of one of those terms; may not contain any word or phrase that implies that it is organized for a purpose other than contained in the Articles; may not be the same as, or deceptively similar to, another corporation; if not in English, shall be transliterated into letters of the English alphabet; may not contain certain words relating to "engineer" unless the purpose is to practice professional engineering.

Name Check/name reservation: May be reserved for a period of 120 days for a $15 fee; may be checked by telephone, but this is not a guarantee that the name is available.

How to File: Incorporators must sign two originals using Form CD-1 *West Virginia Articles of Incorporation.* The filing fee is $10 plus the "Attorney-In-Fact Fee." That fee is required if the principal place of business is outside the state, and ranges from $3 to $12 depending on the month of the filing. After receiving the incorporation certificate from the Secretary and one original copy of the Articles, the copy must be filed within 60 days with the county clerk in W. Va. where the principal place of business is located.

Other Filings/reports: An annual report is required, due between January 1 and March 31. This report discloses general information, including the names and addresses of directors and officers, and a brief statement of the character of affairs conducted.

LOBBYING

Contact:

> West Virginia Ethics Commission
> 1207 Quarrier Street
> Charleston, WV 25301
> (304) 558-0664

Citation: West Virginia Code Sections 6B; WV Ethics Commission Legislative Rules: Series 12 Lobbying, 158-12-1.

Registration required: Lobbyists must register with the Commission before engaging in lobbying. The application requires a *Lobbyist Registration Statement,* two recent 2" by 2" passport style photos, a *Lobbyist Employer Authorization* for each employer, and a $20 registration fee. Registration expires before the second Monday in January of each odd-numbered year. Photos must be submitted with re-registration.

Reporting requirements: All lobbyists must file an annual report on or before the second Monday in January of their activities for the prior year. Reports must also be filed on or before the 45th day of the regular session covering activities from the first of the year through the 42nd day of the session, on or before the 21st day after adjournment of the regular session covering activities from the first of the year or since their last report, and on or before the 21st day after the adjournment of any extraordinary session covering activities from the first of the year or since filing their last report.

TAX EXEMPTIONS

Contact:

Department of Tax and Revenue
Taxpayer Services Division
PO Box 3784
Charleston, WV 25337-3784
1-800-982-8297 (in W.Va)
(304) 558-3333

Citation: Taxation, § 11-24-5—Corporate Net Income Tax; §11-15-9—Consumers Sales Tax.

Publications: A copy of the statute and *Special Sales and Use Tax Rules for Nonprofit Organizations* flyer are available from the contact office.

Requirements: Corporations with federal 501(c) exemptions are generally exempt from corporate income tax, but this does not apply to unrelated business income. Many 501(c)(3)s and (c)(4)s are exempt from the consumers sales tax or use tax, if four conditions are met. Consult the contact office for details.

Application Procedure: File the *Business Registration Certificate* application with the Department, and include a copy of the IRS determination letter.

CHARITABLE SOLICITATION

Contact:

Office of the Secretary of State
Charitable Organization Registration Division
Building 1. Suite 157K
1900 Kanawha Boulevard, East
Charleston, WV 25305
(304) 558-6000

Citation: Chapter 29, Article 19 of the West Virginia Code, *Solicitation of Charitable Funds Act.*

Initial Registration: All charities except those exempt under §29-19-6 must register annually with the Secretary of State. The registration fee is $15 for organizations collecting less than $1 million, and $50 for those collecting more. The registration form must include a copy of a balance sheet and a report of income and expenses for the preceding year. If more than $50,000 is solicited, an audit by an independent CPA is required showing the kind and amount of funds raised, costs and expenses, and where and for what purposes the funds were disbursed. Registrants must include their IRS 990. They need to attach their IRS determination letter if they are new organizations or if they are not required to file a federal 990.

Annual reports: Renewal of registration requires disclosure of general information, information about professional solicitors and fundraising counsel, copies of contracts with them, information about organization misconduct, information about funds raised and disbursed, and a detailed itemized report of income and expenses.

Organization Solicitation Disclosure requirements: Must disclose in writing the name of a representative of the charity to whom inquiries can be made; the charity's name; the purpose of the solicitation; upon request of the person solicited, the estimated percentage of the money collected that will be applied to the cost of solicitation and administration and how much will be applied directly to the charitable purpose; and the number of any raffle, bingo or other state permit used for fundraising. Every printed solicitation must include the following statement:

"West Virginia residents may obtain a summary of the registration and financial documents from the Secretary of State, State Capitol, Charleston, West Virginia 25305. Registration does not imply endorsement."

The disclosure statement must be conspicuously displayed on any written or printed solicitation. When the solicitation consists of more than one piece, it must be displayed on a prominent part of the materials.

Paid Solicitor Requirements: Must register annually and pay a $100 registration fee and post a $10,000 bond.

Fundraising Counsel Requirements: Must register, pay a $100 fee, and post a $10,000 bond.

Wisconsin

Central Switchboard: (608) 266-2211
State Web Home Page: http://www.state.wi.us/

INCORPORATION

Contact:
> Department of Financial Institutions
> Division of Corporate & Consumer Services
> PO Box 7846
> Madison, WI 53707-7846
> (608) 261-7577

Citation: *Nonstock Corporations*, Chapter 181, Wisconsin Statutes.

Publications Available: A reprint of the statute and *Articles of Incorporation* (Form 102) are available from the contact office; all forms are available at the web site: http://www.wdfi.org

General Requirements: Articles of Incorporation must set forth a statement that the corporation is incorporated under Ch. 181; the corporate name; mailing address of the initial principal office; street address of the initial registered office and the name and address of the registered agent at that address; the name and address of each incorporator; whether the corporation shall have members or no members; and, if the corporation is authorized to make distributions under s. 181.1302(4), a statement to that effect.

Corporate Name: Corporate name must contain the word "corporation," "incorporated," "company" or "limited" or the abbreviation of one of those words.

Name reservation: May reserve a corporate name for 120 days. Application may be made by telephone, but the reservation will be canceled if the department does not receive the proper fee within 15 business days. The fee for a written request is $10; the fee for a telephone request is $20.

How to File: Submit Articles of Incorporation in duplicate, at least one with an original signature of an incorporator. The filing fee is $35, payable by check to *Department of Financial Institutions*.

Other Filings/reports: Corporations are required to continuously maintain a registered agent resident in Wisconsin and to file an annual report. The report must be made on the form provided by the Department. Forms are distributed to each

corporation's registered agent in Wisconsin during the calendar quarter in which they are due for filing. Failure to file the report may establish grounds for administrative dissolution of the corporation.

LOBBYING

Contact:
> Wisconsin Ethics Board
> 44 E. Mifflin Street
> Suite 601
> Madison, WI 53703-2800
> (601) 266-8123

Citation: Wisconsin Statutes, Subchapter III, Chapter 13; § 13.61-13.75.

Publications: Several publications on lobbying rules, a copy of the statute, and relevant forms are available from the contact office.

Registration required: Lobbyists are required to register before the fifth day on which the first lobbying communication occurs. The license expires December 31 every even-numbered year. Lobbyists are required to have only one license regardless of the number of clients they represent; organizations authorizing lobbyists must file registration/authorization forms no later than the fifth day after communication occurs. The license fees are $250 to lobby on behalf of one employer and $400 to lobby for multiple employers. The registration fee is $375 for the organization and $125 for each authorization of a licensed lobbyist. Organizations which have lobbying expenditures not exceeding $500 annually pay a fee of $20 for a two-year period.

Forms to use: *Registration of Organization Employing a Lobbyist and Authorization of Lobbyists* (Eth-806); *Application for Lobby License* (Eth-807); and *Principal's Statement of Lobbying Activities and Expenditures (Eth 810).*

Reporting requirements: Each lobbying organization must report to the Ethics Board each bill or proposed rule number on which the organization makes a lobbying communication, within 15 days of the first lobbying communication. In January and July, each lobbying organization must file a *State-*

ment of Lobbying Activities and Expenditures for the preceding six-month reporting period.

TAX EXEMPTIONS

Contact:

> Department of Revenue
> PO Box 8902
> Madison, WI 53708
> (608) 266-2776

Citation: §77.54, Wisconsin Statutes Annotated—sales and use tax; §71.22 —corporate income tax.

Requirements: Occasional sales of tangible personal property or services by nonprofit organizations may qualify for exemption. Consult the statute or the contact office for more information. Organizations exempt from federal income taxes are exempt from the state corporate income tax, other than on unrelated business income.

Application Procedure: File an S-103 form, *Application for Wisconsin Sales and Use Tax Certificate of Exempt Status*, with the Department and include Articles of Incorporation and bylaws, a statement of expenditures and receipts, and a copy of the IRS determination letter if there is one.

CHARITABLE SOLICITATION

Contact:

> Department of Regulation and Licensing
> PO Box 8935
> Madison, WI 53708-8935
> (608) 266-5511, ext. 441

Citation: Chapter 440, Subchapter III, Stats; Chapter RL 5, Wis. Admin. Code.

Publications: A copy of the statute and forms are available from the contact office.

Initial Registration: Organizations that solicit contributions for a charitable purpose must file a registration statement, along with a $15 filing fee. Each organization must include a copy of its certificate of incorporation, charter, Articles of Incorporation or bylaws; a statement explaining how the contributions will be used; a copy of the organization's IRS determination letter if it has one or a copy of its application for exemption if a determination is pending; its federal 990 annual return or a Form #308 *(Charitable Organization Annual Financial Report)* for those with more than $5,000 in contributions during the most recently completed fiscal year (or a Form #1943 for those with $5,000 or less in contributions); the name and address of any professional fundraiser or fundraising counsel used by the organization; a list of government agencies that have formally autho-

rized the organization to engage in charitable solicitation; and information about organizational misconduct concerning solicitations.

Annual reports: Organizations that raise more than $5,000 must submit, within six months after the end of each fiscal year, a financial report that includes a balance sheet; a statement of support, revenue, expenses, and changes in the fund balance; and a statement of functional expenses divided into, at least at a minimum, categories of management and general, program services, and fundraising. Organizations that raise more than $100,000 during the fiscal year must submit an audited financial statement within six months after the end of that fiscal year, consistent with generally accepted accounting principles. Financial reports must be made on approved forms and are provided automatically by the Department within two weeks of the close of the organization's fiscal year. Organizations that raise less than $5,000 must file Form 1942, *Affidavit In Lieu of Annual Financial Report.*

Organization Solicitation Disclosure requirements: Those required to register must, at the time of the solicitation, disclose the name and location of the charitable organization; that a financial statement disclosing assets, liabilities, fund balances, revenue and expenses of the preceding fiscal year will be provided upon request; and a clear description of the primary charitable purpose for which the solicitation is made. This does not apply to those organizations that solicit less than $50,000 in their fiscal year and limits solicitation to the county where they are headquartered.

Paid Solicitor Requirements: Must register by paying a $50 fee and posting at least a $20,000 bond ($5,000 bond if they do not have custody of funds), must have a written contract with the charitable organization, and must file a solicitation notice with the Department disclosing information about the terms of the solicitation.

Fundraising Counsel Requirements: May not have custody of contributions unless they are registered, must pay a $50 registration fee and have a bond of at least $20,000, and must have a written contract with the charitable organization.

Wyoming

Central Switchboard: (307) 777-7011
State Web Home Page: http://www.state.wy.us/

INCORPORATION

Contact:
>   Secretary of State
>   Corporations Division
>   State Capitol
>   Cheyenne, WY 82002-0020
>   (307) 777-7311/7312

Citation: *Wyoming Nonprofit Corporation Act,* Wyoming Statutes 17-19-101 et seq.

Publications Available: Forms are available from the contact office and the web site: http://www.soswy.state.wy.us/

General Requirements: Articles of Incorporation must set forth the corporate name; whether it is a religious, mutual benefit or public benefit corporation; the street address of the initial registered office and the name of the initial registered agent at that office; the name and address of the incorporator; whether it will have members; provisions regarding the distribution of assets upon dissolution; and, for name availability purposes, the type of business the corporation will be conducting.

Corporate Name: May not contain language stating or implying that it is organized for a purpose other than permitted by law or its Articles of Incorporation; shall not be the same as, or deceptively similar to, the name of any trademark or service mark registered, and shall be distinguishable upon the records from other registered business names.

Name reservation: May be reserved for a non-renewable, 120-day period for a fee of $3.

How to File: File Articles of Incorporation with one conformed copy and a *Consent to Appointment by Registered Agent* form with a $10 filing fee.

Other Filings/reports: An annual report must be filed disclosing general information, and any profit or pecuniary advantage paid directly or indirectly to any officer or director. The report is due on the first day of the month of corporate registration of every year. There is a $10 license fee for filing.

LOBBYING

Contact:
>   Secretary of State
>   State of Wyoming
>   State Capitol
>   Cheyenne, WY 82002
>   (307) 777-7186

Citation: Title 28, Chapter 7, Sections 101 et seq.

Publications: Forms may be accessed at the web site: http://soswy.state.wy.us/election/forms.htm or obtained from the contact office.

Registration required: Lobbyists must register with the Office within 48 hours of commencing lobbying activity. The registration fee is $25, but a $5 fee applies if reimbursement or compensation is expected to be less than $500 or if the lobbyist receives only travel and per diem expenses.

Reporting requirements: Lobbyist activity reports are due by June 30 for activities during the preceding May 1-April 30. Activity reports include the date of expenditure, the lobbyist's source of funding, the item or activity, the name of the recipient, and the amount of the expense.

TAX EXEMPTIONS

Contact:

Department of Revenue
Herschler Building
2nd Floor West
122 W. 25th Street
Cheyenne, WY 82002-0110
(307) 777-7961

Citation: §39-15-105 (a)(iv)(A-G).

Requirements: Religious and charitable organizations, and nonprofits providing meals or services to senior citizens, are exempt from sales/use tax on their purchases. There is an exemption from the sales tax for occasional sales made by religious and charitable organizations for fundraising purposes.

Application Procedure: Organizations seeking tax-exempt status must demonstrate the characteristics of their organization, and include Articles of Incorporation; printed descriptions of accomplishments; and provide descriptions of their services, sales, and applicable fee schedules. Submit a copy of the IRS determination letter or advise the Department that no determination has been issued, if that is the case.

There is no corporate income or franchise tax for in-state corporations.

CHARITABLE SOLICITATION

Note: There is no registration/reporting law.

Appendix A

Sample Bylaws for a Nonprofit Corporation

BASED ON THE BYLAWS OF THE PENNSYLVANIA JEWISH COALITION

(reprinted with permission)

BYLAWS
OF
(INSERT NAME OF ORGANIZATION)

ARTICLE I - CORPORATE NAME

1. The name of the corporation shall be (insert).

ARTICLE II - PURPOSE

1. The corporation shall have unlimited powers to engage in and do any lawful act concerning any and all lawful activity for which non-profit corporations may be incorporated under the Act of (insert), under the provisions of which the corporation is incorporated.

2. The corporation shall undertake such acts as it deems necessary to (insert purpose of the corporation).

ARTICLE III - OFFICES

1. The principal office of the corporation shall be located in (insert).

2. The corporation may also have offices at such other places as the Board of Directors may from time to time appoint or the activities of the corporation may require.

ARTICLE IV - SEALS

1. The corporate seal shall have inscribed thereon the name of the corporation, the year of its organization and the words "Corporate Seal, (insert name of state)."

ARTICLE V - MEMBERS

1. The corporation shall have no members. All powers, obligations and rights of members provided by law shall reside in the Board of Directors.

ARTICLE VI - DIRECTORS

1. The business and affairs of this corporation shall be managed by its Board of Directors. The number of directors shall not exceed (insert number). The minimum qualifications of members of the Board of Directors shall be (insert).

2. In addition to the powers and authorities by these Bylaws expressly conferred upon them, the Board of Directors shall have the maximum power and authority now or hereafter provided or permitted under the laws of the (insert state) to Directors of nsert state) non-profit corporations acting as a Board.

3. The Annual Meeting of the Board of Directors shall be held annually during the calendar year at such time and place as the Board of Directors shall designate in the notice of the meeting.

4. Regular meetings of the Board of Directors shall occur at least (insert) at such times and places as it shall designate from time to time.

5. Special meetings of the Board of Directors may be called by the Chairperson at such times as the Chairperson shall deem necessary.

6. Written or personal notice of every meeting of the Board of Directors shall be given to each Director at least five (5) days prior to the day named for the meeting.

7. A quorum for the transaction of business shall consist of (insert). The acts of a majority of directors present and eligible to vote at a Board meeting shall be the acts of the Board of Directors. Any action which may be taken at a meeting of the Directors may be taken without a meeting, if the consent or consents in writing setting forth the action so taken shall be signed by at least a majority of all directors in office, and shall be filed with the Secretary of the corporation.

8. Except where inconsistent with law or these bylaws, corporate proceedings shall be governed by the latest edition of Robert's Rules of Order.

9. The Board of Directors may, by resolution adopted by a majority of the Directors in office, establish one or more committees to consist of one or more Directors of the corporation to report back to the Board on the matter(s) within the committee's jurisdiction. A quorum for the purpose of holding and acting at any meeting of a committee shall be a simple majority of the members thereof.

10. All Board members shall be nominated and elected to serve on the Board. The Board may designate one or more directors as alternate members of any committee, who may replace any absent or disqualified member at any meeting of the committee. In the absence or disqualification of a member of a committee, the member or members thereof present at any meeting and not disqualified from voting, whether or not he, she or they constitute a quorum, may unanimously appoint another director to act at the meeting in the place of any such absent or disqualified member. Each committee of the Board shall serve at the pleasure of the Board.

11. The Board of Directors may, by resolution adopted by a majority of the Directors in office, establish an Advisory Committee to advise and assist the Board of Directors in carrying out its responsibilities. The Advisory committee shall consist of (insert).

12. One or more persons may participate in a meeting of the Board or a committee of the Board by means of the conference telephone or similar communications equipment by means of which all persons participating in the meeting can hear each other. Participation in a meeting pursuant to this section shall constitute presence in person at such meeting.

13. The Board of Directors may declare vacant the office of a director if he or she is declared of unsound mind by the order of court or is convicted of felony, or if within sixty (60) days after notice of his or her selection, he or she does not accept such office either in writing or by attending a meeting of the Board of Directors, and fulfill each other requirements of a qualification as the Bylaws may specify.

14. Any Director or Officer of the corporation is authorized to receive reasonable compensation from the corporation for services rendered and for actual expenses incurred when authorized by the Board of Directors or its designee. No director of the corporation shall receive compensation merely for acting as a director.

ARTICLE VII - OFFICERS

1. The executive officers of the corporations shall be natural persons of full age, shall be chosen by the Board, and shall be a Chairperson, Vice Chairperson, Secretary, Treasurer and such other officers and assistant officers as the needs of the corporation may require. They shall hold their offices for a term of (insert) and shall have such authority and shall perform such duties as are provided by the Bylaws and as shall from time to time be prescribed by the Board. The Board of Directors may secure the fidelity of any or all such officers by bond or otherwise. There shall be no limit on the number or terms an officer can serve.

2. Any officer or agent may be removed by the Board of Directors whenever in its judgment the best interests of the corporation will be served thereby but such removal shall be without prejudice to the contract rights of any person removed.

3. The Chairperson shall be the chief executive officer of the corporation; he or she shall preside at all meetings of the Directors; he or she shall have general and active management of the affairs of the corporation; shall see that all orders and resolutions of the Board are carried into effect, subject, however, to the right of the Directors to delegate any specific powers, except as may be by statute exclusively conferred on the Chairperson to any other officer or officers of the corporation. He or she shall execute all documents requiring a seal, under the seal of the corporation. He or she shall be EX-OFFICIO a member of all committees and shall have the general powers and duties of supervision and management usually vested in the office of Chairperson.

4. The Vice Chairperson shall act in all cases for and as the Chairperson in the latter's absence or incapacity, and shall perform such other duties as he or she may be required to do from time to time.

5. The Secretary shall attend all sessions of the Board and act as clerk thereof, and record all the votes of the corporation and the minutes of all its transactions in a book to be kept for that purpose; and shall perform like duties for all committees of the Board of Directors when required. He or she shall give, or cause to be given, notice of all meetings of the Board of Directors, and shall perform such other duties as may be prescribed by the Board of Directors or Chairperson, under whose supervision he or she shall be. He or she shall keep in safe custody, the corporate seal of the corporation, and when authorized by the Board, affix the same to any instrument requiring it.

6. The Treasurer shall have custody of the corporate funds and securities and shall keep full and accurate accounts or receipts and disbursements in books belonging to the corporation, and shall keep the moneys of the corporation in a separate account to the credit of the corporation. He or she shall disburse the funds of the corporation as may be ordered by the Board, taking proper vouchers for such disbursements, and shall render to the Chairperson and Directors, at the regular meeting of the Board, or whenever they may require it, an account of all his or her transactions as Treasurer and of the financial condition of the corporation.

7. Elections of officers shall be held every (insert) at the Annual Meeting of the Board of Directors.

ARTICLE VIII - VACANCIES

1. If the office of any officer or agent, one or more, becomes vacant for any reason, the Board of Directors may choose a successor or successors, who shall hold office for the unexpired term in respect of which such vacancy occurred.

2. Vacancies in the Board of Directors shall be filled in the same manner as provided for the designation of Directors in Article VI - Directors.

ARTICLE IX - BOOKS AND RECORDS

1. The corporation shall keep an original or duplicate record of the proceeding of the Directors, the original or a copy of its Bylaws, including all amendments thereto to date, certified by the Secretary of the corporation, and an original or a duplicate Board register, giving the names of the Directors, and showing their respective addresses. The corporation shall also keep appropriate, complete and accurate books or records of account which shall be reviewed on an annual basis. The records provided for herein shall be kept at either the registered office of the corporation in this Commonwealth, or at its principal place of business wherever situated.

ARTICLE X - FISCAL YEAR AND ANNUAL REPORT

1. The fiscal year of the corporation shall commence on (insert) and end on the following (insert).

2. The Board of Directors shall cause a report of the activities of the corporation to be prepared annually and sent to such persons as the Board of Directors shall determine.

ARTICLE XI - AMENDMENTS

1. The Board of Directors may alter, amend, suspend or repeal these Bylaws at any regular or special meeting called for that purpose, except as restricted by (insert reference to state law).

ARTICLE XII - LIMITED LIABILITY OF DIRECTORS

1. A director shall not be personally liable for monetary damages as such for any action taken, or any failure to take any action, unless the director has breached or failed to perform the duties of his or her office under (insert state law relating to standard of care and justifiable reliance); and the breach or failure to perform constitutes self-dealing, willful misconduct or recklessness. The provision of this section shall not apply to the responsibility or liability of a director pursuant to any criminal statute; or the liability of a director for the payment of taxes pursuant to local, State or Federal Law.

Appendix B
About the Author...

Gary M. Grobman (B.S. Drexel University, M.P.A. Harvard University, Kennedy School of Government) is special projects director for White Hat Communications, a Harrisburg-based publishing and nonprofit consulting organization formed in 1993. Mr. Grobman is a doctoral student at The Penn State University. He served as the executive director of the Pennsylvania Jewish Coalition from 1983-1996. Prior to that, he was a senior legislative assistant in Washington for two members of Congress, a news reporter, and a political humor columnist for *Roll Call*. He also served as a lobbyist for public transit agencies. In 1987, he founded the Non-Profit Advocacy Network (NPAN), which consists of more than 50 statewide associations that represent Pennsylvania charities. He currently is the Harrisburg Contributing Editor for *Pennsylvania Nonprofit Report* and the Internet site reviewer for the *International Journal of Nonprofit and Voluntary Sector Marketing.*

He serves on the board of directors of the Greater Harrisburg Concert Band as Vice President. He also served on the board of directors of the Citizen Service Project, and was the Treasurer of that 501(c)(3), which was established to promote citizen service in Pennsylvania. He is the author of *The Holocaust—A Guide for Pennsylvania Teachers (1990)*, *The Non-Profit Handbook* (1996), *The Non-Profit Internet Handbook* (1998, co-authored with Gary Grant), and *Improving Quality and Performance in Your Non-Profit Organization* (1999).

For information about speaking engagements or consulting projects, contact Mr. Grobman at: **White Hat Communications, P.O. Box 5390, Harrisburg, PA 17110-0390. Telephone: (717) 238-3787; Fax: (717) 238-2090.**

Appendix C

Nonprofit Handbook—Second Edition
Reader Survey/Order Form

Return Survey To:
White Hat Communications
PO Box 5390
Harrisburg, PA 17110-0390

My name and address (please print legibly):

1. I would like to suggest the following corrections:

2. I would like to suggest the following topics for inclusion in a future edition:

3. I have the following comments, suggestions, or criticisms:

4. I would like to order ____ additional copies @$29.95 each plus $3.50 shipping and handling first book, $1 each additional book. Pennsylvania tax-exempt organizations please add 6% sales tax or include a copy of exemption certificate from the Pennsylvania Department of Revenue. Note: Quantity discounts are available.

Bibliography

A comprehensive bibliography for all aspects of nonprofit organization formation and operation can be found in a three-volume work:

Derrickson, Margaret Chandler, et. al. *The Literature of the Nonprofit Sector* (3 volumes), New York, NY: The Foundation Center, 1989.

Chapter 1/Chapter 2

Conners, Tracy D. (ed.). *The Nonprofit Organization Handbook*. New York, NY: McGraw-Hill Book Co., 1980.

Debnam, Robert J. *Handbook of Legal Liabilities for Nonprofit Executives*. Washington, DC: Rural America.

Hopkins, Bruce R. *Starting and Managing a Nonprofit Organization: A Legal Guide*. New York, NY: Wiley & Sons, 1989.

Kirschten, Barbara L. *Nonprofit Corporate Forms Handbook*. New York, NY: Clark Boardman Co., 1990.

Lane, Marc J. *Legal Handbook for Nonprofit Organizations*. New York, NY: Amacon, 1980.

Mancuso, Anthony. *How To Form Your Own Nonprofit Corporation*. Berkeley, CA: Nolo Press, 1990.

Mandel Center for Nonprofit Organizations. *Legal Issues in Nonprofit Organizations*. Mandel Center for Nonprofit Organizations Discussion Paper Series. Cleveland, OH: Case Western Reserve University, 1988.

Majmudes, Carol S. and Weiss, Ellen. (eds.). *Tax-Exempt Organizations* (2 vol.). Englewood Cliffs, NJ: Prentice-Hall, 1988.

Ott, J. Steven and Shafitz, Jay M. *The Facts on File Dictionary of Nonprofit Organization Management*. New York, NY: Facts on File Publications, 1986.

Philadelphia Volunteer Lawyers for the Arts. *Guide to Forming a Non-Profit, Tax-Exempt Organization*. Philadelphia, PA: Philadelphia Volunteer Lawyers for the Arts, 1980.

Treusch, Paul E. and Sugarman, Norman A. *Tax-Exempt Organizations*. Philadelphia, PA: American Law Institute, 1983.

Whitaker, Fred A. *How to Form Your Own Non-Profit Corporation in One Day*. Oakland, CA: Minority Management Institute, 1979.

Chapter 3

Broadwell, Martin M. *Supervisory Handbook: A Management Guide to Principles and Applications*. New York, NY: Wiley, Inc., 1985.

Conners, Tracy D. (ed.). *The Nonprofit Organization Handbook*. New York, NY: McGraw-Hill Book Co., 1980.

Hopkins, Bruce R. *Starting and Managing a Nonprofit Organization: A Legal Guide*. New York, NY: Wiley & Sons, 1989.

Mancuso, Anthony. *How To Form Your Own Nonprofit Corporation*. Berkeley, CA: Nolo Press, 1990.

Ott, J. Steven and Shafitz, Jay M. *The Facts on File Dictionary of Nonprofit Organization Management*. New York, NY: Facts on File Publications, 1986.

Robert, III, Henry M. and Evans, William J. (eds.). *Robert's Rules of Order Newly Revised* (1990 Edition). Glenview, IL: Scott, Foresman and Co., 1990.

Conners, Tracy D. (ed.). *The Nonprofit Organization Handbook.* New York, NY: McGraw-Hill Book Co., 1980.

Chapter 4

Anthes, Earl, et. al. (ed.). *The Nonprofit Board Book.* Independent Community Consultants, West Memphis, Ark., Independent Community Consultants, 1985.

Bates, Don. *How to Be a Better Board Member: Guidelines for Trustees.* Voluntary Action Leadership (Winter 1983).

Black, Ralph. *What Do You Do With a Do-Nothing Board Member?* American Symphony Orchestra League (1987).

Brooklyn In-Touch Information Center. *Building a Board of Directors.* Brooklyn, NY: Brooklyn In-Touch Information Center, 1984.

————-*How To Conduct a Meeting.* 1988.

————-*How To Develop a Board of Directors.* 1988.

Conrad, William R. Jr. and Glenn, William E. *The Effective Voluntary Board of Directors: What is it and How it Works.* Chicago, IL: Swallow Press, 1983.

Duca, Diane J. *Nonprofit Boards: A Practical Guide to Roles, Responsibilities and Performance.* Phoenix, AZ: Oryx Press, 1986.

Hopkins, Bruce R. *Starting and Managing a Nonprofit Organization: A Legal Guide.* New York, NY: Wiley & Sons, 1989.

Independent Community Consultants. *The Nonprofit Board Book: Strategies for Organizational Success.* West Memphis, Ark: Independent Community Consultants, 1983.

Kirk, W. Astor. *Nonprofit Organization Governance: A Challenge in Turbulent Times.* New York, NY: Carlton Press, 1986.

O'Connell, Brian. *The Role of the Board and Board Members.* Nonprofit Management Series (#1). Washington, DC: Independent Sector, 1988.

———— *Finding, Developing and Rewarding Good Board Members.* Nonprofit Management Series (#2). Washington, DC: Independent Sector, 1988.

———— *The Board Member's Book: Making a Difference in Voluntary Organizations.* New York, NY: The Foundation Center, 1985.

Ott, J. Steven and Shafitz, Jay M. *The Facts on File Dictionary of Nonprofit Organization Management.* New York, NY: Facts on File Publications, 1986.

Chapter 5

Albert, K. J, editor. *The Strategic Management Handbook.* New York: McGraw-Hill, 1983.

Department. of Hospital Planning and Society for Hospital Planning. *Compendium of Resources for Strategic Planning in Hospitals.* Chicago, IL: American Hospital Association, 1981.

Armstrong, J. S. *The Value of Formal Planning for Strategic Decisions: Review of Empirical Research.* Strategic Management Journal (Ill, 1982:197-211).

Barry, Brian W. *Strategic Planning Workbook for Nonprofit Organizations.* St. Paul, Minn: Amherst H. Wilder Foundation, 1986.

Bryson, J. M.*Strategic Planning for Public and Nonprofit Organizations.* San Francisco: Jossey-Bass, 1988.

Mintzburg, Henry. *The Rise and Fall of Strategic Planning.* NY, NY: MacMillan, 1994.

Newman, W. H., Summer, C. E. and Warren, E. K.*The Process of Management.*Englewood Cliffs, NJ: Prentice Hall, 1982.

Pennings, J. M. *Organizational Strategy and Change.* San Francisco, CA: Jossey-Bass, 1985.

Peters, J. P.*A Guide to Strategic Planning for Hospitals.*Chicago, IL: American Hospital Association, 1979.

Rhenmann, E. *Organizational Theory for Long-Range Planning.* NY, NY: Wiley & Sons, 1973.

Steiner, G. A. *Strategic Planning: What Every Manager Must Know.* NY, NY: Free Press, 1979.

Chapter 6

Carver, John. *Boards That Make a Difference.* San Francisco, CA: Josey-Bass, 1990.

Chapter 7

Independent Sector. *Ethics and the Nation's Voluntary and Philanthropic Community.* Washington, DC.

Josephson Institute of Ethics. *Making Ethical Decisions.* Marina del Rey, CA.

Chapter 8

Conners, Tracy D. (ed.).*The Nonprofit Organization Handbook.* New York, NY: McGraw-Hill Book Co., 1980.

Godfrey, Howard. *Handbook on Tax-Exempt Organizations.* Englewood Cliffs, NJ: Prentice-Hall, 1983.

Hansmann, Henry. *The Rationale for Exempting Nonprofit Organizations From Corporate Income Taxation.* New Haven, CT: Institute for Social Policy Studies, 1981.

Harmon, Gail and Ferster, Andrea. *"Dealing With the IRS."* Nonprofit Times (May 1988).

Hopkins, Bruce R. *Starting and Managing a Nonprofit Organization: A Legal Guide.* New York, NY: Wiley & Sons, 1989.

Kirschten, Barbara L. *Nonprofit Corporate Forms Handbook.* New York: Clark Boardman Co., 1990.

Larson, Martin A., and Lowell, C. Stanley. *Praise the Lord for Tax Exemption.* Washington, DC: Robert B. Luce, 1969.

Mancuso, Anthony. *How To Form Your Own Nonprofit Corporation.* Berkeley, CA: Nolo Press, 1990.

Ott, J. Steven and Shafitz, Jay M.*The Facts on File Dictionary of Nonprofit Organization Management.* New York, NY: Facts on File Publications, 1986.

Skousen, Mark. *Tax-Free.* Merrifield, VA: Mark Skousen, 1982.

Stralton, Debra J. *"A Guide for Dealing With the IRS."* Association Management (August 1979).

Trompeter, Jean E. *"Formation and Qualification of a Charitable Organization."* Milwaukee Lawyer (Fall 1983).

Chapter 9

Brooklyn In-Touch Information Center. *How to Assess Board Liability. Fact Sheet for Nonprofit Managers* (#6). Brooklyn, NY: Brooklyn In-Touch Information Center, 1988.

Chapman, Terry S.; Lai, Mary L; and Steinbock, Elmer L. *Am I Covered For? A Guide to Insurance for Nonprofit Organizations.* San Jose, CA: Consortium for Human Resources, 1984.

Conners, Tracy D. (ed.). *The Nonprofit Organization Handbook.* New York, NY: McGraw-Hill Book Co., 1980.

Council on Foundations. *Directors and Officers Liability Insurance.* Washington, DC: Council on Foundations, 1983.

Davis, Pamela. *Nonprofit Organizations and Liability Insurance: Problems, Options and Prospects.* Los Angeles, CA: California Community Foundation, 1987.

Drucker, Peter F. *Managing the Nonprofit Organization.* New York, NY: Harper Collins, 1990.

Johnson, R. Bradley. *Risk Management Guide for Nonprofits.* Alexandria, VA: United Way of America, 1987.

Ott, J. Steven and Shafitz, Jay M. *The Facts on File Dictionary of Nonprofit Organization Management.* New York, NY: Facts on File Publications, 1986.

Peat, Marwick, Mitchell and Co. *Directors' and Officers' Liability: A Crisis in the Making.* New York, NY: Peat, Marwick, Mitchell and Co., 1987.

Chapter 10

American Institute of Certified Public Accountants. *Audits of Certain Nonprofit Organizations.* New York, NY: American Institute of Certified Public Accountants, 1981.

Brooklyn In-Touch Information Center. *How To Prepare a Budget.* New York, NY: Brooklyn In-Touch Information Center, 1988.

Conners, Tracy D. (ed.). *The Nonprofit Organization Handbook.* New York, NY: McGraw-Hill Book Co., 1980.

Drucker, Peter F. *Managing the Nonprofit Organization.* New York, NY: Harper Collins, 1990.

Gross, Jr., Malvern J. and Warshauer, William. *Financial and Accounting Guide for Nonprofit Organizations.* New York, NY: John Wiley, 1983.

Matthews, Lawrence M. *Practical Operating Budgeting.* New York: McGraw-Hill, 1977.

Olenick, Arnold J. and Olenick, Philip R. *Making the Non-Profit Organization Work: A Financial, Legal and Tax Guide for Administrators.* Englewood Cliffs, NJ: Institute for Business Planning, 1983.

Ott, J. Steven and Shafitz, Jay M. *The Facts on File Dictionary of Nonprofit Organization Management.* New York, NY: Facts on File Publications, 1986.

Public Management Institute. *Bookkeeping for Nonprofits.* San Francisco, CA: Institute for Business Planning, 1983.

————- *Budgeting for Nonprofits.* San Francisco, CA: Institute for Business Planning, 1980.

Quint, Barbara Gilder. *Clear and Simple Guide to Bookkeeping.* New York: Monarch Press, 1981.

Ragan, Robert C. *Step-By-Step Bookkeeping.* New York, NY: Sterling Publications, 1987.

Sladek, Frea E. and Stein, Eugene L. *Grant Budgeting and Finance.* New York, NY: Plenum Press, 1981.

Vinter, Robert D. and Kikish, Rhea K. *Budgeting for Not-for-Profit Organizations.* New York, NY: Free Press, 1984.

Wacht, Richard F. *Financial Management in Nonprofit Organizations.* Atlanta, GA: Georgia State University, 1984.

Waldo, Charles N. *A Working Guide for Directors of Not-for-Profit Organizations.* Westport, CT: Greenwood Press, 1986.

Chapter 11

Anthes, Earl W. and Cronin, Jerry (eds.). *Personnel Matters in the Nonprofit Organization.* West Memphis, AR: Independent Community Consultants, 1987.

Anthony, Robert N. and Herzlinger, Regina E. *Management Control in Nonprofit Organizations.* Chicago, IL: Richard D. Irwin, 1975.

Becker, Sarah and Glenn, Donna. *Off Your Duffs and Up the Assets: Common Sense for Non-Profit Managers.* Rockville, NY: Farnsworth Publishing Co., 1988.

Borst, Diane and Montana, Patrick J. (eds.). *Managing Nonprofit Organizations.* New York, NY: Amacon, 1977.

Broadwell, Martin M. *Supervisory Handbook: A Management Guide to Principles and Applications.* New York, NY: Wiley, Inc., 1985.

Brown, James Douglas. *The Human Nature of Organizations.* New York, NY: Amacon, 1973.

Chruden, Herbert J. *Personnel Management.* Cincinnati, OH: South-Western Publications, 1976.

Conners, Tracy D. (ed.). *The Nonprofit Organization Handbook.* New York, NY: McGraw-Hill Book Co., 1980.

Drucker, Peter F. *Managing the Nonprofit Organization.* New York, NY: Harper Collins, 1990.

Goldberg/Rosenthal, Montgomery, Mc Cracken, Walker & Rhoads, and Paychex, Inc. *Accounting, Legal and Payroll Tax Guide for Nonprofit Organizations.* Philadelphia: Community Accountants, 1991.

Hopkins, Bruce R. *Starting and Managing a Nonprofit Organization: A Legal Guide.* New York, NY: Wiley & Sons, 1989.

Chapter 12

Bagley, Esq., Bruce. *Necessary v. Nosey—Guidelines and Strategies for Hiring.* PA Society of Association Executives' *Society News.* April 1996. pp. 20.

Gelatt, James P. *Managing Nonprofit Organizations in the 21ˢᵗ Century.* Phoenix, AZ: The Oryx Press, 1992.

Half, Robert. *On Hiring.* New York, NY: Crown Publishers, 1985.

Hopkins, Bruce R. *Starting and Managing a Nonprofit Organization— A Legal Guide.* New York, NY: Wiley & Sons; 1989.

Pennsylvania Human Relations Commission. *Pre-Employment Inquiries: What May I Ask? What Must I Answer?* Harrisburg, PA.

Rogers, Henry C. *The One Hat Solution—Rogers' Strategy for Creative Middle Management.* New York, NY: St. Martin's Press, 1986.

Thompson, Brad. *The New Manager's Handbook.* Burr Ridge, IL: Irwin Professional Publishing, 1995.

Chapter 13

Adams, Katherine. *"Investing in Volunteers: A Guide to Effective Volunteer Management."* Conserve Neighborhoods (1985).

Brown, Kathleen M. *Keys to Making a Volunteer Program Work.* Richmond, CA: Arden Publications, 1982.

Conners, Tracy D. (ed.). *The Nonprofit Organization Handbook.* New York, NY: McGraw-Hill Book Co., 1980.

de Harven, Gerry Ann. *"Fostering the Voluntary Spirit: Motivating People to Serve."* Fund Raising Management (March 1984).

Flanagan, Joan. *The Successful Volunteer Organization: Getting Started and Getting Results in Nonprofit, Charitable, Grassroots and Community Groups.* Chicago, IL: Contemporary Books, 1984.

Fletcher, Kathleen Brown. *The 9 Keys To Successful Volunteer Programs.* Taft Group: Rockville, MD., 1987.

Independent Sector. *Americans Volunteer, 1981.* Washington, DC: Independent Sector, 1982.

Lauffer, Armand and Gorodezky, Sarah. *Volunteers.* Beverly Hills, CA: Sage Publications, 1977.

London, Mark. *"Effective Use of Volunteers: Who, Why, When and How."* Fund Raising Management (August 1985).

McCurley, Stephen H. *"Protecting Volunteers From Suit: A Look At State Legislation."* Voluntary Action Leadership (Spring-Summer 1987).

O'Connell, Brian. *America's Voluntary Spirit.* New York, NY: The Foundation Center, 1983.

Rauner, Judy. *Helping People Volunteer.* San Diego, CA: Marlborough Publications, 1980.

Stafford, J. et. al. *Fundamentals of Association Management: The Volunteer.* Washington, DC: American Society of Association Executives, 1982.

Taylor, Shirley H. and Wild, Peggy. *"How to Match Volunteer Motivation With Job Demands."* Voluntary Action Leadership (Summer 1984).

Van Til, Jon. *Mapping the Third Sector: Volunteerism in a Changing Social Economy.* New York, NY: The Foundation Center, 1988.

Volunteer—The National Center. *New Challenges for Employee Volunteering.* Arlington, VA: Volunteer—The National Center, 1982.

Chapter 14

Conners, Tracy D. (ed.). *The Nonprofit Organization Handbook.* New York, NY: McGraw-Hill Book Co., 1980.

Mercer, Eric. (1999). The *Unified Registration Statement.* World Wide Web site of the Internet Nonprofit Center (updated May 5, 1999): *http://www.nonprofits.org/library/gov/urs/*

Wickham, Kenneth. *Testimony Presented to House Finance Committee Regarding HB 2046 and HB 2047: November 1, 1989.* Harrisburg, PA: United Way of Pennsylvania, 1989.

Chapter 15

Conners, Tracy D. (ed.). *The Nonprofit Organization Handbook.* New York, NY: McGraw-Hill Book Co., 1980.

Dannelley, Paul. *Fundraising and Public Relations.* Norman, OK: Univ. of Oklahoma Press, 1986.

Des Marais, Philip. *How To Get Government Grants.* New York, NY: Public Service Materials Center, 1975.

Kletzien, S. Damon, ed. *Directory of Pennsylvania Foundations.* Springfield, PA: Triadvocates Press, 1990.

Margolin, Judith B. (ed.). *The Foundation Center's User Friendly Guide—Grant Seeker's Guide to Resources.* New York, NY: The Foundation Center, 1990.

Nelson, Paula. *Where to Get Money for Everything.* New York, NY: William Morris & Co., 1982.

Raybin, Arthur D. *How to Hire the Right Fundraising Consultant.* Washington, DC: Taft Group, 1985.

Seltzer, Michael. *Securing Your Organization's Future: A Complete Guide to Fundraising Strategies.* New York, NY: The Foundation Center, 1987.

White, Virginia (ed.). *Grant Proposals That Succeeded.* New York, NY: Plenum Press, 1983.

Chapter 16

Blum, Laurie. *The Complete Guide to Getting a Grant.* New York, NY: Poseidon Press, 1993.

Chelekis, George C. *The Action Guide to Government Grants, Loans and Giveaways.* New York, NY: Perigee Books, 1993.

Dermer, Joseph. *How to Write Successful Foundation Presentations.* New York, NY: Public Service Materials Center, 1984.

Dumouchel, J. Robert. *Government Assistance Almanac.* Washington, DC: Foggy Bottom Publications, 1985.

Educational Funding Research Council. *Funding Database Handbook.* Arlington, VA: Funding Research Institute, 1992.

Geever, Jane C. *The Foundation Center's Guide to Proposal Writing.* New York, NY: The Foundation Center, 1993.

Hillman, Howard and Chamberlain, Majorie. *The Art of Winning Corporate Grants.* New York, NY: Vanguard Press, 1980.

Margolis, Judith. *Foundation Fundamentals: A Guide for Grantseekers.* New York: Foundation Center, 1991.

_____ *The Foundation Center's User Friendly Guide: Grantseeker's Guide to Resources.* New York: The Foundation Center, 1992.

Smith, Craig W. and Skjei, Eric W. *Getting Grants.* New York: Harper and Row, 1979.

Chapter 17

Brandt, Sanford F. *Tax-Exempt Organizations' Lobbying and Political Activities Accountability Act of 1987: A Guide for Volunteers and Staff of Nonprofit Organizations.* Washington, DC: Independent Sector, 1988.

Caplan, Marc and Nader, Ralph. *Ralph Nader Presents a Citizen's Guide to Lobbying.* New York, NY: Dembner Books, 1983.

Conners, Tracy D. (ed.). *The Nonprofit Organization Handbook.* New York, NY: McGraw-Hill Book Co., 1980.

Gaby, Patricia V. and Gaby, Daniel M. *Nonprofit Organization Handbook: A Guide to Fundraising, Grants, Lobbying, Membership Building, Publicity and Public Relations.* Englewood Cliffs, NJ: Prentice-Hall, 1979.

Independent Sector. *Advocacy Is Sometimes an Agency's Best Service: Opportunities and Limits Within Federal Law.* Washington, DC: Independent Sector, 1984.

Mental Health Association. *A Layman's Guide to Lobbying Without Losing Your Tax Exempt Status.* Roslyn, VA: Mental Health Association. 1976.

Migdail, Rhonda G. *"Lobbying and Political Activities: What Every Nonprofit Should Know."* Nonprofit World Report 3 (May-June 1983).

Speeter, Greg. *Playing Their Game Our Way. Using the Political Process to Meet Community Needs.* Amherst, MA: University of Massachusetts, 1978.

Suhrke, Henry C. *" 'Political' Advocacy by Non-Profits."* Philanthropy Monthly (Feb 1983).

United States House of Representatives, Ways and Means Committee, Subcommittee on Oversight. *Tax Administration: Information on Lobbying and Political Activities of Tax-Exempt Organizations.* Gaithersburg, MD: U.S. General Accounting Office, 1987.

Webster, George D. and Krebs, Frederick. *Associations and Lobbying: A Guide for Non-Profit Organizations.* Washington, DC: Chamber of Commerce of the United States, 1979.

Chapter 18

Gates, Lowell, J.D. (Killian and Gephart). *Political, Lobbying and Grassroots Activities of 501(c)(3) Organizations.* LTC Legal Briefs; July 28, 1988.

Harvard Law Review. *Political Activities of Non-Profit Corporations;* May 1992.

Independent Sector. *Update on Permissible Activities of 501(c)(3) Organizations During a Political Campaign.* July 29, 1988.

Montgomery, Richard C. *Charitable Organizations and Prohibited Political Activities.* Pennsylvania Bar Association Quarterly; April 1992.

Wharton, Linda. *Guidelines for 501(c)(3) and 501(c)(4) Organizations Regarding Electoral Activities Under the Federal Tax Laws.* Memorandum of March 1, 1990.

Chapter 19

Committee to Defend Reproductive Rights of the Coalition for the Medical Rights of Women. *The Media Book: Making the Media Work for Your Grassroots Group.* San Francisco, CA: Committee to Defend Reproductive Rights, 1981.

Conners, Tracy D. (ed.). *The Nonprofit Organization Handbook.* New York, NY: McGraw-Hill Book Co., 1980.

Council on Foundations. *Communications and Public Affairs Guide.* Washington, DC: Council on Foundations, 1984.

Dannelley, Paul. *Fundraising and Public Relations.* Norman, OK: Univ. of Oklahoma Press, 1986.

Drucker, Peter F. *Managing the Nonprofit Organization.* New York, NY: Harper Collins: 1990.

Foundation for American Communication. *Media Resource Guide.* Los Angeles, CA: Foundation for American Communications, 1981.

Gaby, Patricia V. and Gaby, Daniel M. *Nonprofit Organization Handbook: A Guide to Fundraising, Grants, Lobbying, Membership Building, Publicity and Public Relations.* Englewood Cliffs, NJ: Prentice-Hall, 1979.

Green, Alan. *Communicating in the '80s: New Options for the Nonprofit Community.* Washington, DC: Benton Foundation, 1983.

Gross, Sallie and Viet, Carol H. *For Immediate Release: A Public Relations Manual.* Philadelphia, PA: Greater Philadelphia Cultural Alliance, 1982.

Ott, J. Steven and Shafitz, Jay M. *The Facts on File Dictionary of Nonprofit Organization Management.* New York, NY: Facts on File Publications, 1986.

Chapter 20

Gerwig, Kate. *Putting Your Mark on the Web.* NetGuide Vol. 3 No. 2 (February 1996) pp. 87

Grant, Gary; Grobman, Gary; and Roller, Steve. (1999). *The Wilder Nonprofit Field Guide to Fundraising on the Internet.* St. Paul, MN: Amhurst H. Wilder Foundation.

Grobman, Gary and Grant, Gary. (1999). *The Wilder Nonprofit Field Guide to Getting Started on the Internet.* St. Paul, MN: Amhurst H. Wilder Foundation.

Gilster, Paul. *The New Internet Navigator.* NY, NY: Wiley & Sons, 1995.

Grobman, Gary and Grant, Gary. (1998). *The Non-Profit Internet Handbook.* Harrisburg, PA: White Hat Communications.

Chapter 21

Brown, Cherie R. *The Art of Coalition Building— A Guide for Community Leaders.*
New York: American Jewish Committee, 1984.

Kahn, Si. *Organizing: A Guide for Grassroots Leaders.* Washington, DC: NASW Press, 1991 (Revised Edition)

MacEchern, Diane. *No Coalition, No Returns.* Washington, DC: Environmental Action.

Tydeman, Ann. *A Guide to Coalition Building.* Washington, DC: National Citizen's Coalition for Nursing Home Reform, 1979.

Chapter 22

Conners, Tracy D. (ed.). *The Nonprofit Organization Handbook.* New York, NY: McGraw-Hill Book Co., 1980.

Kirschten, Barbara L. *Nonprofit Corporate Forms Handbook.* New York, NY: Clark Boardman Co., 1990.

Mancuso, Anthony. *How To Form Your Own Nonprofit Corporation.* Berkeley, CA: Nolo Press, 1990.

Norsworthy, Alex (ed.). *The Nonprofit Computer Sourcebook.* Rockville, MD: The Taft Group, 1990.

Ott, J. Steven and Shafitz, Jay M. *The Facts on File Dictionary of Nonprofit Organization Management.* New York, NY: Facts on File Publications, 1986.

Chapter 23

Conners, Tracy D. (ed.). *The Nonprofit Organization Handbook.* New York, NY: McGraw-Hill Book Co., 1980.

Deja, Sandy. *"Nonprofit Organizations, Business Ventures, and the IRS: Your Guide to the Unrelated Business Income Tax Law."* Whole Nonprofit Catalog 6 (Spring 1988).

Dewan, Bradford N. *"Operation of a Business by Non-Profit Tax-Exempt Organizations."* Economic Development and Law Center (March-April 1986).

Gallaway, Joseph M. *The Unrelated Business Income Tax.* New York, NY: John Wiley, 1982.

Grobman, Gary. *"The Issue of Competition Between Non-Profit and For-Profit Corporations"* Harrisburg, PA: Pennsylvania Jewish Coalition, 1994.

Hopkins, Bruce. *"Hearings on Nonprofit 'Competition' ".* Nonprofit World 5 (Sept-Oct. 1987).

Kotler, Philip and Andreasen, Alan R. *Strategic Marketing for Nonprofit Organizations.* Englewood Cliffs, NJ: Prentiss-Hall, Inc., 1987.

Lehrfeld, William J. *"More Unrelated Business Tax Issues.* Philanthropy Monthly (October 1984).

Skloot, Edward (ed.). *The Nonprofit Entrepreneur.* New York, NY: The Foundation Center: 1988.

United States Congress, Joint Committee on Taxation. *Tax Policy: Competition Between Taxable Businesses and Tax-Exempt Organizations.* Gaithersburg, MD: U.S. General Accounting Office. 1987.

Wellford, Harrison and Gallagher, Janne. *The Myth of Unfair Competition by Nonprofit Organizations.* New York, NY: Family Service Association of America, 1985.

Chapter 24

Grobman, Gary. *"The Issue of Tax-Exempt Status for Pennsylvania Non-Profit Charities."* Harrisburg, PA: Pennsylvania Jewish Coalition, 1994.

National Council of Nonprofit Associations. *State Tax Trends.* Volume 2, No. 4; Summer 1994.

Wellford, Harrison and Gallagher, Janne. *The Myth of Unfair Competition by Nonprofit Organizations.* New York, NY: Family Service Association of America, 1985.

Chapter 25

Bookman, Mark. *Protecting Your Organization's Tax-Exempt Status.* San Francisco: Jossey Bass, 1992.

Gillespie, Catherine H. *Court Denies Tax Exemption for Nonprofit Nursing Home.* Nonprofit Issues, Philadelphia, PA: Montgomery, McCracken, Walker and Rhoads, March 1992.

Hopkins, Bruce. *The Law and Tax-Exempt Organizations, 6th edition.* New York: John Wiley and Sons. 1992.

Stepneski, Rob. *Rising Tax Pressure Hits Nonprofits.* NonProfit Times: April 1993.

Van Til, Jon. *Tax Exemptions Reconsidered.* NonProfit Times: June 1993.

Chapter 26

Cavadel, Joel. Nonprofit Mergers. Unpublished report on legal consideration relating to non-profit mergers in Pennsylvania, 1996.

La Pinana, David. *Nonprofit Mergers: The Board's Responsibility to Consider the Unthinkable.* Washington, DC: Center for Nonprofit Boards, 1994.

Morgan, William, Mattaini, Paul and Doliner, Ann. *Is a Merger in Your Future?* Presentation to the Pennsylvania Association of Nonprofit Organizations (PANO), 1996.

Chapter 27

Anonymous. *The Year 2000 Challenge for United Ways.* Alexandria, VA: United Way of America, 1998.

Batchilder, Melissa. *Computer Bug Lurking for Nonprofits' Systems.* The Nonprofit Times. July 1998.

Greene, Stephen. *Preparing for the 2000 Bug.* The Chronicle of Philanthropy. v.XI, No. 4, December 3, 1998, p. 1.

Halpern, Charles, Friedman, Paul, and Korpivaara, Ari. *The Year 2000 Challenge: A Socially Responsive Way to Prepare for Disruptions in Computer-Reliant Systems,* New York: Nathan Cummings Foundation, 1998.

Levin, Amanda. *Are Hospitals Ready for Y2K?* National Underwriter (Property & Casualty/Risk & Benefits Management). v102 n40. Oct 5, 1998. p.9-10.

O'Riley, Paloma, et al. *Y2K Citizen's Action Guide. Minneapolis, MN: Utne Reader Books, 1998.*

Rea, Alan. *Frequently Asked Questions (FAQ) About the Y2K Problem.* http://unix.cc.wmich.edu/rea/Y2K/FAQ.html, 1998.

Chapter 28

Crosby, Philip B. *Quality is Free.* New York: McGraw Hill, 1979.

Garvin, David A. *Management Quality: The Strategic and Competitive Edge.* New York: Free Press, 1988.

Grobman, Gary. *Improving Quality and Performance in Your Non-Profit Organization.* Harrisburg, PA: White Hat Communications, 1999.

Martin, Lawrence. *TQM in Human Service Organizations.* San Francisco: Jossey-Bass, 1993.

Chapter 29

Bunker, Barbara Benedict and Alban, Billie T. *Large Group Interventions: Engaging the Whole System for Rapid Change.* San Francisco: Jossey-Bass, 1997.

Bunker, Barbara Benedict and Alban, Billie T. *What Makes Large Group Interventions Effective?* Journal of Applied Behavioral Science 28(4), 1992.

Carter, Reginald. *The Accountable Agency.* Thousand Oaks, CA: Sage Publications, 1983.

Creech, Bill. *The Five Pillars of TQM: How to Make Total Quality Management Work for You.* New York: Penguin Books, 1994.

Crosby, Philip B. *Quality is Free.* New York: McGraw Hill, 1979.

Deming, W. Edward. *On Some Statistical Aids Toward Economic Production. Interfaces,* v5, n4. Aug. 1975. The Operations Research Society of America and the Institute of Management Sciences, 1975.

Friedman, Mark. *A Guide to Developing and Using Performance Measures in Results-Based Budgeting.* Washington, DC: The Finance Project, 1997.

Greenway, Martha Taylor. *The Status of Research and Indicators On Nonprofit Performance In Human Services.* Alexandria, VA: United Way of America, 1996.

Hammer, Michael. *Reengineering Work: Don't Automate: Obliterate. Harvard Business Review,* July-Aug. 1990, pp. 104-112, 1990.

Hammer, Michael. and Champy, James. *Reengineering the Corporation: A Manifesto for Business.* New York: HarperBusiness, 1993.

Hammer, Michael and Stanton, Steven A. *The Reengineering Revolution: A Handbook.* New York: HarperBusiness, 1994.

Peters, Thomas J. and Waterman, Jr., Robert H. *In Search of Excellence: Lessons from America's Best-Run Companies.* New York: Harper and Row, 1982.

Richmond, Frederick and Hunnemann, Eleanor. *What Every Board Member Needs to Know About Outcomes.* Management and Technical Assistance Publication Series n2, Harrisburg, PA: Positive Outcomes, 1996.

Rouda, R. & Kusy, M., Jr. *Organization Development—The Management of Change. Tappi Journal* 78(8): 253 ,1995.

Steckel, Richard and Lehman, Jennifer. *In Search of America's Best Non-Profits.* San Francisco: Jossey-Bass, 1997.

Watson, Gregory H. *The Benchmarking Workbook: Adapting Best Practices for Performance Improvement.* Portland, OR: Productivity Press, 1992.

KEY WORD INDEX

A

accrual basis of accounting, 77
American Cancer Society, 11
annual meeting, 26
annual report, 19, 31, 105, 121, 129, 142, 143, 157, 171, 174
applications (general),
    for employer identification number, 69, 89
    for 501(c)(3) status, 68-69, 70, 111, 223
    for funding and grants, 31, 32, 36, 42, 114, 116, 118-125, 159, 161
    for internet address, 157
Articles of incorporation, 17, 18, 19, 21, 22, 23, 24, 31, 67, 70, 111, 170, 171
Articles of dissolution, 24
Articles of merger, 13, 14, 24, 49
articles, op-ed, 144, 145
audits, 18, 31, 52, 53, 57, 77, 78, 79, 110, 125, 184, 199, 205, 217, 222
awards, 94, 104, 106, 130, 135, 138, 141, 154, 213

B

benchmarking, 211, 215-216
board development, 31, 33
board minutes, 18, 19, 26, 30, 31, 34, 35, 36, 43, 52, 56
board of directors, 15, 16, 18, 21, 22, 23, 25, 27, 28, 29-37, 43, 44, 48, 52, 53, 55, 56, 57, 58, 60, 61, 63, 64, 81, 86, 91, 94, 97, 109, 130, 135, 138, 140, 147, 148, 169, 171, 195, 200, 222
board surveys (see surveys, board)
bookkeeping, 18, 26, 77, 81, 93, 169, 171, 173
BPR (see Business Process Reengineering)
budgeting, 16, 18, 19, 31, 32, 41, 42, 49, 53, 56, 63, 77, 80, 81, 82, 101, 111, 112, 124, 125, 160, 164, 169, 170, 171, 173, 188, 189, 199, 218, 222
bulk mail, 13, 169, 174, 175-179
Business Process Reengineering, 211, 213-214, 215, 216, 219
bylaws, 13, 17, 18, 21, 25-28, 29, 30, 31, 32, 33, 34, 36, 97, 171, 186, 199

C

campaigns (political), 24, 129, 133, 135, 136
cash (basis of accounting), 77
chairperson (of the board), 17, 26, 30, 31, 32, 33, 34, 35, 36, 37, 42, 44, 48, 52, 82, 86, 97, 101, 221
change management, 211-220
charitable gift annuities, 48
child labor law, 86, 88
churches and synagogues, 11, 101, 104, 144
coalitions, 140, 163-168
COBRA (Consolidated Budget Reconciliation Act of 1985), 99
colleges and universities, 17, 101, 113, 116, 169, 170, 182, 183
committees (board) 18, 26, 30, 31, 33, 52, 57, 58, 119
    advisory committee, 112, 116
    board development committee, 33
    executive committee, 27-28, 33
    nominations committee, 27, 29, 30, 31
    personnel committee, 32, 33, 83, 86, 94
compensation (general), 26
    of directors, 26, 60, 64, 221-222,
    of staff, 24, 26, 32, 36, 48, 52, 64, 83, 84, 86, 88, 185, 221, 222

workers' insurance (see insurance, workers' compensation)
    unemployment (see insurance, unemployment compensation)
compilations, 77, 78, 79
computers, 53, 77, 105, 112, 125, 136, 145, 147, 169, 170, 171, 172, 173, 174, 176, 182, 201, 202
conferences and workshops, 63, 80, 81, 82, 117, 140, 142-143, 148, 150, 157, 159, 160, 209
consolidations, 197, 198, 200
consultants, 40, 43, 45, 46, 48, 80, 83, 117, 124, 147, 199, 201, 204, 213
contractors, 83, 93
contributions (see disclosure, lobbyists' contributions)
corporate logo (see logo, corporate)
corporate seal, 26
credit card sales (see sales, credit card)

D

day-care centers, 11, 16, 144, 185, 192, 207
discipline, 98
disclosure (general), 98
    of information by nonprofits, 21, 61, 62, 63, 86, 87, 113, 186, 221, 223
    of lobbyists' contributions, 88, 127, 128, 129
dissolution (by corporations), 24

E

e-mail, 97, 105, 139, 147, 149, 150, 151, 153, 156, 157, 158, 159, 160, 173
employer identification number (see applications, for employer identification number)
equal pay, 86, 88
ethics, 52, 54, 56, 58, 59-65, 78, 88, 151, 159, 160, 161, 198, 216
evaluation, 41, 47, 49, 52, 57, 85, 98, 99, 124, 125, 203, 212, 216, 218
executive committee (see committees)
executive director, 16, 17, 31, 32, 33, 34, 35, 36, 37, 41, 42, 43, 44, 48, 52, 53, 55, 56, 57, 58, 60, 61, 63, 64, 81, 86, 91, 94, 97, 109, 130, 135, 138, 140, 147, 148, 169, 171, 195, 200, 222
exemptions (see taxes)

F

Family and Medical Leave, 85, 87
fees, for applications, 70, 80, 174
financial reports/statements, 30, 31, 40, 53, 77, 78, 79, 86, 107, 109, 143
firing (see hiring and firing)
foundations, 12, 15, 16, 17, 62, 63, 68, 79, 89, 114, 116, 119, 120, 121, 150, 151, 159, 160, 167, 205, 208, 216, 217
frames, 155
FTP (see Internet, FTP)
funding applications (see applications, for funding)
fundraising, 13, 19, 20, 29, 31, 32, 48, 49, 53, 56, 57, 62, 64, 79, 107-110, 111-118, 125, 136, 140, 150, 151, 208

G

governance, board, 23, 41, 42, 49, 54, 56, 58, 164

The Non-Profit Internet Handbook

by Gary M. Grobman and Gary B. Grant

The Non-Profit **Internet** *Handbook* is the definitive handbook for non-profit organizations that want to get the most out of the Internet. This is a valuable resource for:

- Non-profit organization executive staff
- Non-profit organization board members
- Those who fund non-profit organizations
- Those who contribute time and money to non-profit organizations.

The Non-Profit **Internet** *Handbook* includes:

- How to connect to the Internet
- How to do effective fund-raising and advocacy on the Internet
- How to develop your organization's World Wide Web site
- How to find information useful to non-profits on the Internet
- How to locate on-line sources of government, foundation, and private corporation grants.

Table of Contents

Plus—
Reviews of more than 250 of the most valuable Internet sites for non-profit organizations!

Internet-related cartoons drawn by the internationally-acclaimed cartoonist Randy Glasbergen, creator of *The Better Half.*

The Non-Profit **Internet** *Handbook* is an essential reference publication for every non-profit organization.

$29.95 plus $3.50 S/H
ISBN 0-9653653-6-0   8½" x 11" softcover
216 pages plus index
Published 1998

White Hat Communications, P.O. Box 5390, Harrisburg, PA 17110-0390 Phone: 717-238-3787 Fax: 717-238-2090

Improving Quality and Performance in Your Non-Profit Organization

by Gary M. Grobman

Managing non-profit organizations in the 21st century will be more challenging and sophisticated than ever before. *Improving Quality and Performance in Your Non-Profit Organization* provides an introduction to innovative, creative, and effective management techniques developed to totally transform your non-profit organization. Reap the benefits of the quality movement that is revolutionizing commercial and non-profit organizations, and make your own organization more competitive.

Read *Improving Quality and Performance in Your Non-Profit Organization* to learn how you can—

- respond to uncertainty and organizational turbulence
- reduce mistakes and infuse your staff with a quality ethic
- rebuild your work processes from the ground up
- find and implement "best practices" of comparable organizations

Improving Quality and Performance in Your Non-Profit Organization is a comprehensive, introductory guide to change management tools and strategies, including—

- Total Quality Management (TQM)
- Business Process Reengineering (BPR)
- Benchmarking/Best Practices
- Outcomes-Based Management (OBM)
- Large Group Interventions (LGI)

It also includes easy-to-read and practical applications of chaos theory and organization theory.
$16.95   5.5" x 8.5"   155 pages   Published January 1999   ISBN: 0-9653653-4-4

ORDER FORM

PLEASE SHIP MY ORDER TO:

NAME _____

ADDRESS _____

ADDRESS _____

CITY/STATE/ZIP _____

TELEPHONE NUMBER _____

❏ Enclosed is a check for $_____ made payable to "White Hat Communications."

❏ Please charge my: ❏ MasterCard ❏ VISA

Card # _____

Expiration Date _____

Name as it appears on card _____

Signature _____

Billing address for credit card (if different from above) _____

Billing City/State/Zip _____

Please send the following publications:

QUANTITY	TITLE		AMOUNT
_____	THE PENNSYLVANIA NONPROFIT HANDBOOK, 5TH EDITION	$27.95	_____
_____	THE NON-PROFIT INTERNET HANDBOOK	$29.95	_____
_____	THE NON-PROFIT HANDBOOK, SECOND EDITION	$29.95	_____
_____	IMPROVING QUALITY AND PERFORMANCE IN YOUR NON-PROFIT ORGANIZATION	$16.95	_____

SHIPPING $ _____
SUBTOTAL $ _____
PA SALES TAX (6%) $ _____
(Pennsylvania orders only)

Shipping charges: $3.50 first book/$1.00 each additional book in U.S. *Please contact us for rates on rush orders, other methods of shipping, or shipping outside the U.S.*
PA Sales tax: 6% tax on books ordered from Pennsylvania, unless accompanied by sales tax exemption certificate

TOTAL DUE $ _____

Federal EIN: 25-1719745

3b1999